Decadence and the Making of Modernism

Decadence and the Making of Modernism

David Weir

University of Massachusetts Press *Amherst*

LC 95-12795
ISBN 0-87023-991-0 (cloth); 992-9 (pbk.)

Designed by Dennis Anderson
Set in Walbaum Book by Keystone Typesetting, Inc.
Printed and bound by Thomson-Shore, Inc.

Library of Congress Cataloging-in-Publication Data

Weir, David, 1947 Apr. 20–
Decadence and the making of modernism / David Weir.
p. cm.
Includes bibliographical references and index.
ISBN 0–87023–991–0 (cloth : alk. paper). — ISBN 0–87023–992–9 (pbk. : alk. paper)
1. Decadence (Literary movement) 2. Modernism (Literature) I. Title.
PN56.D45W45 1996
809′.91–dc20 95–12795
CIP

British Library Cataloguing in Publication data are available.

"a sort of dire happiness . . ."

—Djuna Barnes, *Nightwood*

In memory of David Geoffrey Weir (1973–1991)

Contents

	Acknowledgments	ix
	Preface	xi
	Abbreviations	xxi
1	The Definition of Decadence	1
2	Decadence and Romanticism: Flaubert's *Salammbô*	22
3	Decadence and Naturalism: The Goncourts' *Germinie Lacerteux*	43
4	Decadence and Aestheticism: Pater's *Marius the Epicurean*	59
5	Decadence and *Décadisme: A Rebours* and Afterward	82
6	Decadence and Modernism: Joyce and Gide	119
7	The Decline of Decadence	151
	Postface	192
	Notes	205
	Index	227

Illustrations follow page 104

Acknowledgments

Decadence and degeneration have little in common: one refines corruption and the other corrupts refinement. The decadent, at least, maintains a standard of decline, while the degenerate lets those standards slip. In this book, I have tried to measure up to the level of decadence achieved by my models and mentors, friends and colleagues. But in decadence as in other matters, nothing fails like success: those who are truly decadent do not do. Simply by writing the book I have participated in a process of degeneration and failed to maintain the dark ideal of decadence. But the fault is mine alone (call it negative culpability), and those who should be exonerated of responsibility for the final, flawed form this book assumed include Brian Swann, Karen Duys, Alessandra Maffei, and other colleagues at The Cooper Union; Karin Drew and the apprentice decadents at The New School for Social Research; Professors Anna Balakian and Daniel Javitch of New York University; Professor Theoharis C. Theoharis of Harvard University; Professor Michael Seidel of Columbia University; and Clark Dougan and the staff of the University of Massachusetts Press. I thank them all for enlightenment and encouragement, but most of all I thank my wife, Camille—for living up to her nineteenth-century name.

A small portion of this book appeared in earlier form in the *James Joyce Quarterly:* some passages in chapter 6 were first published as "Stephen Dedalus: Rimbaud or Baudelaire" (Fall 1980). That chapter also contains some paragraphs originally published as "Moore's Young Man" in the *James Joyce Broadsheet* (February 1985). Permission to reprint this material is gratefully acknowledged. I am also grateful to the Spencer Collection of The New York Public Library, Astor, Lenox and Tilden Foundations, for permission to reproduce illustrations by Auguste Rodin from Octave Mirbeau's *Le Jardin des supplices* (Paris: Ambroise Vollard, 1902).

Preface

In 1856 Charles Baudelaire published the poem "Une Charogne" in *Les Fleurs du mal.* At first, the work seems sentimental and thoroughly conventional: the opening lines present us with a romantic young couple reminiscing about a quiet stroll on a pleasant summer morning ("Ce beau matin d'été si doux").[1] They seem to be lovers because the speaker of the poem, evidently a young man, uses high romantic diction to refer to his companion, calling her his "soul" ("mon âme"). The young man looks back to the past, in typical romantic fashion, and asks his lover to recall one of their earlier moments together—when they happened across a rotten carcass of an animal putrefying in the sun ("une charogne infâme"). The convention of romantic recollection usually involves remembrance of things past that are pleasant or even perfect (anything from childhood to a prior, Platonic state of existence), but here the poet disorients his readers by asking them to recall, not the past, but the future the flesh is heir to: memento mori. Then the reader is faced with another disorienting paradox: the carcass we are asked to recall is dead all right, but animated by a curious, lively process of decay. The dead animal with its legs stiff in the air is compared to a prostitute ("une femme lubrique"), the fluid that oozes from the lifeless body suggesting a woman in a state of sexual arousal. The swollen belly of the corpse ("ce ventre putride") is fairly pregnant with decay, writhing with the motion of the maggots within, which together with the flies buzzing over the body, make a strange, whispering sound ("une étrange musique"). The "music" that comes from the carrion leads to a brief comparison of the gradually decomposing corpse to a fading canvas by some forgotten artist. This artistic meditation comes to a halt when the young man notices a dog behind the rocks and realizes that the dead animal is food for the live one, whereupon he turns to his beloved, his angel, his passion ("Vous, mon ange et ma passion"), and tells her that she, too, will one day be no more than a mass of decomposing flesh ("vous serez semblable à cette ordure") like the one before them. He also tells her that the ceremonies of religion will be ineffective against the strange, erotic power of decay: after the rituals, the worms will "kiss" her body away to nothingness as it lies underground. The church may have the last rites, but Baudelaire has the last word. The poet, at least, will do what he can to preserve something of the form and essence of all his lost, decomposed lovers ("j'ai gardé la forme et l'essence divine / De mes amours décomposés").

Baudelaire's "Une Charogne" stands as the epitaph to this study of decadence for several reasons. First, the poem presents in microcosm the larger paradox of the late nineteenth century: never before have so many artists and writers been so obsessed with various processes and manifestations of decay—and drawn so much life, so much creative energy, from the very decadence they decry. In this trope, civilization itself is the corpse upon which the decadent sensibility feeds, nourished by the prospect of its own annihilation. From the relatively benign melancholy at the beginning of the nineteenth century to the anxious millenialism at the end, from *mal du siècle* to fin de siècle, decline is accompanied by delight. Without question, this attraction to corruption is evident in "Une Charogne": Baudelaire is positively inspired by negation in the poem, celebrating mortality and decay in lively metaphors and rich, resonant language. Like the carrion creature in Baudelaire's poem, decadence makes for some strange music.

A second reason for invoking Baudelaire's "Une Charogne" here concerns the conflict of romanticism and realism that the poem captures. This conflict is significant because the aesthetic terms "romanticism" and "realism" mask a larger tension between religion and science, Christianity and Darwinism. Baudelaire's sarcastic attitude toward the conventions of romanticism is an implicit attack on religion as well, because the romantic movement was strongly connected to Christianity in France, at least after Chateaubriand. "Une Charogne" suggests the development of a new sensibility, an early form of modernism that includes the hard, unblinking realism necessary for the detailed description of the corpse and the arch, ironic commentary on the comforts of religion. Although the first edition of *Les Fleurs du mal* precedes Darwin's *Origin of Species* (1859) by three years, the poet's attitude anticipates some of the cultural interpretations and misinterpretations of Darwin in the late nineteenth century. The scientific neutrality of Darwin's "descent with modification" was misinterpreted as progressive "evolution" by the optimists, and as literal descent or decline by the pessimists. The latter attitude is more complicated, as it involves a grudging acceptance of Darwin's discovery that leads to a kind of enlightened despair. The negation of spirituality and the pessimistic acceptance of the reality that man is an animal and not an angel may be cause for despair, but, at the same time, outright acceptance of mortality as an end in itself can be liberating. Although Baudelaire was never able to believe in mortality as completely as he implies in "Une Charogne," the poem looks at death with a scientist's eye, and sees the decaying corpse, not merely as a fact, but as the *only* fact, a new absolute whose power exceeds that of religion. This sentiment is strongest in the stanza where the speaker of the poem tells the young woman what will happen to her after she receives the last rites of the Catholic faith. There is no talk of choirs of seraphim and life after death, only the "erotic" process of decomposition whereby the woman's dead body is eaten away by the "kisses" of the worms ("la vermine / Qui vous mangera de baisers"). This reading can be expanded to include the poem as a whole if we take the poet literally when he says "mon âme." That is, "Une Charogne" can be read as Baudelaire's apostrophe to his own soul, which he likens to the decaying corpse of an animal—a "Darwinian" reading, indeed.

Another reading of the poem brings us to a third element that is typical of decadence in a larger sense, namely, the superiority of art to nature. This newly established hierarchy is not so simple as it seems, largely because the incorporation of realism into aesthetic expression involves a greater attention to nature than ever before. What the realist notices about nature, however, ends up negating it. Baudelaire's poem is a good example of this process. The romantic artist looked at nature from a distance and saw something sublime, something behind or beyond nature. The realist artist examines nature more closely and sees only surfaces, dead matter, or, at best, living matter in decay. "Une Charogne" celebrates the negation of life and the reality of decay in an interesting fashion. The suggestion at the end of the poem that all reality is subsumed by art argues for the superiority of artifice to nature: the natural process of decomposition described in the poem is no match for the immaculate composition of the poem itself. At first, art does not seem to be any different from the process of decay the poem describes: the gradual degeneration of the carrion body of the animal on the ground is compared to the gradual fading-away of an artist's design on a painted canvas. But this comparison also suggests that artistic creation and decay are somehow in league. Degeneration will go on in any event, but the artist has something to gain by acknowledging it and even by participating in its processes. In the end, after the ineffectual religious rites, and even after the worms, all that is left of *une charogne* is "Une Charogne." Art is superior to romantic "nature" when decadent reality is part of the picture.

The last reason I have for using "Une Charogne" as an epitaph concerns Baudelaire's attitude in the poem toward women, that is, his misogyny. The poet's comparison of the rotting corpse to a prostitute with her legs in the air and then to a pregnant woman giving "birth" to a seething mass of decay has lost none of its power to shock since 1856. But the poem has probably gained in its power to offend because we are no longer able to regard misogyny as simply one more "element" of decadence, like aestheticism, say, as Mario Praz did in 1930, when he took "The Beauty of the Medusa" as a straightforward fact of the fin de siècle. Most of the writers discussed in this book are male, and most of them are misogynistic in the extreme. Indeed, what Roger Williams calls "the horror of life" is largely a horror of procreation, which inevitably entails the hatred of the woman who makes procreation possible.[2] This alignment of philosophical pessimism and misogyny is an important part of the meaning of nineteenth-century decadence. In addition, part of Baudelaire's meaning in "Une Charogne" concerns the hatred of the creature who breeds not only death but disease, the seemingly inevitable result of sexual contact in nineteenth-century artistic and poetic circles. Indeed, *une charogne* is a slang term meaning "slut," so the paradox that makes a dead body into the living corpse of a woman is announced early on. Further, the female gender of the corpse (body) comes into play later in the poem when we are told that another female ("une chienne inquiète") has been feeding off the body ("corps"). Here is a rather gruesome treatment of Baudelaire's obsession with *les femmes damnées.* The oblique reference to lesbian love in a poem about a corpse is corroborated by the allusion to the dead body of Sappho in "Lesbos" ("Le cadavre adoré de Sapho") and by Hippolyte's confession of her anxiety to Delphine in "Femmes Damnées" ("je suis inquiète"), which recalls the anxious bitch ("une chienne inquiète") of "Une Charogne." The "lesbian" element of the poem, together with the eroticizing of death that is the extreme of sadism, brings the poem to a pitch of perversity that, for all of its misogyny, must be recognized as an important theme of decadent literature. Indeed, love of perversity (however defined) and hatred of woman harmonize with the larger paradox of decadence that finds a positive value in corruption, negation, pessimism, and decay.

This self-contradictory, oxymoronic quality of decadence is addressed in Chapter 1 of this book, where I attempt to say what decadence is. However, the reader should also know at the outset what decadence is not. Because I establish decadence as an aesthetic category, I distinguish it from bohemianism, which has more to do with life than art. As an "artistic" life-style, bohemianism may or may not be assumed by the decadent writer: Baudelaire did, Mallarmé did not. In addition, the bohemian is closely affiliated with romanticism, or at least some urban variation of it, whereas the decadent is only indirectly associated with that movement. Decadence and bohemianism are literary neighborhoods with boundaries that sometimes touch or overlap, but separate locales nonetheless. Similarly, the boundaries of decadence and the belle époque also touch, but the ladies and gentlemen of that era are altogether too energetic and optimistic for the decadent. Also, many figures associated with the belle époque (mainly Jarry and Apollinaire) boast a highly experimental form of literature that does not harmonize completely with decadence, whose writers are more guarded about their avant-gardism. Still, bohemia and belle époque are helpful terms to use in discriminating the meaning of decadence. In many ways, the decadent sensibility, in France at least, is bracketed by the other two. As an aesthetic category, decadence is situated somewhere between romantic bohemia and avant-garde belle époque. Decadence falls between these two phenomena in social terms as well. The bohemian artist is always at the lower end of the socioeconomic scale, either in reality or in imagination. The belle époque, on the other hand, is more conducive to aristocratic pretensions (or, as Roger Shattuck says, to the squandering of "the last vestiges of aristocracy").[3] Sometimes the decadent may pursue a bohemian life-style, but he always imagines himself a cultural aristocrat, while being, at base, thoroughly bourgeois. Here again Baudelaire appears as the archetypal decadent figure, not to mention such bourgeois bourgeoisiephobes as Flaubert and the Goncourt brothers. Thus, while decadence is neither bohemian nor belle époque, it has some cultural and social affinities with both. This positioning is consistent with the central thesis of this book, that decadence makes simultaneous appeals, aesthetic and otherwise, to both the past and the future.

Two other terms often associated with decadence are *fin de siècle* and *diabolism.* I have some use for the first problematic phrase, but the second term is not very relevant to this study. While some decadent writers also had an interest in the diabolic (Huysmans is best known in this regard, since he provided a model for decadence in *A Rebours* and a model for satanism in *Là-Bas*), decadence and diabolism are not synonymous. Their relationship does not come into play in this book until Chapter 7, when I entertain the idea of a "decline" of decadence, exemplified by the American writers James Huneker and Ben Hecht. Fin de siècle requires more extended consideration because the term is not a purely temporal designation; the "end" of the century is not strictly chronological, but cultural and social as well. For some reason, "the end of the century" in English does not convey so strong a sense of cultural collapse or secular millenialism as "fin de siècle." According to one critic, the nuance of decline that the French phrase conveys makes it, paradoxically, more appropriate as a descriptive term for the end of the nineteenth century in England rather than France.[4] A recent book by Eugen Weber casts some doubt on this assertion,[5] though it is generally true that the innovations of the avant-garde in France during the last decade of the nineteenth century suggest the renewal of culture rather than the end. These paradoxes and contradictions do not trouble me: if fin de siècle implies both decline and renewal, such a mixture is consistent with the transitional ferment of decadence.

Indeed, "transition" may be the simplest synonym for "decadence," but the problem of defining the word is more complicated than such synonymity suggests. I address this problem in Chapter 1, "The Definition of Decadence," a historical survey of the meaning of the term itself. At different points in this book I may refer to decadence as cultural decline, philosophical pessimism, scientific alarmism (the "heat-death" theory of the end of the universe),[6] physical degeneration, and "immorality" (including *le vice anglais*), but mainly I develop the idea that decadence is transition, and argue that the various nineteenth-century movements that proliferate in the period between romanticism and modernism (naturalism, symbolism, Parnassianism, Pre-Raphaelitism, aestheticism, *décadisme,* and others) can best be understood if they are all seen as grounded in some concept of decadence or decadentism. Decadence, in other words, provides a conceptual focus that helps to unify the cultural transition from romanticism to modernism. This thesis is demonstrated in the five chapters that follow the definition chapter through discussions of particular movements and analyses of exemplary or "touchstone" texts. These texts are all novels, in which I trace the emergence of modernity through different varieties of nineteenth-century decadence, for literary modernism surely owes a debt to decadence with regard to the novel. Consider, for example, the importance of decadent themes (sickness, decay, perversion, artificiality, aestheticism) to virtually all the modern masters of the novel: Proust, Mann, Joyce, Gide, and so on. What I propose here is that decadence was as crucial to the development of the modern novel as symbolism (a movement parallel to decadence and sometimes in competition with it) was to the development of modern poetry.

In presenting decadence as a cultural mode of transition from romanticism to modernism, I am aware that the period labels I employ are enormously problematical and difficult to define. Nevertheless, a critical consensus does exist regarding the relevance of both terms to the historical periods they are intended to cover. The recent debate over the limits of modernism—the question of when, temporally, or how, conceptually, modernism begins to shade into postmodernism—does nothing to alter this consensus. On the contrary, debates about postmodernism show how consistently important students of cultural history consider period labels to be. In fact, contemporary uncertainty about the boundaries of modernism and postmodernism recapitulates an earlier indecision about the boundaries of romanticism and modernism. Granting the obvious fact that the temporal limits of romanticism and modernism are inexact, it is still a truism of literary history that Goethe and Byron have something in common that we have seen fit to call "romanticism," and will no doubt continue to call "romanticism" for some time to come. By the same token, Joyce and Mann are likely to remain "modernists" regardless of the difficulties of saying precisely what "modernism" means. Between romanticism and modernism, however, there is no unifying period concept. During the last half of the nineteenth century, literary movements, schools, cenacles, and "isms" proliferate. My position is that decadence is the common denominator underlying the extremely complex and diverse literary activities in the mid- to late nineteenth century, and that this substratum of decadence is crucial to the development of the modern novel. Several critics share the view that decadence underlies a number of literary trends,[7] but they do not undertake a full demonstration of the thesis, as I do here. Nor do those earlier critics think of decadence in generative or developmental terms, as having an active, dynamic role in the transition from romantic to modernist literature.

If this is an exercise in literary history, it is undertaken with the knowledge that the enterprise should not be, as Geoffrey Hartman remarks, a series of "picaresque adventures in pseudo causality" in which one literary work is seen as the effect of a previous one.[8] I argue the significance of decadence to the development of the modern novel through the analysis of specific novels, showing how each one relates to a particular nineteenth-century aesthetic trend, and how these trends, in turn, relate to decadence. Chapter 2, "Decadence and Romanticism," shows how certain ideas associated with romanticism (recovery of the primary, lost *archē* or origin; fascination with the past, with the exotic, with death, and so on) are modified in the process of a transition to modernity that is characterized as decadent. The exemplary text is Flaubert's *Salammbô,* which is read as the confluence of several contradictory movements: Parnassianism, l'art pour l'art, and realism. Chapter 3, "Decadence and Naturalism," argues that the origins of Zola's naturalism and the Médan school of the *roman expérimental* are to be found in the Goncourt brothers' novel *Germinie Lacerteux.* Again, the text is read as the interference of contradictory movements that have in common a substratum of decadence: in this case naturalism and *écriture artiste* (the Goncourts' variation of l'art pour l'art). Chapter 4, "Decadence and Aestheticism," reads Walter Pater's *Marius the Epicurean* as a kind of confluence of romanticism and naturalism. The subjectivism of the former and the objective, "experimental" nature of the latter combine into Pater's aestheticism. I also note that aestheticism has roots in dandyism and pick up another theme from the previous two chapters: sadism. Thus I read the novel as a mixture of artificiality and brutality, refinement and degeneration: the paradoxical, double essence of decadence. Chapter 5, "Decadence and *Décadisme,*" is subtitled "*A Rebours* and Afterward" and is a discussion of Huysmans and his influence: from the short-lived movement known as *décadisme* to the D'Annunzio cult and the English "art for art's sake" sensibility. In addition to Huysmans' all-important "bible" of decadence, I discuss D'Annunzio's *Il Piacere,* Oscar Wilde's *The Picture of Dorian Gray,* and George Moore's *Confessions of a Young Man.* Chapter 6, "Decadence and Modernism," treats modernism as a self-contradictory development of decadence and uses two quite dissimilar texts to make the argument: Joyce's *A Portrait of the Artist as a Young Man* and Gide's *L'Immoraliste.* I read Joyce's novel in terms of the reception, or perhaps absorption, of prior decadences (those of Pater, Wilde, D'Annunzio, and George Moore), whereas Gide's novel is read as a Nietzschean self-overcoming of decadence. Thus, the paradoxical double essence of decadence, the combination of refinement and brutality, splits into two contradictory strains of modernism, one termed "hypercultural," and the other "primitive." The decadent's passive "urge" to be revitalized by barbarism is something discussed in previous chapters, so the modernist's double interest in an overabundance of culture and in an imaginary, acultural "primitivism" is treated as a coherent development of decadence. Chapter 7, "The Decline of Decadence," looks at the way decadence became decadentism, a set of conventions that could be exploited and parodied. I also examine the rather oxymoronic idea of American decadence in this chapter, which leads to a discussion of a curious form of noncanonical modernism that continues the decadent tradition in a debased, belated form at the same time that the more familiar expatriate Americans, the ones who have been canonized as modernists, were making it new. I end with a postmodern Postface that treats postmodernism as yet another belated variation of the decadent sensibility.

The foregoing summary conveys only one of two important points I wish to make here: that a number of literary movements and tendencies developed through decadence, either by reacting against its characteristic styles and themes, or by extending them in some way. The second point is that decadence itself developed as an independent movement at the same time that other, better known movements were developing through it. The dynamics of decadence as the medium of cultural transition between romanticism and modernism is complicated by this double movement. In one sense, decadence is like the mystical sphere whose circumference is everywhere but whose center is nowhere: naturalism, Parnassianism, aestheticism, and the rest are all arrayed "around" decadence, but they do not point toward a common center. In another sense, the center and the circumference are the same: decadence as an independent movement is a sphere closed and contracted upon itself. The meaning of decadence depends, in part, on whether the term is used to describe some aspect of another movement, or to describe an independent development. Thus, it means one thing to speak of the decadent elements in aestheticism or in naturalism, and something else again to speak of those elements in the aggregate as forming a literary sensibility separate from such movements as aestheticism and naturalism.

As the meaning of decadence expands and contracts to cover major movements and minor trends, the critic of decadence seems to have only two choices: to clarify with categories or to titillate with anecdotes. Although the latter, narrower approach is the more traditional one among critics writing in English, the broader view also has its appeal, especially now that another century is nearing its end. No one, as far as I know, has used the phrase *nouvelle fin de siècle* to describe the end of the twentieth century, but there is no doubt that the 1990s have already occasioned much concern over cultural decline. In fact, for some cultural critics the previous fin de siècle is now a frame of reference for the current one. This is an interesting phenomenon in itself (which I take up more fully in the Postface), largely because the same thing happened at the end of the last century. Looking to a prior decadence as a means of defining a contemporary cultural sensibility is nothing new. Once again, anxiety over decline is expressed as a longing for renewal that can only come about if the state of decadence is admitted and acknowledged. Once again, as the contemporary fin de siècle cycles to its conclusion, the end of history is repeating itself.

Abbreviations

B James Gibbons Huneker, *Bedouins* (New York: Scribner, 1926)

BT Friedrich Nietzsche, *The Birth of Tragedy*, in *The Birth of Tragedy and The Case of Wagner*, trans. Walter Kaufmann (New York: Random House, 1967)

C George Moore, *Confessions of a Young Man*, ed. Susan Dick (Montreal: McGill-Queen's University Press, 1972)

CC Ben Hecht, *A Child of the Century* (New York: Simon and Schuster, 1954)

CW Friedrich Nietzsche, *The Case of Wagner*, in *The Birth of Tragedy and The Case of Wagner*, trans. Walter Kaufmann (New York: Random House, 1967)

CWJJ James Joyce, *The Critical Writings of James Joyce*, ed. Ellsworth Mason and Richard Ellmann (New York: Viking, 1959)

D James Joyce, *Dubliners*, ed. Robert Scholes, in consultation with Richard Ellmann (New York: Viking, 1967)

EH Friedrich Nietzsche, *On the Genealogy of Morals and Ecce Homo*, trans. Walter Kaufmann (New York: Random House, 1967)

FM Ben Hecht, *Fantazius Mallare: A Mysterious Oath* (Chicago: Covici-McGee, 1922)

G Ben Hecht, *Gargoyles* (New York: Boni and Liveright, 1922)

GL Walter Pater, *Gaston de Latour: An Unfinished Romance*, ed. Charles L. Shadwell (London: Macmillan, 1922)

IA James Gibbons Huneker, *Ivory Apes and Peacocks* (New York: Scribner, 1915)

KE Ben Hecht, *The Kingdom of Evil: A Continuation of the Journal of Fantazius Mallare* (Chicago: Pascal Covici, 1924)

ME Walter Pater, *Marius the Epicurean,* ed. Michael Levey (New York: Viking Penguin, 1985)

NC Friedrich Nietzsche, *Nietzsche contra Wagner* in *The Portable Nietzsche,* trans. Walter Kaufmann (New York: Viking, 1954)

O James Gibbons Huneker, *Overtones: A Book of Temperaments* (New York: Scribner, 1922)

P James Joyce, *A Portrait of the Artist as a Young Man,* corrected from the Dublin holograph by Chester G. Anderson (New York: Viking, 1964)

PV James Gibbons Huneker, *Painted Veils* (New York: Modern Library, 1930)

SH James Joyce, *Stephen Hero,* ed. Theodore Spencer, with additional material edited by John J. Slocum and Herbert Cahoon (New York: New Directions, 1959)

SW Walter Pater, *Selected Writings of Walter Pater,* ed. Harold Bloom (New York: Columbia University Press, 1974)

Decadence and the Making of Modernism

1

The Definition of Decadence

Practically everyone who writes about decadence begins with the disclaimer that the word itself is annoyingly resistant to definition. Critics have a hard time finding "objective content" for the term,[1] and what was apparent to G. L. Van Roosbroeck in 1927 seems no less relevant today: "Turning to the critics for a definition of Decadence is much like listening to the famous orchestra of the King of Siam, where each musician plays the way he wants to and without regard for the score. It may even seem a superfluous cruelty to require that the word have a definite connotation in esthetics. It has done very well without it, and even today the critic seems to understand it as he likes."[2] Camille Paglia's *Sexual Personae,* a book of cultural criticism that achieved best-seller status in the early 1990s, is a recent example of the kind of loose, personal usage of the word *decadence* that Van Roosbroeck describes. Subtitled *Art and Decadence from Nefertiti to Emily Dickinson,* Paglia's study aims to make "decadence" part of a dialectic of nature and culture that spans practically the entire history of Western civilization. Most of the time, Paglia employs a Nietzschean vocabulary that makes "decadence" synonymous with "Apollonian objectification," a "*disease of the eye,* a sexual intensification of artistic voyeurism." For some reason, this Apollonian fascination with the visible is uniquely Western and specifically male. At other times, however, "decadence" is associated with "chthonic" or "daemonic" forces that are primarily female. For example, Euripides is called "the first decadent artist" who "substitutes a bloody moon for the golden Apollonian sun" by creating Medea, "nature's revenge." Elsewhere, "the feminine" is termed "a symptom of decadence." "Dionysian pluralism" is said to be "uncontrolled and eventually decadent," but "decadence" is also "a counterreaction within Romanticism, correcting its tilt toward Dionysus." This same corrective "decadence" "invents harsh new limits, . . . disciplining and intensifying the rogue western eye." Despite this discipline, excess or "toomuchness" is the "hallmark of decadence." At another point, however, "precision of bleakness and elegance" is said to be "decadent," but then Paglia returns to the idea of "decadence" as "a style of excess and extravagance."[3] By making "decadence" alternately Apollonian and Dionysian, male and female, uncontrolled and disciplined, profuse and precise, Paglia follows in a long tradition of cultural critics who use the word *decadence* in a way that is not only inexact, but often self-contradictory. Such usage is not necessarily a bad thing if it is acknowledged and examined. Indeed, the paradoxical nature of decadence and its resistance to definition are among the most important elements of its meaning. This point can be illustrated by a sampling of opinions from various critics, whose explanations all reflect the difficulty of definition and show how the problem of definition itself can illuminate the meaning of decadence.

One of the most comprehensive studies of the history of the idea of decadence is Koenraad W. Swart's *The Sense of Decadence in Nineteenth-Century France.* Despite the implications of this title, Swart provides a considerable explanation of the general notion of decadence prior to the nineteenth century, and not just in France. According to Swart, the origins of the concept of decadence as a universal principle of decay or decline can be traced to the earliest myths of both Eastern and Western culture, from the Indian "age of Kali, in which man was biologically, intellectually, ethnically, and socially far inferior to his ancestors," to the Iron Age of Greek and Roman mythology, "when civil strife, greed and other evils of civilization were rampant."[4] Swart shows that even in ages customarily regarded as energetically optimistic, a parallel sense of decadence was profoundly felt. The point is illustrated by observing that the idea of decadence was far from dead during the Renaissance: "The wide response to Savonarola's virulent denunciations of Renaissance society . . . indicates that many Italians at the end of the fifteenth century still looked upon their age as a period of crisis and corruption. In other words the exuberant optimism of the Renaissance is little more than a myth" (19). From such comments it is evident that Swart identifies decadence with a feeling of pessimism that is usually, though not always, a response to some historical reality—such as a military defeat, or a perception on the part of a populace that their country is undergoing a period of decline or outright ruin. Such was the case, for example, during the year 1870 in France, the *année terrible* when the defeat of the French army by the Prussians, the ensuing civil disturbances, and the reduction of ecclesiastical authority suggested that France had degenerated as a European power (123). In addition to this notion of decadence as historical pessimism, Swart offers this opinion of the meaning of literary decadence: "It was [the] consciously adopted ideology of Satanism, individualism, and estheticism that formed the most important legacy of French Romanticism to the so-called Decadent movement in literature at the end of the nineteenth century" (77). Thus a key to Swart's understanding of literary decadence is its relationship to romanticism. Decadence is therefore a kind of late romanticism, a lesser movement that accentuates elements of the greater one.

In a similar manner Mario Praz sees decadence as an extension of one element of romanticism, the erotic sensibility best typified by Sade. Such sensibility nurtures what Praz calls "The Beauty of the Medusa" and finds fatality attractive: "[T]o such an extent were Beauty and Death looked upon as sisters by the Romantics that they became fused into a sort of two-faced herm filled with corruption and melancholy and fatal in its beauty—a beauty of which, the more bitter the taste, the more abundant the enjoyment."[5] Themes evoking such beauty (for example, Salomé, Byzantium, the Hamlet of the graveyard scene) form the subject matter of the morbidly erotic strain of both romanticism and decadence, the principal difference being a matter of technique, as Praz indicates through his comparison of Delacroix, the romantic, and Gustave Moreau, the decadent:

> Delacroix, as a painter, was fiery and dramatic; Gustave Moreau strove to be cold and static. The former painted gestures, the latter attitudes. Although far apart in artistic merit . . . , they are highly representative of the moral atmosphere of the two periods in which they flourished—of Romanticism, with its fury of frenzied action, and of Decadence, with its sterile contemplation. The subject-matter is almost the same—voluptuous, gory exoticism. But Delacroix lives inside his subject, whereas Moreau worships his from outside, with the result that the first is a painter, the second a decorator. (303)

Praz thus presents a clear schema: decadence and romanticism are closely related on the basis of similar themes, albeit presented in dissimilar styles.

Somewhat at variance with Swart and Praz is A. E. Carter, who sees decadence not as an extension of romanticism but a reaction to it: "[T]he badness of civilization and the virtues of nature became part of a new sensibility, which we usually call Romantic; so much a part of it, in fact, that any revolt against Romanticism—when it came—was bound to be a revolt against the primitive and the natural. The cult of decadence is just such a revolt."[6] This does not mean, Carter argues, that the decadent mentality accepts the artificial as somehow "better" than the natural. On the contrary, the decadent does not dispute the romantic's claim that nature is good; he simply opts for the artificial. While never really denying the goodness of nature, the decadent prefers not to participate in it:

> Artificiality . . . is the chief characteristic of decadence as the nineteenth century understood the word. By a voluntary contradiction of the nature-cult, writers were able to see all the traditional Romantic themes in a new light and a new perspective. Their whole approach, of course, was entirely deliberate: from Gautier to Mirbeau, everybody who took up a pen realized that he was going "against the grain." . . . They accept civilization as corrupt, but take a perverse pleasure in that very corruption, preferring the civilized to the primitive and the artificial to the natural. They add nothing new to Rousseau's premise; they simply adopt a different attitude. (25)

Thus Carter's idea of the relationship of decadence to romanticism is, as he says, paradoxical (4), although fundamentally he interprets decadence not as an extension of romanticism but as a reaction to one aspect of it, the cult of nature.

Phillip Stephan, in *Paul Verlaine and the Decadence,* borrows heavily from Carter in defining decadence as a paradoxical reaction to romanticism: "The notion of decadence involves a sustained paradox, for, unable to choose between two opposing ideas, it cordially accepts both. Decadent thinkers accepted Rousseau's idea that nature is good and civilisation bad, yet they enthusiastically preferred the artificial: such perverse enjoyment of what is thought to be evil characterizes decadence."[7] This paradox involves the rejection of the natural on the one hand and on the other the acceptance of the unpleasant, the perverse, the morbid. This latter tendency is close to Praz's idea of Medusan beauty, and is clearly a part of the heritage of romanticism, or at least that element of romanticism that seeks "to revel in its own sufferings." Stephan elaborates: "Chateaubriand's René, the Lamartine of *Meditations poétiques,* and Musset suffered from their ill-fated loves, yet rather than seeking effective relief, they cultivated their misfortune as a source of inspiration. Decadent critics would refer back to the *mal du siècle* as an antecedent of their own pessimism.... Thus decadence was both a revolt against one kind of Romanticism and a continuation of another Romanticism's perversely deliberate choice of what is unpleasant" (18). This levelheaded approach takes account of romanticism as a complex concept with multiple tendencies. Stephan, then, is able to present decadence as a kind of synthesis of Carter's and Praz's views: as both a revolt against some of the programs of romanticism and a continuation of others.

The aforementioned critics all regard decadence as a literary "period" whose temporal limits, though varying to a degree, extend from the mid-nineteenth century (or slightly earlier) to the 1880s and 1890s, the fin de siècle. Swart, Praz, Carter, and Stephan all think of decadence as having a primary relationship with some aspect of romanticism. This is logical enough, since the backward glance seems implicit in the concept of decadence: all is before, nothing is after. The Russian poet Vyacheslav Ivanov saw decadence as "the feeling, at once oppressive and exalting, of being the last in a series."[8] The opposite point of view is taken by other critics, including Matei Calinescu, who regards decadence as looking forward instead of backward, as having a primary relationship not with an earlier period but with a later one. Decadence, to Calinescu, is one of the "faces of modernity," along with avant-garde, kitsch, and postmodernism. Much of Calinescu's argument about the emergence of decadence as a kind of premodernism is related to decadent style, whose principal theoretician seems to be Paul Bourget. Bourget was perhaps the first to take a theoretical interest in literary decadence, establishing "an analogy between the social evolution toward individualism and the 'individualistic' manifestations of artistic language, which are typical of '*le style de décadence.*'"[9] Calinescu translates Bourget's definition of the decadent style as follows: "One law governs both the development and the decadence of [the] organism which is language. A style of decadence is one in which the unity of the book breaks down to make place for the independence of the page, in which the page breaks down to make place for the independence of the sentence and in which the sentence breaks down to make place for the independence of the word" (170). Calinescu agrees with Bourget "that the concept of individualism is central to any definition of decadence" (170), and he draws the conclusion that individualism is the key to the aesthetic relationship of decadence to modernism: "A style of decadence is simply a style favorable to the unrestricted manifestation of aesthetic individualism, a style that has done away with traditional authoritarian requirements such as unity, hierarchy, objectivity, etc. Decadence thus understood and modernity coincide in their rejection of the tyranny of tradition" (171).

Calinescu's remarks about the resistance of decadence to tradition bring to mind Renato Poggioli's comments about the antagonistic anti-traditionalism of the avant-garde.[10] Within Poggioli's theoretical frame of reference on the avant-garde, however, decadence is seen as agonistic rather than antagonistic: "[A] passive agonism dominates the decadent mentality, the pure and simple sense of agony. Decadence means no more than a morbid complacency in feeling oneself passé: a sentiment that also, unconsciously, inspires the burnt offerings of the avant-garde to the cultural future" (76). Decadence, then, is an avant-garde spirit drained of the futuristic energy of the avant-garde: "[W]hile the futurist mentality tremulously awaits an artistic palengenesis, preparing for its coming practically and mystically, the decadent mentality resigns itself to awaiting it passively, with anguished fatality and inert anxiety" (75). Poggioli also surmises that decadence is "really an avant-garde movement while still recognizing its general kinship with romanticism," and at one point says that "decadence and avant-gardism are related, if not identical" (74, 75). Though modernism and avant-gardism are by no means identical, both have futuristic implications at odds with the willingness of the decadent mentality to "do nothing but appeal to defunct civilizations, to predecessor and ancient decadences" (74–75). Thus Calinescu's comment about the decadent rejection of tradition is challenged, yet that rejection may be excused as selective: the decadent accepts certain specifically decadent traditions (such as Byzantine Hellenism or Silver Latin). The point here is that—despite some qualifications—both Calinescu and Poggioli think of decadence not as a reaction to an earlier period but as a preparation and perhaps even a catalyst for a later one.

In contrast to all of the above critics, who conceive of decadence as existing in a dynamic relationship with another literary period, either earlier or later, the point of view of most French critics is that decadence is an isolated and rather minor movement, at best a preparation for the larger, more important symbolist movement. "In France . . . notions like *décadent, décadisme,* or *décadentisme* have been unable to shake off the memory of their short period of tremendous popularity."[11] This is the period that Calinescu aptly terms the "Decadent Euphoria," the late 1880s in France when cenacles were formed, manifestoes published, and literary reviews flourished, all under the banner of *décadisme.* Taking this brief period as his subject, Noël Richard in *Le Mouvement décadent* details the activities of Anatole Baju, whose attitude, contrary to Poggioli's idea of decadence as passive and inert, is that of the passionate revolutionary anarchist, as this manifesto makes clear:

> Not to recognize the state of decadence which we are in would be the height of insensibility. Religion, customs, justice, everything decays [*tout décade*].... Society comes apart under the corrosive action of a deliquescent civilization.... We commit this leaf to murdersome innovations, to stupefying audacities, to incoherences of thirty-six atmospheres at the furthest limit of their compatibility with those archaic conventions labeled by the term public morality. We will be the stars of an ideal literature.... In a word, we will be the Mahdis screaming and preaching eternally the dogma of elixir, the quintessential word of triumphant *décadisme.*[12]

The elixir of decadence: there is much fervor in Baju's phrases, and it is largely due to the swagger of such slogans that Richard ultimately defines decadence antiphrastically, as a type of youthful rebelliousness: "Aesthetic decadence must be understood by antiphrase: it is the synonym of lively youthfulness and renewal."[13] Richard owes something to Remy de Gourmont for this paradoxical definition. Just as Richard inverts the denotative meaning of decadence (age and decline become youth and renewal), Gourmont, after saying that "l'idée de décadence est identique à l'idée d'imitation," inverts the notion of imitation and calls decadence innovation: "However, if it is applied to Mallarmé and his literary group, the idea of decadence has been assimilated by its contrary, the very idea of innovation."[14] In both cases the antiphrases result because the conventional meanings of decadence are inadequate to describe the reality of a Baju or a Mallarmé. Both critics are thus addressing the question of decadence within the limited frame of reference provided by the activities of a few literary men in late nineteenth-century France, and this frame inhibits, to some degree, the development of a theory of decadence that is able to embrace the historical phenomenon of *décadisme.*

By contrast, the appearance of Jean Pierrot's *L'Imaginaire décadent* (1977) may mark a new trend in the treatment of decadence by French critics. Though still confining the concept of decadence to the last twenty years of the nineteenth century (with ample attention given, however, to the precursors of decadence), Pierrot enlarges upon it considerably. He takes issue with the traditional way that decadence has been regarded in French criticism, that is, as a transitional period of preparation for the symbolist movement in poetry. He questions this restrictive approach whose principal expositor is Guy Michaud:

> This limited view of decadence as merely an early and gestatory stage of symbolism is put forward and developed, in particular, by Guy Michaud. His classic interpretation presents decadence as a merely negative reaction to naturalism and Parnassianism, in contrast to the positive stance taken by symbolism. As symbolism took over from decadence, Michaud says, the expression of sadness and melancholy was succeeded by that of joy in life, vague emotionalism was replaced by the intellectual rigor of a coherent doctrine, and Verlaine was correspondingly ousted by Mallarmé as the predominant influence. Finally, the introversion of a self imprisoned within its own closed world was succeeded by the discovery of a higher reality at once impersonal and general in character.[15]

Pierrot proceeds to a point-by-point refutation of this oversimplified view of decadence, noting, for example, that the so-called transformation of decadence into symbolism could hardly have been as perceptible and radical as is generally believed since symbolism was never a "coherent doctrine," as Michaud claims (5–6). Pierrot is most emphatic in saying that decadence and symbolism cannot really be seen as rivaling one another for the favor of poets, and that decadence is too large a context for poetry alone: "Above all, however, it would be committing a serious error to regard the decadent movement as being merely a poetic period. In fact, decadence constitutes the common denominator of all the literary trends that emerged during the last decades of the nineteenth century" (7). Pierrot enumerates a number of features that are traditionally decadent, such as pessimism and antiquarianism, and stresses the evolution of a new aesthetic that rejects everyday reality to cultivate the *paradis artificiels* of the dream and drug-induced hallucination (9–11). But Pierrot elevates the status of decadence highest (at least in the context of French criticism) by emphasizing the importance of *l'esthétique décadent* in the evolution of modern literature: "[B]y dissociating art once and for all from the goal that had always been assigned it—the faithful imitation of nature regarded as the supreme norm—the decadent period does constitute an essential line of cleavage between the classical esthetic and the modern esthetic" (11). In so considering decadence as a modernist aesthetic whose theoretical base is antimimetic, Pierrot expands the notion of decadence well beyond historical *décadisme*.

A similar sense of expanded meaning has been evident for some time in Italian criticism, where the concept of *decadentismo* has a history and legitimacy generally lacking in the English and French critical traditions. In fact, *il decadentismo* "constitutes one of the major historical and aesthetic categories in Italian literary scholarship, comparable in complexity and scope with such concepts as romanticism, naturalism, or modernism."[16] Mario Praz's approach, discussed above, is typical of the Italian disposition to treat *il decadentismo* in large terms. But whereas Praz treats decadence as a species of romanticism, more recent Italian critics associate *il decadentismo* closely with modernism, so closely, in fact, that the two concepts are all but interchangeable. For example, Calinescu notes that Elio Gioanola's *Il decadentismo* (1977) "might be taken by an English reader, if its would-be translator were to replace *decadentismo* by 'modernism,' as one more introduction to literary modernism" (219). This is not to say that Italian criticism has abandoned the earlier view that decadence is an aspect of romanticism; it might be said, rather, that *il decadentismo* is now understood, more or less, as a modernization of romanticism. Gioanola, for example, finds in Baudelaire and Dostoevsky the key element of *decadentismo*—the discovery of the unconscious—a discovery that itself derives from romanticism and is later manifested in movements customarily called "modernist" (futurism, expressionism, surrealism, etc.). The crucial point about *decadentismo* in connection with the unconscious is that "decadentism is born when . . . one arrives at the identification of the Self and the World."[17] In other words, romanticism discovered the unconscious, but decadentism brought it to the surface and made it material so that it could then be codified and manipulated in various ways: as "surrealism" or "expressionism" by artists, as "psychology" or "analysis" by scientists. The materialization of the unconscious—identifying the self with the world—saves the self from sentimentality, which makes a great deal of difference as one moves from the expressiveness of the romantics to the interiority of the moderns. Gioanola is able to reach these types of conclusions because he is considering decadence as a concept, freed of such historical phenomena as the behavior of certain individuals deemed "decadent" by their contemporaries. As such, Gioanola's study is similar to Pierrot's, though it differs in degree, whereas a comparison of Gioanola and Richard reveals the more typical differences between Italian and French approaches to decadence: the Italian broad and theoretical, the French limited and documentary.

Looking over these definitions and approaches that are so diverse, we are struck by the contradictory nature of some rather well argued positions. Decadence seems to emerge as both an extension of and a reaction to romanticism; as both a languorous and a rebellious state of mind; as both a decorative, superficial art and a pioneering, profound aesthetic. And it is precisely *because* the definitions are contradictory that we will be able to gain further insight into the concept of decadence.

As the above survey suggests, the problem of defining decadence is not simply one of a plurality of meanings. If such were the case, the question "What is decadence?" could be rephrased as, say, "What are the varieties of decadence?" Thus it would be possible to explain how the same epithet—decadent—can be used to characterize the asceticism of a Schopenhauer and the bohemianism of a Swinburne: the word is valorized in one way by a certain type of philosophy, and in quite a different way by a certain type of behavior. Indeed, types of decadence can be discriminated, and the meaning(s) of decadence in a poem by Verlaine or an essay by Poggioli can be paraphrased, approximated in other language. This is one of the ways definitions are supposed to work, and decadence clearly has its share of equivalent meanings: social decay, historical pessimism, racial degeneration, cultural refinement, and so on. Yet even in so brief a list as this we can recognize the problem beyond the plurality of meanings in the definition of decadence. Certainly the coupling of such terms as *degeneration* and *refinement*, like the terms *asceticism* and *bohemianism* above, points to an underlying instability of meaning, and we must then ask whether this instability is, in turn, fundamental to the definition of decadence. Ultimately, we shall see that the very elusiveness of the notion of decadence is significant; that is, elusiveness signifies meaning.

One way of defining decadence in a relativistic sense is to say that the word functions as a general or all-purpose antonym. Its meaning in a specific context is derived from the exclusion or negation of the concept to which it is opposed, say, decadent versus bourgeois.[18] Such a juxtaposition, however, is never so simple as it seems, and we need only place the two words in a Marxist context to see them shading into one another. Yet there is something significant in the operation whereby the bourgeois mentality regards the bohemian as decadent, even as the Marxist uses the same epithet to describe the bourgeois. In both cases a decline from or opposition to arbitrarily defined norms is thought to be decadent. This relationship to some normative position is significant to the definition of decadence. What is implied by such an operation, at the level of literary art that we are presently to consider, is the transformation or outright subversion of certain literary norms or conventions.

Consider also the literary implications of another traditional juxtaposition: decadence and progress. When decadence is taken as an antonym of progress it connotes retrogression, decline, obsession with ancient, vanished civilizations. Given this context, the decadent is supposed to retreat into the past when faced by the future and its harbingers—science, technology, industrialization. Roger Williams makes the point that the progress of the nineteenth century, compared to earlier periods, was quite real indeed; that it truly was a time when life for the average person was improved by positive developments in various fields: "[D]oes any historian give us a world, before 1789, so celestial and sanitary that we would unhesitatingly opt for it ahead of the nineteenth century?" During this period of progress, Williams goes on, it is "astonishing to see the number of writers, philosophers, and critics who devoted entire careers to deploring the decadence of their age."[19] But in many cases what is deplored is not so much decadence as progress itself—progress as a form of decadence.

The term *decadence,* for instance, is used by French writers to describe English industrial society in the middle of the nineteenth century.[20] We need not refer, however, to this thoroughly documented reality of the working conditions in British factories to expose the opposition decadence/progress as problematical. In other words, the perception of progress as decadence is more than simply a reaction to the conditions under which progress comes about. As Calinescu argues:

> The critique of the myth of progress was started within the romantic movement, but it gained momentum in the antiscientific and antirationalistic reaction that marks the late nineteenth century and prolongs itself well into the twentieth. As a consequence—and by now this has become almost a truism—a high degree of technological development appears perfectly compatible with an acute sense of decadence. The fact of progress is not denied, but increasingly large numbers of people experience the *results* of progress with an anguished sense of loss and alienation. Once again, progress *is* decadence and decadence *is* progress.[21]

Yet we must hesitate over this synonymity as well. The opposition of decadence and progress should not yield fully to an identity of the two concepts. Certainly, elements associated with the idea of progress, such as bourgeois materialism, are incompatible with the aesthetic refinements of decadence. At the same time, other elements of decadence and progress may be distributed over the same field of meaning. For example, as Calinescu suggests, the paradox of progress is that whatever improves our lives alienates us from life: we are uncomfortable with the comfort made possible by progress. Gautier touches on this aspect of the nineteenth century in his essay on Baudelaire when he says that "artificial life has replaced natural life" ["la vie factice a remplacé la vie naturelle"].[22] Decadence and progress share a dehumanizing or antinatural tendency, and an affinity exists between the two concepts in that the decadent's taste for artificiality and the progressive's cultivation of technology are equally inorganic. Again, as with the opposition of decadence and bourgeois, decadence and progress begin to shade into one another, only more so. The notion of decadence as a relativistic antonym thus becomes suspect. The relationship of decadence to those words to which it is opposed may not, paradoxically, be oppositional.

The question of decadence is everywhere complicated by the same sort of instability of meaning. The rhetorical process of definition-by-restriction ends up admitting those very meanings the process is intended to exclude. To take yet another example, the definition of decadence as an antinomy of barbarism seems a perfectly stable reflection of the opposition of culture and nature. Yet when we recognize in the concept of decadence the primary meaning of *decay* we are immediately confronted with a metaphor of organicism: the state of culture decays, tends toward the state of nature represented by barbarism. Decadence and barbarism, like decadence and progress, are fused into a relationship that is reciprocal rather than oppositional. The concept of barbarism may be necessary to the concept of decadence; Poggioli comments on this reciprocity as follows:

> The very notion of decadence, at least its modern version, is practically inconceivable without this psychological compulsion, on the part of either the individual or the group, to become the passive accomplice and willing victim of barbarism.
>
> [A decadent] civilization falls defenseless before the onslaught of barbarism precisely because it envisages that scourge not only as a moral retribution, but also as the only possible biological alternative.
>
> When the hour of decision comes, he [the decadent] discovers all too late that history has reverted to nature; and that the barbarian, being nature's child, is now becoming history's agent. At this point the decadent recognizes that he is left no alternative but to play a passive, and yet theatrical, role on

> history's stage. That role is that of scapegoat or sacrificial victim; and it is by accepting that part, and acting it well, that he seals in blood the strange brotherhood of decadence and barbarism.[23]

Mario Praz further illuminates this "strange brotherhood" in his assessment of D'Annunzio: "D'Annunzio is a barbarian and at the same time a Decadent, and there is lacking in him the temperate zone which . . . is labelled 'humanity.' "[24] In other words, just as decadence and progress meet on the common ground of the antinatural, decadence and barbarism fuse in the notion of dehumanization. Indeed, the antinatural tendency of both decadence and progress could just as well be termed dehumanization. And if we move from the general concept of decadence to its particular manifestation in literary texts, the idea of dehumanization becomes especially significant, since this idea informs one of the more coherent (if conservative) theories of modern art, that of Ortega y Gasset.[25] Thus the traditional opposition of decadence to progress and barbarism does not lead to an identity of the concepts; rather, that opposition points to a commonality of meaning that helps to define decadence as a transition to modernism.

It is time now to assess all these "contradictory" definitions of decadence. First, I have shown through a survey of criticism that there is considerable disagreement as to the meaning of literary decadence. Moreover, the radical nature of this disagreement is striking: one critic views decadence as an extension of romanticism; another as a reaction to it; one calls it sterile imitation one minute, rich invention the next; and so on. Second, I have suggested that this critical disagreement may arise because decadence does not have a clear and stable referent: its meaning is determined by the word to which it is opposed. From these observations we might conclude that the concept of decadence is fundamentally contradictory, but having said this, we have said little that is helpful to an understanding of decadence in literature. On the other hand, if we ask ourselves *why* so many critics have offered contradictory definitions of decadence, and why the word decadence contradicts its meaning with every shift in context, we might arrive at a more useful dialectical tool than "contradiction" alone. For in virtually every case when decadence is examined, whether historically or linguistically, the contradictions in meaning arise because of a basic *interference* of ideas and literary tendencies. The way some nineteenth-century novelists reacted to romanticism by accentuating elements of extreme artificiality, while at the same time continuing the romanticist interest in erotic sensibility, is an obvious example of a more general quality of aesthetic interference that may be important to a definition of decadence. Literary decadence in the nineteenth century may very well be both an extension of and a reaction to romanticism, and the interference of this dual relationship might be observed in the same text (Walter Pater's *Marius the Epicurean,* for example). Similarly, the same text may reveal itself at the stylistic level to be simultaneously innovative and imitative, as strange as this sounds. Flaubert's imitation of epic style in *Salammbô* ends up like no epic ever written, and the result is something new for the novel. The Goncourt brothers' *Germinie Lacerteux* is, ostensibly, a picture of human squalor at its worst, yet this grimly realistic subject is presented in language (*écriture artiste*) that moves well beyond the tradition of realism. In each of these cases the writers are working within an unsettled aesthetic that—consciously or not—is a reaction to or a revision of an earlier literary tradition. But in no case is the break with tradition complete, and as a consequence a certain interference of aesthetic principles is discernible. A less sympathetic term for this literary ferment would be not interference but simple confusion; certainly it must be acknowledged that decadence has never had a good name, and the purpose here is not to undertake some wholesale amelioration of decadent literature. *Salammbô,* by most accounts, is far from being the finest of Flaubert's works, and neither the Goncourts, Pater, nor Huysmans can be credited with writing the great nineteenth-century novel. Let that accolade fall to Balzac, Stendhal, Dickens, Hugo, Tolstoy—whomever. Decadence is transition, a drama of unsettled aesthetics, and the mixture of literary tendencies constituting that transition is at once within and without tradition and convention.

Decadence, in short, amounts to a reformation of the aesthetic code whereby art brings forth its meaning. Christian and classical values are very much in the process of being rejected and replaced during the so-called decadent period; the challenge to the classical notion of art as representation (see Pierrot's argument above) is evidence of this upheaval. Further, the destruction and creation of aesthetic values during the nineteenth century may be the source of that sense of dynamism which leads Poggioli to identify decadence so closely with avant-gardism. An element of innovation does exist in decadent writing, a sense of newness that can easily be overlooked because of the intrinsic appeal of decadence to earlier periods. This penchant for the past is part of the general heritage of romanticism, but the discourse through which this antiquarian tendency is manifested separates itself from the very past it celebrates. In later chapters we shall see how Pater's evocation of Antonine Rome is cast in language that can only be called modern, and how Huysmans's Des Esseintes meditates on the ancients in linguistically inventive, neologistic terms. More and more, the representation of a romantic past is supplanted by the style of that representation, which brings us back to the larger point: that decadence, to modify Nietzsche's celebrated phrase, involves a transvaluation of the values of art. The novel in the hands of the decadent writer, generally speaking, places less value on the conventional devices of realism and naturalism than on the effects of language itself, and, as we shall see, the epithet *decadent* comes to be applied to certain novels for their "failure" to adhere to the aesthetic dictates of realism or to the conventions of some established genre (such as the historical novel, the naturalistic novel, the portrait novel, and so on). If we must have critical terms for this operation, whereby the artifice of realism gives way to the artifice and play of language itself, the words *mimesis* and *poesis* will suffice, though such a pairing suggests a more radical interference than is intended. In some decadent novels, the mimetic element is quite strong indeed, and we can certainly read the Goncourts' *Germinie Lacerteux*, for example, as one more novel in which the conventions of realism perform the mimetic trick of evoking a sense of reality for the reader. But enough of the poetic element is in *Germinie*—fine phrases and turns of style—to point to the poesis of language itself as something that subverts the mimetic effort by interfering with it. Surely the interference of convention and artifice is more radical in *Salammbô,* and the poesis of language there more at odds with the aims of mimesis, but the use of these terms should not imply the polarization of one element by another, lest we lose the sense of interference altogether, and with it, the notion of decadence as transition.

Decadence, then, is less a period of transition than a dynamics of transition. An interference of mimesis and poesis in the late nineteenth century makes up a large part of this dynamics. Dynamics implies movement, and by introducing a more pronounced element of poesis into the novel, decadent writers move away from mimesis as an aesthetic base. Again, Ortega y Gasset's concept of dehumanization aptly describes the decadent element in the transition from romanticism to modernism. What is meant by dehumanization, according to Ortega y Gasset, is a distortion of natural forms, an obscuring of recognizable, human elements in art, such as straightforward, realistic presentations of human situations in the novel and drama. His essay does not indicate a simple equivalent for dehumanization, but instead offers a complex of concepts by way of definition: irony, iconoclasm, aestheticism (i.e., "artistic art"), and so on. But a good part of the meaning of "dehumanization" has to do with distortion and obscurity, for the "new art" (Ortega y Gasset's terminology) is everywhere set in contrast to the straightforward, clear, traditional representations of reality in nineteenth-century art. Ortega y Gasset's presentation of the contrast between new and nineteenth-century art as an "optical problem," as two completely different ways of seeing reality, strongly suggests an affinity between "dehumanization" and distortion of natural forms and situations.[26] It should be borne in mind, however, that Ortega y Gasset is a critic of modernism who is also a modernist critic; and as a modernist himself, his interest in distortion and dehumanization cannot be separated from his promotion of high culture and pure art. His "optics" reinforces his politics, and makes his critical position ideologically consistent with the aesthetics of decadence because of a shared aversion to popular art and populist tastes. Decadence and dehumanization, it seems, are both part of the vast movement from romanticism to modernism that transforms "the folk" into "the masses."

Dehumanization thus involves a movement away from the conventions of realism that is both aesthetic and political. This antimimetic stance is at odds with most of the programs of romanticism, and most emphatically opposes the cult of nature. After all, the romantic "cult of nature" might well be called the culturalization of nature, a recognition that nature should be brought into the human sphere and so become coequal with culture. The romantic "return to nature" is, therefore, more of a revision than a return. The dehumanizing tendencies of modernism amount to the virtual exclusion of nature from culture, for modernism, or at least one rather important strain of modernism, suggests what might be called the hypercultural. We can scarcely read James Joyce, for example, without recognizing references to other literary works and other artifacts of Western culture, without deciphering a remarkably complex cultural code. Decadence takes up the antiquarian tendency in romanticism but abandons the cult of nature, and this combination of antiquarianism and antinaturalism is a clear presage, or transitional process, to the dehumanizing hyperculturalism of modernism.

Decadence functions as part of a dynamics of transition in another way as well. Here we may think of romanticism and decadence as existing in a kind of dialectical relationship (with "natural" and "antinatural" as the key terms in the relationship) that leads to a synthesis in modernism. The romantic culturalization of nature takes as one of its main programs a return to the speech of the common people, the natural rhythms and diction of everyday language—in short, a vernacular style (which, in turn, contributes to the development of realism). Against the grain of the vernacular style the decadent style emerges as fragmented and artificial. In fact, modernist style, or at least the style of the principal Anglo-American and Irish moderns (Joyce, Pound, Eliot), may be understood as the synthesis—or, perhaps, the static—of the romantic vernacular and the decadent artificial: consider Joyce's and Eliot's insistence on the importance of the natural speaking voice while simultaneously maintaining the relationship to high culture. As Geoffrey Hartman says of the principal modernists, "Though their art aimed for the genuine vernacular, it could not resist the appeal of forms associated with high culture, forms that remained an 'ideological' reflex of upper-class mentality."[27] Viewed in this way, decadence appears as that element in modernism which interferes with the vernacular heritage of romanticism.

Another type of decadent interference has to do with time. The relationship of decadence to temporality is perhaps too complex to be fully indicated here, but certainly we must note that the "period" of decadence, the late nineteenth century, is also a *time* of decadence: late, nineteenth, "last in a series." Whether the late nineteenth century was actually a period of decadence is open to debate; but clearly it was perceived as such, as a time when all was over, or almost over: not the end, but the ending. This sense of an ongoing ending helps to account, in yet another way, for the strange affinity between decadence and progress. More to the point is the effect that such a concept of time must have on the narrative art of the novel. After all, a novel cannot be over at the outset: sustaining a sense of chronologically progressive time is part of the artifice of the conventional realistic novel. And the conventional novelist has his ending at the end of the narrative structure, that ending having been prepared by character development, changes of scene, plot complication, and so on. The decadent novelist, on the other hand, is thwarted by his sense of decadence, and he needs something other than a chronologically progressive plot to fill the pages of his novel. The decadent novelist, in short, occupies his time with style, and this interference of a decadent sense of time and narrative time is yet another manifestation of an interference of poesis and mimesis. Huysmans's *A Rebours*, as we shall see, is one example of the way in which a decadent outlook on reality resists the narrative flow of the conventional novel. This suggests that one of the traditional axioms about decadent literature needs revising: that such literature is "characterized by non-creative imitation of a preceding and superior literary expression."[28] As far as the nineteenth-century novel is concerned, decadence occasions a turning away from preceding literary expression, because decadence as a concept and the novel as a form cannot be fully reconciled: newness becomes necessary, imitation no longer suffices.

In addition to formalist and aesthetic varieties of interference (poesis and mimesis, vernacular and artificial style), the movement through decadence toward modernism also involves large sociocultural shifts in the nature of authorship and readership. Elaine Showalter and others have discussed the importance of gender politics in this transition, describing the fin de siècle as a period of "sexual anarchy" when "New Women and male aesthetes redefined the meanings of femininity and masculinity."[29] Earlier in the nineteenth century, the sociological changes that resulted in increased opportunities for education and greater literacy among women than at any other time in history produced a vast new audience for literary art, and also changed the meaning of authorship itself: "In the case of novels . . . women were the main consumers, the main readers. The male artist, then, might be in something of an ideological bind: neither pure artist nor fully masculine."[30] This female gendering of the male writer complicates the idea of decadence in some interesting ways. On the one hand, the male author is heir to the misogynistic tradition of Schopenhauer, which aligns asceticism and aestheticism in such a way that, in theory, women are excluded from any chance of participation in cultural production. On the other hand, the male author, especially the male novelist, finds himself in a profession that, in reality, is becoming more and more a form of woman's work. Decadent writers have no sympathy at all for the vigorous, masculine world of the bourgeois businessman. On the contrary, they willingly accept the idea that they, like women, are outside that world. Flaubert, for example, had no trouble thinking of himself as an "hysterical old woman," and the Goncourt brothers sometimes describe themselves as sisters.[31] But this negative reaction to conventional notions of masculinity does not necessarily involve an endorsement of feminism. Showalter says that "[t]his paradox is at the heart of fin-de-siècle culture. Indeed, strongly anti-patriarchal sentiments could also coexist comfortably with misogyny."[32] Andreas Huyssen, commenting on Sartre's psychosexual study of Flaubert (*L'Idiot de la*

Famille), notes that the novelist (widely believed to have said, "Madame Bovary, c'est moi!") "fetishized his own imaginary femininity while simultaneously sharing his period's hostility toward real women, participating in a pattern of imagination and of behavior all too common in the history of modernism." Like Showalter, Huyssen sees the phenomenon of "imaginary femininity in the male writer" as a historical product of "the increasingly marginal position of literature and the arts in a society in which masculinity is identified with action, enterprise, and progress—with the realms of business, science, and law."[33] The decadent writer's self-idealization of himself as woman coupled with the negative fantasy of woman as the embodiment of all that is natural and therefore antithetical to the art he practices is another pattern of interference important to the concept of decadence itself. In terms of cultural history, this double gendering can be seen as a double negation—of both "male" modernity and "female" romanticism. In any event, the result of this double negation is a form of decadence that ends up participating in patriarchy even as it rejects masculinity. Small wonder, then, at the scarcity of female writers in the canon of decadent-aesthetic literature.

Recent commentary by female writers on the exclusion of women from late nineteenth-century culture is oddly in harmony with the views of the male writers who excluded them in the first place. Showalter notes that "women have traditionally been perceived as figures of disorder," and cites the political historian Carole Pateman's observation that women are regarded as "potential disrupters of masculine boundary systems of all sorts." In this formulation, women cross the border from order to chaos, becoming "inhabitants of a mysterious and frightening wild zone outside of patriarchal culture."[34] This notion of a "wild zone" outside of culture is central to Camille Paglia's thinking on decadence, as noted earlier. Although her usage of "decadence" is shifting and imprecise, Paglia's linkage of women with the chthonic realm of earthy Dionysianism is clear. The association of woman with the creative-destructive chthonic forces that Paglia celebrates is precisely the image of woman that fueled the male artist's misogyny in the late nineteenth century. Because of her ability to engender and sustain life, the woman is viewed by the decadent as more "natural" than man, whose domain is art. Since the natural is antithetical to art, and woman is natural, the artist must of necessity be removed from woman as far as possible. This paradigm of the artist as bachelor continues well into the twentieth century, with Franz Kafka being the best modernist exemplar of the model. The image of woman as the "natural" negation of male art is contradicted by the commercial and artistic success of female writers in the nineteenth century, a fact the decadent artist finds hard to reconcile with his misogynistic view of culture. When George Sand died, Edmond de Goncourt was certain that an autopsy would prove that she had been some kind of hermaphrodite, since no *real* woman could have written the books she did: "I believe that, if there were an autopsy made of women of original talent, like Madame Sand, Madame Viardot, etc., their genitals would be found similar to those of a man, their clitorises somewhat like our penises."[35]

Edmond de Goncourt's inability to reconcile the conventional view of woman as "natural" with George Sand's commercial and cultural success is one more pattern of interference common to the meaning of decadence in a larger sense. Indeed, the general notion of decadent art as something uncontaminated by the literary marketplace is contradicted by the Goncourt brothers' disappointment over the commercial failure of their books, and by the popular readership of Flaubert's novels and the success of Oscar Wilde's plays. This mixture of aesthetic detachment and commercial desire must be included in the general ferment of late nineteenth-century literary activity. Decadence includes this kind of interference, as well as the interference of poesis and mimesis that marks the reformation of the aesthetic code, which leads to such modernist qualities as dehumanization, hyperculturalism, "artistic" art, complexity, obscurity, and so on. To again invoke the organic metaphor at the root of decadence, what is crucial about the notion of decay is not so much the change from a greater to a lesser state, but the changing itself. The time of decadence is a time of transition. Flaubert's entry for "AGE (OUR)" in his *Dictionary of Received Ideas* reads as follows: "Thunder against it. Complain that it is not poetic. Call it a period of transition, of decadence."[36] Baudelaire, also, called Victor Hugo a "compositeur de décadence ou de transition";[37] what is interesting about this statement is that it places Baudelaire himself at a time after the transition. That is, Baudelaire did not perceive himself as decadent, but as preceded by a decadence that was a transition to his own sense of modernity. Paradoxically, this is the way Baudelaire emerges to later critics as decadent—as coming *before* modernity. This is the sense in which decadence should be understood: not reflexively, as a debased and imitative version of something that has gone before, but as a predication toward a later condition, a subsequent sensibility.

For this reason, in the pages to follow, decadence will not be treated as an imitative or "inferior" form of literary expression. That conception of decadence may have its relevance to some nineteenth-century writers, but such a view ultimately depends on standards of judgment that risk being little more than arbitrary preferences, matters of individual taste. Further, I make no attempt here to develop points well established in the critical canon already, such as the ascendant position of the artificial over the natural, or the decadent predisposition toward perversity and morbidity. The significance of such thematic concerns is not to be denied, but that significance will be invoked only on those occasions when the issue of transition arises; my purpose is to show the relationship of decadence to the development of the modern novel. In the succeeding chapters several works will be discussed that seem remarkably dissimilar when they are removed from the context of decadence. Flaubert's *Salammbô*, for example, might appear to have little in common with Pater's *Marius the Epicurean*. What is important are decadent elements in each work that lead to later developments, even though the decadence of Flaubert can scarcely be expected to coincide with the decadence of Pater. But if we can illuminate transition by discussing the decadent elements in *Salammbô* as well as in *Marius*, then we are well on our way to demonstrating that decadence is indeed what we have called it: a substratum that underlies the literary activities of the latter part of the nineteenth century, and that helps us to arrive at literary modernity.

2

Decadence and Romanticism: Flaubert's *Salammbô*

Flaubert's *Salammbô* was published in 1862, some six years after *Madame Bovary.* Then as now, the work defies simple description or ready categorization, for a number of reasons. Principal among them is the odd juxtaposition of Flaubert's first and second published novels: the spare, precise realism of *Madame Bovary,* the lush overabundant romanticism of *Salammbô;* the provincial setting of Yonville-l'Abbaye, the exotic landscape of Carthage; the tormented sensuality of Emma Bovary, the quiescent mysticism of Salammbô. These two novels alone argue Harry Levin's case that *alternativement* "subsumes the creative rhythm of Flaubert's career."[1] Even though such alternation between "realistic spleen" and "romantic ideal"[2] may seem too schematic, the realistic devices that make *Madame Bovary* succeed as a representation of provincial life are hard to find in *Salammbô.* Closely related to this "romanticism or realism" question is the problem of genre. *Salammbô* is a highly poetic work, yet it is clearly not a poem; it has certain epic features, yet it is by no means an epic; it has been called a historical novel, but Georg Lukács follows Sainte-Beuve in arguing that it is not truly historical. More recent efforts at generic classification tend to place the work in the category of the fantastic as defined by Todorov, but certain events in the novel suggest that it has a closer kinship with the marvelous than the fantastic.[3]

From any one of these particular perspectives, *Salammbô* may appear flawed. Judged by the standards of the historical novel set by Sir Walter Scott, Flaubert's work falls short. In the earliest review of the novel, Sainte-Beuve argued that *Salammbô* could not succeed as a historical novel because the historical period Flaubert resuscitates is extremely unfamiliar to the modern reader.[4] Ancient Carthage seems too remote, both culturally and temporally, to appeal to anyone who is not of a strictly archaeological turn of mind. But if this limited view of the work is abandoned, the novel no longer appears as some malformed creation that fails to satisfy the expectations created by a particular genre. Instead, it may be viewed as an aggregate of several traditions and literary tendencies that can be termed "decadent." Decadence, in fact, provides a conceptual unity that is useful to the critical analysis of *Salammbô*. Calling the novel decadent, however, runs the risk of being little more than simple nominalism, so it remains now to show in a more detailed and substantial fashion the meaning of decadence as it relates to *Salammbô*.

Salammbô is decadent not by design but by decree. The work is pronounced "decadent" in Sainte-Beuve's 1862 *Lundi* reviews, where certain stylistic features of Flaubert's prose are compared to those of the writers of the Roman decadence. Thus the epithet "decadent" is a term of reproach at first, a minor swipe of the critic's pen much in the manner of Louis Leroy's derisive label *impressionniste*.[5] As with impressionism, the original term of censure lingers long after the censure itself has given way to praise (though praise of Flaubert's "decadence" is not so unqualified as praise of Monet's "impressionism"). And like impressionism, decadence is not a priori a category into which the work of art is placed, but an evolving aesthetic cotemporal with the creation of those works it seeks to describe. Thus to some degree *Salammbô* defines decadence, and decadence comes to mean more than, say, "mannered imitation," simply by the fortuitous association of the word and the work of art. Another reviewer in 1862 might have used another term to describe *Salammbô*, but this is a moot point. Decadence was Sainte-Beuve's term, and it has come to be ours as well. Our usage, however, is less pejorative than Sainte-Beuve's, who used the word because Flaubert's novel, to him, represented an unacceptable deviation from normative or conventional standards of literary judgment. Such deviation now appears a good thing to us; indeed, most of the novels associated with the idea of decadence in this study move away from the traditional norms of nineteenth-century realism and head in several new directions. Despite this quality of innovation, however, decadence remains an appropriate descriptive term because of certain thematic and stylistic characteristics, and because of the way those characteristics interfere with the narrative itself.

This sense of interference is created by Flaubert's elaborate and extended descriptions of unfamiliar and exotic aspects of life in ancient Carthage. And since *everything* in ancient Carthage is unfamiliar and exotic, the narrative is brought to a halt on every page. Always, something requires description: an ancient structure, an obscure cultural practice, an exotic mode of dress. The description of Salammbô herself is telling: "Her hair, which was powdered with violet sand, and combined into the form of a tower, after the fashion of the Chanaanite maidens, added to her height. Tresses of pearls were fastened to her temples, and fell to the corners of her mouth, which was as rosy as a half-open pomegranate. On her breast was a collection of luminous stones, their variegation imitating the scales of the murena" (1:13). ["Sa chevelure, poudrée d'un sable violet, et réunie en forme de tour selon la mode des vierges chananéennes, la faisait paraître plus grande. Des tresses de perles attachées à ses tempes descendaient jusqu'aux coins de sa bouche, rose comme une grenade entrouverte. Il y avait sur sa poitrine un assemblage de pierres lumineuses, imitant par leur bigarrure les écailles d'une murène" (56).][6] The way the description functions in this brief passage is typical of the book as a whole. Pictorial language and figurative language are always at odds; images are constantly undermined by similes comparing the concrete to the exotic. "Hair combined into the form of a tower" is clear enough, but the clarity dissipates when the simile is extended: "after the fashion of the Chanaanite maidens." This pattern of interference compounds the larger interference of description and narration and makes the plot of the novel secondary to its stylistic surface. Flaubert, in short, does what decadence by definition must always do: he makes the superficial substantial.

A summary of the plot of *Salammbô,* therefore, does a disservice to the novel by substituting substance for surface. Readers who are unfamiliar with the novel should keep this caveat in mind through the following précis (and those who know the novel may pass over it).

Salammbô opens with the contrast of a group of drunken, unruly mercenaries camped at Megara outside the city of Carthage, one of the great centers of Phoenician civilization. The mercenaries are barbarians in the root sense of the word, since they all come from different parts of the ancient world and speak any number of strange tongues incomprehensible to the sophisticated Carthaginians in their walled city. Flaubert places a great deal of emphasis on the linguistic mixture of the mercenary army:

"Beside the heavy Dorian dialect were audible the resonant Celtic syllables rattling like chariots of war, while Ionian terminations conflicted with consonants of the desert as harsh as the jackal's cry" (1:2–3). ["On entendait, à côté du lourd patois dorien, retentir les syllabes celtiques bruissantes comme des chars de bataille, et les terminaisons ioniennes se heurtaient aux consonnes du désert, âpres comme des cris de chacal" (45).] The double image of barbarism and civilization, together with the description of the heteroglot hoards, looks forward to Gautier's description of the decadent style and to Verlaine's sonnet "Langeur," with its contrast between the indolent decadent and the vigorous barbarians massed on the horizon.

The barbarians in *Salammbô* are restless and impatient because they have not been paid their blood-wages for service in the Carthaginians' campaigns of conquest. Their frustration is focused on the absent Carthaginian leader Hamilcar Barca, and they vent this frustration by freeing a number of his slaves, among them the Greek captive Spendius, who sees in the restless mercenaries an opportunity to foment a larger rebellion and gain power for himself. Meanwhile, the Carthaginians try to placate the soldiers by feeding them huge feasts and countless bowls of wine, but this strategy backfires when the mercenaries go on a drunken rampage through Hamilcar's gardens. The climax of this episode comes when the barbarians cook a number of sacred fish taken from the pools in the Barca garden, whereupon Hamilcar's daughter Salammbô appears in her role as priestess of the moon-goddess Tanit to bewail this blasphemous act. She speaks in an ancient Canaanite dialect that the mercenaries cannot understand, but it has its effect nonetheless. The Numidian mercenary Narr'Havas and the Libyan Mâtho are particularly smitten by the display of female beauty and religious mystery, and both want to see more of Salammbô, who promptly disappears.

The Libyan Mâtho is then befriended by the opportunistic Spendius, who helps him get inside the walls of Carthage. The Carthaginian citizens have closed their gates to the restless army, and with good reason: the mercenaries now plan to exact their wages from the city by conquering it. Spendius and Mâtho enter Carthage through the city's aqueduct and make their way to the temple of Tanit, where they steal the mysterious zaïmph, the veil of the moon-goddess herself. Mâtho goes to Salammbô's bedroom wrapped in the veil, hoping to make a gift of it to her. Instead, she cries for help and her servants respond. Since they, like all Carthaginians, are forbidden to touch the sacred veil, Mâtho is safe so long as he keeps it wrapped about him. In this way he makes his escape from Carthage and returns to become the leader of the barbarian army—such is the power conferred on the keeper of the zaïmph.

The Carthaginians are devastated by the loss of the mysterious veil. At this low point Hamilcar Barca returns and engages the mercenary force in battle with a newly formed army. He is on the verge of defeat when the eunuch priest Schahabarim has the ingenious idea of sending Salammbô to seduce Mâtho and so recover the veil, and with it, the fortunes of Carthage. Salammbô prepares herself for this task by performing a ritualistic dance with a sacred python, then makes her way to the barbarian camp. She returns from Mâtho's tent with the veil but without her virginity, which prompts Mâtho's jealous rival Narr'Havas to switch sides and help Hamilcar butcher the barbarians. Hamilcar rewards Narr'Havas for his loyalty with the promise of marriage to his daughter Salammbô.

The description of the ensuing butchery is protracted and exotic, to say the least, and includes the gruesome crucifixion of Hamilcar's degenerate ally Hanno at the hands of the barbarians. When Mâtho is captured, he is sentenced to run a gauntlet of Carthaginian citizens who flay his body and shred his flesh to pulp before a priest rips the still-beating heart from his chest. The mutilation of Mâtho is presented almost as a part of Salammbô's wedding ceremony. She is married to Narr'Havas, as Hamilcar promised, but when she raises her cup to toast Carthage's most recent victory, she drops dead. She did, after all, touch the veil of Tanit.

This summary of *Salammbô* conveys some of the strangeness and remoteness of the novel, but it conceals Flaubert's implicit comparison of ancient Carthage to contemporary France. This comparison was also lost on Sainte-Beuve, who likened the novel to antiquity only on the basis of the book's style, which reminded him of something out of the Roman decadence. But the comparison of a prior decadence to a contemporary one does not extend to the subject matter of the novel, as Sainte-Beuve's comments on the historical remoteness of the Carthaginian material suggest. His charge that ancient Carthage is too unfamiliar to interest most readers assumes that familiarity is grounded in knowledge of antiquity, whereas Flaubert evidently proceeded on the contrary assumption that any antiquity, no matter how remote, could be made familiar to the reader if it included enough parallels with contemporary life. For example, during the feast that opens the novel a rumor starts among the mercenaries that they have been poisoned by the Carthaginian authorities. Since no record in antiquity for this episode exists, Flaubert probably has in mind the rumors that the great cholera epidemics of 1832 and 1848 were somehow created by the French government as a diversion from political problems. Another example of the parallelism of Carthaginian and Parisian society involves Flaubert's deliberate anachronism of having a great aqueduct supply Carthage with its drinking water. The aqueduct most likely has its origins not in antiquity but in Baron Haussmann's plan, dating from 1854, to use a hundred-mile-long aqueduct to introduce fresh drinking water into Paris from the springs at Somme-Sonde. This detail is only the most glaring evidence that Flaubert meant for his readers to see a parallel between the design of ancient Carthage and the redesign of Paris during the Second Empire. Like Haussmann's Paris, Flaubert's Carthage is going through a process of radical rebuilding: temples are moved, ancient walls are torn down, and new ramparts are built using the stones of the old structures. In addition, much of the material in Flaubert's novel concerning the Carthaginian people themselves harmonizes with a number of contemporary racial theories, such as the one developed in the comte de Gobineau's *Essai sur l'inégalité des races humaines* (1853–55). Gobineau attributed the ruin of ancient civilizations to the inherent inferiority of certain races and argued that the fall of Carthage resulted, in part, from the ethnic inferiority of the Phoenician people. The collapse of Carthage is also attributed to the dilution of the "pure" national stock that results from the sort of mingling of the races Flaubert describes in his novel. For Gobineau, the example of Carthage is a cautionary one, since the decadence of the ancient empire suggests the contemporary decline of France. In this, Flaubert follows Gobineau: "*Salammbô* contains this same sense of the inevitability of Carthage's collapse, describing a civilisation which has passed its peak and is moving into the period of religious fanaticism, excessive luxury, immorality and decadence which Gobineau believed to be symptomatic of the last stages of national decline."[7]

Flaubert was not alone in comparing an ancient civilization on the brink of collapse to contemporary French society. However, the usual comparison involved not Carthage but ancient Rome, as the example of Thomas Couture's huge painting *Les Romains de la décadence* (now in the Musée d'Orsay) shows. The canvas was said to have been inspired by a quotation from Juvenal, and Couture drew support for his implicit criticism of French civilization from the Roman satirist's assertion that "the Roman Empire lost its power not through its earlier exertions of war but through its later cultivation of vice during years of peace."[8] The appearance of the painting at the salon of 1847 created a sensation, in part because Couture provided a pictorial commentary, indirect but unmistakable, on the dire state of the nation that had already been announced in print by such writers as Hippolyte Taine and Edgar Quinet, who had both compared mid-century France to decadent Rome. Arsène Houssaye, one of Couture's contemporaries, expressed the typical reaction to the painting when he wrote in his memoirs that the artist had "depicted the *French* of the Decadence. Can't you just see the French orgy?"[9] Flaubert went against this trend when he chose Carthage rather than Rome as the ancient emblem of contemporary French decadence, and his reasons for making the substitution are complicated. In a letter to Maxime du Camp, Flaubert imagines living in Rome at the time of Caesar or Nero and watching a triumphal procession through the city: "Antiquity is where we must live, you see. Only there does one find enough poetic air to fill one's lungs, air like that on a high mountain, so much of it that it sets the heart racing."[10] Here, Flaubert treats Roman antiquity as the idealized site of robust, original art; imagining himself in Rome is Flaubert's way of describing an aesthetic version of *aretē,* a condition of artistic excellence. In this context, the choice of ancient Carthage to represent contemporary decadence is quite logical. By writing about Carthaginian civilization, Flaubert put himself in the strong, metaphorically "Roman" position of taking an entire decadent culture captive. Indeed, Flaubert's fiction and Roman history are contiguous in that the novelist's reconstruction of Carthage implies its imminent destruction, for the city is so weakened by its victory over the barbarians that its fall to imperial Rome is inevitable. The next "chapter" of *Salammbô,* so to speak, is the annihilation of Carthage by the Romans.

If Flaubert's appeal to Carthage as a predecessor of French decadence is idiosyncratic, the appeal in itself is typical of the late nineteenth-century decadent sensibility. As discussed in Chapter 1, anxiety over cultural collapse is frequently accompanied by longing for cultural renewal. Poggioli's observation that the decadent is often willing to suffer immolation at the hands of the barbarians for the sake of cultural regeneration finds added support in Flaubert: "Perhaps we need barbarians. Humanity, the perpetual old man, requires infusions of new blood during his occasional agonies. How low we are! And what universal decrepitude!"[11] The romantic reflex, which regards prior culture as better, and better because it is closer to some mythical *archē* or origin, is turned inside-out by Flaubert's revival of ancient Carthage. In fact, the general impulse to turn to the past in quest of models for decadence is a fundamental perversion of the romantic temperament. In a discussion of Flaubert's complex relationship to romanticism, Eugenio Donato says of *Salammbô* that the novel makes no attempt to revive the past for the sake of some purifying origin: "The perception that Flaubert's France is at the end of a history of which Carthage represents, if not the beginning, then at least a more primitive or even original moment, is illusory. Carthage itself is at the end of history."[12] Flaubert's quasi-romantic revival of Carthage is therefore charged with paradoxes. The corrupt Carthaginians will be swept away, not by barbarians, but by Romans, model decadents for everyone except Flaubert. Also, the "romantic" revival of a civilization at the end of history suggests a longing for the end of French civilization. By taking the past as a model for the future, Flaubert expresses a paradoxical nostalgia for the millennium; that is, the anxious feeling that civilization is about to end is replaced by the concern that it will *not.* At heart, Flaubert fears that the pageant of mediocrity will go on forever, that the age of the triumphal procession is over.

Although Sainte-Beuve did not comment on Flaubert's appeal to Carthage as a prior decadence, he did note the novel's strain of sadism, which the critic claims is Flaubert's "invention," something outside the realm of available archeological evidence.[13] Certainly, the "influence" of the marquis de Sade must be recognized as one aspect of the novel's decadence, and of decadence in a more general sense, as Mario Praz argues in his study of romanticism.[14] However, as Roger Williams says, we should not assume that Flaubert "derived his knowledge of sadism from reading Sade," nor argue too strongly for the place of sadism in *Salammbô.* Other aberrations of human behavior seem more important here: "In no other work did Flaubert more clearly reveal his insight into the association of sexual frustration with hysteria, and with the tendency to seek relief in mysticism or religious fanaticism."[15] Thus in *Salammbô* sadism is not a major theme of the novel, though it does provide an appropriate coda. The note of sadism is sounded, mingled with hysteria, in the final chapter, as Mâtho runs the gauntlet of Carthaginians who tear at his flesh with their fingernails, burn his skin with hot oil, sprinkle glass under his bare feet, and so on:

> In their eyes the body of this victim was something peculiarly theirs, and was adorned with almost religious splendor. They bent forward to see him, especially the women. They burned to gaze upon him who had caused the deaths of their children and husbands; and from the bottom of their souls

there sprang up in spite of themselves an infamous curiosity, a desire to know him completely, a wish mingled with remorse which turned to increasing execration....

A child rent his ear; a young girl, hiding the point of a spindle in her sleeve, split his cheek; they tore handfuls of hair from him and strips of flesh; others smeared his face with sponges steeped in filth and fastened upon sticks....

Excepting his eyes he had no appearance of humanity left; he was a long, perfectly red shape; his broken bonds hung down his thighs, but they could not be distinguished from the tendons of his wrists, which were laid quite bare.... (2:167, 168, 170–71)

[Le corps de cette victime était pour eux une chose particulière et décorée d'une splendeur presque religieuse. Ils se penchaient pour le voir, les femmes surtout. Elles brûlaient de contempler celui qui avait fait mourir leurs enfants et leurs époux; et du fond de leur âme, malgré elles, surgissait une infâme curiosité,—le désir de le connaître complètement, envie mêlée de remords et qui se tournait en un surcroît d'éxecration....

Un enfant lui déchira l'oreille; une jeune fille, dissimulant sous sa manche la pointe d'un fuseau, lui fendit la joue; on lui enlevait des poignées de cheveux, des lambeaux de chair; d'autres avec des bâtons où tenaient des éponges imbibées d'immondices lui tamponnaient le visage....

Il n'avait plus, sauf les yeux, d'apparence humaine; c'était une longue forme complètement rouge; ses liens rompus pendaient le long de ses cuisses, mais on ne les distinguait pas des tendons de ses poignets tout dénudés.... (454–55, 455–56, 458)]

The interest in sadism and hysteria, however, is subordinate to a more general pathological interest, manifested not only in passages like the one above, but throughout the novel, and most emphatically in the descriptions of Hanno's hideous disease: "Ulcers covered the nameless mass; the fat on his legs hid the nails of his feet; from his fingers there hung what looked like greenish strips; and the tears streaming through the tubercles on his cheeks gave to his face an expression of frightful sadness" (2:144–45). ["Des ulcères couvraient cette masse sans nom; la graisse de ses jambes lui cachait les ongles des pieds; il pendait à ses doigts comme des lambeaux verdâtres; et les larmes qui ruisselaient entre les tubercules de ses joues donnaient à son visage quelque chose d'effroyablement triste" (430).] Such concern with sickness and the decay of human flesh—really an index to Flaubert's pessimism—makes up part of the thematics of decadence.[16]

Illness is not, in itself, necessarily decadent, but Hanno's sickness is.

This prompts a peculiar question: "What makes decay *decadent*?" The question is not so redundant as it seems. In Shakespeare's sonnets, human mortality is a cause for melancholy; in any number of romantic works (*La Bohème,* for instance), illness intensifies love. But in *Salammbô,* the sickness of Hanno is not only evidence of inner corruption, it is also the corollary of refined, epicurean tastes. Hanno's body is being eaten away by leprosy, but the body itself is covered by luxurious garments: a scarf, a belt, a large black cloak with double-laced sleeves ["une écharpe, une ceinture et un large manteau noir à doubles manches lacées" (87)]. He also wears earrings, gold clasps, a necklace of blue stones, and sprinkles gold sequins ["des paillettes d'or" (86)] in his hair. His diet includes such delicacies as flamingo tongues seasoned with honeyed poppy seeds ["des langues de phénicoptères avec des graines de pavot assaisonnées au miel" (173)] and a drink made of weasel's ashes and asparagus boiled in vinegar ["la cendre de belette et des asperges bouillies dans du vinaigre" (88)], but his breath still gives off a stench like that of a rotting corpse (176). When his illness worsens, he paints over the sores on his face—"Il avait peint avec du fard les ulcères de sa figure" (195). The idea of putting rouge ("fard") on ulcers is interesting, since *fard* has the more general meaning of "artifice." Decay is decadent, in short, when artifice is used not merely to conceal but to decorate decomposition. In a way, the sequined degeneration of Hanno's body is an apt figure for the body of the text Flaubert has written. In *Salammbô,* Flaubert decorates decline with his stylistic brilliance, studs the narrative with prismatic fragments. When Paul Bourget describes *le style de décadence,* he uses an organic metaphor that likens the composition of the text to the decomposition of the body: the book gives way to the page, the page to the paragraph, paragraph to phrase, phrase to word. In *Salammbô,* the disintegration of decadence is a textual principle that the description of Hanno's crucified dead body only enforces: "His spongy bones had given way under the iron pins, portions of his limbs had come off, and nothing was left on the cross but shapeless remains, like the fragments of animals that are hung up on huntsman's doors" (2:147). ["Ses os spongieux ne tenant pas sous les fiches de fer, des portions de ses membres s'étaient détachées,—et il ne restait à la croix que d'informes débris, pareils à ces fragments d'animaux suspendus contre la porte des chasseurs" (433).] Even here, the shapeless clumps of dead flesh are marked by artifice: at the top of Hanno's cross hangs a broad golden ribbon ["un large ruban d'or brillait" (433)].

In addition to his recognition of this "sadistic" element, Sainte-Beuve noticed certain qualities in *Salammbô* that set it off from other fiction, and while he may have called the work decadent with negative connotations in mind, his observations help to clarify the emergence of a new aesthetic. The particular point in Sainte-Beuve's review where the notion of decadence is invoked concerns Flaubert's use of the phrase "un silence énorme." The critic finds the expression "forced," and goes on to make the analogy with writers of the Roman decadence by saying that such expressions "date" the book and justify comparisons with Lucian or Claudian.[17] Elsewhere, Sainte-Beuve notes that Flaubert's novel underplays the significance of actual political and historical events, as these and other elements of "the grand current of civilization are sacrificed . . . or subordinated entirely to the exorbitantly descriptive side" of things that is called mere "dilettantism."[18] To appreciate that silence can be called enormous and that narrative movement can be subordinated to exorbitant description requires an artifice of reading that has become more fully accepted since Sainte-Beuve.[19] And both these observations point toward a single aesthetic fact about *Salammbô* more comprehensible now than then: spatial elements dominate the temporal; description occupies a place of importance accorded to narration in the past.

Throughout *Salammbô,* the drama of human situations is defused by the ornamentation of language, the narrative flow everywhere arrested by florid descriptive passages:

> Far in the background stood the palace, built of yellow mottled Numidian marble, broad courses supporting its four terraced stories. With its large, straight, ebony staircase, bearing a prow of a vanquished galley at the corners of every step, its red doors quartered with black crosses, its brass gratings protecting it from scorpions below, and its trellises of gilded rods closing the apertures above, it seemed to the soldiers in its haughty opulence as solid and impenetrable as the face of Hamilcar. (1:2)
>
> [Le palais, bâti en marbre numidique tacheté de jaune, superposait tout au fond, sur de larges assises, ses quatre étages en terrasses. Avec son grand escalier droit en bois d'ébène, portant aux angles de chaque marche la proue d'une galère vaincue, avec ses portes rouges écartelées d'une croix noire, ses grillages d'airain qui le défendaient en bas des scorpions, et ses treillis de baguettes dorées qui bouchaient en haut ses ouvertures, il semblait aux soldats, dans son opulence farouche, aussi solennel et impénétrable que le visage d'Hamilcar. (44)]

This description of the palace of Hamilcar, only the fifth paragraph of the novel, illustrates quite well the process repeated to the end of the book.

Our interest in this passage is so taken over by the description of Hamilcar's palace that we hardly notice the characterization of Hamilcar himself. The opening paragraph of the novel tells us that we are in Hamilcar's gardens outside Carthage; the second, that Hamilcar commanded a number of soldiers in Sicily. It is some pages before we infer, more or less, the dramatic situation that opens the novel: a group of mercenaries in the service of the Carthaginians is growing restless because they have not received the payment that is due them. Such straightforward narrative exposition is all but lost in the plethora of bronze breastplates, emerald-jeweled cups, golden amphorae, and the like. Sainte-Beuve called *Salammbô* "[une] espèce de poëme en prose,"[20] and it is certainly true that the way the language is used in the work is rather poetic than prosaic, less a means to some narrative end than an end in itself. That language should be so used in a novel was something relatively new in 1862, so new that Sainte-Beuve could only call it dilettantism and decadence because to him the work was clearly at variance with prevailing novelistic standards. And a principal reason for the association of a particularly poetic novel with the idea of decadence rests in *Salammbô*'s affinity with a particular type of poetry.

If *Salammbô* seems to belong more to the history of poetry than to that of the novel, the school of poetry that can most illuminate the work is *le Parnasse* and the concern with l'art pour l'art. In 1860, Flaubert described his new novel to the Goncourt brothers by saying that "the banner of the Doctrine will be carried openly this time," and that it would "prove nothing, say nothing—neither historical, satirical, nor humorous."[21] These remarks, together with other of Flaubert's pronouncements,[22] leave no doubt that the "Doctrine" to be employed is the idea of l'art pour l'art, and the thrust of Flaubert's statement is that the proposed novel will be an autonomous work, related to nothing so much as itself. Of course, the case can also be made that Flaubert's thinking about the novel owes little to *le Parnasse.* After all, there is the famous letter to Louise Colet of 1852 in which is sounded the Flaubertian aesthetic of pure style and the ideal of writing a "book about nothing" ("un livre sur rien").[23] Such aesthetic purpose makes the Parnassian poet's preoccupation with conventional notions of beauty seem narrow by comparison. Nevertheless, the particular instance of *Salammbô*—and not so much Flaubert's general aesthetic theorizing—suggests certain points of similarity between the novel and *le Parnasse.*

The conception of l'art pour l'art is a key to the larger aesthetic of the

Parnassian poets, originating at least as early as Victor Hugo's 1829 preface to the first edition of *Les Orientales.* There the phrase does not appear, but the essential l'art pour l'art attitude toward poetry and poets does.[24] A few years later, Gautier's preface to *Mademoiselle de Maupin* (1835) makes the point that poetry exists only for beauty, and therein consists its "usefulness": "Nothing is truly beautiful unless it is useless."[25] The real issue at stake is not whether poetry is useful or useless, but whether its purpose is independent of such matters as morality, science, politics, and so on. The relationship of l'art pour l'art to the idea of decadence rests in the opposition of those poets in France in the mid-1850s advocating the position that poetry should help to usher in the new world of progress and industry and those insisting on the pure function of poetry as a vehicle for beauty alone. The lines are drawn most clearly by Maxime du Camp on the one hand and by Leconte de Lisle on the other. Du Camp "emphasized that a new world had been born from the union of science and industry and that literature inherited as its function to act as an interpreter of science as well as a guide to industry."[26] Leconte de Lisle defended poetry on the grounds that its purpose was strictly the evocation of beauty.[27] De Lisle, in fact, decried the "alliance monstrueuse de la poésie et de l'industrie" in his 1855 preface to his *Poëmes et poésies,* saying that "the hymns and odes inspired by the steamboat and the electric telegraph," as well as "all [such] didactic periphrases," were only inspired by mediocrity and had "nothing in common with art."[28] Thus, l'art pour l'art is at one level a reaction to the burgeoning materialism of the nineteenth century, and it is largely because of this opposition to progress that Parnassianism anticipates one of the fundamental aspects of decadence.

The resistance to progress, the weariness with the modern world, and the longing for remote places and exotic times are all basically romantic attitudes adopted by Leconte de Lisle and other Parnassian poets. De Lisle in the 1855 preface advocates an erudite resuscitation of antiquity, "the examination of historical facts and institutions, the serious analysis of customs," and so on.[29] Works inspired by antiquity, de Lisle believed, "will always excite a more profound and lasting interest than the daguerreotype picture of contemporary customs and occurences."[30] These attitudes were shared by Flaubert when he came to write *Salammbô.* In 1857 Flaubert described his incipient novel in these terms: "I am going to write a novel whose action will take place three centuries before Jesus Christ, because I feel the need to leave the modern world, with which my pen is drenched, and whose reproduction wears me out as much as the sight of it disgusts me."[31] This attitude has the result in *Salammbô* of "focusing on a civilization so distinctly out of touch with the world of modern Europe as to ensure an almost hermetic purity."[32] Indeed, this hermetic quality, this concern with pure art, is one of the more obvious aspects of Parnassianism conveyed by the phase l'art pour l'art. And the concern for the purity of art, in turn, leads to an intense attentiveness to artifice, and "ultimately a marked trend toward decadentism."[33]

At least one critic has gone to considerable lengths to relate *Salammbô* and the poetry of *le Parnasse.* Victor Brombert calls the novel a "Parnassian epic" because, he argues, the work exhibits the sort of "sculptural" qualities and plastic effects that the Parnassians attempted in poetry.[34] To a large degree Parnassian poetry was judged effective insofar as it was able to approximate in language the sculptor's art in marble. The aesthetic validity of this variation on the old idea of *ut pictura poesis* is open to debate, but the notion was given considerable credence by Gautier's comparison of poetry and sculpture in the famous poem "L'Art." In the poem Gautier says that the most beautiful art emerges from material that is difficult to work with and offers resistance to the artist: "Vers, marbre, onyx, émail."[35] The comparison of the poet's art to the sculptor's or the enameler's makes the point that the struggle with difficult materials (such as Carrara marble) pays off in precision, in the "pure contour" of form ("Lutte avec le carrare, / Avec le paros dur / Et rare, / Gardiens du contour pur"). Such art outlasts civilizations and empire; in fact, the vanished city and the forgotten emperor are only known through art ("Le buste / Survit à la cité. / Et la médaille austère / . . . Révèle un empereur"). The poem ends with an admonition to the artist-poet to "Sculpte, lime, cisèle" so that his vague dreams may be sealed in the hard, "resistant block" ("Que ton rêve flottant / Se scelle / Dans le bloc résistant!"). Flaubert indicated that in writing *Salammbô* he had "tried to fix a mirage" ("j'ai voulu fixer un mirage"),[36] which sounds like Gautier's admonition "to seal the dream." Other points in the poem seem consonant with Flaubert's aesthetic as well, namely the belief that artistic creation is a difficult struggle with language, and that this struggle is necessary for the sake of precision, whether "le mot juste" or "le contour pur." As Gautier's "L'Art" implies, there is more to the Parnassian aesthetic than a preoccupation with sculptural imagery; the process of writing itself is likened to the sculptor's art as well. Still, sculpture for sculpture's sake is one of the conventions of Parnassianism, so Brombert is right to connect Flaubert's extensive use of sculptural and architectural figures of speech to the poetry of *le Parnasse:*

> Hanno looks like an incompleted stone idol. The crucified Mercenaries look like "red statues." Salammbô, when her father promises her in marriage to Narr'Havas, stands "calm as a statue."
>
> The architectural obsession is particularly striking. Numerous passages suggest a real choreography of geometric figures and patterns. The three levels of a tower are like three "monstrous cylinders." One of Hamilcar's apartments is built in the "form of a cone." . . . Carthage is viewed as a vast amphitheater of "cubic" houses: it is a "mountain of blocks" with innumerable "intersecting" streets which "section" it vertically.[37]

And so on. But this "sculptural" quality goes beyond the simple use of figurative language employing tropes drawn from sculpture and architecture. Such tropes are there, certainly, but since "the vantage point of *Salammbô* is objective rather than subjective, its predominant images are literal rather than metaphorical; they are objects, paraphernalia of the story, to be admired impassively for their own sake, as in the poetry of the Parnasse."[38] Thus, Brombert's observations on the various sculptural effects of *Salammbô* are just, but those effects seem part of a more general imagistic quality related to Parnassianism. And that quality of objective, literal imagery has a bearing on the style of *Salammbô*. Such imagery may produce a static, concentrated effect in poetry, but when images become objects in prose, "to be admired impassively for their own sake," the effect on the narrative is necessarily one of discontinuity, fragmenting the text into any number of separate units. In short, the sculpturelike poetry of *le Parnasse* cannot be grafted onto narrative prose without resulting in *le style de décadence.*

The autonomy of art, the distaste for the bourgeois world, the heightening of artifice, the affinity for sculpture and architecture, the use of exotic imagery in an objective way—all these are general elements of Parnassianism that seem to have found their way into *Salammbô*. More important, these Parnassian elements enunciate the characteristics of a developing aesthetic of decadence that can now be further detailed.

If we expand on the Parnassian use of imagery as it appears in *Salammbô,* we can see that the literal or objective nature of the imagery in the novel is but an index to a more general sense of literality, of a text everywhere manifesting a kind of linguistic opacity. Such is the density of the texture of description, for example, that most readers' pictorial sense is likely to be so undercut by the surfeit of exotic imagery that what they "see" is not, in the following passage, the veil of Tanit but the veil of language:

Then they penetrated into a small and completely circular room, so lofty that it was like the interior of a pillar. In the centre there was a big black stone, of semispherical shape like a tambourine; flames were burning upon it; an ebony cone, bearing a head and two arms, rose behind.

But beyond it seemed as though there were a cloud wherein were twinkling stars; faces appeared in the depths of its folds—Eschmoun with the Kabiri, some of the monsters that had already been seen, the sacred beasts of the Babylonians, and others with which they were not acquainted. It passed beneath the idol's face like a mantle, and spread fully out was drawn up on the wall, to which it was fastened by the corners, appearing at once bluish as the night, yellow as the dawn, purple as the sun, multitudinous, diaphanous, sparkling, light. It was the mantle of the goddess, the holy zaïmph which might not be seen. (1:92–93)

[Alors ils pénétrèrent dans une petite salle toute ronde, et si élevée qu'elle ressemblait à l'intérieur d'une colonne. Il y a avait au milieu une grosse pierre noire à demi sphérique, comme un tambourin; des flammes brûlaient dessus; un cône d'ébène se dressait par-derrière, portant une tête et deux bras.

Mais au-delà on aurait dit un nuage où étincelaient des étoiles; des figures apparaissaient dans les profondeurs de ses plis; Eschmoûn avec les Kabires, quelques-uns des monstres déjà vus, les bêtes sacrées des Babyloniens, puis d'autres qu'ils ne connaissaient pas. Cela passait comme un manteau sous le visage de l'idole, et remontant étalé sur le mur, s'accrochait par les angles, tout à la fois bleuâtre comme la nuit, jaune comme l'aurore, pourpre comme le soleil, nombreux, diaphane, étincelant, léger. C'était là le manteau de la Déesse, le zaïmph saint que l'on ne pouvait voir. (142)]

The argument might be made that this is not a typical passage, that it fails to illustrate the point that descriptive language in *Salammbô* interferes with itself to such a degree that the usual mimetic function of description is destroyed. After all, the object described in this passage is essentially indescribable: it is the veil of a goddess, a pure appearance only, a thing of no substance, supernatural, mystifying. Yet this passage concentrates an activity of the text that is elsewhere diffused perhaps, but nonetheless present. The subject matter of the text, the objects under description, never quite escape from the language to enter fully into the consciousness of the reader as represented reality. Here the veil is yellow, there it is blue, and again, crimson: and as it undulates in the breeze, a kind of narrative appears, a progression of "figures" that emerge only for a moment and then disappear, but without clarity—veiled, quite literally, in exotic obscurity. In this context Flaubert's adamant resistance to his publisher's plans to illustrate the book is particularly telling.[39]

So the veil of Tanit seems a perfect figure for the text as a whole: an image of the unimaginable, the un-image-able.[40] We read *Salammbô* for its rich surface of words, and rarely are we able to pass beyond this surface to the sort of "readerly" experience we have in a novel by Dickens or Balzac, or even the Flaubert of *Madame Bovary*, where we are able to imagine the spare reality of Emma's life.[41] It is this surface quality of *Salammbô* that Alfred Nettement has singled out so succinctly—"Il [Flaubert] a voulu faire une copie sans original"[42]—and that leads Harry Levin to suggest that the novel "be classified within the genre of the 'tapestry novel,' to cite Mann's term which *Death in Venice* formulates."[43] These phrases—copy without an original, tapestry novel—attest to a sense of surface, a literal quality of the text that is at odds with traditional interpretive modes of reading (allegorical, metaphorical, psychological, historical, biographical, and so forth) and that needs further investigation since it is a major element in the decadent aesthetic.

This surface quality may be admired or derided for whatever reason, but rarely has it been better explained than in Georg Lukács's ruminations on the decline of the historical novel. Lukács draws his insights from Sainte-Beuve's remarks that the character Salammbô seemed to him a mere mythologized version of Emma Bovary, an essentially modern, provincial woman in ancient, Carthaginian dress. This thesis is surely problematical, but it may be granted for the sake of Lukács's argument, which leads to some fine observations on the quality of *Salammbô* under discussion here. Lukács's comments must therefore be quoted at length:

> He [Flaubert] chooses an historical subject whose inner social-historical nature is of no concern to him and to which he can only lend the appearance of reality in an external, decorative, picturesque manner by means of the conscientious application of archaeology. But at some point he is forced to establish a contact with both himself and the reader, and this he does by modernizing the psychology of his characters. The proud and bitter paradox which contends that the novel has nothing to do with the present, is simply a defensive paradox contending against the trivialities of his age. We see from Flaubert's explanations . . . that *Salammbô* was more than just an artistic experiment. It is for this reason that the modernization of the characters acquires central importance; it is the only source of movement and life in this frozen, lunar landscape of archaeological precision.
>
> Naturally it is a ghostly illusion of life. And an illusion which dissolves the hyper-objective reality of the objects. In describing the individual objects

> of an historical *milieu* Flaubert is much more exact and plastic than any other writer before him. But these objects have nothing to do with the inner life of the characters. When Scott describes a medieval town or the habitat of a Scottish clan, these material things are part and parcel of the lives and fortunes of people whose whole psychology belongs to the same level of historical development and is a product of the same social-historical ensemble as these material things. This is how the older epic writers produced their "totality of objects." In Flaubert there is no such connection between the outside world and the psychology of the principal characters. And the effect of this lack of connection is to degrade the archaeological exactness of the outer world: it becomes a world of historically exact *costumes and decorations,* no more than a pictorial frame within which a purely modern story is unfolded.[44]

In comparing *Salammbô* unfavorably to the form of the epic, in which mankind is in harmony with the world and experiences a sense of totality, Lukács's assessment suggests that Flaubert's work is a radical illustration of the form of the novel, in which man's relationship to the world breaks down and a "separation between interiority and adventure" results, to use the language of Lukács's earlier work, *The Theory of the Novel.*[45] The separation or disconnectedness between the psychology of characters and their milieu in *Salammbô* certainly contributes to a sense of flatness, but the question arises as to whether the technique of modern psychological characterization is, as Lukács argues, essentially the same as in *Madame Bovary.*

Erich Auerbach's analysis of a "simple" dinner scene involving Charles and Emma Bovary illustrates clearly the technique of subtle and indirect psychological characterization in the earlier novel:

> The paragraph [from part 1, chapter 9, of *Madame Bovary*] itself presents a picture—man and wife together at mealtime. But the picture is not presented in and for itself; it is subordinated to the dominant subject, Emma's despair. Hence it is not put before the reader directly; here two sit at table—there the reader stands watching them. Instead, the reader first sees Emma, who has been much in evidence in the preceding pages, and he sees the picture first through her; directly, he sees only Emma's inner state; he sees what goes on at the meal indirectly, from within her state, in the light of her perception.[46]

This technique of "complete subjectivity," or the carefully controlled illusion of such, is hardly in evidence in *Salammbô.* For example, the psychological situation between Salammbô and the eunuch priest Schabarim is presented in a perfectly direct manner:

> She could not live without the relief of his presence. But she rebelled inwardly against this domination; her feeling towards the priest was one at once of terror, jealousy, hatred, and a species of love, in gratitude for the singular voluptuousness which she experienced by his side.
> . . . His condition established, as it were, the equality of a common sex between them, and he was less angry with the young girl for his inability to possess her than for finding her so beautiful, and above all so pure. Often he saw that she grew weary in following his thought. Then he would turn away sadder than before; he would feel himself more forsaken, more empty, more alone. (2:3, 5)

> [Elle ne pouvait vivre sans le soulagement de sa présence. Mais elle se révoltait intérieurement contre cette domination; elle sentait pour le prêtre tout à la fois de la terreur, de la jalousie, de la haine et une espèce d'amour, en reconnaissance de la singulière volupté qu'elle trouvait près de lui.
> . . . Sa condition établissait entre eux comme l'égalité d'un sexe commun, et il en voulait moins à la jeune fille de ne pouvoir la posséder que de la trouver si belle et surtout si pure. Souvent il voyait bien qu'elle se fatiguait à suivre sa pensée. Alors il s'en retournait plus triste; il se sentait plus abandonné, plus seul, plus vide. (279, 282)]

The string of abstract terms is typical of the characterization throughout *Salammbô: terreur, jalousie, haine, amour,* and so on. Simply speaking, the psychological state of the characters is not revealed dramatically or subjectively through narrative action, but is flatly and objectively labeled. It may be true that the psychological makeup of the characters in *Salammbô* is more modern than ancient, as Lukács says, but simply naming the state of depression ("triste . . . abandonée . . . seul . . . vide"), a touchstone of the modern temper, is only a minimal index to the interiority of character. Perhaps the relationship between psychology and setting is less disconnected than Lukács supposes: it seems that the same exterior, objective technique prevails throughout *Salammbô,* that the surface quality of "costumes and decorations" is uniform, and that one part of the characters' costumes is a "psychological" element that is little more than a mask of abstraction. Emma Bovary's despair colors the world of the novel because she imposes it on everything about her from within, whereas Salammbô's "despair" is a label imposed on her from without.

If the world of *Salammbô* seems flat and lifeless in comparison to the world of *Madame Bovary,* much of this flatness results from the absence of a character's mediating consciousness. Nathalie Sarraute has made the keen observation that Emma Bovary's world is every bit as inauthentic as

Salammbô's, but that the defect of inauthenticity is transformed into a virtue by the mediating consciousness of the principal character: "We all remember that *trompe-l'oeil* universe, the world as seen through the eyes of Madame Bovary: her desires, her imaginings, the dreams on which she seeks to build her existence, all of which are made up of a succession of cheap images drawn from the most debased, discredited forms of romanticism."[47] And *Salammbô* clearly lacks this sort of controlling consciousness: "For here, more than in any of Flaubert's novels, psychology is non-existent, description all-important, and style increasingly his sole concern."[48] We are tempted to call this aspect of *Salammbô* the main element in the aesthetic of decadence—an excessive, even obsessive, concern with style—and to say further that a decadent novel merely elaborates its own systems of language at the expense of the conventional devices by which a realistic novel achieves a sense of *vraisemblance:* psychological characterization, narrative exposition, demotic dialogue, straightforward chronology, and so on. But this is too much a definition of what the novel becomes later in the early twentieth century, when the conventions of nineteenth-century realism are distorted in the service of such modernist programs as ambiguity and obscurity. It is true that the language of decadence as it appears in *Salammbô* is at odds with realistic conventions, but the nature of this opposition is better described as an interference of the artificial and the conventional (here the relationship between decadence and Parnassianism reappears). The use of ornate description has already been cited as one instance of heightened artifice at cross-purposes with conventional narrative exposition. Another example is the use of such times signals as *alors, cependant,* and *tout à coup* to prod the progression of the plot along, the effect of which is paradoxically to reduce the sense of narrative chronology by artificially connecting events in the text, rather than setting them in some causal relation, as in: "Suddenly, without anyone being able to guess from what point he had sprung up, Spendius appeared" (2:47). ["Tout à coup, et sans qu'on pût deviner de quel point il surgissait, Spendius parut" (328).] The narrative of *Salammbô* is difficult to follow not because of some antichronological modernist technique, but because events are artificially connected and not meaningfully related.

To conclude, we can now say that *Salammbô* may be called decadent on a number of counts that pertain to aesthetic issues. In general terms, the conception of decadence as the dominance of the artificial over the natural, of culture over nature, holds true in *Salammbô.* As a novel, the work's decadence consists largely in the incompatibility of heightened artifice and the devices of conventional realistic fiction. Narration gives way to description, and description gives way to effects of language: a descriptive passage in *Salammbô* is not an imaginative picture of life in ancient Carthage, but a pure spectacle of style. The unit of composition in *Salammbô* is not the chapter or even the paragraph, but the brilliant sentence, the finely wrought phrase. If we consider decadence as a transition from romanticism to modernism, *Salammbô* argues that thesis most interestingly. The work is constituted of basically romantic elements: the exotic, the unfamiliar, the "oriental"; the primitive, the ancient, the aboriginal; the fantastic, the grotesque, the bizarre. But the technique is scrupulous, mean, detached, objective—qualities hardly a part of the generally expressive aesthetic of romanticism. Flaubert in pessimistic moments voiced the fear that his tendency to blend romantic subject and realistic style might make of him a kind of "Chateaubrianized Balzac," but he later defended the mixture in his reply to Sainte-Beuve: "Chateaubriand's system seems diametrically opposed to mine. He started from a completely ideal standpoint; he dreamed of *typical* martyrs. I have tried to fix a mirage by applying the methods of the modern novel to antiquity."[49] As a result, *Salammbô* exhibits a modernity of surface only, and to a considerable degree this quality constitutes the novel's decadence. For that surface of words is somehow obscure, and the sense of obscurity does not arise from the mysteries of moon and sun and Tanit and Moloch, but from strange phrases and tricks of style. This obscurity of surface, the opaque, poetic language, is more a confusion of lights, a brilliant display of phrases, than a distorted, expressionistic exploration of the psychic depths, which is what we usually mean by obscurity in a modernist context. But *Salammbô*'s difficulty of access, together with its disregard for realistic devices, its l'art pour l'art hermeticism, its pathological interests—in short, all its decadent elements—herald a different kind of novel and an aesthetic sensibility not too far removed from modernism.

3

Decadence and Naturalism: The Goncourts' *Germinie Lacerteux*

Flaubert's *Salammbô* has some bearing on the development of the modern novel in that it breaks with the realist tradition and introduces into fiction ideas akin to the Parnassian notion of l'art pour l'art. The devices of conventional fiction are so obscured in *Salammbô* that our interest as readers is focused directly on the language of the work itself, rather than on the imaginative projection of a fictional world: we are not drawn through the language, but to it. This sort of stylistic opacity is one feature of decadence, characterized by a taste for artificiality and exoticism at the expense of the natural and the everyday. It may seem odd, therefore, to move from the florid artifice of *Salammbô* to the naturalistic technique of *Germinie Lacerteux* while still using the rubric of decadence. Nevertheless, both these works appealed to the decadents of the 1880s during the high noon of *décadisme*, and the Goncourt brothers simultaneously helped shape both the naturalist school and the so-called decadent movement. Also, while Flaubert's stylistic innovations are inestimably important to the development of modernism, it is likewise true that the social milieu evoked in modern fiction often harkens back to the novels of the Goncourts and Zola. (Joyce, after all, expected to be called the "Irish Zola" at the outset of his career.)[1] Thus, some examination of the relationship of decadence and naturalism is now in order.

Naturalism and decadence have little or much in common, depending on one's point of view. As a sympathetic response to the rise of analytical scientism, the naturalist's investigation of the effects of heredity and environment is opposed to the decadent's less structured, more aesthetic interest in the rarefied mentality of modern man. Certainly, the naturalist school in France during the late nineteenth century is much more in tune with the general scientific and progressive temper of the times than is the decadent mentality, or at least the aspect of decadence that, like Parnassianism, set itself against the burgeoning materialism of the age. On the other hand, this pitting of the scientific naturalist against the artistic decadent is rather too facile when we consider that an attitude of pessimism and a preoccupation with decay or decline are common to both. The difference is largely one of means rather than ends: the vicissitudes of the descendants of Adélaïde Foque in Zola's *Rougon-Macquart* cycle result from a genetic and environmental determinism that is understandable in scientific (or pseudoscientific) terms, whereas the end of Huysmans's Des Esseintes comes about because of a more general malaise—nervous disorders brought on by an excess of civilization. In one case the fruit shrivels and dies because the seed is bad, in the other it grows heavy and falls overripe from the branch.

Naturalism and decadence, in short, are not radically dissimilar; both are predisposed toward pessimism and determinism. During the 1860s, as the Goncourt brothers were writing their early works and Zola was beginning his literary career, several social and historical studies appeared that seemed to confirm the general pessimistic supposition that the human race—and the Gallic species in particular—was doomed to decline and decay. Darwin's *Origin of Species* (1859) furnished French historians with a deterministic interpretation of recent history, as Henri de Ferron's *Théorie du progrès* (1867) demonstrates. One of the first to apply Darwinian theories of natural selection to history, Ferron concluded that the French might not be fit enough to survive in competition with the Anglo-Saxons and Germans.[2] The debacle of 1870–71, when France was defeated by Prussia, must have given credence to such ideas. Another work of the 1860s, and one having a more direct influence on literature, is Hippolyte Taine's *Histoire de la littérature anglaise* (1864). The well-known axiom from Taine's preface—"Le vice et la vertu sont des produits comme le vitriol et le sucre"[3]—appears as an epigraph to the second edition of Zola's *Thérèse Raquin,* written in 1867. Also, the elements of Taine's deterministic formula—*le race, le milieu,* and *le moment*—figure prominently in Zola's theory and practice of naturalism.[4]

In other works, Taine "showed a marked taste for the more alluring aspects of decadence."[5] In *La Fontaine et ses fables* (1853), for example,

Taine found occasion to attribute the depravity of modern man to an excess of civilization at the expense of nature. Taine was particularly disturbed by the way nature had been "mastered and disfigured" in the great cities, where the earth was covered with pavement, buildings blocked out the sky, artificial lights "effaced" the night, and even the streets were encumbered by "ingenious" inventions. Man himself, Taine says, has come to resemble the ingenious and artificial cities he has built.[6] We might question the relevance of this rather Rousseauistic attitude to the development of decadence. What is noteworthy is the perception of society and modern man as decadent, and the isolation of the cause of this decadence as an excessively urban civilization, even though Taine's attitude is not sympathetic and the phenomenon of decadence is viewed from the outside. Still, Paul Bourget, one of the earliest theoreticians of decadence, found sufficient interest in Taine's work to study it carefully.[7] But the relationship of Taine to the rise of decadence is not so direct as it is with the evolution of naturalism, which owes some debt to Taine's deterministic theories. The difference between naturalistic determinism and decadence is the difference between a mechanism for a malaise and the malaise itself, and several other elements besides Taine's theories make up this malaise. One such element is the impact of Schopenhauer's philosophical pessimism; even though the Schopenhauer vogue did not take hold in France until the late 1870s and 1880s,[8] the fashion for the German pessimist has much to do with the philosophical coincidence of naturalism and decadence. In literature, the deterministic ideas of Taine and others influenced the naturalists to cultivate a pessimism not so different from the kind associated with Schopenhauer. For example, passages from Zola's *La Faute de l'Abbé Mouret* seem remarkably Schopenhauerean, as in the abbé Mouret's paean to the virgin where the very existence of the human race is denounced and the death of the species is preferred to the continuing "abomination" of propagating it.[9] The desire for the extinction of the human race is really a radical extension of Schopenhauer's pessimism, adopted by his student Eduard von Hartman, whose work was translated into French in 1877.[10] As the ideas of Schopenhauer and von Hartman were disseminated at about the same time as Zola's naturalism, the decadents of the 1880s could readily see an analogy between Schopenhauer and naturalistic pessimism, and this accounts, in part, for the readiness of some decadents to accept naturalists and to see in them a literary kinship.

Nevertheless, as Philip Stephan observes, "naturalism and decadence are not at all the same thing, since the former proposed to analyze contemporary society . . . with scientific rigor . . . , and the latter sought to express the sentiments of 'modern' man, who was likened to the ancient Romans of the decadence."[11] It would be more precise to say that naturalism is not *décadisme,* although an element of decadence appears in the naturalistic point of view. In 1866, Zola's expression of literary preferences indicates a general sympathy for decadence. His "depraved" taste meant that he liked his "literary stews strongly spiced, the works of decadence where a kind of sickly sensibility substitutes for the robust health of the classical ages."[12] And Huysmans, the quintessential decadent writer of the 1880s and 1890s, began his career as the author of such naturalistic novels as *Marthe* (1876) and *Les Soeurs Vatard* (1879). In the ensuing years, as Stephan mentions, naturalists and decadents "worked alongside each other as friends and collaborators," and had their works published in the same magazines. In the early 1880s, such magazines as *La Revue Indépendante* and *Le Chat Noir* "were congenial to naturalism and decadence equally. *La Revue Independante* included poetry by Verlaine, Mallarmé, Laforgue, Banville, and Heredia; short 'slice of life' sketches, such as Huysmans's 'L'Avenue de la Motte-Picquet,' Paul Hervieu's 'Attentat à la pudeur,' or Frantz Jourdain's 'Ouvriers de bâtiment'; and articles and sketches by Edmond de Goncourt and Emile Zola."[13]

Thus naturalism and decadence coincide on several points, based on both philosophical affinity and historical affiliation. But the principal instance of this coincidence is the early work of the Goncourt brothers, to whom the epithets decadent and naturalistic apply equally.

A crucial point of relationship between naturalism and decadence in the case of the Goncourt brothers is their preoccupation with illness and degeneration. As Roger Williams says, the brothers "enjoyed poor health, or so it would seem from their *Journal,* where they took obvious pleasure in analyzing other people's maladies, as well as their own, in detail."[14] Like the *Journal,* the novels also show the morbid delight the Goncourts took in a variety of diseases, principally those linked to some degeneration of the nervous system. In 1870, they informed Zola that the originality of their work rested on nervous maladies, presumably both their own and those they observed in others.[15] Add to this preference for nervous maladies the brothers' lifelong commitment to literature and art, and an amalgam of naturalism and decadence emerges. To refine this point somewhat, A. E. Carter suggests that "[A] distinction ought to be made between degeneracy and decadence—although Zola and others used both terms synonymously—the one being pathological, the other aesthetic."[16] Carter's point is well made: the major works of naturalism, like the *Rougon-Macquart* cycle, are generally not overconcerned with aesthetic matters, focusing instead on processes of degeneration among social classes removed from artistic circles. The pseudoaristocratic Goncourt brothers, on the other hand, combined pathological interests with artistic sensibilities and so because, as Carter says of Huysmans's Des Esseintes, "both degenerate and decadent, both neurotic and aesthetic" (81). In truth, the brothers Goncourt must be counted among the several models for Huysmans's famed character. At any rate, if later distinctions can be drawn between degeneration and decadence, we might say that the Goncourts are one of the main sources from which the two streams of thought emerged.

This confluence of pathology and aestheticism, however, is by no means original with the Goncourts. Nineteenth-century medical theory tended to confirm the brothers' predilection to regard the artist as necessarily suffering from nervous complications. Of particular importance to this issue is the work of Dr. Joseph Moreau de Tours, who developed the thesis in 1830 that insanity and lesser mental afflictions are produced by heredity. His research led him to note in 1836 that "the most brilliant families, with the largest proportion of geniuses, also contain the largest numbers of neurotics and madmen."[17] By 1859, Dr. Moreau's association of genius and madness had become almost doctrinaire. According to Moreau, the man who distinguished himself from other men through the originality of his ideas could be sure that those ideas had their sources in the same "organic conditions" ("les même conditions organiques") that produce madness and idiocy.[18] Dr. Moreau also taught that men of genius, bordering so near to insanity, "could expect to suffer from all manner of physical and mental torments: neuralgias and nervousness, vague fears and indefinable ailments, insomnia, and anguish in the region of the heart."[19] It follows that the symptoms of literature and lunacy are almost identical: "Dr. Moreau enabled the Goncourts to be convinced that their own illnesses, their neuropathy or neurasthenia, were fundamentally creative. If their visits to hospitals left them in a highly nervous state, so much the better for literature. If piecing together the appalling details of [their maidservant] Rose's life for the story of *Germinie Lacerteux* plunged them into gloom and set their nerves on edge, so much the better for the novel."[20] From all this emerges a version of the artist as a truly decadent creature: "the artist becomes an unbalanced being in whom an excessive delicacy of the sensibility and the nerves, plus a hypertrophied critical intelligence, takes its revenge by destroying the faculty of will and the desire to act."[21]

This conception of the artist was widespread in the 1880s and 1890s in France and elsewhere, and contributes to a core idea of decadence: the paradoxical parallelism of degeneration and refinement. The Goncourts certainly equated sensitivity with sickness well before the idea became popular among the literati of *décadisme,* and it is arguable that the brothers "were the first to recognize the importance of their contemporaries' nervousness and to claim that a morbidly hypersensitive nature was actually a form of superiority."[22] Indeed, the Goncourts' use of a new artistic style in the fictional investigation of nervous maladies earned them the esteem of the principal decadent critics, as this passage from Bourget's *Nouveaux essais de psychologie contemporaine* (1886) demonstrates:

> That rhetoric, derived from painting and sculpture, is a marvelous instrument for carrying out certain analyses, those, for example, concerned with disorders of the nervous system. Under the influence of these disorders, the mental disturbance is accompanied by a succession of strong physical impressions; given that such enervation is the very malady of the present age, the brothers Goncourt have employed their stylistic manner with uncommon success in forceful studies of derangement titled *Manette Salomon, Madame Gervaisais,* [and] *Germinie Lacerteux.* These monographs of neurosis could never have been written in the language we inherited from Voltaire.[23]

The association here of nervous hypersensitivity with stylistic innovation is certainly noteworthy; it helps to account for the fact that the Goncourts were held in high regard by the decadents of the 1880s, and, more important, it helps to define decadence itself as an aesthetic expression of naturalistic degeneration.

By the time the brief decadent movement was launched in 1886 (with the publication of Baju's *Le Décadent*), the Goncourts were recognized as precursors of *décadisme* and as "des décadents de parti pris" (decadents by choice) by Paul Bourget.[24] As early as 1860, the Goncourts were among those writers making the connection between nineteenth-century and Roman decadence. "The anemia we experience," they wrote in *Charles Demailly,* "is obviously an actual fact." The facts as they saw them argued for the "degeneration" of humanity, the same "malady of the Roman empire" that shows through in the faces of some emperors, even in bronze. The Romans, however, had the means whereby they could experience periodic revival: "When society was lost, exhausted from a physiological perspective, an invasion of barbarians arrived to give it a transfusion of young, Herculean blood. Who will save the world from the anemia of the nineteenth century? In a few hundred years, will society experience an invasion of workers?"[25] Although the word "decadence" is not used in this passage, the concept could not be clearer: the Goncourts saw themselves living in an "anemic" age tremulously awaiting the onrush of barbarian hoards. Also, the ideology of the "aristocratic" brothers is made clear in the passage through the reference to workers as barbarians. A few years before the publication of *Charles Demailly*, Jules de Goncourt shortened the anticipated invasion of worker-barbarians from a few hundred to only fifty years: "When stomachs are full and men can no longer copulate, they have fallen to six-foot barbarians from the North. But now that Europe contains no more savages, the workers will do the job of revitalizing civilization in about fifty more years. It will be called the Social Revolution."[26] Indeed, the Goncourts longed for the Old Regime, the days before democracy, "that happy moment before 1789, before mankind embarked upon the vulgarization of life and culture, when life had been charming rather than hateful."[27] Their own despised century, they felt, was altogether too progressive and energetic for the good of mankind: "Since the time mankind exists, its progress, its acquisitions have all been the order of sensibility. Each day, it becomes nervous, hysterical. And in regard to this activity . . . are you certain that modern melancholy does not result from it? Do you know if the sadness of the century does not come from overwork, movement, tremendous effort, furious labor, from its cerebral forces strained to the breaking point, from overproduction in every domain?"[28] "Thus as humanity advances," William comments, "it becomes increasingly neurotic and hysterical; and those who have nothing left but nerves become the finest of our flowers." The Goncourts' distaste for the progressive and democratic nineteenth century, together with their dual interest in art and degeneration, produced a perfect "formula" for decadence: "Democracy equals mediocrity and means barbarism; science deflects us from a true perception of reality; reality is boredom, as only superior writers know; and the superior being is the decadent. To define decadence as vitality, to find mental disease as the root of vigor, is surely to define life as hateful. To hate life, moreover, will be to hate nature, after which the final formula asserts that art is superior to life."[29]

By the 1880s and 1890s, this formula had become quite conventional, and the Goncourts must be recognized as anticipating—and perhaps originating—a number of decadent conventions. Certainly, the publication of the *Journal* in 1887 helped to fuel *décadisme.* In taking the position that the Goncourts exercised an influence on the development of both naturalism and decadence, one is tempted to ascribe to the *Journal* a greater share of decadence, and to give the novels over to the naturalists. After all, Edmond made the claim that *Germinie Lacerteux* provided a complete formula for naturalism.[30] Yet we cannot overlook the fact that the novels were celebrated by such decadent critics as Ernest Raynaud.[31] *Germinie Lacerteux* may well be, as Edmond thought, the first novel of naturalism, but this in no way diminishes its relevance as one of the principal works of decadence.

Germinie Lacerteux has its origins in the Goncourt brothers' investigation of the life of their servant since childhood, one Rose Malingre, who died in 1862. After her death the brothers were confronted with the most appalling evidence that Rose, who had always seemed an exemplary maternal figure of quiet devotion and simple virtue, had for many years lived a separate life of extreme depravity. While maintaining the appearance of a diligent housemaid (indeed, she performed her household duties without stint), Rose pursued a variety of vices, drinking absinthe and brandy to excess and having a succession of affairs once she had been spurned by her lover, whom she had helped support by stealing money from the Goncourts. Rose had even given birth to an illegitimate child who died in infancy, and managed somehow to keep the secret of her pregnancy and her dead infant from the brothers. The shocking details of their beloved maid's existence were revealed only when the Goncourts were solicited by creditors demanding payment for the debts Rose had accumulated as a result of her sexual and alcoholic appetites.[32] In the novel, Rose is replaced by Germinie and the brothers themselves by an elderly spinster, Mlle. de Varandeuil, but the biography of Rose and the story of Germinie are essentially the same: a simple and devoted woman is gradually ruined by an obsessive desire for sex and alcohol.

Germinie Lacerteux thus details the degeneration of an individual, and as such it is broadly naturalistic. In several ways, the novel is a harbinger of later novels of the naturalist school. We have noted Edmond's retrospective awareness that the work broke new ground and provided later authors with a prototype of the naturalist novel: "*Germinie Lacerteux* is the kind of book that has served as a model of everything that has been made since us, under the title of realism, naturalism, etc."[33] One of the things that bears out Edmond's judgment is the brothers' presentation of Germinie's depravity in scientific and specifically physiological terminology, as in the opening of chapter 32: "A normal effect of nervous disorders [of the organism] is to upset human joys and sorrows, take away from them a sense of proportion and balance and push them to their furthest extreme" (99). ["C'est un effet ordinaire des désordres nerveux de l'organisme de dérégler les joies et les peines humaines, de leur ôter la proportion et l'équilibre, et de les pousser à l'extrémité de leur excès" (135).][34] Thus runs the explanation of the "organism's," that is, Germinie's, excesses. Later, the nervous excitability of Germinie is diagnosed as "une sorte d'éréthisme cérébral" (142), which has a rather scientific ring to it. Such scientism is in keeping with the tone established by the novel's preface, which promises not a vulgar or sentimental love story, but a clinical "study": "l'etude qui suit est la clinique de l'Amour" (27). In this famous preface the Goncourts claim for their novel "les études et les devoirs de la science" (28). So both the preface and the main text of the novel suggest that the work has a kind of scientific legitimacy, one of the basic principles of naturalism. The deterministic element that comes to be associated with later naturalistic fiction is also evident in *Germinie Lacerteux,* as Germinie helplessly submits to her animalistic cravings before the entreaties of her exploitative lover, Jupillon: "She came back to him like an animal being pulled back on a lead" (95). ["Elle revint à lui comme une bête ramenée à la main et dont on retire la corde" (130).] Elsewhere, the deterministic theme is sounded even more clearly and at some length:

> A moment came when Germinie gave up the struggle. Her conscience sagged, her will-power folded and she bowed beneath her destiny. What remained of her resolution, energy and courage was vanishing in the face of the feeling, the desperate conviction of her powerlessness to save herself from herself. She felt swept along on the current of something always moving which it was useless, almost impious, to think of arresting. The great world force that brings suffering, the evil power, Fatality, that bears the name of a god on the marble of ancient tragedies and which is called *No luck* on the tattooed brows of convicts, crushed her and Germinie lowered her head beneath its foot. (123)

> [Une heure arrivait dans cette vie où Germinie renonçait à la lutte. Sa conscience se courbait, sa volonté se pliait, elle s'inclinait sous le sort de sa vie. Ce qui lui restait de résolution, d'énergie, de courage, s'en allait sous le sentiment, la conviction désespérée de son impuissance à se sauver d'elle-

même. Elle se sentait dans le courant de quelque chose allant toujours, qu'il était inutile, presque impie, de vouloir arrêter. Cette grande force du monde qui fait souffrir, la puissance mauvaise qui porte le nom d'un dieu sur le marbre des tragédies antiques, et qui s'appelle *Pas-de-Chance* sur le front tatoué des bagnes, la Fatalité l'écrasait, et Germinie baissait la tête sous son pied. (166)]

Thus, in several ways *Germinie Lacerteux* justifies Edmond's claim that the work marks the beginning of naturalism.

In other ways, however, the hybrid or dual character of the work appears, and the unqualified classification of *Germinie Lacerteux* as a naturalistic novel becomes suspect. As Auerbach points out in his chapter on *Germinie Lacerteux* in *Mimesis,* the Goncourt brothers' interest in the depravity and dissolution of an individual is almost completely aesthetic; that is, the terrible story of Germinie exists mainly for stylistic exploitation, as "a matter of the sensory fascination of ugliness."[35] In other words, the Goncourts' pretensions to clinical or scientific analysis are primarily the stance of the coldly detached artist who faithfully renders the most sordid details of the subject in order to arouse new sensations in an audience wearied by the familiar and conventional. We have noted A. E. Carter's supposition that the naturalists' interest in pathology is less aesthetic than the decadents'. Auerbach makes a similar point when he argues that Zola's representation of various working-class milieus is not meant to titillate the aesthete, but to rouse the reader to sympathetic understanding: "Almost every line that he [Zola] wrote showed that all . . . was meant in the highest degree seriously and morally; that the sum total of it was not a pastime or an artistic parlor game but the true portrait of contemporary society as he—Zola—saw it and as the public was being urged in words to see it too" (510). By contrast, the Goncourts make it abundantly clear that their interest in corruption and depravity is not moralistic, but almost a matter of aesthetic appreciation: "Passion for things comes not from the goodness or the pure beauty of those things. One adores only corruption. One will be passionate about a woman for her whorishness, her nastiness, a certain unpleasant laziness of the head, the heart, the senses." At base, they write, they are aroused by corruption and by a kind of "gaminess" ("faisandé") that extends to language as well.[36] After Jules's death, Edmond wrote an entry in the *Journal* that further reveals the uses to which the Goncourts put low social milieux in their novels, and this seems particularly relevant to *Germinie Lacerteux:*

"But why, people will say, choose such locales? Because in the midst of the obliteration of civilization it is at the bottom that the character of things, people, language, everything is conserved. . . . Again I ask why. Perhaps because I am a wellborn writer, and the people, the scum, if you wish, have for me the attraction of unknown and undiscovered peoples, possess a certain *exotic quality*—which travelers undergo a thousand discomforts to seek out in distant lands."[37] In treating the milieu of *Germinie Lacerteux* as an exotic landscape of depravity, the Goncourts separate themselves from the naturalists who followed them. The qualities of *faisandage,* of "gaminess" or overripeness, and of an exoticism contrived of lowness and ugliness, are not really elements of the naturalists' canon—far from it, in fact. Auerbach mentions that passages from Zola's *Germinal*—their moral seriousness aside—have the vitality and robust flavor of seventeenth-century Flemish or Dutch painting.[38] The point here is that the work of the Goncourts is anything but vitalistic, that *Germinie Lacerteux* takes the *natural* out of naturalism. Germinie, unlike many of Zola's heroines, is without earthiness and primitive sensuality. True to the Goncourts' conception of modern life, Germinie lives on in her wasted body by the strength of her nerves alone, "une vitalité nerveuse prodigieuse" (204).

This reduction of the natural is part of an emerging decadent formula that would have art take the place of nature, and the Goncourts thought of themselves primarily as artists and of fiction as *écriture artiste.* After their mother's death in 1848 when the brothers came into their inheritance and were free to pursue whatever career they wished, their initial choice of vocation was not literature but visual art.[39] Marcel Sauvage notes the importance of this fact to the development of the Goncourts' style, and illustrates it by citing the following passage:

> Seven o'clock in the evening. The sky is pale blue, a blue almost green, as if an emerald were dissolved in it; just above, moving slowly, with a movement harmonious and slow, masses of small clouds ["des masses de petits nuages"] are swept up, like shredded cotton, violet in color, as delicate as smoke in a sunset. Some of them are rose at the tips, like the peaks of glaciers in pink light. In front of me, on the opposite bank, rows ["lignes"] of trees, their leaves still yellow and hot from the sun, are soaking and bathing in the warmth and the dust of the shades of evening, in the glaze of gold that covers the earth just before the dusk. In the water, rippled by a strip of straw a man wets to wrap around his sheaf of oats, the rushes, the trees, the sky, are reflected along with the blocks of buildings ["des solidités denses"]. Under

> the last arch of the old bridge, close to me, a curved shadow seems to cut in half a russet cow that is slowly drinking; when she has finished, she raises her head and stares, her white muzzle streaming with rivulets of water.
>
> [Sept heures du soir. Le ciel est bleu pâle, d'un bleu presque vert, comme si une émeraude y était fondue; là-dessus, marchent doucement, d'une marche harmonieuse et lente, des masses de petits nuages balayés, ouateux et déchirés, d'un violet aussi tendre que des fumées dans un soleil qui se couche; quelque-unes de leurs cimes sont roses, comme des hauts de glacier, d'un rose de lumière. Devant moi, sur la rive en face, des lignes d'arbres, à la verdure jaune et chaude encore de soleil, trempent et baignent dans la chaleur et la poussière des tons du soir, dans ces glacis d'or qui enveloppent la terre avant le crépuscule. Dans l'eau, ridée par une botte de paille qu'un homme trempe au lavoir pour lier l'avoine, les joncs, les arbres, le ciel, se reflètent avec des solidités denses, et sous la dernière arche du vieux pont, près de moi, de l'arc de son ombre se détache la moitié d'une vache rousse, lente à boire et qui, quand elle a bu, relevant son mufle blanc bavant des fils d'eau, regarde.][40]

Sauvage, echoing Sainte-Beuve, comments that the passage is like a page taken from the album of a painter.[41] One might also say that such passages are merely precious, exercises in the excesses of description, that nothing is truly comparably to visual art in these lines of purple verbiage. On the other hand, the use of such terms as *masses, lignes,* and *solidités denses* suggest an affinity with landscape painting; a strong element of visual composition is evident in the passage. In short, the Goncourts tend to describe a landscape as if it were a painting of a landscape.

In practice, the Goncourt brothers intended their artistic prose style, or *écriture artiste,* to demonstrate the same sensitivity to light, color, and form as that achieved by the fine art of painting. One of the ironies of this practice is that descriptive passages in the Goncourts' novels suggest the work of the impressionists, with whom the brothers shared no common artistic ground at all. Nonetheless, whenever Germinie and Jupillon go walking out of doors the scenic description suggests impressionist canvases: "Far away the country stretched out, shining but vague, melting into the gold-dust of seven o'clock. Everything was floating in the powdered daylight that the day leaves behind on the verdure it effaces and the buildings it turns rose pink" (58). ["La campagne, au loin, s'étendait, étincelante et vague, perdue dans le poudroiement d'or de sept heures. Tout flottait dans cette poussière de jour que le jour laisse derrière lui sur la verdure qu'il efface et les maisons qu'il fait roses" (84).] Impressionistic effects are not limited to the countryside, however; when Germinie and Jupillon return from their walk the city is subjected to the same treatment: "The sun had gone, the sky was grey below, pink in the middle and blue above. The horizons were darkening, the greens were getting deeper and less distinct, the zinc roofs of the pubs shone as with moonlight, lights came on in the darkness, the crowd looked grey, white skirts became blue" (61). ["Il n'y avait plus de soleil. Le ciel était gris en bas, rose au milieu, bleuâtre en haut. Les horizons s'assombrissaient; les verdures se fonçaient, s'assourdissaient, les toits de zinc des cabarets prenaient des lumières de lune, des feux commençaient à piquer l'ombre, la foule devenait grisâtre, les blancs de ligne devenaient bleus" (187).] In a journal entry dated 8 May 1888, Edmond de Goncourt dismissed impressionist artists as incapable of realizing anything other than sketches and "spots": "Yes, these sketchers, these markers of spots, and still more spots that they haven't invented, spots stolen from Goya and the Japanese."[42] Elsewhere, the Goncourts liken these "spots" and the impasto technique of some impressionists to the mottled and peeling skin of syphilis victims.[43] The approximation of impressionist style in *Germinie Lacerteux* may therefore be part of a more general aesthetic effect, the purpose of which is not to create the "impression" of light, but of disease. In any event, the Goncourt brothers anticipate the theories of Max Nordau, who saw impressionist art as evidence of pathological degeneration: "The degenerate artist who suffers from *nystagmus*, or trembling of the eyeball, will, in fact, perceive the phenomena of nature trembling, restless, devoid of firm outline." Lacking "normal vision," the impressionist artist, with his vibrating eyeballs and defective retinas, paints what he sees, but because of "all sorts of gaps in his field of vision . . . he will be inclined to place in juxtaposition larger or smaller points or spots which are completely or partially dissociated."[44] Since both the Goncourts and Nordau are in agreement in their low estimation of impressionist artists as nothing more than "spot makers," it is somewhat ironical to find Nordau using the Goncourt brothers to illustrate "impressionism in literature," which is said to be "an example of that atavism which we have noticed as the most distinctive feature in the mental life of degenerates." Nordau claims that literary impressionism produces only "sense-stimulation," not concepts (485–86).

Later critics have been much more receptive to the Goncourt brothers' attempts at *écriture artiste*. Enzo Caramaschi singles out *Germinie Lacerteux* as a work rich in painterly techniques, especially in the use of seasonal description for psychological purposes:

> On the whole, it is by painting in prose (I would say in *plein air* impressionism) that the Goncourts attain their most fulfilling poetry. Even in their realism one finds an artistic completeness in the rendering that is at the same time "stenographic" and expressive of popular language. They subtly match their landscapes to the state of the soul of their characters: it is springtime when spring is in the soul of Germinie; it is muddy autumn when her soul agonizes and her body contracts phthisis in the pursuit of the past or in the wait for a man; winter descends at the hour of her death, and the snow is there to cover the meager handful of earth that has been thrown over her body.[45]

Again, the comparison to visual art is not immediately obvious; Caramaschi's commentary could well be taken as one more analysis of what is usually called "atmosphere," the use of setting to evoke a mood. With the Goncourts, however, such formalist labels are not quite adequate to cover the activity of the text. For example, the Goncourts are rarely more artistic or "painterly" than in the closing chapter of *Germinie Lacerteux,* after Germinie's death, in the description of the cemetery at Montmartre:

> The sky was leaden, colour-washed, as it were, by the bluish, cold tones of ink spread with a brush; it had for light a break over Montmartre all yellow, the colour of the Seine after heavy rains. On this wintry streak the sails of a concealed windmill went round and round, slow sails unvarying in their motion, which seemed to be marking eternity. (168)

> [Le ciel était plombé, lavé des tons bleuâtres et froids de l'encre étendue au pinceau: il avait pour lumière une éclaircie sur Montmartre, toute jaune, de la couleur de l'eau de la Seine après les grandes pluies. Sur ce rayon d'hiver, passaient et repassaient les ailes d'un moulin caché, des ailes lentes, invariables dans le mouvement, et qui semblaient tourner l'éternité. (223)]

The metaphor comparing the sky over Montmartre with an artist's canvas washed with ink is more than a mere trope; it serves to underscore the decadent predisposition to replace nature with art, and to use style at a distance from subject matter traditionally handled in the realist mode.

This stylistic removal from realism is another decadent feature of *Germinie Lacerteux,* and has its complement in the aesthetic elevation of ugliness and depravity, as the Goncourts use a heightened style in the presentation of subjects traditionally considered "low" or "unacceptable." Take, for instance, the following description of Germinie early in the novel:

> Germinie was ugly. Her hair, a dark mousey colour that looked black, was crimped and curled in recalcitrant waves, little hard rebellious wisps stick-

> ing up loose on her head in spite of the pomade on her smoothed coils. Her low, shining, round forehead stood out from the shadow of deep sockets in which her eyes were sunk almost unhealthily, sharp, glistening little eyes, made smaller and more glistening by a girlish blinking which moistened them and made them sparkle when she laughed. The eyes looked neither brown nor blue, they were of an indefinable and ever-changing grey that was not a colour at all, but a light. Emotion showed in them in a feverish fire, pleasure in the blaze of a kind of intoxication, passion in phosphorescence. (45)
>
> [Germinie était laide. Ses cheveux, d'un châtain foncé et qui paraissaient noirs, frisottaient et se tortillaient en ondes revêches, en petites mèches dures et rebelles, échappées et soulevées sur sa tête malgré la pommade de ses bandeaux lissés. Son front petit, poli, bombé, s'avançait de l'ombre d'orbites profondes où s'enfonçaient et se cavaient presque maladivement ses yeux, de petits yeux éveillés, scintillants, rapetissés et ravivés par un clignement de petite fille qui mouillait et allumait leur rire. Ces yeux on ne les voyait ni bruns ni bleus: ils étaient d'un gris indéfinissable et changeant, d'un gris qui n'était pas une couleur, mais une lumière. L'émotion y passait dans le feu de la fièvre, le plaisir dans l'éclair d'une sorte d'ivresse, la passion dans une phosphorescence. (66–67)]

The description of Germinie's ugliness is similar in hue and tone to the description of Montmartre cited above, as both suggest colors of gray and yellow. This color motif is one indication of the aesthetic integration of the work, but it also makes attractive what is conventionally unattractive or even repellent. Here, the misogyny of the Goncourt brothers suggests that from their point of view, women are not attractive, but the hatred of women is. The description of Germinie's ugliness is quite lengthy, extending two richly detailed paragraphs beyond the one quoted, but the description culminates on an unexpected note—with the declaration that such ugliness is far from repellent, but rather provocative and seductive: "Everything in her, mouth, eyes, even her very ugliness, was a provocation and solicitation" (45). ["Tout en elle, sa bouche, ses yeux, sa laideur même, avait une provocation et une sollicitation" (67).] The use of a precious and careful style in the presentation of ugliness could be called the antisublime, and the term may serve as one more approximate synonym of decadence. Indeed, in *Mimesis,* Auerbach sees the preface of *Germinie Lacerteux* as "a radical and bitter protest against the forms of an idealizing and palliating elevated style, whether of classical or romantic origin, which despite its decline continued to govern the average taste of the public" (499). By the time of the Goncourts, classical and romantic sublimity had become, albeit in debased form, elements of middle-class literary tastes that such works as *Germinie Lacerteux* challenged and resisted: *épater le bourgeois*, one of the slogans of *décadisme*,[46] has its partial origins with the brothers Goncourt.

Germinie Lacerteux is therefore one of the earliest books of naturalism as it is one of the principal works of decadence. But the importance of the novel goes well beyond the "influence" it may have exercised on this or that writer or literary school. The work marks an aesthetic shift in the direction of modernism by virtue of its highly artistic approach to a subject that is not inherently so. The aestheticization of ugliness, the pathological explanation of depravity, and the subtle but certain elevation of art over nature are all elements of decadence that will become more pronounced later. And if those elements of decadence seem muddled with the quasi-scientific spirit of naturalism, such a confluence is consistent with the notion of transition, wherein the movement of literary currents is not necessarily progressive, but often retrograde, resistant to the main flow of things. Indeed, the reactionary Goncourts, who come to modernity by way of the ancien régime, who become the literary approximations of the impressionists while idolizing Watteau and Fragonard, suggest again that perhaps the main characteristic of literary decadence is an interference of aesthetic tendencies. And this suggests, in turn, that the time of decadence, of decadence as a kind of aesthetic discovery, is a time before convention, before the stabilization of aesthetic concepts, a time of transition. Such is the time of the Goncourts.

4

Decadence and Aestheticism: Pater's *Marius the Epicurean*

The examples of *Salammbô* and *Germinie Lacerteux* make it possible to enumerate several elements that can be called decadent. Both texts are almost obsessively pathological in their evocation of cruelty, disease, and decay, from the horrible flagellation of Mâtho to the gradual ruin of Germinie. The jeweled style of *Salammbô* and the Goncourts' *écriture artiste* are early instances of *le style de décadence*, or at least move in the direction of that style. Also, both texts transform the stuff of romance into perversely erotic subject matter; sadism and hysteria infiltrate and ultimately destroy whatever may be potentially romantic in the story of Salammbô and Mâtho, and nothing is sentimentally romantic about Germinie and Jupillon, as the Goncourts announce in the preface of the novel. In this decadent context, the work of Walter Pater raises a number of problematic issues. As we shall see, *Marius the Epicurean* merely touches upon the pathological preoccupations that so concerned Flaubert and the Goncourt brothers, and the monkish Marius can hardly be called erotic. The matter of decadent style is less problematic, but here again Pater appears to be outside the emerging tradition of decadence that received its impetus from certain works by Flaubert, Baudelaire, Gautier, and the Goncourts. The question, in short, is how Pater and British aestheticism relate to those tendencies in French literature that acquire the name of decadence in the 1880s and then modulate into modernism by the early twentieth century.

This question is complicated by the seeming vagueness of the term *aestheticism,* hardly comparable semantically, for example, to *décadisme,* which refers to a clearly defined movement, albeit a minor and short-lived one, with its own theoreticians, manifestoes, reviews, and coterie of artists. There was never an aesthetic movement, though there were, perhaps, a number of aesthetes. In *The Aesthetes: A Sourcebook* (1979), Ian Small anthologizes selections from Swinburne, Pater, Whistler, and Wilde under "Aesthetic Criticism and Polemic," and places works from those same writers, adding Lionel Johnson but deleting Whistler, under "Works of Aestheticism."[1] Even though other writers of the English fin de siècle, such as Ernest Dowson and George Moore, might be added to this list, most critics would agree with Small that these are the names that come up when the topic of aestheticism arises, but the task of saying what aestheticism is still lies before us. "Aesthetic school" is preferable to "aesthetic movement," since a school implies a small group of individuals who share common interests and look to one person as master and leader, as the Médan school of naturalists looked to Zola. The master of the aesthetic school is clearly Walter Pater, but even this designation is made difficult because Pater's disciples did not always acknowledge his influence or require his guidance. Pater's most truant student, Oscar Wilde, understood his master not wisely but too well, turning subtleties into epigrams and making aestheticism seem flat and formulaic as a result: Wilde, not Pater, is the English Gautier. By the time aestheticism reaches the 1890s, borne across the Channel by Wilde, George Moore, and Arthur Symons, an admixture of *décadisme* and Francophilia has so obscured the original Paterian ideas that the problem of sorting out the meaning of aestheticism and its relation to the subsuming idea of decadence is considerable.

If we are trying to show that Pater's aestheticism is one of the characteristics of decadence that leads to the development of the modern novel, a basic dissociation must be made: between Pater's influence on the writers of the English decadence (Wilde, Swinburne, Moore, and Symons, among others), and his influence on the modernists who followed them. As we shall see in a later chapter, James Joyce was not content to emulate the elements of aestheticism that his countrymen Wilde and Moore passed on to him, but returned to Pater for raw materials for his own fiction. At the same time, that variety of aestheticism (Graham Hough, following George Moore, calls it "The New Aestheticism")[2] imagined by the writers of the nineties has an important place in the modulation of decadence into modernity, and the topic will be treated in time. But first, the literary relationship between France and England with respect to the idea of decadence must be articulated, and the place of Pater and of aestheticism in that relationship clarified.

The general conception of the literary relationship between France and England during the late nineteenth century is that British writers were isolated from happenings in Europe until the 1880s and early 1890s. Such is the assessment of Maurice Beebe, whose opinion is typical: "[T]he Aesthetic movement in England was for the most part an insular phenomenon not appreciably influenced by happenings on the Continent."[3] The notion that French literature worked as a catalyst on an English tradition in need of new directions is commonplace, as is the idea that the stimulus occurred around 1890 or so. This view of literary history is by and large correct, though such broad views always run the risk of oversimplifying literary developments and sometimes lead to erroneous conclusions. Pierrot, for example, has this to say about Oscar Wilde's part in the introduction of French literature into England: "It is clear from the many critical articles of his that appeared in London periodicals during the period from 1885 to 1895 that he had taken on the task of introducing ['il se fait l'introducteur'] French literature to Britain and championing its cause with the British reading public. So much so that he was soon acknowledged as ringleader of the group of young, francophile writers that was to launch the Aesthetic School ['le mouvement esthétique'] during the 1890s."[4] Few would argue with the point that Wilde's role as *introducteur* was substantial, but the last phrase of the quotation illustrates precisely the problem at hand. Pierrot most likely has been misled by a confused critical tradition when he has Oscar Wilde launching the "aesthetic movement" in the 1890s, and the confusion is manifold: "mouvement" is inaccurate (significantly, the translator of Pierrot's book uses "school"), the originator of the aesthetic school is not Wilde, and the suggestion that English writers had to wait for Wilde to discover French literature is somewhat misleading. Further, the assumption that the traffic of literary influence flowed exclusively from France to England is mistaken. Without question, English literature underwent a profound transformation as a result of French ideas disseminated by Wilde, Symons, and others, but those very ideas owed at least some of their originality to earlier English traditions and fashions.

For example, the decadent taste for artificiality finds considerable precedence in the dandyism of early nineteenth-century England. As Ellen

Moers tells us, in the person of George Bryan Brummel (1778–1840), the original dandy, man becomes a "creature perfect in externals and careless of anything below the surface, a man dedicated to his own perfection through a ritual of taste."[5] And the dandy's perfection, Moeurs continues, consists mainly in his resistance to nature: "To the dandy the self is not an animal, but a gentleman. Instinctual reactions, passions and enthusiasms are animal, and thus abominable. Here the dandy temperament diverges most widely from the romantic" (18). It should be noted that the dandy as exemplified by Beau Brummel cultivated a style of dress simple and rigorous in the extreme. The true dandy was not interested in a flamboyant wardrobe or decorative accessories, but in creating a style, though "legend is confused about the nature of that style. The popular version has always been that he dressed too obviously well, with fantastic colours and frills, exotic jewels and perfumes. The accurate (and important) report declares that he dressed in a style more austere, manly, and dignified than any before or since" (31). So defined, dandyism found its place in France around 1815 with the return of the Bourbons and with French anglophilia after the victory of Wellington. The temporary revival of a mannered society coincided with receptivity to English fashion, and *le dandysme* enters the vocabulary of French intellectuals (108–9). In 1845, Barbey d'Aurevilly published *Du Dandysme et de Georges Brummel*, a book that helped Baudelaire formulate his conception of the artist. As Moers points out, Baudelaire's critics "have labelled as dandyism his passions for artificiality, for perfection, for refinement, and his antipathies to vulgarity, to sentimentalism and to extravagance" (276). Thus, the dandyism of Baudelaire, so important to the formation of the decadent aesthetic that had such an impact on the young British Francophiles of the fin de siècle, is itself traceable to British culture. Maurice Beebe notes that "one of Pater's contributions to the Aesthetic movement is his development of the esthete as a new kind of being, not unlike Baudelaire's dandy,"[6] and it would seem that this aspect of Pater's aestheticism need not have developed, necessarily, as a result of French influences.

Other instances of British influence on French decadentism are less obvious than the importation of the English dandy, but helped to contribute, nonetheless, to the formation of a new aesthetic in France. Pierrot, for example, emphasizes the place of Thomas De Quincey as a forerunner of decadence in France. De Quincey's *Confessions of an English Opium Eater* (1822), translated by Musset as early as 1828, was read and appreciated by Baudelaire, whose *Les Paradis artificiels* (1860) contributed to the fashion for opium and other drugs among the decadents of the 1880s and 1890s.[7] The use of drugs at that time was by no means simply a matter of social rebellion or a way of resisting the values of the bourgeoisie. Speaking of De Quincey's influence on Paul Bourget, Pierrot notes that "the use of drugs was regarded as one of the possible means of escaping from reality in order to transfigure it, and the attitude and the writings of De Quincey seemed to him to be exemplary guides on that new path" (36). And the transfiguration of reality, rather than the classical aesthetic of representation of reality, is an important quality of decadence advanced by Bourget in his theoretical writings. Pierrot also notes that Bourget traveled in England and there discovered the Pre-Raphaelites, "whose influence on French decadent literature is indisputable" (13). Along with the Pre-Raphaelites', Swinburne's work found a favorable audience in France. Although both the Pre-Raphaelites and Swinburne are related more to the development of symbolist poetry than to decadent prose,[8] their influence, along with De Quincey's, is ample illustration of the point that British writers contributed in large measure to the formation of the literary sensibility in France that so affected the English Francophiles at the end of the nineteenth century.

This is not to say that English writers prior to the fin de siècle were unaffected by Continental literature. Pater in particular can be seen as a kind of avant-garde figure in this respect, for his interest in French literature antedates by a generation the discoveries of Wilde and Symons and Moore. In his 1888 essay on "Style," Pater expressed the greatest admiration for Flaubert as the master of literary prose: "If all high things have their martyrs, Gustave Flaubert might perhaps rank as the martyr of literary style" (*SW*, 115). But Pater's knowledge of Flaubert dates back much earlier, to the period of his Oxford matriculation (1858–62). At Oxford, a recent biographer says, Pater "apparently made a regular habit of translating" not only Flaubert but Sainte-Beuve as well.[9] The thoroughness of Pater's knowledge and understanding of French literature is most evident in the essay from *Appreciations* titled "Romanticism" (1876). Here, Pater demonstrates a familiarity with the French tradition that is quite complete, ranging from Racine to Rousseau to a number of nineteenth-century writers: Balzac, Stendahl, Hugo, Gautier, and others. What is most important about this essay, however, is the evidence it offers for the place of French literature in Pater's own thought.[10] In this essay Pater offers his succinct definition of romanticism as "the addition of strangeness to beauty" and identifies the "romantic temper" as "the addition of curiosity to [the] desire of beauty" (*SW*, 211). Pater turns to French romantic writers to lend support to this definition, supplementing it with Sainte-Beuve's statement that a "genuine classic" must be "[*é*]*nergigue,* frais, et dispos" (*SW*, 212). These qualities of "energy, freshness, [and] comely order" (*SW*, 214) in the best romantic art combine with strangeness so that beauty is intensified by the interaction of contrary elements; the simplest terms for these opposing elements in Pater's vocabulary are the *grotesque* (the extreme of strangeness) and *sweetness* (which encompasses energy, freshness, and comely order) (*SW*, 212). Gautier and Victor Hugo, in particular, are representative romantics in Pater's view, but even more telling is his admiration of Chateaubriand. In Chateaubriand's *Génie du Christianisme,* Pater finds a "refuge from a tarnished actual present, a present of disillusion, into a world of strength and beauty in the Middle Age. . . . It is to minds in this spiritual situation, weary of the present, but yearning for the spectacle of beauty and strength, that the works of French romanticism appeal" (*SW*, 215). The language here strongly suggests that Pater's understanding of French romanticism contributed to his own aesthetic ideal of combining a "comely decadence" with the "charm of *ascēsis*" (*SW*, 20), and that a balance of strength and sweetness, of strangeness and beauty, is a large part of the aesthetic program that Pater imagined. This much is obvious from the concluding passages of the "Romanticism" essay, where the critical tone shifts from the descriptive to the prescriptive: "[I]n literature as in other matters it is well to unite as many diverse elements as may be: that the individual writer or artist, certainly, is to be estimated by the number of graces he combines, and his power of interpenetrating them in a given work" (*SW*, 220). Pater drew from his knowledge of French literature a conception of the totality of literary art, an art combining apparent opposites into an overriding aesthetic unity.

The "Romanticism" essay, in short, illustrates a more complete influence of French literature on Pater than is usually allowed by his critics, one of whom, for example, says that "Pater's aesthetic gospel could not have been preached if Gautier . . . had not initiated the doctrine of '*l'art pour l'art*'—the phrase which Pater himself translates as 'art for art's sake.'"[11] This overestimates the impact of Gautier on Pater; surely it would be a mistake to say that Pater was simply the British expositor of Gautier's ideas. Pater garnered more from French literature than an isolated slogan. Moreover, the case of Pater illustrates that there was no paucity of French influence on English writers well before the 1890s. The receptivity of Pater to that influence helped to frame the minds of the generation to follow, whose openness to French literature was complete. But even though the intense interaction of French and British writers in the late 1880s and the 1890s is an unquestionable fact of literary history, the "aestheticism" of that period is not quite the same as the Paterian original. And we need to understand Pater's aestheticism in particular if we are to understand the variations and distortions of it that followed.

Ruth Z. Temple has declared that "[A]esthetic as a label for a literary movement had better be discarded,"[12] and there is good cause for this consideration. One reason for Temple's conclusion is the diversity of the writers usually labelled "aesthetic" (Temple's list: "Swinburne, early Tennyson, Pater, Symons, Dowson, Wilde" [218–19]); such diversity certainly violates the notion of a movement. Another reason aestheticism is suspect as a literary term is the faddish dilettantism that evolved under the name of aestheticism during the English fin de siècle. There *was* an aesthetic movement, but it was a movement of fashion and taste, not of literature. Blue china, kneebreeches, peacock feathers, lilies and sunflowers were among the paraphernalia required by the fashionable aesthete, and such affectations of taste and dress were frequently lampooned in *Punch* by the well-known satirist George Du Maurier.[13] In the following passage, Postlethwaite, one of Du Maurier's typical aesthetes, offers a sampling of what the proper British public thought the aesthetic style to be:

> The Aesthetic Young Man rose languidly from his seat, and leaning against a bookcase, with the Lily in his hand, and the Peacock's Feather in his hair, he read aloud. . . .
>
> 'You have never heard of MAUDLE and Mrs. CIMABUE BROWN? I dare say not. To know them is a Joy, and the privileges of a select and chosen few; for they are simply Perfect. Yet in their respective perfection, they differentiate from each other with a quite ineffably subtle exquisiteness.
>
> For *She* is Supremely Consummate—whereas *He* is Consummately Supreme. I constantly tell them so, and they agree with me.'[14]

Such ridicule has obscured the usefulness of aestheticism as a literary term. Temple discusses the problem of definition and notes that the venerable *Oxford English Dictionary* preserves the Victorian bias against aestheticism: "Recent extravagances in the adoption of a sentimental archaism as the ideal of beauty have [helped to remove] *aesthetic* and its derivatives from their etymological and purely philosophical meaning."[15] The reference to "sentimental archaism" suggests that what the *OED* editors had in mind was not Walter Pater's aestheticism at all, but Rossetti's Pre-Raphaelitism and the choice of medieval subjects to embody a vague ideal of beauty. For while it is true that Pater does move away from a "purely philosophical meaning" of aesthetic, he restores to the word its etymological connotations.

Pater's recovery of the root sense of aesthetic occurs in the preface to *The Renaissance,* which must be read against the background of a philosophical tradition that had long sought to investigate the idea of beauty in metaphysical terms. Though this tradition is much older than the work of its principal proponent, the German philosopher Baumgarten, his use of the word *aesthetica* to mean "criticism of taste"[16] helped to popularize aesthetics as the particular branch of philosophy concerned with beauty as a subject of metaphysical speculation. Much of Pater's originality, as well as his importance to the development of modernism, concerns his resistance to the metaphysical interpretation of beauty in favor of what has come to be called the phenomenological:

> Beauty, like all other qualities presented to human experience, is relative; and the definition of it becomes unmeaning and useless in proportion to its abstractness. To define beauty, not in the most abstract, but in the most concrete terms possible, to find, not a universal formula for it, but the formula which expresses most adequately this or that special manifestation of it, is the aim of the true student of aesthetics.
>
> "To see the object as in itself it really is," has been justly said to be the aim of all true criticism whatever; and in aesthetic criticism the first step towards seeing one's object as it really is, is to know one's own impression as it really is, to discriminate it, to realise it distinctly. (*SW,* 17)

The "object" under discussion in the above passage is the work of art, and all works of art for Pater the aesthetic critic are "powers or forces producing pleasurable sensations" (*SW,* 18). In so emphasizing the sensuous nature of art, Pater reminds us that *aesthetic* defines itself etymologically as *perception,* and that the principal forms of perception are feeling and seeing, or as Pater usually says, "observation": "The service of philosophy, of speculative culture, towards the human spirit is to rouse, to startle it into sharp and eager observation" (*SW,* 60). As Harold Bloom says: "We owe to Pater our characteristic modern use of 'aesthetic,' for he emancipated the word from its bondage to philosophy . . . when he spoke of the 'aesthetic critic' in his 'Preface' to *The Renaissance.* . . . Pater had to endure the debasement of 'aesthete' as a term, and we endure it still. Pater meant us always to remember what mostly we have forgotten: that 'aesthete' is from the Greek *aisthetes,* 'one who perceives.' "[17]

Aestheticism, then, is largely a matter of the sensuous perception of works of art, and such perception gains in importance when reality is no longer anchored, in Pater's view, by the absolutes of conventional Victorian morality. In a sense, Pater aims to save the perceiver from his own perceptions, to help him discriminate finely among the multiple and fleeting impressions of a world in constant flux. Ian Small, commenting on the conclusion to *The Renaissance,* notes that the "simple phenomenological proposition behind Pater's work is that the perceiver is certain only of his *own* impressions, and the individual, although celebrating his individuality, is consequently isolated in the 'chamber' of his own mind, a victim of his own impressions of the world beyond."[18] What saves the perceiver from the onslaught of phenomena is art, for the experience of art is superior in quality to everyday experience: "[A]rt comes to you proposing frankly to give nothing but the highest quality to your moments as they pass, and simply for those moments' sake" (*SW,* 62). Thus, aestheticism comes to be defined not as a pure concept but as a complete program for a life devoted to the refined appreciation of great works of art. Such a definition may have little application to any nineteenth-century writer other than Pater, since those he inspired made of aestheticism something rather different from what Pater had proposed.

The aesthetic program as Pater imagined it depends heavily on a discriminating and disciplined taste, on temperance and control. Pater's aestheticism is also rooted in the real world of concrete objects and genuine sensations, though his refined and often ethereal style occasionally belies this fact. Pater manages an odd fusion of the delicious and the disciplined, of decadence and *ascēsis,* those two qualities that he saw as separate in the preface to *The Renaissance:* "[T]he Renaissance put . . . forth in France an aftermath, a wonderful later growth, the products of which have to the full that subtle and delicate sweetness which belongs to a refined and comely decadence; just as its earliest phases have the freshness which belongs to all periods of growth in art, the charm of *ascēsis,* of the austere and serious girding of the loins in youth" (*SW,* 20). As Bloom puts it, "Pater's strange achievement is to have assimilated Wordsworth to Lucretius, to have compounded an idealistic naturalism with a corrective materialism."[19] The fusion of contradictory qualities appears uniquely Paterian, and this is what his so-called disciples evidently missed. Commenting on the hedonistic habits of Wilde's Dorian Gray, Graham Hough argues that aestheticism is more than a strategy to "beguile the tedium of life. It is of course the putting into practice of part of the Paterian ideal, but without the element of *ascēsis*, the real devotion to the best that life has to give, that saves Pater from deliquescence."[20] This is not to say, however, that Pater's austere aestheticism cannot be extended and distorted into the decadent posturing and self-conscious immorality that is associated with Wilde and his hero, Dorian Gray. Pater is an advocate of experience of the real world, but it is the check of perception that controls and refines experience and prevents its becoming a simplistic and hedonistic *indulgence* in the real world. Without the aesthetic check of perception, the way is open for the Wildean hero, a way unwittingly prepared by Pater.[21]

Another effect of the reduction and oversimplification of Pater's aestheticism was a tendency away from the appreciation of great works of art and toward the cultivation of artificiality in any form whatsoever. As a reduction or trivialization of aestheticism, the love of artifice for artifice's sake gained impetus from Huysmans's *A Rebours* and from the formulations of *décadisme*. Thus, Pater's strict aestheticism may be an intermediate stage in a more general modulation of romanticism into decadence; that is, Pater's aestheticism expresses a preference for works of art as objects of perception, but by no means are the creations of nature rejected, as *Marius* illustrates (see below).[22] In short, Pater's place in this schema is that of the revisionist, to adopt the vocabulary of Harold Bloom. Bloom, in fact, stresses the significance of Pater as a pivotal figure when he offers his own scenario of transition: "Pater is the heir of a tradition already too wealthy to have required much extension or variation when it reached him. He revised that tradition, turning the Victorian continuation of High Romanticism into the late Romanticism or 'Decadence' that prolonged itself as what variously might be called Modernism, Post-Romanticism, or, self-deceivingly, Anti-Romanticism."[23] The centrality of Pater becomes evident when his aestheticism is compared to the imitations of Wilde, whose work seems clearly decadent when set against Pater's.

The proof of this point can be readily observed by a comparison of the style of the two writers. The epigrammatic style of Wilde needs little commentary; examples from *The Picture of Dorian Gray* could be cited at length: "Women are a decorative sex. They never have anything to say, but they say it charmingly. Women represent the triumph of matter over mind, just as men represent the triumph of mind over morals" (48).[24] This is not far removed from the language of Samuel Johnson: though Wilde may be at odds with Dr. Johnson philosophically (their shared misogyny notwithstanding), he is well within the rhetorical tradition of the eighteenth century. Throughout the dialogue of the novel, "Wilde on the whole proves himself a late descendant of the eighteenth-century playwrights, making one pun after another."[25] And this is exactly the point: the decadence of Wilde consists largely in that there is nothing *new* about an epigrammatic style. He is indeed a "late descendant," an imitator of an earlier tradition. More important, such a style reveals a worldview hardly consonant with the changing reality of the nineteenth century. That is, an epigrammatic style possesses the qualities of succinctness, brevity, directness, and assurance, so that anyone who writes an epigram does so with an air of certainty and confidence. There is more to Wilde than epigrams, however, and in certain of his critical and polemical writings, notably *The Soul of Man Under Socialism* (1891), Wilde's sensitivity to the complexities of the nineteenth century are more pronounced than in his imaginative prose. His criticism, in fact, is often remarkable for the way it announces or anticipates any number of aesthetic trends important to the development of modernism. This is the case with at least three of the essays published in *Intentions* (1891): Through its title and cryptic ending "The Truth of Masks" seems to anticipate the idea of the persona taken up later by several modernist poets; "The Critic as Artist" urges a return to personal voice at the same time that it encourages self-consciousness over self-expressiveness; and "The Decay of Lying" presents a strong critique of the naturalist-realist tradition, as Wilde calls for a return to "imaginative power" (974) that would elevate artistic prose over slavish documentation: "Art finds her own perfection within, and not outside of, herself. She is not to be judged by any external standard of resemblance" (982). But Wilde leads later writers into modernism more by precept than by example, as the example of his only novel shows. In *Dorian Gray* Wilde responded to the changes about him mainly at the moral level; in so doing he appears, sometimes, almost as dogmatic as his opponents: not the contrary (to use the language of William Blake), but the negation of Victorian consciousness.

The style of Walter Pater, on the other hand, reveals completely his sensitivity to change, and his affinity with Heraclitus and other philosophers of change is well known. Pater analyzing the stuff of experience is a study in instability, the flow of sentences tentative, hesitant, unsure of destination or conclusion, with none of Wilde's predictable finish:

> Analysis goes a step farther still, and assures us that those impressions of the individual mind to which, for each one of us, experience dwindles down, are in perpetual flight; that each of them is limited by time, and that as time is infinitely divisible, each of them is infinitely divisible also; all that is actual in it being a single moment, gone while we try to apprehend it, of which it may ever be more truly said that it has ceased to be than that it is. To such a tremulous wisp constantly reforming itself on the stream, to a single sharp impression, with a sense in it, a relic more or less fleeting, of such moments gone by, what is real in our life fines itself down. It is with this movement, with the passage and dissolution of impressions, images, sensations, that analysis leaves off—that continual vanishing away, that strange perpetual weaving and unweaving of ourselves. (*SW*, 60)

Pater's great distinction is his recognition of such prose as "being the special art of the modern world" because of its capabilities of expressing the instability of that world:

> That imaginative prose should be the special and opportune art of the modern world results from two important facts about the latter: first, the chaotic variety and complexity of its interests, making the intellectual issue, the really master currents of the present time incalculable—a condition of mind little susceptible to the restraint proper to verse form, so that the most characteristic verse of the nineteenth century has been lawless verse; and secondly, an all-pervading naturalism, a curiosity about everything whatever as it really is, involving a certain humility of attitude, cognate to what must, after all, be the less ambitious form of literature. And prose thus asserting itself as the special and privileged artistic faculty of the present day, will be, . . . as varied in its excellence as humanity itself reflecting on the facts of its latest experience—an instrument of many stops, meditative, observant, descriptive, eloquent, analytic, plaintive, fervid. (*SW*, 106–7)

Pater's perception of reality as flux and his recognition that such a view of reality required an equally fluid form of artistic expression contribute, in the end, to the difficulties of defining aestheticism. After all, the *-ism* suffix suggests something coherent and systematic, "adherence to a system or a class of principles,"[26] and it is difficult to see how the aesthetic admonition to "burn always with a hard, gemlike flame" can be part of any system at all, especially since the flame is an Heraclitean emblem of change. It would be better, perhaps, to drop the *-ism* altogether, to admit that the concept we are dealing with does not have the substance and stability of a noun, that to accord it substance and stability is to miss the point completely. One should probably speak instead of the aesthetic attitude, the aesthetic frame of mind, the aesthetic spirit, and so on. Indeed, the curious grammar of Pater's aesthetic style depends less on the substantive than the adjective, the lagging qualifier, the added phrase. What is true of language in general is true of Pater in particular: that meaning is modified into existence. Existence, however, is not the best word, for the meaning is all in the modification: Pater's language brings nothing forth except itself. One embodiment of this operation is *Marius the Epicurean,* where the aesthetic ideal of refined perception is constantly wedded to the reality of a changing world. As a result, Marius, considered as a conventional fictional character, means a great deal, though he hardly exists at all.

Marius the Epicurean is a *Bildungsroman* that traces the intellectual, aesthetic, and spiritual development of a young man living in the Roman Empire in the second century, during the reign of Marcus Aurelius. The first part of the book concerns the growth of Marius from a devout boy with a deep, meditative love of pagan ritual to a budding *littérateur* whose main interest is the ornate, "euphuistic" style of Apuleius. He is introduced to Apuleius's golden book at Pisa by his schoolfriend Flavian, who has courted corruption in some obscure way and dies of fever. The link between refined literary taste and physical decay is unmistakable, as Flavian undertakes to write poetry throughout his long death agony. The death of Flavian turns Marius away from literature and, at the same time, extinguishes the religion of his childhood.

In the second section of the novel, Marius begins to pursue his "natural Epicureanism" in earnest and now finds some "aesthetic charm" in the "cold austerity of mind" (*ME,* 105–6) such philosophy fosters. His study of philosophy ultimately brings him back to literature, but only as one element in a larger " 'aesthetic' education" in "those aspects of things which affect us pleasurably through sensation" (*ME,* 117–18). This "new Cyrenaicism" is not, however, hedonistic, but "heroic, impassioned, ideal" (*ME,* 120). His character thus reformed in this manner, Marius receives a summons to Rome, where he is to serve as secretary to the emperor. He is accompanied on the journey from Pisa by Cornelius, a young soldier who has converted to Christianity. Cornelius is also attached to the royal house, and his quiet Christianity provides a contrast to both the Stoicism of Marcus Aurelius and the hedonism of the emperor's brother Lucius Verus. The Epicureanism of Marius seems to combine the finer elements of all three "faiths." The second part of the book ends with the bloody spectacle of the gladiatorial contests, which helps to persuade the inexperienced Marius that "evil was a real thing" (*ME,* 171).

The brief third section of the novel concentrates, at first, on the problem of morality, as Marius begins to doubt whether his Epicurean philosophy provides sufficient guard against the reality of evil. He also intuits the inadequacy of the emperor's stoicism when Marcus Aurelius suffers the death of his son and then sets off on a military campaign. Marius is struck by the contrast of the emperor's drained face against his splendid armor, an obvious figure for stoical philosophy. The intellectual climax of the novel comes in the chapter that closes this section, titled "The Will as Vision." Here, Marius's materialist philosophy breaks down as a series of idealist insights make themselves felt: "The purely material world, that close, impassioned prison-wall, seemed just then the unreal thing, to be actually dissolving away all around him" (*ME,* 212).

The long fourth section of the novel takes place some time after this "fortunate hour" when many things are compressed into "one central act of vision" (*ME,* 217). Marius is a changed man. His old curiosity about the world is diminished, for the world itself "looked further off, was weaker in its hold, and, in a sense, less real to him than ever" (*ME,* 217). The Christian community about Rome has gotten stronger, and Marius is drawn to it in an oddly materialistic way for one who has so thoroughly adopted the doctrine of idealism. He finds his friend Cornelius at the house of the Christian woman Cecilia and, by chance, witnesses the celebration of the Eucharist. Marius would seem to be ripe for conversion, but the ceremonies of the church paradoxically revive his earlier aesthetic interests as he finds the rituals more sensuous than sacred. A second visit to Cecilia's house allows Marius to witness the burial ceremony of a child. The contrast between the Christians' joyful response to the child's death and the emperor's despair in the earlier episode makes an impression on Marius, who is ever more mindful of death. In this frame of mind he returns to his childhood home and visits the family mausoleum, where he rearranges the bones of his ancestors. Cornelius finds him there and they set off again for Rome, as they did in their youth. On the way they are joined by a group of Christians who are attacked by a band of superstitious pagans. Cornelius and Marius are arrested, but Marius bribes the guards to release Cornelius, who sets off to secure his friend's legal defense. The Christians, Marius with them, are sent on a forced march to the place of trial. Marius falls ill with fever on the way and is left to die in a small village. The local Christians find him and, knowing that he has saved Cornelius, administer the last rites and regard him as a martyr. There is some irony in the situation that has a Roman pagan receiving a Christian martyr's funeral. Marius dies without really embracing the faith: his interest in Christianity all along has been mainly a matter of aesthetic curiosity rather than spiritual conviction.

Marius the Epicurean is, therefore, an aesthetic novel set in a time of decadence. *Aesthetic* here has the Paterian meaning of refined and sensitive perception, while *decadence* refers to a historical period of transition perceived as a decline from perfection to corruption, though the last two terms become curiously mingled in the mind of Marius. This mingling of opposites establishes the tone of the novel as one of tension and refined irresolution. Marius thus finds that his sensations of the real world, even in their more repellent aspects, have something attractive about them, as when the youthful Marius finds himself fascinated by the repugnance he feels at the sight of two snakes breeding in the summer: "He wondered at himself indeed, trying to puzzle out the secret of that repugnance, having no particular dread of a snake's bite. . . . A kind of pity even mingled with his aversions, and he could hardly have killed or injured the animals, which seemed already to suffer by the very circumstances of their life, being what they were" (*ME,* 48). That Marius is capable of wondering and puzzling over his sensations marks him off from the stoical Marcus Aurelius, a man of abstract principles only who fails to come to terms with his own perceptions of the material universe. The emperor's indifference to the cruelties of the arena slaughter that closes part 2 of the novel indicates the distance between the purely intellectual and the aesthetic man, and the episode confirms the rightness of Marius's philosophy: "His chosen philosophy had said, —Trust the eye: Strive to be right always in regard to concrete experience: Beware of falsifying your impressions" (*ME,* 170). Hence the meaning of the subtitle, *His Sensations and Ideas:* sensations have only a slightly privileged place in Marius's consciousness; the mind of Marius, like the novel itself, is in suspense between the abstract and the concrete, even as Marius himself at the arena is positioned between the indifferent emperor and Lucius Verus, the sensualist who relishes all that he sees at the "great slaughter house . . . with loud shouts of applause" (*ME,* 169). By allowing this interplay of opposites, Pater manages to suggest a special kind of Epicureanism. As Bloom notes, even though Marius supposedly entertains a number of different philosophies, "in the broad sense [he], like Pater, lives and dies an Epicurean. For the Epicureanism involved is simply the inevitable religion of the Paterian version of sensibility, or the 'aesthetic philosophy' proper."[27] This type of "aesthetic Epicureanism" places the greatest premium on completeness, which any choice, any coming-to-rest on the side of either sensations or ideas, would obviously negate: "Not pleasure, but a general completeness of life, was the practical ideal to which this anti-metaphysical metaphysic really pointed. And towards such a full or complete life, a life of various yet select sensation, the most direct and effective auxiliary must be in a word, Insight" (*ME,* 115). This, in broad terms, explains the implications of the title and indicates the relevance of aestheticism to the text as a whole.

The sense of suspense that gives the work a philosophical "center" that floats and hovers throughout also has implications for the form of the novel. Despite its relation to the *Bildungsroman* tradition, the novel does not really trace the maturation of Marius in the usual sense of progress or development. Each intellectual phase that Marius enters remains connected in some way to those preceding, so that the chronology of the narrative is retarded by its origins. Thus, at the end of the novel Marius has "progressed" to his point of departure, and the intermixture of simplicity, art, and religion represented by the early Christian Cecilia echoes those same qualities embodied at the outset of the novel in the figure of Marius's mother. *Marius* begins and ends at the home of Marius, with Cecilia taking the place of the mother: "His [Marius's] beginning foreshadows his end, and his end enfolds his beginning. This symmetrical bracketing of the chronological progression of his life suggests the dissolution of origins into repetitions, of a reality which refuses to yield an attainable ground of being apart from the dialectic between consciousness and language."[28] Marius, in fact, recognizes that reality cannot be structured to provide a "satisfactory basis of certainty" since such structures are "after all only a fixity of language" and thus he "fall[s] back upon direct sensation" (*ME,* 113). The structure of the novel reflects Marius's refusal to fix reality artificially through language, for the work is without narrative destination. Again, the novel is not "plotted" to chart the progressive, linear development of the hero. Such a schema would be too much at odds with Pater's minutely qualified vision of a reality that refuses to accept any preconceived logical structure, including the structure of conventional narrative.

Pater's willingness to accept the problematic nature of reality, to see the world in phenomenological rather than metaphysical terms, is one of the things that distinguishes him as a precursor of modernism. Pater accepts the instability of the new world that nineteenth-century science discovered, and the attitude is certainly shown by the style of *Marius*, where the sentences are so tentative, qualified, self-conscious. Just as the narrative of *Marius* is without destination, so Pater's sentences seem without "rhetorical predisposition," free of any "preconceived structural formulation."[29] The art of reading *Marius the Epicurean* is analogous to slowly feeling one's way along in a dark room filled with unfamiliar objects, for Pater's style provides the reader with few of the conventional rhetorical devices of earlier English prose. The style itself, in other words, is consonant with the notion of flux, and Pater's language offers only momentary stays against instability. One critic notes that Pater "creates in *Marius* a structure of awareness that carefully dislocates all possibility of dogmatic center and places the protagonist, the narrator/commentator, and the reader in a state of spiritual community in that they are all on their own, all fallible, and all engaged (while the book lasts) in a conscientious effort at personal renewal."[30] This operation can be illustrated by citing virtually any passage of *Marius*, where every paragraph is studded with qualifiers, such as "somewhat," "sort of," "rather," "perhaps," and so on, and the verbs are more often than not conditional:

> It was intelligible that this "aesthetic" philosophy might find itself (theoretically, at least, and by way of a curious question in casuistry, legitimate from its own point of view) weighing the claims of that eager, concentrated, impassioned realization of experience, against those of the received morality. Conceiving its own function in a somewhat desperate temper, and becoming, as every high-strung form of sentiment, as the religious sentiment itself, may become, somewhat antinomian, when, in its effort toward the order of experiences it prefers, it is confronted with the traditional and popular morality, at points where that morality may look very like a convention, or a mere stage-property of the world, it would be found, from time to time, breaking beyond the limits of the actual moral order; perhaps not without some pleasurable excitement in so bold a venture. (*ME*, 119)

Here the absence of an unqualified "dogmatic center" might be attributed to a cautious attitude on Pater's part because of the sensation created by the conclusion of *The Renaissance;* Pater is clearly writing as much about the "received morality" of his own age as about that of Antonine Rome. But what is described above is Marius's "New Cyrenaicism" and Pater hedges here as elsewhere for the same reason: no interpretation of reality and no philosophy of life can be final and conclusive. Pater's rhetoric of reticence is elusive in the service of the elusiveness of reality. Much of that elusive quality inheres in the idea of transition, both in Pater's choice of subject and in the suggested analogy between the earlier age and his own.

There is no question that Pater was mindful of his own times when he set himself to write *Marius.* The choice of Antonine Rome as a subject relevant to late nineteenth-century Britain was perhaps influenced by Pater's reading of Matthew Arnold, who had suggested the analogy in an essay on Marcus Aurelius in *Victoria Magazine* in 1863. There Arnold claimed that Marcus Aurelius was "a man like ourselves" and that the second century was an age "akin to our own."[31] In *Marius,* the analogy is ever-present and stated on occasion quite explicitly: "That age and our own have much in common—many difficulties and hopes. Let the reader pardon me if here and there I seem to be passing from Marius to his modern representatives—from Rome, to Paris or London" (*ME,* 181). As Bloom says, "Pater's *Marius* is founded on a . . . convincing and troubling resemblance, between Victorian England in the 1880s and Rome in the Age of the Antonines, two summits of power and civilization sloping downward in decadence. The aesthetic humanism of Marius, poised just outside of a Christianity Pater felt to be purer than anything available to himself, is precisely the desperately noble and hopeless doctrine set forth in the conclusion to *The Renaissance.*"[32] It has even been suggested that *Marius* was written partly as an apologetic corrective to the famous conclusion, to make clear to anyone who had been misled by the earlier work that the aesthetic philosophy is not to be equated with some kind of vulgar hedonism.[33] The clearest analogy between Pater's Antonines and the Victorians revolves about the "Euphuism" of Marius's friend Flavian, for such "euphuism" has "obvious topical relevance to the creed of Art for Art's sake."[34] Flavian's literary ambitions and Marius's literary interests are heightened by the *Metamorphoses* of Apuleius, which is Marius's golden book just as *The Renaissance* had become the golden book for Wilde and Moore. Pater's description of Apuleius's golden style, moreover, is often close to Gautier's description of *le style de décadence.* Apuleius's style is said to be heterogenous, a mixture of old idioms and new phrases, of literary and nonliterary language: full of "archaisms" and "quaint terms," "the lifelike phrases of some lost poet," "racy morsels of the vernacular and studied prettiness" (*ME,* 67). Similarly, Gautier describes the decadent style as an aesthetic mixture, combining different "technical" vocabularies and taking "colors from every palette and notes from every keyboard" ["empruntant à tous les vocabulaires techniques, prenant des couleurs à toutes les palettes, des notes à tous les claviers" (124)].[35] The euphuistic style of Apuleius also includes "a certain tincture of 'neology' in expression" (*ME,* 68). Gautier is more forceful on the presence of neology in the decadent style, insisting that "new ideas" require "new forms" and "words never before heard" ["il exprime des idées neuves avec des formes nouvelles et des mots qu'on n'a pas entendus encore" (125)]. This implicit comparison of literary tastes in second-century Rome and Second Empire France becomes quite direct when Pater shifts from the style to the substance of decadence, "into what French writers call the *macabre*—that species of almost insane preoccupation with the materialities of our mouldering flesh, that luxury of disgust in gazing on corruption" (*ME,* 70). Certain scenes in Apuleius's golden book, in fact, are said to be "worthy of Théophile Gautier" (*ME,* 70).

The incorporation of these references to the tradition of the golden book shows that Pater manipulated his own fairly recent literary infamy into the text of *Marius.* The death of Flavian at the end of section 1 shows in dramatic form Pater's belief that "fatality . . . lies in the quest for beauty," and that "art for art's sake" offers only "a partial and limited solution" to the problems of life.[36] Thus, from the end of the first section onward Pater provides his contemporaries with an extended supplement to the misread *Renaissance* and puts forth the true aesthetic doctrine of Marius/Pater. However, the corrective had little effect on those who transformed Pater's austere aestheticism into the dandified decadentism of the 1890s. On the contrary, *Marius* is filled with passages and phrases that, taken out of their highly qualified Paterian context, could only give impetus to the "new aestheticism's" tendency toward decadentism. The "cloistral or monastic" setting of White-Nights (*ME,* 47); the dual fascination with the ancient world's "depth of corruption" and its "perfection of form" (*ME,* 65); the "preoccupation of the *dilettante* with . . . mere details of form" (*ME,* 92); the delight in "a mediocrity for once really golden" (*ME,* 163); the sadism of the arena slaughters ("[T]here would be a certain curious interest in the dexterously contrived escape of the young from their mothers' torn bosoms; as many pregnant animals as possible being carefully selected for the purpose" [*ME,* 168]); the love of liturgy and ritual for its own sake ("The aesthetic charm of the catholic church . . . we may see already" [*ME,* 242]); the Baudelairean image of the world "as a hospital of sick persons" (*ME,* 270); and the pervasive sense of morbidity in Marius's sensibility ("throughout it had been something of a *meditatio mortis*" [*ME,* 288]): All of these elements would readily find a place in the mind-set of the English fin de siècle.

Thus, Pater's importance is twofold: as an immediate influence on the minor writers of the English fin de siècle and as a pivotal figure in the transition from romanticism to modernism. The modernity of *Marius* includes a thematic and stylistic predisposition to acknowledge the relativism and instability of the modernist worldview. In more specific literary terms, *Marius* amounts to a radical revision of the form of the novel, so much so that the traditional categories of generic classification seem irrelevant. *Bildungsroman* and "portrait novel," conventionally the genre to which *Marius* supposedly belongs, do very little to describe the novel. It is possible to see the work as part of a tradition of nineteenth-century "semifiction" that would include Robert Southey's *Colloquies on Society*, Carlyle's *Sartor Resartus*, and Walter Savage Landor's *Imaginary Conversations*,[37] but Pater's unique style effectively separates him from earlier traditions of English prose. And the break with the conventional nineteenth-century realistic novel is also complete: "The fixed antagonism that conventional fiction accepts as permanent between the real and the imaginary and that it attempts to bridge by a willing suspension of disbelief, Pater's fiction disavows."[38] Pater's importance for the development of the modern novel consists in this disavowal, and in his assimilation of the tradition of English poetry, particularly Wordsworth's, into the tradition of English prose, which amounts to the invention of a new prose idiom capable of expressing a new sensibility. That sensibility involves more than anything else an articulation of interiority, subjectivity, the unconscious: "This . . . is the most relevant context in which to read *Marius the Epicurean*. *Marius* is the masterpiece of things-in-their-farewell, the great document in English of the historical moment when the unconscious came painfully to its birth. Where Wordsworth and Keats, followed by Mill and Arnold, fought imaginatively against excessive self-consciousness, Pater welcomes it, and by this welcome inaugurates, for writers and readers in English, the decadent phase of Romanticism."[39] Like his character Marius, Pater seems fully aware of the necessity and difficulty of such transition: "Certainly, the most wonderful, the unique, point, about the Greek genius, in literature as in everything else, was the entire absence of imitation in its productions. How had the burden of precedent, laid upon every artist, increased since then! . . . There might seem to be no place left for novelty or originality,—place only for a patient, an infinite, faultlessness" (*ME*, 91). This is a fair description of Pater's own achievement, the novelty of which is not in newness, paradoxically, but in the reinvention of tradition. The tradition of Romantic poetry, reinvented by Pater in the form of prose, becomes the medium through which the form of the novel is likewise reinvented. Pater thus illustrates as well as anyone that quality of interference that characterizes decadence, and shows again the curious affinity of decadence with the avant-garde. The perfect figure of this interference of old and new, and of Pater's accomplishment, is found in *Marius,* in the marmoreal description late in the novel of graves in an early Christian cemetery: "All alike were carefully closed, and with all the delicate costliness at command; some with simple tiles of baked clay, many with slabs of marble, enriched by fair inscriptions: marble taken, in some cases, from older pagan tombs—the inscriptions sometimes a *palimpsest,* the new epitaph being woven into the faded letters of an earlier one" (*ME,* 229–30).

This figure of interference is given more extended narrative treatment in *Gaston de Latour* (1896), Pater's posthumous novel about a young nobleman's intellectual and aesthetic growth in sixteenth-century France. In this "Unfinished Romance," so called, Gaston decides on an ecclesiastical career, even though the choice of the religious life might "end the race of Latour altogether" (*GL,* 8–9). As in *Marius,* Pater turns religious "Observance" (*GL,* 13) into an ambiguous practice that includes aesthetic appreciation of the visible world. In fact, religious observance and aesthetic perception gradually merge into "two neighbourly apprehensions of a single ideal" (*GL,* 23). Clearly, Gaston de Latour is, like Marius, another aesthetic hero living in a time of decadence, not Antonine Rome this time, but the waning of the Middle Ages. Also, the later novel treats the culture of an earlier transitional age as a parable of the changes taking place during Pater's own time. The novelist is probably right in thinking of the erosion of religious faith during the Victorian period as the intellectual equivalent of the Forty Years' War, which forms the turbulent background of Gaston de Latour's tranquil life. At any rate, Gaston (who dies in 1594) is living in a medieval fin de siècle that is the cultural cognate of the late nineteenth century. Gaston himself is an anachronistic figure, not only because of his Paterian aestheticism, but also because of a decadent sensibility that recalls Verlaine: "Physical twilight we most of us love, in its season. To him, that perpetual twilight [of a "dusky church"] came in close identity with its moral or intellectual counterpart, as the welcome requisite for that part of the *soul* which loves twilight, and is, in truth, never quite at rest out of it" (*GL,* 31).

This anachronistic treatment continues in a chapter titled "Modernity," in which Gaston experiences a secular conversion by reading the poetry of Pierre de Ronsard, who then becomes one of the young nobleman's culture heroes (along with Montaigne and Giordano Bruno). Reading Ronsard's poetry allows Gaston to see reality in a fresh way: "Things were become at once more deeply sensuous and more deeply ideal" (*GL,* 54). What Gaston experiences here is said to be "the function of contemporary poetry to effect anew for sensitive youth in each succeeding generation. The truant and irregular poetry of his own nature . . . found an external and authorised mouthpiece" (*GL,* 51). In short, Gaston is awakened to a sense of modernity in himself, and he is unaware of his own contemporary sensibility until he sees it reflected in the pages of a book: "The age renews itself; and in immediate derivation from it a novel poetry also grows superb and large, to fill a certain mental situation made ready in advance" (*GL,* 53). In the phrase "novel poetry" Pater may be punning on his own poetic use of language in the novel. What is clear is that "the power of 'modernity'" in Ronsard is virtually identical to the power of Pater's impressionistic aestheticism: "Here, was a discovery, a new faculty, a privileged apprehension" that succeeds in "asserting the latent poetic rights of the transitory, the fugitive, the contingent" (*GL,* 57). At this point, the transformation of the medieval "decadent" Gaston de Latour by the "modernity" of Ronsard seems to be complete.

This unqualified modernity is partly contradicted when Gaston goes out of his way to meet Ronsard himself. When he does, we learn that the sense of youthful energy and freshness that Gaston finds in the "Odes"—which Pater explicitly terms "modernity"—has its underpinnings in that same anachronistic decadence that gives Gaston his taste for twilight. Ronsard reminisces about his earlier life as a court poet and shares "memories of that 'Bohemia'" (*GL,* 65) when he consorted with other members of the Pleiade, including Joachim du Bellay. Du Bellay also seems to belong more to the English decadence than to the French Renaissance: "Pensive, plaintive, refined by sickness, of exceeding delicacy" (*GL,* 66). Gaston is hopeful that Ronsard can help him attain "his intellectual furtherance" by bringing about "the addition of 'manly power' to a 'grace' of mind" (*GL,* 69). The last phrase sounds like an echo of the combination of *ascēsis* and "comely decadence" that Pater took as an aesthetic ideal himself. But when Pater describes a portrait of that same Ronsard admired by Gaston for his "modernity" of expression in the "Odes," the decadence is anything but comely: "In spite of his pretension to the Epicurean conquest of kingly indifference of mind, the portrait of twenty years ago betrayed, not less than the living face . . . the haggard soul of a haggard generation, whose eagerly sought refinements had been after all little more than a theatrical make-believe—an age of wild people, of insane impulse, of homicidal mania. . . . Even in youth nervous distress had been the chief facial characteristic" (*GL,* 67). This is the portrait of the agent of "modernity," a Renaissance poet who influences Gaston de Latour as Pater himself was affected by Baudelaire. The "Baudelairean" influence of Ronsard is suggested when Gaston thinks of the newly discovered religion of art and his old faith as "two rival claimants upon him": "Might that new religion be a religion not altogether of goodness, a profane religion, in spite of its poetic fervors? There were 'flowers of evil,' among the rest. It came in part, avowedly, as a kind of consecration of evil, and seemed to give it the beauty of holiness" (*GL,* 71).

By the end of the chapter on "Modernity," the list of nineteenth-century decadent features in Pater's portrait of the sixteenth-century Renaissance poet is quite extensive: Ronsard is acquainted with "Bohemia," the refinements of sickness, nervous distress, and "the flowers of evil." This is not, however, anachronism for anachronism's sake; rather, Pater uses a prior period of transition as a means of expressing anxieties about the age of transition in which he finds himself. The earlier decadences of Carthage, Rome, and even medieval France are all available to later decadent writers as cultural models for the predication toward modernity. In some ways, the decadent-aesthetic novel of the nineteenth century may be understood as a variant of the *roman expérimental,* though not in the sense that Zola intended. That is, the novel in the hands of Flaubert or Pater becomes a fictional laboratory where the writer may employ an earlier culture to "experiment" with his own, using prior decadences as a way of working out, and working toward, the subsequent state of modernity. Certainly Pater, by weaving a Baudelairean epitaph into the faded letters of Pleiad poetry, makes his own palimpsest of modern life.

5

Decadence and *Décadisme:* *A Rebours* and Afterward

The preceding chapter argues that Walter Pater's place in the history of decadence is highly dependent upon later literary developments. Not until the appearance of *A Rebours* (1884) and the subsequent phenomenon of *décadisme* in France did English writers of the 1880s and 1890s begin to see Pater in a decadent context and to think of him as a precursor of their own decadentism. This vision of Pater would not have been possible had not some affinity existed between aestheticism and decadence, but it is unlikely that such writers as Wilde and George Moore would have seized upon this affinity without the example of Huysmans, Bourget, and others who contributed to the development of decadence as a specifically literary sensibility. For it is during the 1880s in France that such a sense of decadence as a legitimate literary tradition begins to emerge: Huysmans's *A Rebours* and the advent of *décadisme* made it possible to incorporate the isolated decadentism of earlier writers into a more comprehensive idea of decadence.

Both *A Rebours* and the manifestoes that appeared in *Le Décadent* furnished readers and writers with a checklist of the decadent sensibility. It is one thing to work within an emerging aesthetic of decadence, and something else to announce, articulate, and develop that aesthetic. In putting forth a program of decadence through *A Rebours,* Huysmans helped bring into focus several literary developments that otherwise lacked any common ground. By using Des Esseintes to articulate the decadent strain in

Baudelaire, in Flaubert, in Mallarmé, and even in his rejected mentor Zola, Huysmans furnished his contemporaries with a paradigm of decadence, a singular model that might be emulated or obliterated, but had, somehow, to be reckoned with: "A thousand pathways open up, a thousand possibilities become available from 1884 on, when Huysmans publishes *A Rebours.* Aesthetes, mystics, captives of a purely verbal absolute, men ravaged by their senses, *littérateurs*—all were equally entitled to claim the book as their own. But in this thicket, Huysmans alone was able to continue along the path he had opened up."[1] So runs the argument of François Livi, and it does seem that Huysmans created a great many possibilities for literary expression while at the same time remaining a one-man movement. *A Rebours* amounts to a manifesto,[2] for it is as much as anything else a fictional forum for literary criticism. This distinction is significant, because manifestoes provide a clear point of departure: they mark the spot on which transition turns. Generally speaking, whenever a literary manifesto appears, a change is in the offing, a change occasionally quite different from whatever the manifesto advertises. In those cases where the manifesto is merely an a posteriori formulation of some literary direction followed unconsciously in the past, the manifesto may be the sign, paradoxically, that whatever is announced as new is really over, or almost over. The Médan school breaks up, for example, when Zola's prescriptions for the naturalistic novel become clearest. Similarly, *A Rebours,* and to a lesser extent the manifestoes that appeared in *Le Décadent,* assured that literary decadence would enter a new phase. In this case, that new phase was largely a conventionalization of decadence, an inevitable result of *A Rebours* and the various rituals of decadent sensibility depicted therein. After *A Rebours,* "there was little more to be said."[3] But there is more to *A Rebours* than "decadent sensibility," and while the work did inspire *décadisme* and lead to the conventions of the 1890s, it also illustrates how the concept of decadence necessarily implies a transformation of the novel.

In his 1903 preface to *A Rebours,* Huysmans indicated that one of his main concerns in 1884 (and earlier—the novel was begun in 1881)[4] had been to shake off artistic prejudices about the form of the novel, to break "les limites du roman" by using the form as a frame ("cadre") for something more serious ("de plus sérieux travaux"), including "l'art, la science, l'histoire" (55).[5] Even though Huysmans's retrospective assessment of his earlier intentions may be colored in various ways by his later conversion to Catholicism (which accounts for the strange transformation of a revolutionary, irreverent novel into "serious work"), his comments show that *A Rebours,* like the Goncourt brothers' *Germinie Lacerteux,* is a self-conscious departure from the popular novel, and in Huysmans's case, from the naturalistic novel as well. In several ways, *A Rebours* presages the modern novel, particularly since Huysmans equates decadence with modernity.[6] But the modernity of *A Rebours* is more than thematic, more than an exercise of the idea that a decadent attitude is the only appropriate response to modern times. The concept of decadence in Huysmans's novel profoundly alters the conventional notion of character in fiction, while at the same time affecting style and, most significant, structure.

Much has been said of Des Esseintes as an archetype of the "decadent hero." Though the phrase may be an oxymoron, "decadent hero" describes with some accuracy a new type of character in fiction distinguishable from earlier romantic types: "Unlike the dynamic romantic hero, the decadent is the ideal man of passivity and inactivity."[7] The decadent hero, as Pierrot says, is largely a study in psychopathology with a profound pessimism at the root of his actions, or lack of them: "Boredom, melancholy, disillusion, discouragement, such were the effects of this pessimism on the decadent sensibility, and also the essential elements in the makeup of the fin-de-siècle hero."[8] The decadent hero belongs to what Edmond de Goncourt called "la littérature de la tristesse," something rather different from romantic *mal du siècle:*

> This sadness was much more profound, and more dramatic . . . than the romantic melancholy of which it constitutes the extreme aggravation. Like Baudelaire's "spleen" it has physical and physiological foundations. Contemporary observers regarded it as stemming from . . . individual or collective pathological disturbances . . . : the decline of nations exhausted by the senility of civilization; the physical instability caused by the ever more artificial conditions of modern life; and the exacerbation of their nervous sensibilities that led artists to live in a state of constant mental erethism; an atrophy of the will eventually resulting in the triumph of uncontrolled association of ideas and anarchic reverie. And it is a fact that most decadent heroes are clearly abulic in character, unable to make any decision, gnawed by doubt, living wholly isolated from society, like des Esseintes. . . .[9]

Indeed, the more perceptive of Huysmans's contemporaries recognized in Des Esseintes something more than romantic melancholy, as Barbey d'Aurevilly observed:

> Des Esseintes is not a character organized along the lines of Obermann, René, or Adolphe, those heroes of human books, passionate and guilty. He is a deranged mechanism. Nothing more. . . . In writing the autobiography of his hero, he [Huysmans] has made nothing more than the unusual confession of a depraved and solitary personality; but, in the same stroke, he has written for us the nosology of a society made rotten by materialism. . . . Indeed, for a decadent of that force to have been produced, and for something like M. Huysmans' book to have sprouted in the head of a human being, it would have to be necessary for us to have become what we are—a race in its final hour.[10]

Though d'Aurevilly's last remarks are rather apocalyptic, nevertheless they are strong evidence that Des Esseintes was perceived as an exemplary character typical of the modern age.

Des Esseintes's typicality as a decadent hero does not mean, however, that the character type is original with Huysmans. The obvious literary debt is to Baudelaire. Mario Praz suggests that the title was derived from Baudelaire's informal musings on the logic of contrariety, summed up in the phrase *à rebours:* "To apply to pleasure, to the sensation of being alive, the idea of the hyperacuity of the senses, that Poe applied to pain. To effect a creation through the pure logic of contrariety. The path is already marked, in the opposite direction ["à rebours"]."[11] In the text of *A Rebours* itself Baudelaire emerges as the principal model for Des Esseintes's decadent tastes in literature: "Baudelaire . . . had descended to the bottom of the inexhaustible mine, had picked his way along abandoned or unexplored galleries, and had finally reached those districts of the soul where the monstrous vegetations of the sick mind flourish" (146). ["Baudelaire . . . était descendu jusqu'au fond de l'inépulsable mine, s'était engagé à travers des galeries abandonnées ou inconnues, avait abouti à ces districts de l'âme où se ramifient les végétations monstrueuses de la pensée" (177).] Further, Des Esseintes, and by implication, Huysmans as well, sees Baudelaire as a literary innovator who has opened up new possibilities *for the novel.* In the following passages, the reference to Balzac indicates that Huysmans is suggesting that the novel is in need of the same sort of complexity that Baudelaire brought to poetry:

> His [Des Esseintes'] admiration for this writer [Baudelaire] knew no bounds. In his opinion, writers had hitherto confined themselves to exploring the surface of the soul, or such underground passages as were easily accessible and well lit, measuring here and there the deposits of the seven deadly sins, studying the lie of the lodes and their development, recording, for instance,

as Balzac did, the stratification of a soul possessed by some monomaniacal passion—ambition or avarice, paternal love or senile lust. (146)

[Son admiration pour cet écrivain était sans borne. Selon lui, en littérature, on s'était jusqu'alors borné à explorer les superficies de l'âme ou à pénétrer dans ses souterrains accessibles et éclairés, relevant, ça et là, les gisements des péchés capitaux, étudiant leurs filons, leur croissance, notant, ainsi que Balzac, par exemple, les stratifications de l'âme possédée par la monomanie d'une passion, par l'ambition, par l'avarice, par la bêtise paternelle, par l'amour sénile. (177)]

In contrast to such simplistic motivations, "la psychologie morbide" is celebrated as a Baudelairean discovery:

He [Baudelaire] had laid bare the morbid psychology of the mind that had reached the October of its sensations, and had listed the symptoms of souls visited by sorrow, singled out by spleen; he had shown how blight affects the emotions at a time when the enthusiasms and beliefs of youth have drained away, and nothing remains but the barren hardships, tyranies, and slights, suffered at the behest of a despotic and freakish fate. (147)

[Il avait révélé la psychologie morbide de l'esprit qui a atteint l'octobre de ses sensations; raconté les symptômes des âmes requises par la douleur, privilégiées par le spleen; montré la carie grandissante des impressions, alors que les enthousiasmes, les croyances de la jeunesse sont taris, alors qu'il ne reste plus que l'aride souvenir des misères supportées, des intolérances subies, des froissements encourus, par des intelligences qu'opprime un sort absurde. (177–78)]

Throughout Des Esseintes's (or Huysmans's) reflections on Baudelaire runs the commentary that literature has been facile and simplistic when it comes to the examination of human psychology, and this commentary is phrased in language that suggests that by "littérature" is meant mainly the novel:

In a period when literature attributed man's unhappiness almost exclusively to the misfortunes of unrequited love or the jealousies engendered by adulterous love, hc had ignored these childish ailments and sounded instead those deeper, deadlier, longer-lasting wounds that are inflicted by satiety, disillusion, and contempt. (147–48)

[A une époque où la littérature attribuait presque exclusivement la douleur de vivre aux malchances d'un amour méconnu ou aux jalousies de l'adultère, il avait négligé ces maladies infantiles et sondé ces plaies plus incurables, plus vivaces, plus profondes, qui sont creusées par la satiété, la désillusion, le mépris. (178)]

The sort of thing described here as the "literature of the age" sounds rather like a novel by Paul de Kock or some other popular writer. At any rate, the key point is that simplistic motivations such as "jalousies de l'adultère" no longer have a place in the novel and should give way to more complex motivations experienced by a new type of character capable of a Baudelairean view of the world.

Des Esseintes, however, is not merely a "Baudelairean" character. He has other literary—and strictly fictional—ancestors, such as Poe's Usher, who resembles him in being the last scion of a once-noble, now-decaying aristocratic family. Moreover, a sketch of Des Esseintes' attributes leads us to associate his character with several other nineteenth-century antecedents: "[Des Esseintes] unites every characteristic of decadent sensibility: he has all the dandy's anti-socialism and lust for domination, and all the neurotic's fear of reality and love of artifice and sterile revery. He spends his days closed in his library, hating the nineteenth century and at the same time enjoying the corrupt beauties it produces. Like any Rougon-Macquart, he is the victim of hereditary neurosis. His resemblance to D'Albert, Fortunio, Poe's creatures, Igitur, Samuel Cramer, Amaury, Calixte Sombreval, is obvious from first to last."[12] Of these, Des Esseintes's resemblance to Mallarmé's Igitur is most striking, for in *Igitur* we find another last descendant of a decaying family, and in his passivity and isolation Igitur anticipates Huysmans's character. Though *Igitur* is only a fragment that has no direct historical bearing on Huysmans's work, with it and *A Rebours* we are introduced to two static, cerebral heroes, and the transition has begun to a new kind of character in the novel. Most of *A Rebours* is, in fact, simply a record of what Des Esseintes *thinks* of things. "As the century draws to a close, the disease of thinking becomes an ever more insistent theme of a literature haunted by the notion of decadence,"[13] notes Victor Brombert, and his phrase "intellectual hero" can surely be applied to Des Esseintes. Moreover, a less aesthetic version of Des Esseintes might qualify him as a Dostoevskean anti-hero—the point of this conjecture being that Huysmans's character inches us forward in the direction of the modern novel the more we think about him.[14] By introducing such a character into fiction, Huysmans automatically negates for himself most of the options a more conventional novelist leaves open. In a more calculated manner than is evident in Flaubert's *Sa-*

lammbô, the focus of Huysmans's novel shifts from the dramatic to the poetic, from action to language.

The language of *A Rebours* is cast in a style that is self-consciously decadent. By the time Huysmans wrote *A Rebours* the idea of a decadent style had already been announced by Sainte-Beuve, in his review of Flaubert's *Salammbô,* and by Gautier, in his review of the third edition of Baudelaire's *Les Fleurs du mal* (see Chapter 2). In fact, the stylistic elements of decadent art had been enumerated even earlier than Saint-Beuve's article. The critic Désiré Nisard published his *Études de moeurs et de critique sur les poètes latins de la décadence* in 1834, whose ideas are summarized by "his view that a 'decadent style' of art places such emphasis on detail that the normal relationship of a work's parts to its whole is destroyed, the work disintegrating into a multitude of overwrought fragments."[15] The idea that a decadent style is necessarily fragmented was echoed in 1881 by Paul Bourget, in his articles on Baudelaire in the *Nouvelle Revue.*[16] Though Bourget's notion of a fragmented style of decadence is more sympathetic than Nisard's, it is difficult to imagine a complete aesthetic dependent on fragmentation alone. Hence, the most important statement about decadent style remains Gautier's 1868 preface to Baudelaire's *Les Fleurs du mal,* which is a veritable *ars poetica* of decadence. But Gautier is uncomfortable with the phrase "le style de décadence" ["Le poète des *Fleurs du mal* aimait ce qu'on appelle improprement le style de décadence" (124)] because the style itself is not decadent in relation to some earlier style; instead, the so-called decadent style is *necessary* ["l'idiome nécessaire" (125)] to express the condition "of peoples and of civilizations where the factitious life has replaced the natural life and developed in them unknown needs" ["des peuples et des civilisations où la vie factice a remplacé la vie naturelle et développe chex des besoins inconnus" (125)].[18]

Thus, in Gautier's view Baudelaire's style is decadent in a special sense, for it is the *only* style or idiom capable of representing the complexities of modern life in the late stages of empire, when civilization itself is in a state of decay or decadence. The modern idiom, or the decadent style, is a complex, heterogenous mixture of literary and nonliterary "vocabularies," as Gautier puts it, not unlike the late Latin of the Roman decadence, "marbled by green streaks of decomposition" ["la langue marbrée déjà des verdeurs de la décomposition et faisandée du bas-empire romain" (125)]. Gautier's metaphor of decomposition, in which a disintegrating language is likened to a decaying body, suggests the fragmentation that is the focus of Nisard's and Bourget's understanding of the decadent style. But Gautier's metaphor of decomposition is richer than this: the marbled language he describes is figuratively *growing* out of decay, it is the verbal verdure of decomposition. This phrase—"les verdures de la décomposition"—echoes Baudelaire's title, and implies that Gautier imagines the poetry of *Les Fleurs du mal* as the paradoxical flowering of sickness and decay. Indeed, the *mal* of Baudelaire's title seems to convey, for Gautier at least, the sense of "illness" rather than "evil," the customary English translation. The distinction is important, for illness includes "the subtle confidences of neurosis" ["les confidences subtiles de la névrose" (124)] that the decadent style is fully capable of communicating. Even though the decadent style was construed by later critics (primarily Bourget and Nietzsche) as indicative of a disintegrating society, Gautire apparently thought of the style mainly in psychological rather than social terms. The notion of a psychologically sensitive style that can "convey the most inexpressible thoughts" ["à rendre la pensée dans ce qu'elle a de plus ineffable" (124)] is powerfully suggestive of later stylistic developments. Gautier describes a style of poetry, but if his insights are applied to prose, the way is open for the fragmented phrases that make up the *monologue intérieur* practiced by Dujardin, George Moore, and James Joyce. Huysmans also appears to have grasped the psychological dimensions of the decadent style, in addition to the other elements that Gautier enumerates: neologistic language, technical vocabularies, synaesthesia, the thematic preoccupation with depravity, and so on. Further, it is significant that Huysmans's novel and Bourget's theoretical writings—with their critical reformulation of Gautier's ideas—are contemporary with each other:[18] the novelist provided the decadent work, the critic provided a sympathetic analysis of decadence that helped educate an audience to accept it.

A distinction should be made, however, between Huysmans's style of decadence and his rhetoric of decadence, as Calinescu puts it.[19] "Rhetoric" here has the debased meaning of inflammatory grandiloquence, as in the following declamation on the poetry of Mallarmé:

> The truth of the matter was that the decadence of French literature, a literature attacked by organic diseases, weakened by intellectual senility, exhausted by syntactical excesses, sensitive only to the curious whims that excite the sick, and yet eager to express itself completely in its last hours,

> determined to make up for all the pleasures it had missed, afflicted on its death-bed with a desire to leave behind the subtlest memories of suffering, had been embodied in Mallarmé in the most consummate and exquisite fashion. (199)
>
> [En effet, la décadence d'une littérature, irréparablement atteinte dans son organisme, affaiblie par l'âge des idées, épuisée par les excès de la syntaxe, sensible seulement aux curiosités qui enfièvrent les malades et cependant pressée de tout exprimer à son déclin, acharnée à vouloir réparer toutes les omissions de jouissance, à léguer les plus subtils souvenirs de douleur, à son lit de mort, s'était incarnée en Mallarmé, de la façon la plus consommée et la plus exquise. (222–23)]

We might argue that the length and complexity of this sentence, whose subject and verb ("la décadence . . . s'était incarnée") are at opposite ends, fragments its unity through excessive modification, and that this illustrates decadent style. In fact, Huysmans's syntactical separation of subject and verb is one of the main elements of the decadent style, as has been often observed. François Livi, choosing to call the effect of this syntactic disruption instability rather than fragmentation, remarks as follows: "In effect, Huysmans' sentences, like his thoughts, are always out of balance ["en équilibre instable"]: the adverbial phrase constitutes an excellent means of accentuating that insecurity. But these forms of modification are hardly superficial. Above all, Huysmans attacks the structure of the sentence by altering as often as possible the subject-verb-complement order."[20] While all this may be perfectly true, such a style is distinguishable from the rhetoric at work in the passage quoted above, which exploits a common trope by personifying language as an exhausted and decaying organism. The passage from Barbey d'Aurevilly cited earlier, in which he bewails a "race in its final hour," is decadent rhetoric, a kind of self-conscious doom-saying practiced by any number of late nineteenth-century critics, but it is not decadent style. Huysmans's remarks about Mallarmé likewise illustrate decadent rhetoric, but the rhetoric is cast in a decadent style, and the style, in fact, rescues the rhetoric from becoming mere apocalyptic bombast. The distinction between rhetoric and style has been extended by the critic John R. Reed, who makes a valuable categorical dissociation of fin-de-siècle fiction into novels of decadence and decadent novels. Joséphin Péladan's *Le Vice suprême,* published the same year as *A Rebours,* is a novel of decadence because of its rhetorical stress on perversity, androgyny, degeneration, and the rest. Because these themes are cast in a commonplace, conventional style, *Le Vice suprême* is not a decadent novel, like *A Rebours,* which not only catalogues the themes but does so in a style that "embodies Decadent aesthetic assumptions."[21]

In developing a true decadent style, Huysmans follows the model established by Nisard and Sainte-Beuve and takes the style of the Roman decadence as exemplary, but unlike the critics, he sees value in imitating that style. Chapter 3 of *A Rebours* is a compendium of comments about decadent Latin style, with the greatest admiration reserved for Apuleius (88)—as in Pater's *Marius*—and Petronius (86), mainly because of their refusal to use an accepted and polished "literary" style, opting instead for neologisms and slang expressions:

> Huysmans seems to have looked on himself as a sort of modern Petronius, utilizing all the varied terms which the juxtaposition of cultures has poured into nineteenth-century Paris. . . . Huysmans wrote slang, combining it with learned, foreign, or classical words, whenever he wanted a "decadent" effect—which was quite often. To describe the reek of a female armpit (*Croquis parisiens*), for example, every sort of locution is employed: "The aroma of valeral ammonia and urine is sometimes accentuated quite savagely, and often even a light flower of prussic acid, a faint whiff of peach, bruised and really overripe, drifts by with the sigh of essences of flowers and powders. . . . It is a range of odors covering the whole keyboard of the sense of smell."
>
> ["L'arome du valérianate d'ammoniaque et de l'urine s'accentue brutalement parfois et souvent même un léger fleur d'acide prussique, une faible bouffée de pêche talée et par trop mûre passe dans le soupir des extraits de fleurs et des poudres. . . . C'est une gamme parcourant tout le clavier de l'odorat."][22]

The use of slang is certainly an element of Huysmans's decadent style, but what accentuates the quality of decadence (as Carter, above, suggests) is the interference of slangish and elitist language, of the ordinary and the erudite.

This principle of linguistic interference occurs with some frequency in *A Rebours,* as scholarly passages stand alongside the language of the street (though the alternation is by no means regular and the language tends toward the scholarly and erudite).[23] For example, the memorable passage where Des Esseintes engages a prostitute who is also a ventriloquist (whose talents, in bizarre fashion, temporarily excite the hero and allow him to overcome his impotence) involves the use of dialogue that anticipates the harsh language of, say, Céline: "Open up, damn you! I know you've got a cully in there with you! But just you wait a minute, you slut, and you'll get what's coming to you!" (115). ["Ouvriras-tu? je sais bien que t'es avec un miché, attends, attends un peu, salope!" (149).] In contrast to such earthiness is the exotic catalogue of Des Esseintes' cosmetic collection a few pages later, a virtual orgy of language rich and strange:

> There, lacquered jars inlaid with mother-of-pearl held Japanese gold and Athens green the colour of a blister-fly's wing, golds and greens that turn dark crimson as soon as they are moistened. And beside pots of filbert paste, of harem serkis, of Kashmir-lily emulsions, of strawberry and elder-berry lotions for the skin, next to little bottles full of China-ink and rose-water solutions for the eyes, lay an assortment of instruments fashioned out of ivory and mother-of-pearl, silver and steel, mixed up with lucern brushes for the gums—pincers, scissors, strigils, stumps, hair-pads, powder-puffs, back-scratchers, beauty-spots, and files. (126)
>
> [là, des laques, incrustés de burgau, renfermaient de l'or Japonais et du vert d'Athènes, couleur d'aile de cantharide, des ors et des verts qui se transmuent en une pourpre profonde dès qu'on les mouille; près de pots pleins de pâte d'aveline, de serkis du harem, d'émulsines au lys de kachemyr, de lotions d'eau de fraise et de sureau pour le teint, et près de petites bouteilles remplies de solutions d'encre de Chine et d'eau rose à l'usage des yeux, des instruments en ivoire, en nacre, en acier, en argent, s'étalaient éparpillés avec des brosses en luzerne pour les gencives: des pinces, des ciseaux, des strigiles, des estompes, des crêpons et des houppes, des gratte-dos, des mouches et des limes. (159)]

These two extremes of vocabulary, of crude and cultured diction, typify the contradictory quality apparently inherent in the concept of decadence. The language, in fact, manifests the two directions away from the natural or normative state of being which the decadent, in his attempt to escape from nature, may pursue. One route of escape leads *through* nature, so to speak, to an obsessive concern with various types of physical pleasure, mainly sexual, that are usually termed immoral or unnatural. Within the boundaries of physical sensation, in other words, something natural is so manipulated and controlled that it becomes unnatural, distorted, debased. Along these lines, the ultimate debasement of nature in *A Rebours* comes when Des Esseintes takes his "nourishment" through exotically concocted enemas. The other route of escape leads not through nature but away from it in favor of artificiality in various forms, and this is the course that Des Esseintes takes more often, cultivating sensations rather cerebral than physical. The former avenue of escape, however, is always open to the decadent and should not be overlooked in gauging the appeal and influence of *A Rebours:* Huysmans, unlike Pater, furnished his readers with a more complete spectrum of the decadent sensibility.

Such sensibility in Huysmans's hands becomes almost an ideology of decadence, and this ideology affects the structure and texture of the novel. Decadent "ideology" appears as the interference of aristocratic and democratic values, and as the simultaneous affirmation and denial of the progressive materialism of the nineteenth century. On the one hand, Des Esseintes's removal to Fontenay might be construed as an elitist, aristocratic rejection of democratic society; on the other hand, the removal is motivated by a desire for radical self-reliance and the expression of intense individualism. No one is likely to mistake Des Esseintes for the persona presented by Henry David Thoreau in *Walden,* but at the same time Fontenay and Walden Pond have something in common: the freedom of the individual that democratic society encourages. This freedom is necessary for the cultivation of the aristocratic, esoteric activities that form the core of the novel, and that one critic calls "the final, exhausted exercise of democratic individualism itself."[24] The "ideology" of decadence that makes the aristocratic Des Esseintes into an aesthetic version of Thoreau also accepts the progressive materialism of the nineteenth century, but not for progressive reasons. This point is best illustrated by Des Esseintes's celebration of the steam locomotive as an *aesthetic* marvel, a great invention "au point de vue de la beauté plastique" (80): "Does there exist, anywhere on this earth, a being conceived in the joys of fornication and born in the throes of motherhood who is more dazzlingly, more outstandingly beautiful that the two locomotives recently put into service on the Northern Railway?" (37). ["[E]st-ce qu'il existe, ici-bas, un être conçu dans les joies d'une fornication et sorti des douleurs d'une matrice dont le modèle, dont le type soit plus éblouissant, plus splendide que celui de ces deux locomotives adoptées sur la ligne du chemin de fer du Nord" (80–81)."] Even the most monumentally useful of nineteenth-century developments can be regarded with a detached Parnassian gaze as something useless, and therefore beautiful, after all. This aesthetic appreciation of progress, however, does not extend to the narrative line of the novel itself, whose artistic design negates the possibility of progress altogether.

The structure of *A Rebours* is, to say the least, unlike that of the conventional, realistic novel, and the work is difficult to define in generic terms.

Nevertheless, *A Rebours* can be called a revival of "the ancient, elusive *genre* which Northrop Frye has labeled 'anatomy' and which he and Bakhtin have also called 'Menippean satire.' Anatomy consists of a rich compendium of opinion. Its unity is thematic rather than mimetic. It grows out of what one might call an author's encyclopedic ambitions."[25] Since the use of a decadent hero in fiction involves an abrogation of action and plot, and since such a character is necessarily passive and cerebral, the encyclopedic anatomy emerges as an appropriate vehicle for the decadent sensibility. What Frye calls a "magpie instinct to collect facts" is part of a French tradition of exhaustively encyclopedic erudition that runs from Rabelais to Flaubert (and is quite evident in *Bouvard et Pecuchet*).[26] Thus, *A Rebours* might be regarded as an anatomical dissection of decadence along the lines of Burton's *Anatomy of Melancholy*. Such generic classification, however, does little to illuminate the structure of *A Rebours* and does nothing to show the interaction of decadent "ideology" and novelistic form in this particular work.

A more insightful analysis of the structure of *A Rebours* has been provided by Joseph Halpern, who observes that the very beginning of the novel, the "Notice" that precedes the first chapter, announces that the narrative we are about to read is really over, in a sense. The "Notice" acquaints us with the "story" of Des Esseintes, told through a succession of old portraits of the young man's ancestors, and indicates that he has come to such a state of hereditary degeneration that little is left of him. Des Esseintes is the last of his line, and, we might say, the last of the narrative line as well, because narrative development ends as the novel opens. It is this sense of overness at the outset that affects the structure of the work. As the opening pages conclude the narrative history of Des Esseintes, very little happens afterward, and the succeeding chapters could very well be in any order whatsoever, as far as traditional plot is concerned. Decadence, quite simply, implies finality, and this implication is at odds with the conventional novel, with its elaborate devices that work to delay finality. Basically, decadence all but negates dramatic complication and resolution, and *A Rebours* certainly verifies this negation: the novel is virtually without conflict, save in a few retrospective episodes (such as the scene, alluded to above, with the ventriloquist/prostitute), and then only minimally. The novel does involve some basic conflict toward the end with the introduction of the doctor who revives Des Esseintes and convinces him to return to Paris and involvement with the world. Thus, there is a summary narrative at the beginning of the novel, and a potential narrative at the end, but very little in between. As Halpern says: "'Decadence' expresses itself here as the imminence of an ending which thrusts itself into the narrative from the very beginning, and as the *process* of falling, a Schopenhauerian life as a constant dying. Des Esseintes—the last of his line—represents an ending in himself, his *impuissance* is a finality in itself."[27] Indeed, what happens after the "Notice" is remarkably simple: Des Esseintes moves to his house at Fontenay and indulges in the exercise of decadent artificiality, and the chapters on literature, interior decoration, perfumery, and so on, become structurally interchangeable. "The House [at Fontenay] serves as the impetus for the continuation of the story and the extension of the text. Yet when des Esseintes disappears into the house, so does narrative development."[28]

The house at Fontenay, then, may be taken as a kind of figure for the structure of the work. The conventional and temporal dimension of the novel is limited to the "Notice" and to the very end of the text, with the atemporal and encyclopedic substance of the novel within those boundaries, just as Des Esseintes's "activities" are confined, for the most part, to the house itself. Further, this sense of atemporality contained or bracketed by temporality is replicated by the ship's cabin that Des Esseintes has constructed *within* an existing room: "Like those Japanese boxes that fit one inside the other, this room had been inserted into a larger one, which was the real dining room planned by the architect" (33). ["Ainsi que ces boîtes du Japon qui entrent, les unes dans les autres, cette pièce était insérée dans une pièce plus grande, qui était la véritable salle à manger bâtie par l'architecte" (77).] Des Esseintes within the cabin *within* the dining room imaginatively removes himself from his removal to Fontenay—by "voyaging" through his books and his memories of past experiences. Of course, having a character shut himself up in a house does not in itself negate the possibilities of conventional narrative development: certainly many a mystery novel has been written, for example, in which such a limited setting in no way impinges upon an author's exercise of intrigue, suspense, surprise, and other effects of plot complication. The fact that such complications do *not* occur at Fontenay suggests that Huysmans uses the house not as a conventional setting or scene but as a spatial model for the structure of the novel itself.

One of the basic critical insights about the modern novel is that the reader's sense of time when confronted with a modernist text is likely to be disrupted to the point that chronological progression ceases to be of any value to an understanding of the work at hand. Narrative discontinuity, fractured chronology, simultaneity, and outright atemporality distinguish practically all modern fiction, from Joyce's *Ulysses* to the stories of Borges and the novels of Beckett. The idea that the structure of the modern novel typically adheres to some spatial rather than a temporal model is quite sound, and has been discussed in detail by Joseph Frank and by Sharon Spencer.[29] Though *A Rebours* does not substitute the spatial for the temporal paradigm as radically as some twentieth-century works do, Huysmans's novel "embodies exactly Joseph Frank's oft-cited thesis that works of the modern period have exchanged temporal structure for what he called spatial form."[30] As David Mickelson says, "More than traditional, sequential forms, spatial form forces the reader to be backward-looking. He is less concerned with what-happens-next than with fitting the latest disparate piece into the complex of what-has-gone-before."[31] For the most part, it is true that in reading *A Rebours* we are hardly interested in "what-happens-next," focusing instead on the static discourse of decadence that articulates the ramifications of Des Esseintes's bizarre exploration of artificiality. As Sharon Spencer points out, the use of a spatial model necessarily proscribes or limits the traditional role taken by character, but such spatialization does much more than simply inhibit convention:

> [M]ore important than this general reduction of the role of the character is a definite change in the way in which the author uses the character. The literary spatialist wishes to exploit the character's point of view of the reality of the world the novelist is creating. Thus, characters are chosen or invented less because they are interesting or important in their own right than because they are capable of providing various masks for the author. Generally, characters are used by the literary spatialist as perspectives, as points of reference from which the subject of the book is perceived.[32]

This seems to be the case with *A Rebours,* where the subject is decadence and Des Esseintes is little more than a vehicle for approaching and exploiting that subject. Indeed, Des Esseintes *as a character* disappears from the text for pages at a time, while this or that aspect of decadent taste is explored—the Latin of Petronius, the philosophy of Schopenhauer, the artificiality of exotic plants, the nuances of strange combinations of colors and odors, and so on. The implications of spatiality in *A Rebours* suggest that it is one of the earlier experiments in a form that will be exercised more fully in the twentieth century.

A Rebours thus realizes Huysmans's announced goal of transforming the novel by passing beyond the limits of convention. The key to this transformation is the overriding idea of decadence, which contributed to the creation of a new type of character, occasioned the use of a new type of language, and almost necessarily required a new type of literary structure for its expression. Des Esseintes as a decadent hero is a precursor of the inert, cerebral anti-hero of twentieth-century fiction; the language of *A Rebours,* through syntactic inventiveness and a highly textured interference of varied vocabularies and different levels of diction, continues and develops the Flaubertian emphasis on style as an end in itself; and the structure of the novel, with narrative development subordinate in the extreme, anticipates the atemporal, spatial constructions of the modern period. These aspects of the novel are ultimately more important to the transition toward literary modernity than the decadent sensibility that serves as the subject of *A Rebours.* The transformation of the form of the novel that developed, in part, out of the idea of decadence, means more to the evolution of modernism than does decadence itself, as an isolated literary phenomenon of the nineteenth century. The rhetoric of decadence is of little importance to early modernists, but the style of decadence, the style that developed because of decadence, is something to be reckoned with. At the same time, the more immediate effect of *A Rebours*—as manifesto, as checklist of decadent tastes and sensibilities—has a place in the movement toward modernism. Huysmans's novel, after all, contributed as much as anything else to the popularization of decadent attitudes during the period immediately after its publication, the period usually labeled fin de siècle or simply "The Decadence," and though the works of this period are slight, they too have an impact on the development of the modern novel. Before addressing the fiction of the fin de siècle, however, a parenthesis needs to be inserted on the topic of *décadisme,* a movement that in itself produced no great writers, but did direct attention to the idea of decadence and did much to articulate a thematics of decadence.

Huysmans's *A Rebours* marks a point in the development of the modern novel by illustrating how a deeply felt sense of decadence can affect and even alter the conventions of fiction. But the novel's immediate impact was on the development of *décadisme;* the book served as a "*summa* of decadence, an encyclopedia of decadent tastes and idiosyncrasies in matters covering the whole range from cuisine to literature."[33] Along with Bourget's article on Baudelaire (reprinted in *Essais de psychologie contemporaine*) and Verlaine's sonnet "Langueur," both published a year earlier than *A Rebours,* Huysmans's novel imparted an aesthetic legitimacy to the idea of decadence, and the moment was ripe for someone to exploit that legitimacy and organize a movement. That someone was Anatole Baju, who published *Le Décadent* from 1886 to 1889, proclaiming in virtually every issue "le triomphe du Décadisme" as the principal literary school of the day. That *décadisme* was anything but triumphant is clear enough now, but no study of decadence would be complete without some consideration of this minor and predominantly polemical movement.

The early issues of *Le Décadent* are noteworthy because they bring into clear focus the feeling that the nineteenth century was a time of decadence that demanded a new perspective: "Not to acknowledge the state of decadence we are in would be the height of insensibility. Religion, customs, justice, everything decays. . . . Society disintegrates under the corrosive action of a deliquescent civilization. Modern man is an apathetic creature ["un blasé"]. Refinements of desire, of sensation, of taste, of luxury, of pleasure; neurosis, hysteria, hypnotism, drug addiction ["morphinomanie"], scientific charlatanism, extreme schopenhauerianism: such are the symptoms of social evolution."[34] The last phrase hints at an aspect of *décadisme* not coincident with the usual idea of decadence, that is, a sense of social and political involvement. This aspect becomes more pronounced in later issues of *Le Décadent* as Baju became increasingly interested in politics, particularly socialism. But the poetry and fiction published in the earlier issues of the journal are concerned mainly with the presentation of a relatively uncomplicated sense of decadent tastes and manners: "The first number contains a serial . . . , *La Grande Roulotte,* by Luc Vajarnet. It is stuffed with material from *Maupin,* and describes the Lesbian relations of a neurotic Countess and her maid. *L'Espado negro* by Paul Pradet and *Le Sceptique* by Lucien de Sably deal with pederasty. . . . An article by Ernest Raynaud (June 15, 1888), 'Causerie morale,' stresses the role played by Gautier and Baudelaire in introducing homosexual themes into literature."[35] By espousing a literature of what was then called "perversity," Baju makes clear that his version of literary decadence is largely a matter of thematics, of treating subject matter that had been traditionally forbidden. No doubt this thematic focus is one reason for the collapse of *Le Décadent,* for Baju evidently failed to realize, as Huysmans and Bourget did, that the concept of decadence implies the possibility of a new poetics of style and structure.

Just about the only passages of any genuine literary interest in *Le Décadent* were provided by Paul Verlaine, whose famous sonnet "Langueur" may have inspired the name of Baju's review.[36] In that sonnet, Verlaine employed the trope of personification to give voice to the declining Roman Empire itself, creating a mood of decadence despairing in its very weariness. The languid cadence of the poem says as much as the words themselves about an empire so jaded and bored that nothing—not even its own impending destruction by the invading barbarians—offers relief from ennui: "Je suis l'Empire à la fin de la décadence, / Qui regarde passer les grands Barbares blancs."[37] Since the poem established Verlaine, at least in Baju's mind, as the one poet most responsive to the phenomenon of literary decadence, his support of *Le Décadent* was welcomed and exploited in rather shameless fashion. Verlaine's most significant contribution to *Le Décadent* is probably his "Lettre au 'décadent,'" which appeared in the first issue of 1888. What is significant about this "Lettre" is Verlaine's praise of the word *décadisme* as a liberation from the pejorative connotations of decadence:

> *Décadisme* is a word of genius, an amusing discovery which will remain in literary history; this barbarism is a miraculous sign. It is short, convenient, *handy*, and removes in a stroke the degrading connotations ["l'idée abaissante"] of decadence; it sounds literary but not pedantic. . . . The sense of the term stressed in this passage clearly indicates, I think, what you and I mean by Décadisme, which is characteristically a brilliant literature for a time of decadence, one that does not march in step with its age, but always and completely against it ["à rebours"], to rebel against it, to react to the delicate, the well-bred ["l'éléve"], the refined, if you will, . . . against the platitudes and turpitudes, literary and otherwise, that are in the air ["ambiantes"].[38]

In the next issue of *Le Décadent*, Baju wrote an article in which he hailed Verlaine's letter as a condemnation of *symbolisme* and other "hérésies littéraires," and called Verlaine's pronouncements "the light so long awaited by young writers seeking their own direction."[39] Verlaine's letter is taken as evidence of the poet's outright sponsorship of *décadisme* as the true literary path that all young writers should follow, particularly if they have been led astray by rival schools such as naturalism and symbolism. Because of such exploitation, the affiliation of Verlaine and *décadisme* was to be short-lived, as Calinescu explains: "By 1888, those who declared themselves decadents tended to be identified simply as followers of Anatole Baju, whose own literary reputation was in no way capable of giving credibility to a true literary movement. Baju had probably been conscious of that when he tried to use Verlaine's name to boost his magazine and the tendencies it represented. But, understandably, Verlaine was quite reluctant to play a role that he was being forced into for reasons of literary tactics."[40] With the loss of Verlaine's support, and with Baju's heightened political ardor, the disciples of *décadisme* drifted away and *Le Décadent* lost its status as a review devoted to a particular literary movement: the last three issues, in fact, are not called *Le Décadent* but *La France Littéraire*, attesting to a loss of focus virtually complete.

The importance of *décadisme*, then, does not rest in the literature it produced, which was little more than filigree work in topics broadly decadent because of their perversity or morbidity. At least some importance should be ascribed to the invention of the term *décadisme*, which does help to ameliorate the concept of decadence in its application to literature, as Verlaine said. Most important, however, is the way *décadisme* fuses decadence and modernity: "[D]ecadence, the readers of the second issue of *Le Décadent* learn, is simply awareness and acceptance of modernity. And even more, the true decadent will not only try to harmonize his work with the most outstanding features of modern civilization but will also resolutely and courageously express a progressive creed. . . . In other words, the decadent is in the avant-garde."[41] This sort of decadent requires special attention, for such outright avant-gardism is not typical of decadence generally, only of certain historical manifestations of it. After all, those who were involved with the rather strident *Le Décadent* "belonged to a younger literary generation than Bourget and Huysmans, and their political and philosophical ideas were more radical and modernistic."[42] Noël Richard terms these progressive decadents "bajutien," and the phrase seems to fit: "Far from being pessimists, the bajutien Decadents are men of action, animated by faith in progress."[43] This strange kinship of decadence and progress, along with Baju's vigorous polemic, is the clearest example yet of the willingness of decadence to merge with its apparent opposite, the avant-garde. It is an affinity that Poggioli has discussed at some length:

> The old Russian poet Vyacheslav Ivanov . . . defined decadence as "the feeling, at once oppressive and exalting, of being the last of a series." Bontempelli . . . believes the mission and function of the avant-garde to be the opening of a new series, or at least the preparing of its way.
>
> These two definitions represent two extremes and as such they touch, showing that decadence and avant-gardism are related, if not identical. The implicit distinction is a secondary one, limited to recognizing that, while the futurist mentality tremulously awaits an artistic palingenesis, preparing for

> its coming practically and mystically, the decadent mentality resigns itself to awaiting it passively, with anguished fatality and inert anxiety. Bontempelli considers the avant-garde's aim and ideal to be the establishing of a primitive or primordial condition which makes possible a grand future renascence. But in the decadent spirit one can also perceive a profound and disturbed nostalgia for a new primitiveness: the wait with mixed fear and hope for the coming of a new "return to barbarism." Paul Verlaine had already sensed this sentimental and dialectical contrast when he closed his sonnet "Décadence" [*sic*] with the vision of a mob of "huge white barbarians" at the horizon of that sky over the sinking Roman Empire.[44]

Poggioli's comments are broadly theoretical: every instance of decadent literature need not demonstrate his thesis, but the particular case of *décadisme* does show that decadence can have an avant-garde edge to it. *Décadisme* thus illustrates again that process of interference common to periods of transition. Decadence in reaction to itself tends toward the avant-garde and realizes literary modernity, or at least begins that realization. But what is missing from *décadisme* are the literary works in which this interference and reaction may be observed to operate. For this reason, we must turn from the idea of decadence that is *décadisme* to the literature of decadence that makes up the fin de siècle.

The expiration of Baju's *Le Décadent* marks the end of *décadisme* as a limited polemic whose rhetoric may have been inspired by literary decadence, but ultimately had little to do with literature. *Décadisme* dies, ironically, at the historical moment when literary decadence is most alive and when such earlier writers as Pater and Huysmans are widely regarded as the authors of aesthetic "bibles" to be admired and imitated by the young men of the nineties. Indeed, the phrase "young men" is one of the keys to understanding the fiction of the period, as a number of fin de siècle novels focus on the young man, or more specifically, the refined and artistic young man and his place in late nineteenth-century society. Even though this sort of fiction is often slight, its appearance marks a major shift in the history of the novel, and is one noteworthy development in the transition to modernism. The centrality of character and the limitation of episodic action and plot complication resulted, in part, from the incompatibility of the idea of decadence and narrative development, as already said. However, it would be simplistic to regard the emergence of the modern novel as merely a sophisticated development of decadent emphasis on the young artist or aesthete. As we shall see more fully in Chapter 6, distinctions can be made between those works that lead logically to modernism because of the centrality of character, and those works that give rise to modernism as a reaction to the conventions of decadence. Such works as Wilde's *The Picture of Dorian Gray* and D'Annunzio's *Il Piacere,* for example, take Pater's aestheticism and Huysmans's decadence to such eccentric extremes that little room for development is left. In these works, decadence becomes little more than literary paraphernalia, so equipped are they with convention.

Certain works of early modernism can thus be seen as antidecadent, such as Gide's *L'Immoraliste,* a text that turns away from decadence as a metaphorical sickness and, instead, embraces modernity as a form of health and newness. On the other hand, a number of early modernists accept fully the *Zeitgeist* of decadence and work it thoroughly into the fabric of their fiction; the obvious authors in this case are Joyce, Proust, and Mann. Joyce, for example, owes much to Pater and at least something to George Moore, whose early works, now virtually unread, opened up new possibilities for the novel in English. The same is true of some of Moore's criticism, in which he tried to move the novel away from oppressive Victorian conventions: "In a controversial essay of 1885 called 'Literature at Nurse,' George Moore protested against the censorship, decorum, and restraint on the novelist's art imposed by the dictatorship of the libraries and family readership."[45] This kind of activist involvement in literary politics probably encouraged literary modernity as much as Moore's aesthetic program did. In any event, Moore's activism and aestheticism both contributed in some measure to the artistic growth of James Joyce. As Graham Hough says, it is unlikely that either "the title [or] the content of Joyce's *Portrait of the Artist as a Young Man* would have been quite the same in 1916 if it had not been for the prior existence of George Moore's *Confessions of a Young Man* in 1886."[46] Indeed, Moore's *Confessions* is one of those texts that illustrates a type of literary decadence that is not a closed system of conventions, but a basis for further development. The relative absence of conventionality; the lack of a clear generic identity; a varied and inventive style; a shifting, contradictory thematic focus; and a certain simple but invaluable documentary quality make Moore's *Confessions* an extremely malleable text—incomplete in itself, but a mine of possibility. As such, it belongs not so much to the end of the old century as the beginning of the new. The same cannot be said of Wilde's *Dorian Gray* and D'Annunzio's *Il Piacere,* two works that belong permanently to the fin de siècle because in them decadence becomes something stable and identifiable. Wilde and D'Annunzio do not write with decadence behind them, so to speak, but in front of them: it is there for them to observe and describe, a known quantity with identifiable characteristics, and not, as it was for Moore, an aesthetic impetus to move in a new direction.

The early work of Gabriele D'Annunzio illustrates a separation of decadent conventions from the idea of decadence that led to those conventions. In *A Rebours,* for example, an erudite aestheticism and a jaded sense of ennui form the very core of the novel: it is the center from which Des Esseintes's decadent sensibility emanates, and all of his eccentric pursuits are related to this center. Moreover, Des Esseintes's resistance to things natural is one measure of Huysmans's distance from earlier forms of romantic expression. In D'Annunzio's *Il Piacere,* on the other hand, certain elements of decadence serve merely as accessory to adventure and romantic intrigue, so that the novel's decadence is all on the outside, and not deeply a part of the work. Mario Praz, for example, in his *Romantic Agony,* finds D'Annunzio incapable of "penetrating into [the] subtleties or shades of meaning" in the decadent writers who were his models (401). D'Annunzio, in Praz's estimation, is essentially a primitive (401), a kind of literary barbarian who invaded France and was paradoxically conquered by decadence but who could never make that culture truly his own. In particular, Praz mentions D'Annunzio's receptivity to the key Parisian trends of the 1880s—the Schopenhauer vogue, the *Revue Wagnérienne,* the fascination with English Pre-Raphaelitism and the cult of beauty, Huysmans's *A Rebours,* and so on (401, 323). D'Annunzio may indeed be "the most monumental figure of the Decadent Movement" (399), but he is not its best representative. This monumentality comes in large measure from the hedonistic energy displayed in D'Annunzio's novels, and his work is "decadent" in this and in a few other limited senses. In addition to a thoroughgoing treatment of "decadent" or immoral sensuality, a fair number of decadent conventions are evident in the early novels, which makes for an interesting mixture. The immorality of Des Esseintes, by contrast, is a rather ascetic affair: his erotic conquests are all in the past and ordinary sensuality is merely one more thing that bores him; his senses stir only when he is touched by something exotic and excessively refined. D'Annunzio's Andrea Sperelli (the hero of *Il Piacere*) is, on the other hand, a dual creature: a sensualist driven by instinct, an aesthetic idealist moved by the high calling of art.

Il Piacere was published in Italian in 1889, translated into French as

L'Enfant de volupté (in the *Revue de Paris;* by Calmann-Levy in 1895), and published in English in 1898 as *The Child of Pleasure.* D'Annunzio's greatest popularity at this time was achieved in France, where criticism of his excessive sensuality was less severe than in Italy.[47] In England, D'Annunzio was praised by Arthur Symons, who did the renderings of the poetry that appeared in the English translation of the novel.[48] All this is testament to the fact that a kind of D'Annunzio vogue occurred in the 1890s, and not just among the literati. This in itself is interesting in the context of decadence, which usually involves an elitist rejection of literature as a form of popular entertainment. Perhaps the popularization of decadence is specific to the fin de siècle, and may in fact furnish that term with some meaning in addition to its obvious temporal significance. At any rate, the popularization of decadence in D'Annunzio is one more aspect of the aesthetic mixture that is *Il Piacere.*

Decadent elements are easy enough to isolate in D'Annunzio's novel. Like Des Esseintes, D'Annunzio's hero is "l'ultimo discendente d'una razza intellettuale" (36); Count Sperelli is the lone survivor of an aristocratic lineage that includes artists, poets, eccentric epicureans. The character thus combines those qualities of decline and aestheticism that are the requisite features of the decadent hero. Less general references to an established system of decadence are equally clear. For example, the painting of Moreau, celebrated in *A Rebours,* is taken as a standard of feminine beauty: "I lineamenti gai del volto rammentavano certi profili feminini ne'disegni del Moreau giovine" (41–42). The text is also abloom with the exotic flora of decadence and aestheticism, as Sperelli sports a gardenia in his buttonhole (42), and Elena Muti, the work's resident femme fatale, admires the orchid as a "fior diabolico" (46). Elsewhere, we find gardenias displayed in the aesthete's essential blue china: "gardenie fresche in piccoli vasi di porcellana azzura" (74). The novel does owe something to English aestheticism and Pre-Raphaelitism (or the French assimilation of those two separate but related phenomena) in that Sperelli takes late medieval art as his inspiration ("pittori che precorrono il Rinascimento" [95]) and becomes devoted to "il culto passionato della bellezza" (36). Although the cult of beauty in *Il Piacere* is not always part of the decadent formula for replacing nature by artificiality, the theme is sounded often enough, and is even reconciled to the more prominent theme of sensuality through allusions to hermaphroditism. Sperelli himself is said to be the author of the much-admired "*Favola d'Ermafrodito*" (44), and though the content of this work is never fully detailed, it is mentioned several times.

The decadent novelist usually makes realistic representation secondary to stylistic experimentation. Nothing could be further from the pictorial tradition than *le style de décadence.* Despite this fact, illustrators have been drawn to decadent novels again and again, no doubt because of popular assumptions that the subject matter of decadence is always sensational, excessive, erotic, or immoral. In the examples presented here, my own description of decadence as the interference of conflicting artistic traditions holds true. In most cases, the novels themselves point toward modernism, while the illustrations *in* the novels seem permanently fixed in the fin de siècle.

This design from a 1925 edition of *The Picture of Dorian Gray* is clearly inspired by *Les Fleurs du mal.* Sick and bleeding, this "flower of evil" suggests both refinement and degeneration, the hybrid sensibility cultivated by the decadents after Baudelaire.

This and the next two illustrations from an 1897 edition of *Germinie Lacerteux* date from 1885. Taken together, they capture the narrative of Germinie's decline. Here, Germinie is shown in her ball gown, before her troubles begin, as her elderly employer, Mlle. Varandeuil, looks on.

Germinie confronts her lover Jupillon at a cabaret with another woman. The illustrator may have drawn some inspiration from post-impressionist art for the festive cabaret setting, but a face as grim as Germinie's would never appear on a post-impressionist canvas.

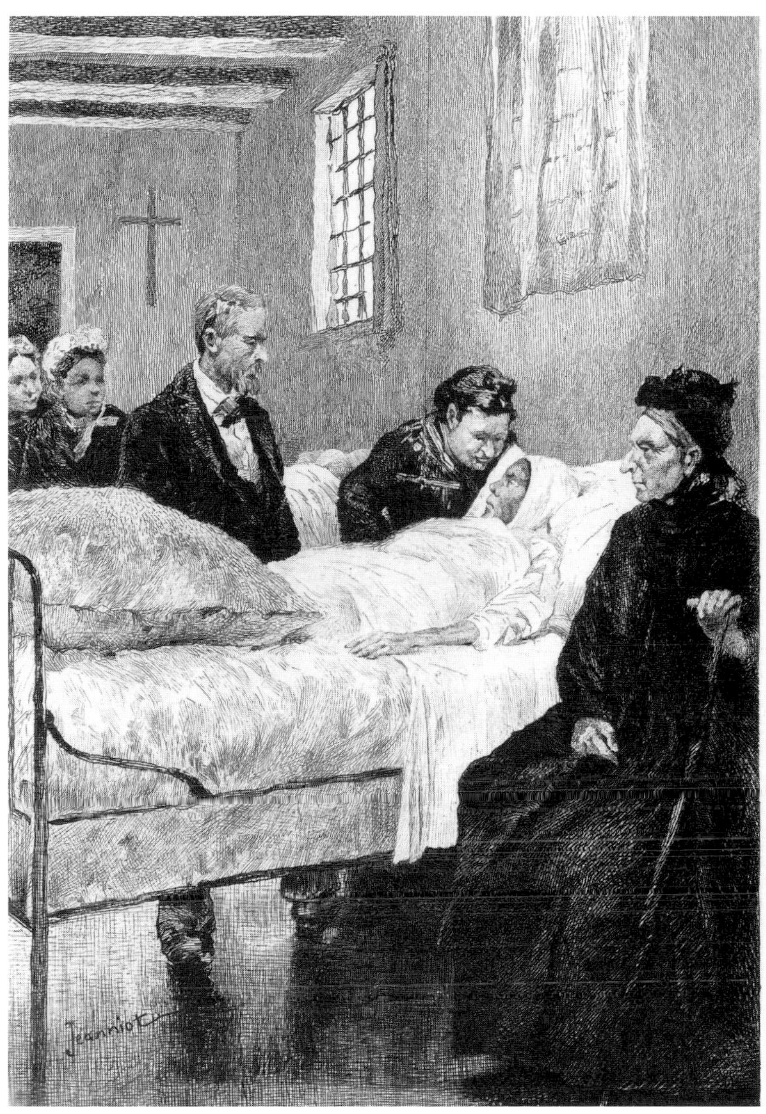

Here, the face of Germinie has gone from grim to feral. The evident "Darwinism" of the illustrator, who depicts the dying woman with an animalistic, apelike face, harmonizes with the determinism of the Goncourt brothers.

A crowned vulture drinking from a jeweled goblet: the deference shown to the bird of death makes an appropriate illustration for Flaubert's *Salammbô,* even though the scene is not in the novel.

Another line illustration by Clare Victor Dwigging from a 1904 edition of Flaubert's novel suggests the simultaneous influence of the Pre-Raphaelites, their idol Botticelli, and possibly Dwigging's contemporary, the dancer Loie Fuller.

Salammbô's ritual with the sacred python is a favorite scene with illustrators.

Walter Pater's *Marius the Epicurean* has not attracted many illustrators, which is not surprising: despite the author's aesthetic obsession with the visual world, the novel is hardly imagistic. This illustration of Marius himself, by Thomas MacKenzie, suggests a sensibility more ascetic than aesthetic.

This illustration, also by MacKenzie from a 1929 edition of Pater's novel, is inspired by this passage: "Some jaded women of fashion, especially, found in certain oriental devotions, at once relief for their religiously tearful souls and an opportunity for personal display; preferring this or that 'mystery' chiefly because the attire required in it was suitable to their particular manner of beauty."

Here, two of the better known scenes from *A Rebours* are illustrated in woodcuts by Arthur Zaidenberg from a 1931 edition: Des Esseintes with his collection of artificial-looking natural plants, and Des Esseintes in his study with his jeweled tortoise.

Aubrey Beardsley may be the one artist most closely associated with fin-de-siècle decadence, yet he did not illustrate any decadent novels. He is represented here because of his association with Oscar Wilde, whose stylized face appears as the "woman in the moon" in this illustration for *Salome,* Wilde's play.

Two images by the illustrator Majeska from a 1930 edition of *The Picture of Dorian Gray* capture the progression of the hero's corruption: the first shows Dorian posing for the portrait; the second illustrates the portrait itself in a late stage of degeneration.

These illustrations from a deluxe edition of *The Happy Hypocrite* published in 1915 represent the two women in Lord George Hell's life. The simple cameo design by George Sheringham captures the innocence of Jenny Mere ("her arms full of buns"), but the corruption of La Gambogi is not so easily contained, as the elaborate *art nouveau* design spills out of its boundaries.

Ornate designs may not be the best means of conveying reflective moods: here, Sheringham's *art nouveau* elegance cannot really capture the depression of the downcast Lord George.

Baudelaire called lesbian lovers *les femmes damnées,* and Mirbeau picks up the theme in *Le Jardin des supplices.* But this drawing of two lesbian lovers by Auguste Rodin from a 1902 edition of the novel suggests not damnation, but dignity. (Spencer Collection, New York Public Library, Astor, Lenox and Tilden Foundations)

Less dignified is Rodin's illustration of the torture master's ability to transform a woman into a man. (Spencer Collection, New York Public Library, Astor, Lenox and Tilden Foundation)

This illustration by Edy Legrand from a 1935 edition of *Le Jardin des supplices* presents a horrible scene in a highly decorative style, making Mirbeau's garden of punishment appear more Parisian than "Asian."

This drawing by Wallace Smith for Ben Hecht's *Fantazius Mallare* may have been inspired by Mirbeau's gratuitous descriptions of sadistic torture in the earlier novel.

Smith's rendition of the three principals of *Fantazius Mallare:* Mallare, the hump-backed dwarf Goliath, and the gypsy girl Rita, whose white body is reflected in a black mirror—an apt figure for the paradoxes and reversals in Hecht's novel.

Here, Hecht and Smith offer a literalist reading of Barbey d'Aurevilly's comment about Huysmans—that after decadence and diabolism the only choices are "the barrel of a pistol or the foot of the cross."

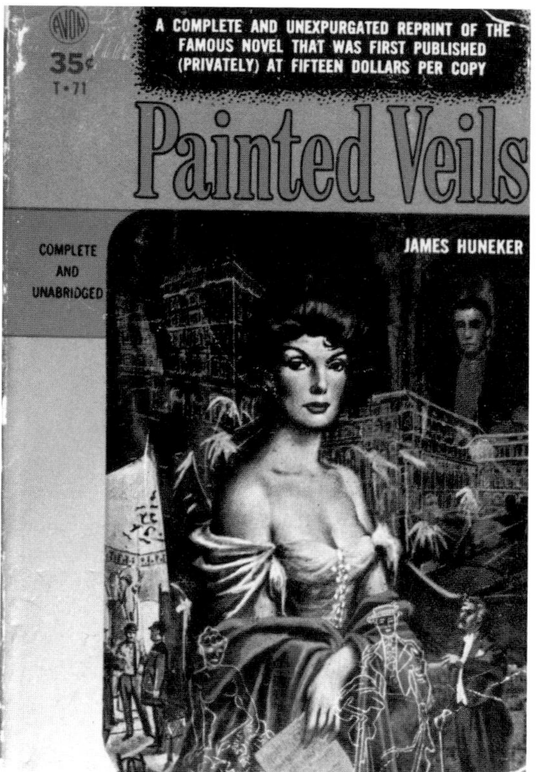

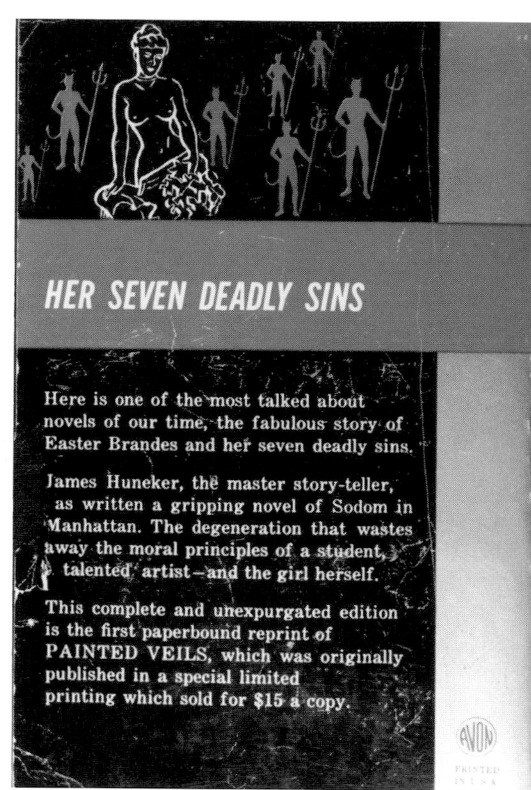

The decline of decadence begun by Mirbeau and continued by Hecht reaches its nadir with James Huneker's *Painted Veils.* The front cover of this 1954 paperback edition of the novel presents the heroine Easter Brandes, "the Great Singing Whore of Modern Babylon," in the guise of a 1950s sex goddess. The blurb on the back, however, suggests current fin-de-siècle concerns with moral decay and social corruption.

The theme of hermaphroditism is sounded most clearly through the person of one Bébé Silva, a character of intermediate or indeterminate sex:

> Bébé Silva had lighted a cigarette and was eating oysters, while she let the smoke curl through her nostrils. She was like a restless schoolboy, a little depraved hermaphrodite; pale and thin, the brightness of her eyes heightened by fever and kohl, with lips that were too red, and short and rather woolly hair that covered her head like an astrachan cap. Fixed tightly in her left eye was a single eyeglass; she wore a high stiff collar, a white necktie, an open waistcoat, a little black coat of masculine cut and a gardenia in her button-hole. She affected the manners of a dandy and spoke in a deep husky voice. And just therein lay the secret of her attraction—in this imprint of vice, of depravity, of abnormality in her appearance, her attitudes and her words. (186)

> [La Silva aveva accesa una sigaretta; e inghiottiva le ostriche mentre il fumo le usciva dalle narici. Ella somigliava un collegiale senza sesso, un piccolo ermafrodito vizioso: pallida, magra, con gli occhi avvivati dalla febbre e dal carbone, con la bocca troppa rossa, con i capelli corti, lanosi, un po'ricci, che le coprivano la testa a guisa d'un caschetto d'*astrakan*. Teneva incastrata nell'occhiaia sinistra una lente rotonda; portava un alto solino inamidato, la cravatta bianca, il panciotto aperto, una giacca nera di taglio maschile, una gardenia all'occhiello, affettando le maniere d'un *dandy*, parlando con una voce rauca. E attirava, tentava, per quella impronta di vizio, di depravazione, di mostruosità, ch'era nel suo aspetto, nelle sue attitudini, nelle sue parole. (252–53)]

The hermaphrodite, as Praz has pointed out at length, is the "artistic sex *par excellence*" whose appeal to the decadent mentality involves an assumed combination of artificiality and depravity. The most complete expression of the hermaphrodite theme is found in the novels of Péladan, whose influence on D'Annunzio is almost unquestionable.[49] At any rate, the hermaphrodite theme in *Il Piacere* is one of the clearest indicators of a decadent context manifestly literary in nature; it suggests that decadence in D'Annunzio's novel is something approached from the outside, as a matter of convention.

But more than one kind of decadence is at work in the text of *Il Piacere*. The derivations from Péladan, Huysmans, the Pre-Raphaelites, and a debased version of aestheticism (that is, "aesthetic" fashion and the "religion" of art)—in short, all the conventions cited above—do not adequately convey what can only be called a specifically D'Annunzian sense of decadence that arises from the style of the work. In the following passage, for example, such essential "aesthetic" elements as gardenias and blue china do not in themselves justify the epithet *decadent,* but the overall richness of detail does:

> He went into an adjoining octagonal room to dress, the most luxurious and comfortable dressing-room any young man of fashion could possibly desire. On a great Roman sarcophagus, transformed with much taste into a toilet table, were ranged a selection of cambric handkerchiefs, evening gloves, card and cigarette cases, bottles of scent, and five or six fresh gardenias in separate little pale blue china vases—all these frivolous and fragile things on this mass of stone, on which a funeral *cortège* was sculptured by a masterly hand! (37)

> [Egli andò a vestirsi, nella camera ottagonale ch'era, in verità, il più elegante e comodo spogliatoio desiderabile per un giovine signore moderno. Vestendosi, aveva una infinità di minute cure della sua persona. Sopra un gran sarcofago romano, transformato con molto gusto in una tavola per abbigliamento, erano disposti in ordine i fazzoletti di batista, i guanti da ballo, i portafogli, gli astucci delle sigarette, le fiale delle essenze, e cinque o sei gardenie freshe in piccoli vasi di porcellana azzura. Egli scelse un fazzoletto con le cifre bianche e ci versò due o tre gocce di *pao rosa;* non prese alcuna gardenia perché l'avrebbe trovata alla mensa di casa Doria; empì di sigarette russe un astuccio d'oro martellato, sottilissimo, ornato d'uno zaffiro su la sporgenza della molla, un po' curvo per aderire alla coscia nella tasca de' calzoni. Quindi uscì. (74–75)]

Here, the description of Andrea Sperelli's dressing room does not function as description typically does in a realistic novel. The room itself is abstract, geometric, a "camera ottagonale." It is simply the sort of room that "un giovine signore moderno" would be expected to have, and the reader must summon up that image for himself. True, we are told that the room contains a sarcophagus transformed into a *toilette,* and we are subjected to an extensive list of bric-a-brac that lies on top of it, yet these details are not there for reasons of realism or verisimilitude, but as attributes of Sperelli's character. Such phrases as "cinque o sei" and "due o tre" reveal an imprecision we would not expect to find in realistic description. Compare, for example, the slavish exactitude and spatial organization in this descriptive passage by a typical American naturalist of the nineties: "It was an ordinary little room. A clean white matting was on the floor; gray paper, spotted with pink and green flowers, covered the walls. In one corner, under a white netting, was a little bed, the woodwork gayly painted with knots of bright flowers. Near it, against the wall, was a black walnut bureau. A work-table with spiral legs stood by the window, which was hung with a green and gold window curtain. Opposite the window the closet door stood ajar, while in the corner across from the bed was a tiny washstand with two clean towels."[50] This description of Trina's room from Frank Norris's *McTeague* differs from D'Annunzio's description of Sperelli's room in that Norris reduces the reader's efforts at visualization: the details are there for him to "see." That the objects described are exotic in one case and ordinary in another has something to do with the radical difference in verisimilar effect, but the exoticism of D'Annunzio's details defeats or reduces the quality of verisimilitude mainly because those details have their own richness: they are isolated images, paradoxically detached from the purported description and connected to one another only by an arbitrary seriality. Not surprisingly, the translator of *Il Piacere* omits the details from the latter half of the paragraph quoted above, offering instead a rather bombastic summary: "all these frivolous and fragile things on this mass of stone, on which a funeral *cortège* was sculptured by a masterly hand." The omission underscores the point that D'Annunzio's accumulation of exotic details serves no "useful" realistic purpose. They contribute instead to the extensive elaboration of the decadentism of the novel's hero.

In addition to the stylistic and conventional manifestations of decadence, the novel displays a more general sense of decadence that goes beyond convention, a universal despair arising from the inescapable fact of death, and it is against this background that Sperelli's extravagant sensuality is displayed. The presence of death in *Il Piacere* means that its hero's sensuality is at once necessary and futile, a form of escape that only emphasizes the inevitable truth that escape is impossible. An awareness of death combines with Sperelli's erotic adventures at every turn, and this gives the theme of sensuality its decadent coloration. For example, the earliest interaction between Sperelli and Elena Muti occurs when she presides at an auction of precious and exotic objets d'art. The item she recommends for his purchase is a grotesque clock built into a death's head carved in ivory, and this gesture is full of erotic significance. The clock itself has an erotic history, having been a gift of some unknown artist to his mistress ("offerta d'un artefice misterioso alla sua donna" [70]) that must have served as a warning symbol to the lovers ("col suo simbolo ammonire gli spiriti amanti" [70]). The first passionate exchange between Sperelli and Elena Muti takes place when she is lying in her sickbed amid an odor of chloroform (85). Amorous scenes are recounted when Sperelli covers Elena's recumbent body with flowers, an unmistakably funereal tableau, especially since Sperelli's tastes run along such macabre lines: his own dressing room, after all, is furnished with a large Roman sarcophagus (74). After Elena Muti temporarily disappears from the story (to resolve her financial problems by marrying the wealthy Lord Heathfield, an erudite bibliophile who treasures his collection of erotic books and decadent Roman texts), the confluence of sensuality and morbidity continues, with some variations, as Sperelli is wounded in a duel and recovers in the company of Donna Maria. As the name suggests, Maria is a rather idealized female type, a contrast to the openly carnal Elena Muti. Nevertheless, she falls in love with the wounded, convalescent Sperelli, suggesting that sickness is a seductive force in the novel, since any evocation of physical pleasure involves a heightened awareness of death. The most eloquent expression of this point comes when Sperelli resolves upon a plan to regain the newly married Elena Muti's affections, a scheme whereby he hopes to intoxicate her with the ideal in order to renew her friendship and then lead her back into a more sensual relationship. Plotting out this amorous intrigue, Sperelli finds his thoughts moving away from sensuality and toward death:

> Thus Andrea Sperelli reasoned, sitting in front of the fire which had glowed upon Elena, laughing among the scattered rose leaves. A boundless lassitude weighed upon him, a lassitude which did not invite sleep, a sense of weariness, so empty, so disconsolate as to be almost a longing for death; while the fire died out on the hearth and the tea grew cold in the cup. (217)
>
> [Così ragionava Andrea Sperelli, d'innanzi al camino che aveva illuminata l'amante Elena ignuda, avvolta nel drappo dello Zodiaco, ridente tra le rose sparse. E l'occupava una stanchezza immensa, una stanchezza che non chiedeva il sonno, una stanchezza così vacua e sconsolata che quasi pareva un bisogno di morire; mentre il fuoco spegnevasi in su gli alari e la bevanda freddavasi nella tazza. (271)]

Such weariness and longing for death is a more profoundly decadent characteristic of the novel than the one emphasized by the narrator: Sperelli's moral degradation as he involves himself in the double pursuit of both Elena Muti and Maria Ferres. The resolution of this plot comes when Sperelli learns that Elena has rejected him, not for her husband but for a rival lover; he then turns to the idealist Maria as a substitute for the sensualist Elena, calls out Elena's name while he is in Maria's arms, and Maria leaves him without a word. The novel ends with Sperelli doubly rejected and completely alone, a victim of his own moral depravity. This may be an "appropriate" ending, satisfying certain moral expectations of one type of nineteenth-century audience, but it should not be mistaken for a satisfactory statement about the meaning of decadence. As we have seen, *immorality* is a poor equivalent for the word *decadence*. D'Annunzio's Sperelli is not decadent simply because he is a "child of pleasure," but because of a more complex interaction of sexuality and death. More than a child of pleasure, he is, as Wilde says of Dorian Gray, a "son of Love and Death" (41).[51]

The Picture of Dorian Gray does bear some resemblance to *Il Piacere* in that both novels explore the moralistic theme that excessive devotion to the life of the senses leads to ruin, and in both this theme is supplemented by decadent aestheticism. Further, *Dorian Gray* and *Il Piacere* both draw on earlier works of decadence without contributing much to the development of decadence as an aesthetic category. Both works are highly conventional, although it has been said that *Il Piacere* should not be dismissed too lightly, "for it does reflect the break with the traditions of *verismo* and the historical novel."[52] In general, however, neither D'Annunzio nor Wilde realizes the potential that the idea of decadence holds for the form of the novel. Both *Il Piacere* and *Dorian Gray* belong permanently to the fin de siècle and have little to do with the transition to modernity, except that both suggest a terminus, a dead end of decadence, and point out the need for new directions.

In *The Picture of Dorian Gray* the most pronounced element of decadence is the elevation of art over nature. The opening pages of the novel juxtapose art and nature by pairing the dandified Lord Henry Wotton and the as yet uncorrupted Dorian Gray, first in Basil Hallward's studio, then in his garden. The dual setting (studio/garden) suggests a balance of art and nature, a balance that is transposed by Basil Hallward into a yearning for a "harmony of soul and body" that will be the basis of a "fresh school" (24) of art. Dorian Gray is for Basil, the artist, the visible symbol of this ideal, but for Lord Henry, the aesthete, he becomes the "visible symbol" of "a new Hedonism" (32) whose basis is pure sensation. Lord Henry's influence is complete: instead of harmonizing soul and body, art becomes a means of separating them, as the device of the portrait illustrates. Art is therefore a corruptive force, dividing rather than unifying reality. The decadent elevation of art over nature is thus allied to the theme of moral degradation, as Dorian's affair with the actress Sybil Vane illustrates. He does not love the real woman but the actress in her various roles, and when art gives way to reality—when Sybil Vane ceases to act and asks that Dorian love her as she is—he is coldly indifferent. The possibility of aesthetic sensation no longer exists, until she commits suicide and "pass[es] again into the sphere of art," dying "as Juliet might have died" (90).

Further impetus to Dorian Gray's corruption through art is given when Lord Henry sends him a copy of a book that closely resembles *A Rebours*. Huysmans's novel is not named outright in the text of *Dorian Gray*, but the description of "the young Parisian, who spent his life trying to realize in the nineteenth century all the passions and modes of thought that belonged to every century but his own" (101), leaves no doubt that the character is Des Esseintes. The eleventh chapter of *Dorian Gray* is heavily indebted to *A Rebours*, as Dorian studies one artificial and erudite subject after another: jewels, perfumes, obscure oriental texts, and so on. The catalogue of precious gems is perhaps the one passage where Wilde comes nearest to Huysmans's exotic diction:

> On one occasion he took up the study of jewels. . . . This taste enthralled him for years, and, indeed, may be said never to have left him. He would often spend a whole day settling and resettling in their cases the various stones that he had collected, such as the olive-green chrysoberyl that turns red by lamplight, the cymophane with its wirelike line of silver, the pistachio-colored peridot, rose-pink and wine-yellow topazes, carbuncles of fiery scarlet with tremulous four-rayed stars, flame-red cinnamon stones, orange and violet spinels, and amethysts with their alternate layers of ruby and sapphire. . . . (107)

Nothing is terribly striking here, as elsewhere, about the style, as it has none of Huysmans's syntactic inventiveness. Moreover, despite the "influence" of *A Rebours*, Dorian Gray has little in common with Huysmans's hero, whose moral degradation is hardly of interest to us, having been disposed of in summary fashion at the beginning of the novel as little more than background information.

The sources of Dorian Gray should therefore be sought elsewhere, not because source-hunting is necessarily valuable in itself, but because those sources indicate that Wilde's relationship to literary decadence is largely tangential. Indeed, Wilde's novel is more easily reconciled to larger traditions and movements, than to the relatively narrow confines of literary decadence. The myth of the Garden of Eden, of innocence giving way to an evil tempter, is clearly suggested at the outset of the novel, as is the Faust legend, when Dorian expresses the desire to exchange his soul for eternal youth (34). The device of the mysterious portrait is traceable to the *Doppelgänger* theme of German romanticism, as developed by Jean-Paul and Hoffmann. Wilde, however, need not have gone back to the origins of this theme, as more recent examples were available to him in the form of Poe's short story "William Wilson," Stevenson's *The Strange Case of Dr. Jekyll and Mr. Hyde,* and Maturin's *Melmoth the Wanderer* (of which more presently). Richard Aldington pointed to Disraeli's forgotten first novel, *Vivian Grey,* as the source not only of the portrait device, but also of Dorian Gray's name and character type—a kind of "intellectual Don Juan" or "spiritual libertine."[53] Edouard Roditi makes a convincing case for Melmoth as the primary ancestor of Dorian,[54] and in so doing he hits upon the essential element that most distances Wilde's novel from literary decadence. Roditi stresses the development of the Byronic hero from the proud but passive Promethean type (as in *Manfred*) to the more vigorous Satanic character who pursues evil in all its forms. The most extreme development of the Satanic type is unquestionably Lautréamont's Maldoror,[55] whose evil is fueled by a crudely Darwinian awareness of the animalistic nature of human beings. Now Dorian Gray is not a Satanist in the extreme sense that a Maldoror is, but the kinship is evident, and equally evident is the fact that the Satanist and the decadent have little in common. The difference can be explained by contrasting two mythic aspects of the fallen angel, as Satan, the vigorous archfiend, and as Lucifer, the Promethean light-bringer whose rebellion is illuminated by cunning and artifice. The difference between Satan and Lucifer is the difference between Lautréamont's creation and Huysmans's. The Satanist continually repeats the gesture of rebellion in the energetic exercise of evil, while the Luciferian quits the active rebellion and goes about the task of building his hell in heaven's despite. The Satanist, in short, is part of the romantic field of energy, while the Luciferian looms on the horizon of modernism as a precursor of the ironic anti-hero. Thus Dorian Gray, "callous, concentrated on evil, with stained mien, and soul hungry for rebellion" (144), repeats the Satanic gesture of defiance and moves into a squalid life of degradation, altogether different from the refined world of decadence.

This contrast between decadence and degradation is also played out in the novel's coded commentary on homosexual love. The decadent Lord Henry Wotton imagines Dorian Gray as a representative type in the tradition of male beauty: "Grace was his, and the white purity of boyhood, and beauty such as old Greek marbles kept for us" (41). Homosexuality thus aestheticized is certified by a history that includes Plato and Michelangelo, but Wilde hedges just enough to allow the reader to make the choice between aestheticism and eroticism in passages like the following, where the antecedent of the pronoun *it* is intentionally indeterminate: "[H]ow strange it all was! He remembered something like it in history. Was it not Plato, that artist in thought, who had first analysed it? Was it not Buonarotti who had carved it in the coloured marbles of a sonnet sequence? But in our own century it was strange" (41). The novel can be read as a conflict of this "higher," aesthetic sense of homosexuality that is represented by Dorian Gray in the flesh, and the "low" or "degrading" reality of active homosexual pursuits, whose effects are registered by the portrait. There is no question that homosexual acts are among the "vices" practiced by Dorian Gray, as the long list of "ruined" young men supplied by Basil Hallward suggests: "Why is your friendship so fatal to young men? There was that wretched boy in the Guard who committed suicide. You were his great friend. There was Sir Henry Ashton, who had to leave England, with a tarnished name. You and he were inseparable" (117). And so on. Just as the naive but inquisitive Basil asks why Dorian's friendship is fatal to young men, well-to-do society people look at Dorian "as though they were determined to discover his secret" (112). All of this emphasis on some secret, unspoken element of Dorian Gray's corruption leaves little doubt that Wilde intends an oblique reference to "the love that dare not speak its name." And since the deteriorating portrait is kept closeted away, the "secret" of homosexuality seems part of its meaning. That homosexuality is regarded as a form of degradation, and is even set alongside criminality as one of the features of Dorian's secret soul, is a sad comment on Victorian society. There is also something sadly prophetic in Wilde's allegory of the fatal homosexual soul that so degrades the aesthetic ideal. In *De Profundis* (1905), the long letter to Lord Alfred Douglas written from Reading Gaol, Wilde insists that Douglas was only interested in degradation ("The gutter and the things that live in it had begun to fascinate you" [874]), and that their association was, for that reason, fatal to Wilde's art: "While you were with me you were the absolute ruin of my Art, and in allowing you to stand persistently between Art and myself I give to myself shame and blame to the fullest degree" (876); "But most of all I blame myself for the entire ethical degradation I allowed you to bring on me" (877).

The last phrase shows that Wilde himself was hardly capable of making the moral choice between the refinements of decadence and the excesses of degradation. Whether Wilde's self-destructive psychology had an impact on his aesthetic choices is hard to say, but the choice of degradation over decadence in *Dorian Gray* has considerable implications as far as the structure of the novel is concerned. As we have seen, the idea of decadence is resistant to conventional novelistic structure. The subject of degradation, on the other hand, is completely compatible with the notion of a chronologically progressive narrative: Dorian Gray moves from one *gradus* or step in the process of his moral corruption to the next, each step progressively more corrupt than the last. This simple narrative format, however, is disrupted by several contrivances, notably when Dorian Gray accidentally meets James Vane, the dead actress's brother who has sworn to avenge his sister's death; and when Vane is accidentally shot to death after somehow discovering the whereabouts of Dorian. Such improbabilities must discomfit even the unsophisticated reader, and they point out just how crudely the craft of fiction is handled in *Dorian Gray.* This novel, therefore, has little to say to later writers: romantic characterization, epigrammatic style, and conventional structure are not the stuff of modernism.

By contrast, George Moore's *Confessions of a Young Man* demonstrates the positive relationship between decadence and literary modernity. First, the book is a fairly complete record of decadent tastes, and the work has considerable documentary value in that it illustrates in fine detail the sensibility of a young man living in a period of literary ferment and experimentation. One of Moore's letters to his friend Edouard Dujardin summarizes this aspect of the book: "I am writing a book called 'The Confessions of a Young Man.' The young man goes to Paris to study painting, and I trace the development of his character in the three schools—romantic, naturalist and symbolist. He returns to London, and I show what becomes of him when he finds himself in the midst of English painting and literature. The idea? To contrast art in London with art in Paris."[56] Even in this brief statement we can observe a significant operation: the author has distanced himself from his biographical and documentary subject, and has begun to think of it in structural and fictional terms. The *Confessions,* then, is more than a record of decadence, and the added dimension comes from the introduction of new fictional techniques that grew out of Moore's decadent aestheticism. The centrality of one type of character (the artistic young man) is a significant development, as noted earlier; another is Moore's experimentation with the *monologue intérieur,* derived from his familiarity with Dujardin's work. With this blend of experimentation and documentation Moore's *Confessions* matters a great deal in the transition to modernity.

Confessions of a Young Man, begun in 1886, was first published in book form in 1888 as a semi-autobiographical account of Moore's experiences in the Paris of the 1870s. In several ways the *Confessions* is not purely autobiographical, and the "young man" of the title is not always George Moore. Edward Dayne, as he is called in the 1888 edition, is an idealized version of "the young man of refined mind" (91),[57] the habitué of café society who is a kind of civilized bohemian: "Each century has its special ideal, the ideal of the nineteenth is a young man" (176). Edward Dayne's fictional nature is underscored by several eccentricities that seem to be drawn not from Moore's experiences in the 1870s but from Huysmans's *A Rebours,* which Moore had reread in 1886 shortly before he began work on his *Confessions:* "Des Esseintes . . . expresses contempt for the bourgeois, love of the artificial and arcane; he admires the poetry of Baudelaire, Verlaine, and Mallarmé and the opera of Wagner. To complete his decadent tastes, he endorses a Schopenhauerian outlook on life. All of these themes have a place in the intricate fabric of *Confessions* and recreate for English audiences the aura of decadence which was to transform the artistic world of the 1890s."[58] For example, Moore's description of the salon shared by Dayne and his friend Marshall suggests the exotic and artificial atmosphere favored by Des Esseintes:

> The drawing room was in cardinal red, hung from the middle of the ceiling and looped up to give the appearance of a tent; a faun, in terra cotta, laughed in the red gloom, and there were Turkish couches and lamps. In another room you faced an altar, a Buddhist temple, a statue of Apollo, and a bust of Shelley. The bedrooms were made unconventual with cushioned seats and rich canopies; and in picturesque corners there were censers, great church candlesticks, and palms; then think of the smell of burning incense and wax and you will have imagined the sentiment of our apartment. . . . I bought a Persian cat, and a python that made a monthly meal off guinea pigs; Marshall, who did not care for pets, filled his rooms with flowers—he used to sleep beneath a tree of gardenias in full bloom. (75–76)

Several elements in this passage contribute to the overall sense of decadence: the laughing faun and the Turkish couches suggest sensuality made exotic by an oriental setting. The oriental connotations shade into the next sentence, but here the juxtaposition of Buddhist temple and bust of Shelley intimates that art has the same sublime status as religion. The next sentence shifts back to the theme of exotic and opulent sensuality, but as soon as it is sounded it blends with the ecclesiastical motif of burning censers and church candlesticks. The mention of the python and the tree of gardenias rounds out the amalgam of sensuality, exoticism, mysticism, and art.

Throughout the text of *Confessions* are similar indications of a type of decadent mentality that George Moore may have known quite well as a writer in the late 1880s, but which appears anachronistic in a young man just off the boat from Ireland in the 1870s. Edward Dayne, for example, finds "feminine depravities" in his character: "I am feminine, morbid, perverse. But above all perverse, almost everything perverse interests, fascinates me" (76). Such rhetoric is obviously derived from a rather one-dimensional conception of Baudelaire as the great popularizer of the perverse. Baudelaire, Dayne believes, is a "mock priest" of perversity, a "cynical libertine": "[T]he children of the nineteenth century go to you, O Baudelaire, and having tasted of your deadly delight all hope of repentance is vain. Flowers, beautiful in your sublime decay, I press you to my lips" (80–81). Dayne develops an "appetite for the strange, abnormal and unhealthy in art" and turns to Verlaine to satisfy this urge: "The royal magnificences of the sunset have passed, the solemn beatitude of the night is at hand but not yet here; the ways are veiled with shadow, and lit with dresses, white, that the hour has touched with blue, yellow, green, mauve, and undecided purple; the voices? strange contraltos; the forms? not those of men and women, but mystic, hybrid creatures, with hands nervous and pale, and eyes charged with eager and fitful light . . . '*un soir équivoque d'automne,*' . . . '*les belles pendent rêveuses à nos bras*' . . . and they whisper '*les mots spéciaux et tout bas*' " (87). Such passages as these, perhaps better than in any English work of the period, communicate the characteristic tone of decadence, the weariness of endings about to happen ("at hand but not yet here"), a state of being not clearly defined ("undecided . . . hybrid").

Moore's appreciation of Verlaine, however, illustrates more than a vague taste for twilit decadence. The language itself, with its rhythmic, assonant phrasing ("ways are veiled with shadow"), its inventive syntax ("lit with dresses, white"), and other poetic effects ("hour has touched"; "undecided purple"), indicates a strong sense of style that Moore developed in large measure from his reading of Pater: " 'Marius the Epicurean' . . . was the first book in English prose I had come across that procured for me any genuine pleasure derived in the language itself, in the combination of words for silver or gold chime, and unconventional cadence" (166). Moore's Paterian style is the perfect medium for the transmission of his experiences of French literature, and for this reason the *Confessions* must be counted among the catalysts for the creation of a new type of English fiction. Others may have helped to introduce the new literature to England, but Moore was almost alone in mastering a new idiom to go along with it. Such Francophiles as Swinburne and Wilde lacked the type of language needed to bring the French authors they admired into the tradition of English prose. Could Wilde with his epigrams or Swinburne with his alliterative effects have rendered Mallarmé into English the way Moore did? "I have passed whole days alone with my cat; and, alone with one of the last authors of the Latin decadence; for since that white creature is no more, strange and singularly I have loved all that the word *fall* expresses. In such wise that my favourite season of the year is the last weary days of summer, which immediately precede autumn, and the hour I choose to walk in is when the sun rests before disappearing, with rays of yellow copper on the grey walls and red copper on the tiles" (170). More of Pater than of Mallarmé may be in this passage, and if so it only gives the same point a slightly different emphasis: Moore adopts an idiom to accommodate the French sense of decadence that other styles of English prose would have excluded. Wilde's epigrams and Swinburne's metrical effects, to answer the question posed above, are two very different but equally inappropriate idioms to approach the mood of decadence in Mallarmé. Moore, on the other hand, manages to evoke this mood by slowing the cadence of the language, an effect achieved through the use of monosyllabic words, the repetition of long vowels ("whole . . . alone"; "rays . . . grey"), and the insertion of words that in any other context would draw the criticism of verbosity (compare the languorous rhythm of Moore's "and the hour I choose to walk in is when the sun rests before disappearing" with this too-efficient version of the same clause—"and I walk when the sun rests before disappearing," or even "and I walk before the sun disappears").

In addition to finding the right idiom in English to express the mood of decadence, Moore in the *Confessions* helps introduce the innovations of Edouard Dujardin by using a new English prose style to approximate the *monologue intérieur*. Moore used the device only a year after Dujardin's *Les Lauriers sont coupés* began appearing in *La Revue Indépendante* in 1887. The subjective condition of Dujardin's novel, set entirely in the mind of a Parisian dandy in amorous pursuit of a young actress, was suggested by Wagner's music, as Dujardin "sought to capture the *leitmotifs* of consciousness, the orchestra of the inner man."[59] When Moore read Dujardin's work in *La Revue Indépendante,* he wrote to him and praised the book: "Your story is very good, uncommonly good: the daily life of the soul unveiled for the first time; a kind of symphony in full stops and commas."[60] Although Moore does not make extensive use of the interior monologue in the *Confessions,* its presence marks what is probably the first appearance of the device in English prose. In the following passage, the *monologue intérieur* suggests a moment of boredom felt by Edward Dayne, as his mind flits from subject to subject:

> How different is the present to the past! I hate with my whole soul this London lodging, and all that concerns it—Emma, and eggs and bacon, the fat lascivious landlady and her lascivious daughter; I am sick of the sentimental actress who lives upstairs, I swear I will never go out to talk to her on the landing again. Then there is failure—I can do nothing, nothing; my novel I know is worthless; my life is a weak leaf, it will flutter out of sight presently. I am sick of everything; I wish I were back in Paris; I am sick of reading; I have nothing to read. Flaubert bores me. What nonsense has been talked about him! Impersonal! Nonsense, he is the most personal writer I know. That odious pessimism! How sick I am of it. . . . Happily, I have "A Rebours" to read, that prodigious book, that beautiful mosaic. Huysmans is quite right, ideas are well enough until you are twenty, afterwards only words are bearable . . . a new idea, what can be more insipid—fit for members of parliament. . . . Shall I go to bed? No. . . . I wish I had a volume of Verlaine, or something of Mallarmé's to read—Mallarmé for preference. I remember Huysmans speaks of Mallarmé in "A Rebours." In hours like these a page of Huysmans is as a dose of opium, a glass of some exquisite and powerful liqueur. (168–69)

This passage has been quoted at length to illustrate the subtle ways the interior monologue has been used. The subject is Edward Dayne's dissatisfaction with his life in London as compared to his earlier life in Paris. The present life in London, with its odious images of eggs and bacon and lascivious landladies, is contrasted with the refined literary life that Dayne had known in Paris. "Eggs and bacon" typify the ordinary present, "a dose of opium" and "a glass of . . . liqueur" the exquisite past to which Dayne turns for a moment of imaginary escape. The movement from one extreme to the other occurs in stages, each stage of dissatisfaction marked by the word "sick": first the life in the London lodging, then Dayne's fruitless literary efforts, and finally literature in general and Flaubert in particular. Since the word "Emma" is invoked at the outset of the series, Dayne most likely finds Flaubert in his realist mode offensive, so he turns to *A Rebours* for relief—not only from reality, but from realism as well. The entire interior monologue, in fact, is used to introduce several quotations from Huysmans's novel. The *monologue intérieur* is not used extensively in the *Confessions,* but as the above passage suggests, Moore was able to handle the device with a degree of sophistication that goes beyond gratuitous experimentation; in so doing he helps introduce a new fictional technique.

The appearance of the *monologue intérieur* in Moore's work may have stimulated Joyce's interest in the device. Susan Dick notes that "Moore's friendship with Dujardin led James Joyce to read *Les Lauriers* in 1903,"[61] and Joyce himself always claimed that he had derived the technique of the interior monologue from Dujardin and not from Freud's discovery of the unconscious, as some critics claimed.[62] Moore's role in the development of the interior monologue may be limited, but its appearance in the *Confessions* adds significance to the work as a transitional text. *Confessions of a Young Man* leads in the direction of the twentieth-century novel with the artist-hero at its center, emphasizing the subjective state of an unusually sensitive protagonist. Further, Moore in the *Confessions* assimilates the style of Pater and modifies his native English idiom in such a way that the language becomes a more appropriate medium to accommodate the mood of decadence. Unlike Wilde, Moore creates a sense of decadence to match the milieu, and he does this through a carefully cadenced and modulated style. Without this style, the *Confessions* would be little more than a typical fin de siècle pastiche of decadent tastes and fashions. That aspect of decadence is represented, as the Huysmanesque descriptions of Edward Dayne's "oriental" boudoir illustrate; at the same time, however, the experimental strain in the text plays counterpoint to convention, saving Moore's decadence from the typicality we have observed in D'Annunzio and Wilde. *Confessions of a Young Man* is Moore's remembrance of a brief "hour of artistic convulsion and renewal" (107–8), and the work communicates that spirit of renewal: it is a reminiscence that looks forward to the future.

6

Decadence and Modernism: Joyce and Gide

All of the texts previously discussed in this study can be called decadent with some justification, although the decadence of one text never coincides precisely with the decadence of another. As noted at the outset, the term *decadence* is too unstable to carry with it any exact and specific reference: it is a word rich in connotation, poor in denotation. Yet some decadent impulse is behind the stylistic opacity of *Salammbô,* the pathological thematics of *Germinie Lacerteux,* the antinatural artifice of *A Rebours,* and so on. None of these novels completely embodies all that decadence implies, but all of them have in common a quality of resistance to aesthetic norms, an opposition to literary convention. The customary idea of decadence is quite different from this; that is, decadence is usually regarded as an *excess* of convention, unoriginal imitation of earlier forms of literary expression. Except for a couple of fin de siècle texts (*Dorian Gray, Il Piacere*), the novels discussed in this study suggest that nineteenth-century decadence is an aesthetic category in its own right, not a debased imitation of some antecedent period or movement. Despite the problematic relationship (reaction/continuation) of decadence to romanticism, something is self-contained about decadence, the proof of this being that conventions evolved *within* the phenomenon of literary decadence. The oft-noted phenomenon of aesthetic interference notwithstanding, a tradition of decadence emerges in the nineteenth century that is autonomous—with its own systems, images, laws, assumptions, conventions, and so forth—and not a diffuse aggregate of aesthetic tendencies. By the beginning of the twentieth century, this tradition of decadence is influential in a special sense: decadence is at once a subject and a way of approaching that subject. To accept the thematics of decadence is also to accept the poetics of decadence, as one implies the other. Such themes as artificiality and decay affect the style and structure of the novel, resulting in a greater focus on purely linguistic effects and less interest in conventional narrative development.

It would be an oversimplification to say that the modern novel "developed" out of decadence in a strictly causal sense. Nevertheless, the structural, stylistic, and thematic implications of decadence have a strong bearing on the emergence of an important strain of modernist fiction. For example, the idea of decadence looks forward to the kind of modernism typified by James Joyce in at least two ways. First, the poetics of decadence is antagonistic to the conventional narrative, and we have reason to believe that Joyce's early interest in writers affiliated with decadence shifted his interest away from the art of the traditional narrative. Second, what was earlier called the hyperculturalism of decadence, together with the general notion of decay or decline, is close to the thematic concerns of Joyce. Even though Joyce did not adopt the thematics of decadence without subjecting it to ironic treatment, he still seems somewhat sympathetic to the fin de siècle. As we shall see, *A Portrait of the Artist as a Young Man* may play upon decadence ironically at times, but the text is far from being an outright rejection of the same decadent interests that had preoccupied Pater and Moore.

By contrast, the early work of André Gide illustrates how the existence of a poetics and a thematics of decadence influenced the development of a different strain of modernism. Again, it would be an oversimplification to attribute the modernism of Gide to decadence alone, but the type of fiction invented by Gide at the beginning of the twentieth century is based to a considerable extent on a reaction to literary decadence, a reaction that could only have come about as a result of a deep appreciation and understanding of decadent literature. Joyce's and Gide's relationship to decadence becomes all the more interesting when we consider that these two writers, who each shaped the development of the modern novel in quite different ways, were almost exact contemporaries, living in Paris at a time when that city was the hub of European literary activity. What is remarkable about this fact is that both men were largely untouched by this activity. The period that saw the modulation of symbolism into surrealism and the birth of a true avant-garde affected Joyce and Gide little, if at all. Indeed, the avant-gardism of the early twentieth century now seems isolated and eccentric, whereas the modernism of Joyce and Gide endures (indeed, Joyce and Gide seem to be weathering the recent ideological critiques of modernism better than, say, T. S. Eliot and Céline). For this reason, it is instructive to turn to decadence to articulate the place of that literature in the work of these two writers. Ultimately, we shall see how the early work of Joyce and Gide argues for the place of literary decadence not only in the emergence of the modern novel, but in subsequent fictional developments as well.

James Joyce is rightly regarded as a radically inventive modernist who invigorated the art of prose fiction and changed forever the form of the novel. Too often, however, Joyce's literary origins are obscured and overlooked because of his later innovations, perpetuating the myth that the man was born full-grown out of his own head. The early influence of Ibsen is well known; but the argument might be made that Joyce responded to the playwright more as artist than writer; that is, as Richard Ellmann proposes, Ibsen helped Joyce to decide on a career in literature and suggested to him what an artist should be like,[1] but with the possible exception of the play *Exiles,* it is difficult to see how Joyce's writing is indebted to Ibsen. On the other hand, like any young man with literary ambitions coming of age during the fin de siècle, Joyce immersed himself in the fiction that we have associated with the idea of decadence. Ellmann says that Joyce "read so widely it is hard to say definitely of any important creative work published in the late nineteenth century that Joyce had not read it" (75). Early interests included Huysmans and D'Annunzio, whose style Joyce managed to imitate (75–76, 59). His fellow Irishmen Moore and Wilde he read with some skepticism,[2] though this does not diminish the importance of Moore's *Confessions of a Young Man* to Joyce's *Portrait.* The strongest early influence on Joyce the writer, however, remains the prose of Walter Pater. Passages from Pater and Joyce can be set side by side and their stylistic resemblances noted with some clarity. In short, Joyce owes much more to a native Irish-English tradition of decadent literature than is generally supposed.

Joyce experimented with Paterian rhythms and diction as an undergraduate in 1902, writing an essay on the Irish poet James Clarence Mangan (1803–49) in language blatantly derivative of Pater's *Renaissance.* Joyce qua Pater evokes in this youthful essay some vague ideal of woman,

"Vittoria Colonna and Laura and Beatrice—even she upon whose face many lives have cast that shadowy delicacy, as of one who broods upon distant terrors and riotous dreams, and that strange stillness before which love is silent, Mona Lisa . . ." (*CWJJ,* 79). Whether this could have been written without the precedent of Pater's famous passages on *La Gioconda* is doubtful: "Hers is the head upon which all 'the ends of the world have come,' and the eyelids are a little weary. It is a beauty wrought out from within upon the flesh, the deposit . . . of strange thoughts and fantastic reveries and exquisite passions" (*SW,* 46). Joyce's "shadowy delicacy" and "riotous dreams" are but slight transpositions of Pater's weary-liddedness and "fantastic reveries," but the imitation goes beyond such semantic echoes (compare also the syntactical similarity of "even she upon whose face" and "Hers is the head upon which") into an overall emulation of mood and tone. Joyce's early facility at mimicking the Paterian manner was to be put to use later to achieve a variety of effects; thematically as well as stylistically, Joyce's *Portrait* owes much to *Marius,* Pater's portrait novel.

Although the influence of Pater on Joyce is widely acknowledged by critics, it is rarely studied in detail; only a few article-length studies of the relationship between the two writers exist.[3] But the relationship seems quite complex and deserving of further investigation, for several bases of comparison point to the evident influence of Pater on Joyce. The stylistic similarities to Pater's prose, noted above, are repeated in the *Portrait.* For example, the mixture of sensuality and spirituality in *Marius* is expressed in language that will not yield to a fully unqualified affirmation of either element of the mixture, to spirit or flesh, ideas or sensations: "It was to the sentiment of the body, and the affections it defined—the flesh, of whose force and colour that wandering Platonic soul was but so frail a residue or abstract—he must cling. The various pathetic traits of the beloved, suffering, perished body of Flavian, so deeply pondered, had made him a materialist, but with something of the temper of a devotee" (*ME,* 106). The last phrase refers to a specifically religious devotion, and the spiritual cast given off by material objects is consonant with the conception of Marius as a kind of artist-priest. This image of the artist as an occupant of a holy office, as well as the language reflecting the ambiguous merger of physical sensations and spiritual ideas, is so basic a part of Joyce's *Portrait* that the novel would be unthinkable without it. Joyce's Stephen Dedalus is "a priest of eternal imagination, transmuting the daily bread of experience into the radiant body of everliving life" (*P,* 221). For Stephen Dedalus, not only are generally sensuous experiences translated into ecclesiastical language, but specifically sensual ones as well: "Her image [i.e., Emma's, Stephen's beloved] had passed into his soul for ever and no word had broken the holy silence of his ecstacy" (*P,* 172). This is the point where Joyce's use of Paterian language becomes ironical: when sensation gives way to sensuality an affirmation of the physical world occurs that is not part of Pater's highly qualified aestheticism. Pater's Marius devotes himself to perception of the physical world, but refrains from participation in it.

In the passage from *Marius* quoted above, the death of Flavian arouses in Marius an awareness merely of the sentiment of the body, so he is far from being the frustrated adolescent sensualist that Joyce's hero often is. The language of the two writers, however, is similar in that both evoke tentative states of consciousness not fully understood by the central characters of either work. Indeed, each work is allied to the tradition of the *Bildungsroman,* and it is appropriate that the language in both novels communicates the subtleties and difficulties involved in the various stages of awareness that the characters must go through. The following passages from Joyce describe Stephen Dedalus's somewhat desperate awakening to the awareness of the body, but the language suggests something almost mystical: "He felt some dark presence moving irresistibly upon him from the darkness, a presence subtle and murmurous as a flood filling him wholly with itself. Its murmur besieged his ears like the murmur of some multitude in sleep" (*P,* 100). This is a rather mannered imitation of Pater's alliterative, repetitious diction; compare, for example, this passage from *Marius:* "[H]e felt a quite hope, a quiet joy dawning faintly, in the dawning of this doctrine" (*ME,* 212). (Joyce also delights in participle-adverb clusters like Pater's "dawning faintly" throughout the *Portrait*—"fading slowly" [*P,* 103], "falling continually" [*P,* 142], "wielding calmly" [*P,* 158], and so forth. Note also the concluding sentence of "The Dead": "His soul swooned slowly as he heard the snow falling faintly through the universe and faintly falling" [*D,* 224]). What keeps Joyce's imitation of Pater's diction from being merely imitative is the ironical use of the Paterian idiom to express pure sensuality and even outright crudity. For example, the mystical passage featuring some "dark presence" continues in the same lush aesthetic vein as above, but only for a while: "He stretched his arms in the street to hold fast the frail swooning form that eluded him and incited him: and the cry that he had strangled for so long in his throat issued from his lips. It broke from him like a wail of despair from a hell of sufferers and died in a wail of furious entreaty, a cry for an iniquitous abandonment, a cry which was but the echo of an obscene scrawl which he had read on the oozing wall of a urinal" (*P*, 100). The distance from "frail swooning form" to "oozing wall of a urinal" is considerable, to say the least, but the extreme difference in diction is more than a mere rhetorical effect used to shock an unsuspecting reader. The opposition of style and subject creates a sense of dramatic irony by juxtaposing Stephen Dedalus's aesthetic consciousness and the less-than-aesthetic context within which that consciousness attempts to operate. Simply stated, in *Marius* the aesthetic hero[4] does not appear as an ironic figure because he is not out of place in his environment, whereas in the *Portrait* he does because he is.

The examples above show what is obvious of many passages in the *Portrait:* that Joyce echoed the style of Pater and used the Paterian idiom for ironic effect. Even so, the question of how Joyce's imitations of Pater link the *Portrait* to the phenomenon of decadence remains. As we have already observed, Pater himself has only an indirect, almost accidental, bearing on the development of decadence in its highly artificial, fin de siècle form. Pater gets into the *Zeitgeist* of the nineties mainly because of the oversimplifications and misinterpretations of Wilde and Moore. The "new aestheticism" of the nineties is removed from the true aestheticism of Pater because the former lacks the quality of *ascēsis* essential to the latter, and because a taste for unqualified artificiality takes the place of Pater's discriminating aestheticism. Aestheticism, strictly speaking, has little to do with the cult of artificiality that characterizes fin de siècle decadence. The place of Joyce in all this can be summarized as follows: Joyce relates to decadence *through* Pater in much the same way that Wilde and Moore do, but with a crucial difference. Joyce's misinterpretation in the *Portrait* is deliberate and self-conscious: indeed, it is the very stuff of the novel; the character Stephen Dedalus is a hopelessly "Paterian" devotee of art who almost completely inverts the Paterian ideas that make the devotion possible.

This inversion becomes clear when the well-known but rarely understood idea of the Joycean epiphany is examined and compared to a similar notion in Pater's *Marius.* The definition of epiphany is given in *Stephen Hero,* the preliminary version of the *Portrait:* "By an epiphany he [Stephen] meant a sudden spiritual manifestation, whether in the vulgarity of speech or of gesture or in a memorable phase of the mind itself. He believed that it was for the man of letters to record these epiphanies with extreme care, seeing that they themselves are the most delicate and evanescent of moments" (*SH*, 211). This "sudden spiritual manifestation" is mainly a revelation of the essence of an object (or gesture, or whatever is perceived) that "leaps to us from the vestment of its appearance" (*SH*, 212). Joyce modifies Aquinas so that this perception of the essence, the *quidditas* or "whatness" (*SH*, 213) of the object, comes in stages that parallel the "three things requisite for beauty," according to Aquinas; that is, "integrity . . . symmetry and radiance" (*SH*, 212), the final quality (radiance or *claritas*) being equated with *quidditas*. "What this tries to do," S. L. Goldberg has noted, "is . . . show how something in the object, its true inner nature, corresponds to a stage of its perception by a subject."[5] The aesthetic developed in *Stephen Hero* is therefore epistemological, and the epiphanic "leap" through which the essence or whatness of the object is known is effectively a mediation between subject and object that makes insight and appreciation possible. Thus, the aesthetic is rooted in concrete *things* and manages, as Goldberg notes, a correspondence of subject and object: "The soul of the commonest object . . . seems to us radiant. The object achieves its epiphany" (*SH*, 213). Hugh Kenner elaborates: "The object achieves *its* [Kenner's emphasis] epiphany. What the scrutinizer comes to know is the thing itself in its irreducible otherness."[6] It should be obvious by now that the idea of the epiphany is completely dependent on perception, and not simply ordinary perception, but the refined perception of an artist's eye—in short, aestheticism in the true Paterian sense.

Pater's Marius gradually develops a philosophy of perception that is analogous to the idea of epiphany articulated in *Stephen Hero* (I shall comment presently on the absence of the epiphany theory in the *Portrait*). Like the Joycean epiphany, what Marius eventually terms *vision* is an intense revelation of the reality of the concrete world: "It seemed just then as if the desire of the artist in him—that old longing to produce—might be satisfied by the exact and literal transcript of what was then passing around him, in simple prose, arresting the desirable moment as it passed, and prolonging its life a little.—To live in the concrete!" (*ME*, 127). The moment of epiphany or vision in *Marius*, as in *Stephen Hero*, is marked by what Joyce calls the radiance of the object: "[I]t was a reconciliation to the world of sense, the visible world. From the hopefulness of this gracious presence, all visible things around him, even the commonest subjects of everyday life—if they [Marius and Cornelius] but stood together to warm their hands at the same fire—took for him a new poetry, a delicate fresh bloom, and interest. It was as if his bodily eyes had been indeed mystically washed, renewed, strengthened" (*ME*, 166). Following this mystical renewal is Marius's enlightened understanding of a principal aspect of Cyrenaic philosophy: "the pleasure of the 'Ideal Now,' . . . certain moments [that are] high-pitched, passionately coloured, intent with sensation, and a kind of knowledge which, in its vivid clearness, was like sensation" (*ME*, 185). This type of intense awareness is strikingly like Joyce's idea of the epiphany. Moreover, at the conclusion of the climactic chapter titled "The Will as Vision," Marius experiences what can justifiably be called an epiphany (Pater calls it "one central act of vision" [*ME*, 217]) when he resolves to search out "the equivalent of [the] Ideal, among so-called actual things—a gathering together of every trace or token of it, which his actual experience might present" (*ME*, 213). All of this is ample illustration that Joyce's theory of epiphany has considerable precedence in Pater's *Marius;* indeed, the idea of the epiphany in *Stephen Hero* seems little more than Pater's ideal of vision dressed up in the language of Scholasticism. The key point here is that the epiphany in *Stephen Hero* is quite Paterian and clearly not a distortion or misinterpretation of Pater's thought.

The *Portrait,* on the other hand, completely misrepresents and virtually inverts the Paterian concept developed in *Stephen Hero.* As the above quotations from *Marius* and *Stephen Hero* illustrate, vision or epiphany is rooted in perception, in an acute realization of the world of concrete things. The term *epiphany* is not used in the *Portrait,* and with good reason; the term applies to a process of mediation between artistic perception and the world perceived by the artist, precisely the process absent from the *Portrait* theory. The aesthetic philosophy of Stephen Dedalus in the finished novel is much more formalistic than the one Stephen Daedalus presents in the earlier manuscript, being mainly a series of divagations based primarily on Aristotle's *Poetics:* "The esthetic emotion . . . is . . . static. The mind is arrested and raised above desire or loathing" (*P,* 205). Stephen never uses the word *catharsis* outright, but the phrase "raised above" implies a kind of purification of the mind as it is freed from the "kinetic" (*P,* 205) emotions of desire and loathing by an aesthetic stasis of pity and fear. How then is the effect of stasis that a work of art "ought to awaken" (*P,* 206) brought about? It is "called forth," Stephen says, "prolonged and at last dissolved by . . . the rhythm of beauty" (*P,* 206). The tortured definition of *rhythm* that follows ("the first formal esthetic relation of part to part in any esthetic whole or of an esthetic whole to its parts or of any part to the esthetic whole of which it is a part" [*P,* 206]) leaves no doubt that the aesthetic is highly formalistic and related more to rationalistic than to empirical modes of thinking. Apparently the desired stasis is to be "called forth" by formal *relations* of beauty in some absolute sense, and is not necessarily related to beautiful *things.* The Latin sentence that is used to define "beauty" in the *Portrait* is "Pulcra sunt quae visa placent," which Stephen translates as "that is beautiful the apprehension of which pleases" (*P,* 207). Joyce in the Pola notebook, however, uses a more precise translation: "Those *things* [my emphasis] are beautiful the apprehension of which pleases" (*CWJJ,* 147). This is a slight but significant change, and like the omission of the concept of the epiphany from the *Portrait* theory, it suggests that Stephen Dedalus's idea of beauty is detached from the concrete. Despite his remarks to the contrary (*P,* 213), as Stephen's theory progresses it becomes increasingly apparent that his aesthetic theory depends upon an aesthetic ideal, a near-Platonic conception of Beauty in some absolute sense.

As Kenner mentions, in *Dublin's Joyce,* an aesthetic theory requires an epistemological theory (138). When Stephen says that the "first step in the direction of beauty is to understand the frame and scope of the imagination, to understand the act itself of esthetic apprehension" (*P,* 208), the language comes close to the idea of perception in Pater. But when we come to the application of Aquinas's thought that led Stephen in *Stephen Hero* to the all-important epiphany, we find that element of "esthetic apprehension" missing. In both *Stephen Hero* and the *Portrait* the Aquinian attributes of beauty are the same ("wholeness, harmony, and radiance" [*P,* 212]), and in both the correspondence of these attributes to the "phases of apprehension" (*P,* 212) is the same. But what follows from this in the *Portrait* is quite different: The "supreme quality" of radiance, *claritas, quidditas,* or "whatness" is only "felt by the artist when the esthetic image is first conceived in his imagination" (*P,* 213). This suggests that the "esthetic image" has its own *quidditas* or "whatness" that is distinct from the "whatness" of an apprehended object: the epiphanic leap from the object perceived to the perceiving subject is missing from the *Portrait* aesthetic. The term *imagination* as Stephen uses it clearly refers to a faculty on the part of the artist that enables him to invent or conceive images that are apparently divorced from concrete objects. In the Paris notebook, Joyce translates Aristotle's *hē tekhnē mimeitai tēn physin* not as "art is an imitation of nature" but as "art imitates Nature" (*CWJJ,* 145), that is, the activity of art imitates the activity of nature. This seems the case in the *Portrait:* the "esthetic image" is not an imitation of an object in nature made possible by acute perception of the object; the "esthetic image" is brought forth from the artist's imagination and has the same ontological status as an object in nature. In other words, art imitates nature simply by bringing objects into existence, and what results is what David Daiches has called the "ontological fallacy," the idea that "a work of art fulfills its purpose and achieves its value simply by *being*."[7]

When the actual process of poetic composition is described in the *Portrait*, the aesthetic in operation clearly produces objects of art ontologically analogous to objects in nature. The give-and-take between subject and object that is the idea of epiphany does not appear. As Stephen writes his villanelle, the isolation of the subjective mind is complete: "In the virgin womb of the imagination the word was made flesh" (*P*, 217). This "virgin womb" of imagination at first appears as a kind of tabula rasa on which have been written experiences with and memories of the "beloved" (*P*, 215), the young girl called Emma or E.C. who is the subject of the villanelle. But the poetic process as it is described here is not really so empirical as it first seems: Stephen feels an "instant of inspiration" (*P*, 217), and the experience of concrete reality is transmuted and dominated by some vague ideal of beauty. Stephen the theorizer denies that beauty is "a light from some other world" (*P*, 213), but the villanelle betrays his "desire to press in [his] arms the loveliness which has not yet come into the world" (*P*, 251). The last phrase finally identifies the Neoplatonic strain in Stephen's aesthetic that is implicit in the theory itself, though never admitted and articulated. The "esthetic image" does not "come into the world" until it is conceived within Stephen's imagination. His subjective "experience" is somehow outside the world of concrete, sensible objects, and the beauty of this art is only a positivist concept unrelated to phenomenal reality.

Thus, Stephen Dedalus in the novel is a different sort of character from his predecessor in the manuscript precisely because he is made to misrepresent and misunderstand the aestheticism of Pater and so becomes not an artist but an aesthete in the fin de siècle sense. Without this misrepresentation, Stephen Dedalus would not be the ironic figure he is. He would instead be a straightforward artist-hero in the manner of Stephen Daedelus in *Stephen Hero* (hence the name), and the self-righteousness of the character would not have been diffused by the self-consciousness of the author.

Stephen Dedalus's relationship to Pater's Marius is quite complex, and without *Stephen Hero* and Joyce's notebooks we would not be able to see how the Stephen Dedalus character evolved in a direction away from

Pater's aestheticism. A more direct relationship can be observed between the *Portrait* and George Moore's *Confessions of a Young Man,* where the conventional fin de siècle sensibility is more obviously displayed. First, the similarity of the titles of the two works suggests that the nineteenth-century ideal of the "young man" is very much a part of Joyce's novel. This aspect of the *Portrait* is often overlooked, owing perhaps to the legacy of early Joyce criticism that was largely biographical in nature, and would have us identify the phrase "young man" with "young Joyce."[8] The title *A Portrait of the Artist as a Young Man* does suggest that "young man" might refer to a chronological stage in the development of an artist; however, "young man" may also be taken to mean not only a phase of development, but a role, a self-conscious pose. Read in this way, *artist* and *young man* cease to signify the progressive temporality of the *Bildungsroman* and become instead the terms of an antithesis. "Young man" and "artist" appear then as separate states of being, and the temporal relationship between the two shifts from the simple biographical to the complex psychological. In other words, "young man" becomes not only a stage that the artist goes through, but a mentality that he must overcome. This interpretation of the meaning of the phrase "young man" makes much of the *Portrait* more comprehensible than the customary *Bildungsroman* context allows, and helps explain some troubling facts of the text. In particular, the transformation of Stephen Dedalus from a sensitive youth to a romantic rebel-artist seems quite inconsistent: "As a bewildered child or a schoolboy buffeted by the storms of puberty, Stephen is a victim who automatically enlists our support; it is only when he begins to assert himself that we start having our doubts."[9] These doubts are fueled by Stephen's grandiose and egotistical claims about himself as an artist and his all but total failure to give substance to those claims. The only evidence of Stephen's artistic prowess is a rather precious piece of moody romanticism, languid of cadence and vague of subject: "Are you not weary of ardent ways, / Lure of the fallen seraphim? / Tell no more of enchanted days" (*P,* 223), and so on. "Are such unimportant verses," one critic asks, "the result of such exalted intentions and the best a cunning priest of the imagination can do?"[10] The rift between Stephen's artistic intentions and his artistic performance becomes less puzzling once we are aware that Stephen is *not* an artist but a "young man" in the sense that George Moore's Edward Dayne is.

The young man of Moore's *Confessions,* the "special ideal" (*C,* 176) of the nineteenth century, differs from Stephen Dedalus in that Moore's hero operates at a higher level of society and is admitted to circles from which Joyce's hero would be excluded. But Stephen Dedalus has many of the same tastes and aristocratic pretensions as Edward Dayne. When Stephen has money in his pockets from a prizewinning essay, he exercises these tastes "to build a breakwater of order and elegance against the sordid tide of life without him" (*P*, 98). Here, early in the text, Stephen's efforts to emulate the ideal of the artistic young man sound earnest and poignant, but as Stephen persists in the pose he appears dandified and pretentious: "Good morning, everybody, said Stephen, smiling and kissing the tips of his fingers in adieu" (*P*, 175). The context here could not illustrate more fully the "sordid tide of life" that Stephen had earlier tried to stem, but his gesture at this point cannot be seen as a heroic effort to resist the sordidness of his surroundings; it is a petty rebellion at best, and elegance has given way to affectation. Ultimately, not rebellion but exile becomes the only way for Stephen to acquire the ideal of order and elegance through art that he desires. In this, Joyce's and Moore's young men are almost identical, and Joyce's text echoes Moore's quite closely. Edward Dayne says that the "two dominant notes" in his character are "an original hatred of my native country, and a brutal loathing of the religion I was brought up in" (*C*, 109). These issues are treated much more subtly in the *Portrait*, but they are precisely the issues that occasion the need for exile. Dayne also notes that "those who loved literature the most purely . . . were marked out for persecution, and . . . driven into exile" (*C*, 168). Clearly, Stephen Dedalus feels himself persecuted for the sake of art (it is often noted that the character's name combines martyrdom and artifice in the double allusion to Saint Stephen and to Ovid's Daedalus), and plans to defend himself using "the only arms I allow myself to use—silence, exile, and cunning" (*P*, 247). Stephen at novel's end is set to voyage to Paris, the haven of refined young men, where he "intends to forge in the smithy of my soul the uncreated conscience of my race" (*P*, 253). To accomplish this, exile is necessary, and for this reason: "When the soul of a man is born in this country there are nets flung at it to hold it back from flight. You [Davin, a nationalistic Irishman] talk to me of nationality, language, religion. I shall try to fly by those nets" (*P*, 203). How similar are Stephen's aims to those of Edward Dayne, the young man in Paris "striving heart and soul to identify himself with his environment, to shake himself free from race and language and to recreate himself as it were in the womb of a new nationality" (*C*, 129). In one sense, the theme of exile is specifically Irish, but the problem of Irish nationalism only accentuates the issue of the autonomy of art in both the *Portrait* and the *Confessions.* In both, the political situation in Ireland at the turn of the century, and the concomitant mentality that would have art serve as the handmaiden of nationalism, serves as the context that brings the theme of art for art's sake into sharper focus.

In addition to these general similarities involving the "young man" as a character type and the scenario of exile necessitated by a lack of native sympathy to art, both texts have in common several points clearly related to the phenomenon of nineteenth-century decadence. The superficial—but nonetheless significant—conception of Baudelaire as the poet of perversity finds its way into both texts. We have already noted Moore's reference to the "mock priest" in the *Confessions* and his extended appreciation of Baudelaire as a "cynical libertine" (*C,* 80). Joyce's "priest of eternal imagination" seems to owe something to the "mock priest" Baudelaire as well. Stephen Dedalus, in fact, goes through what can only be called a Baudelairean phase, prowling the streets of the brothel district called Nighttown and cultivating a sense of sin: "The whores would be just coming out of their houses making ready for the night, yawning lazily in their sleep and settling the hairpins in their clusters of hair. He would pass by them calmly waiting for a sudden movement of his own will or a sudden call to his sinloving soul from their soft perfumed flesh" (*P,* 102). In addition to the alliance of art and depravity, the pervasive romantic dualism that runs through the *Portrait* helps to link Stephen Dedalus to Baudelaire. The alternation of emotional highs and lows in the *Portrait,* of scenes of sublimity and squalor (e.g., the ending of chapter 4 and the beginning of chapter 5), is similar to the Baudelairean vacillation between *idéal* and *spleen.* Stephen's poetic-erotic ecstasy, with "choirs of seraphim . . . falling from heaven" (*P,* 217) is later balanced against a splenetic "spasm of despair" and "lice falling from the air" (*P,* 234). These lice seem clearly Baudelairean, recalling the *vermine* of "Au Lecteur": "His mind bred vermin. His thoughts were lice born of the sweat of sloth" (*P,* 234). Baudelaire, however, is not the only writer related to the decadent context of both the *Portrait* and the *Confessions.* Those artists who "loved literature most purely" and who were "driven into exile," according to Edward Dayne, are Byron and Shelley (Dayne also names George Moore!) (*C,* 168). Byron and Shelley, Moore writes, are "my poets [that] were taken to school, because it pleased me to read 'Queen Mab' and 'Cain' amid the priests and ignorance of a hateful Roman Catholic college" (*C,* 50). Stephen Dedalus is likewise a defender of Byron against the accusations of his Catholic schoolmates, who claim that the English poet is a heretic (*P*, 80–81). Byron, in short, has value to both Dayne and Dedalus as the great rebel, while Shelley is appreciated for his ability to create moods of ethereality and languor. Moore calls Shelley "my soul" whose "craft [is] fashioned of mother o' pearl, with starlight at the helm and moonbeams for sails" (*C*, 78). The same vocabulary surfaces in the text of the *Portrait* when the subject is Shelley: "The music came nearer and he recalled the words, the words of Shelley's fragment upon the moon wandering companionless, pale for weariness. The stars began to crumble and a cloud of fine stardust fell through space" (*P*, 103). But neither text needs recourse to Shelley to sound the decadent note of weariness and imminent decline. "I have loved all that the word *fall* expresses" (*C*, 170), runs Moore's translation of Mallarmé, and the same sense of weary decadence is present in the *Portrait:* "Not to fall was too hard, too hard: and he felt the silent lapse of his soul, as it would be at some instant to come, falling, falling but not yet fallen, still unfallen but about to fall" (*P*, 162). Even though this passage has religious implications, the "overtone of weariness" (*P*, 163) and the overall feeling of decadence are more important to an understanding of the *Portrait* as a text related to a particular fin de siècle mood. Stephen Dedalus is a young man whose sense of age in youth or youthful senescence betrays a deeply felt sense of decadence: "All seemed weary of life even before entering upon it" (*P*, 164). Sentiments such as this, along with Joyce's use of Paterian language and his exploration of the "young man" as a character type, leave no doubt that the *Zeitgeist* of 1890s decadence has a place in *A Portrait of the Artist as a Young Man.*

To say that Joyce was as sympathetic to the decadent milieu as was George Moore would be incorrect. Joyce, after all, belonged to a later generation than Moore's, and his role in the phenomenon of decadence is diminished. Thus, Joyce's relationship to the decadent period that preceded him has more to do with its usefulness as raw material for the creation of fiction than as an aesthetic in its own right. In Pater and Moore, Joyce found substance and style to supplement his own experience of the fin de siècle mentality that went into the creation of Stephen Dedalus, but he remains outside the decadentism of Moore and the aestheticism of Pater. Joyce's artistic position is always that of the exiled observer, and even though Joyce would never advertise himself as an aesthete or a decadent, it is hard to imagine the *Portrait* in its final ironical form without the precedence of *Marius* and the *Confessions.* This is tantamount to saying that Joyce's modernism proceeded from a sense of decadence, despite Joyce's own distance and detachment from that sense. Full sympathy is not requisite to continue an earlier aesthetic trend. However altered and self-consciously undercut, the preoccupations of Pater and Moore are perpetuated in the work of the early Joyce.

Joyce's receptive attitude toward the phenomenon of decadence is attributable to at least two causes. First, decadence never enjoyed in England or Ireland the coherence that it did in France. For a brief time, decadence and *décadisme*, as we have seen, became sufficiently manifest and clear to invite both imitation and dismissal. If Joyce did not react to decadence in an oppositional manner, this may be due to the relative lack of any clearly defined set of conventions that could be comprehended as decadent. Second, the influence of Nietzsche in the English-speaking countries at the turn of the century was slight and superficial compared to his impact in France and Italy. George Moore mentioned in his 1904 preface to the *Confessions of a Young Man* that he detected an "exalted individualism" in the book "which in certain passages leads the reader to the sundered rocks about the cave of Zarathustra" (*C*, 40–41), but this is only a retrospective comment, an attempt to interpret Edward Dayne in Nietzschean terms. (Moore had not read Nietzsche when he wrote the *Confessions* [*C*, 41].) Joyce indulged in some Nietzschean posturings for a while,[11] and signed a letter in 1904 as "James Overman,"[12] but evidently Nietzsche exerted no real influence on Joyce's work: "Joyce . . . , like Moore, went through a period of temporary infatuation with Nietzsche which left no mark of any consequence on his creative work."[13] The inconsequentiality of Nietzsche to any writer of the early modern period is significant, for Nietzsche provided a complete paradigm of antidecadence. We shall see how the Nietzschean model provided Gide with the necessary framework on which to create a different type of modern novel than that produced by Joyce, a difference highly dependent on a rejection of decadence. This is not to say that Nietzsche occupied for Gide the same position that Pater and Moore occupied for Joyce; Gide's response to decadence did not depend exclusively upon his reading of Nietzsche. By no means did Gide need to experience his decadence vicariously, since he was himself acquainted firsthand with the decadent milieu of the 1890s via his affiliation with such figures as Mallarmé and Oscar Wilde. But Nietzsche is profoundly influential because of the way he *complicated* the idea of decadence, enriched it dialectically, and paradoxically came to admire certain qualities of decadence that he attempted to deny. What

Nietzsche thought of decadence and what he imagined in its place thus become important to the transition to modernity, and to understanding Gide's place in that transition.

Nietzsche is not the philosopher of decadence (that epithet Nietzsche himself applied to Schopenhauer), but he is the philosopher who has thought most deeply about the phenomenon of decadence, including the relationship between decadence and art. "Nothing has occupied me more profoundly than the problem of decadence" (*CW*, 155), he says in *The Case of Wagner*, and in the same passage he equates decadence and morality on the basis of common negative values: "impoverished life, the will to the end, the great weariness. Morality negates life" (*CW*, 155). Similarly, in *Ecce Homo* (1888) morality is defined as "the idiosyncrasy of decadents, with the ulterior motive of revenging oneself against life—successfully" (*EH*, 333). Decadence and Christian morality share the spirit of negation, and this spirit leads also to the production of decadent art. Nietzsche's great example of decadence is Richard Wagner, as he illustrates most completely the morality of negation, the rejection of life: "To do justice to this essay [*The Case of Wagner*], one has to suffer of the fate of music as an open wound.—Of *what* do I suffer when I suffer the fate of music? That music has been done out of its world-transfiguring, Yes-saying character, so that it is music of decadence and no longer the flute of Dionysus" (*EH*, 317).

We can easily be misled by such statements into thinking that Nietzsche's definition of decadence is merely a matter of setting no against yes, the decadent versus the Dionysian. On the contrary, an element of decadence occurs in what Nietzsche calls Dionysian art: an art that is at once affirmative and tragic and "wishes to convince us of the eternal joy of existence" by finding joy "not in phenomena, but behind them," so that even in the face of decay and decline we experience the "exuberant fertility of the universal will" (*BT*, 104). While decadent and Dionysian art are contraries (or "antipodes," as Nietzsche says of himself and Wagner [*NC*, 662]), Nietzsche does not *reject* decadence even though he sets himself against it. Rather, it is the decadent who rejects the Dionysian, and a key element of Dionysian art is the quality of overfulness or abundance that can *include* decline, decadence, negation: "He that is richest in the fullness of life, the Dionysian god and man, can afford not only the *sight* of the terrible and the questionable, but even the terrible deed and any luxury of destruction, decomposition, and negation" (*NC*, 670). Again, the decadent and the Dionysian are opposed, but it is the decadent who is "doing" the opposing because of his passive attitude of rejection and negation.

The nearest analogy to this operation, this complication of the usual notion of contrariety, is the "opposition" of Apollonian and Dionysian art in *The Birth of Tragedy* (1872). When these two famous terms are paired they are sometimes misunderstood as synonyms for such hackneyed phrases as "classic and romantic" or "rational and emotional." In truth, Apollo and Dionysus are opposed, in Nietzsche's view, only in the earlier Doric period, when the "majestically rejecting attitude of Apollo is immortalized" (*BT,* 39). Later, this rejecting attitude gives way to partial acceptance, and when the myth-making powers of the Apollonian dreamer are wedded to the Dionysian spirit of intoxication, Attic tragedy is born. This reconciliation is really the Apollonian's discovery that the Dionysian "was actually not so very alien to him after all, in fact, that it was only his Apollonian consciousness which, like a veil, hid this Dionysian world from his vision" (*BT,* 41). Nietzsche's earlier, Doric Apollonian has only the *attitude* of rejection in common with the Wagnerian decadent; the quality of the rejection differs, however, because the Apollonian's initial denial of the Dionysian is based on the blissful peace of the inner world of dreams. The decadent's rejection is allied to idealism, other-worldliness—something cultural and acquired. The dreams of the Doric Apollonian are primordial and natural, and thus spring from the same source as the Dionysian's rhythmic frenzy. When the two "opposites" are reconciled, the plastic and the visual nature of the Apollonian is animated by the music and dance of the Dionysian, while at the same time the Dionysian spirit is given concrete form. Attic tragedy is therefore an art of the whole; it is constituted of contraries that do not reject one another, even as Nietzsche, the latter-day Dionysian, does not reject that which he most opposes—decadence.

When Nietzsche describes the style of decadence, the issue of aesthetic wholeness is again central. Because the decadent spirit rejects that which is unlike itself, that is, nature, it lacks any power of organic synthesis or assimilation. The attitude of rejection leads necessarily to an art of separation, division, fragmentation:

> For the present I merely dwell on the question of *style.*—What is the sign of every *literary decadence?* That life no longer dwells in the whole. The word becomes sovereign and leaps out of the sentence, the sentence reaches out

> and obscures the meaning of the page, the page gains life at the expense of the whole—the whole is no longer a whole. But this is the simile of every style of *decadence:* every time, the anarchy of atoms, disgregation of the will, "freedom of the individual," to use moral terms—expanded into a political theory, "*equal* rights for all." Life, *equal* vitality, the vibration and exuberance of life pushed back into the smallest forms, the rest, *poor* in life. Everywhere paralysis, arduousness, torpidity *or* hostility and chaos: both more and more obvious the higher one ascends in forms of organization. The whole no longer lives at all: it is composite, calculated, artificial, and artifact. (*CW*, 170)

This description begins as a paraphrase of Bourget's definition of *le style de décadence*, but as Calinescu says, the passage does much more than simply echo the French critic: "The striking fact about this borrowed passage is that, read in the context of *Der Fall Wagner* and the other works of Nietzsche's last period, it both sounds and *is* original; and this is so because it is enriched by the complex and dialectically ambivalent significances that Nietzsche attaches to the idea of decadence."[14] It might be added that Nietzsche's originality lies in his understanding of the internal workings of decadence, its roots and causes, in his ability to make what he called the "backward inference . . . from every way of thinking and valuing to the *want* that prompts it" (*NC*, 670). Bourget, by contrast, *observed* decadent art from the outside and saw fragmentation on its surface, but made no deeper inference (attributing this fragmentation to individuality is little more than an analogy, a comparison of one surface observation with another; that is, fragmented text: democratic society). Nietzsche's deeper insight enabled him to elaborate fully upon the decadent's negation of life, and to see the fragmented, atomistic text as one of several effects of that negation. Other aesthetic requirements arising from the spirit of the decadent no-sayer are "the sublime, the profound, the overwhelming" (*CW*, 167). These aesthetic effects are precisely that: effects only, effects made necessary by the absence of totality, nature, health. "Wagner's art is sick," Nietzsche says, because of the "problems he presents on stage—all of them problems of hysterics—the convulsive nature of his affects, his overexcited sensibility" (*CW*, 166). In the absence of Dionysian health and wholeness, aesthetic effects become the equivalent of stimulants on the nervous system, and the only artistic experiences available to the decadent are those resulting from such stimulation: "In his [Wagner's] art all the modern world requires most urgently is mixed in the most seductive manner: the three great *stimulantia* of the exhausted—

the *brutal*, the *artificial*, and the *innocent* (idiotic)" (*CW*, 166). Thus in Nietzsche's view Wagner's music—and all decadent art—is at best a series of separate, unconnected moments: "Wagner was unable to create from a totality; he had no choice, he had to make patchwork, 'motifs,' gestures" (*CW*, 177). Along these lines, Nietzsche praises the expansive Wagner as "our greatest *miniaturist* in music who crowds into the smallest space an infinity of sense and sweetness" (*CW*, 171). In fact, Nietzsche admires these qualities "to such an extent that afterward almost all other musicians seem too robust" (*CW*, 171). That Nietzsche can admire Wagner's beautiful fragments and consider the excessively robust unattractive illustrates how close Nietzsche himself is to the "Wagnerian" decadence he describes. He understood decadence because he had been through it and, as he says, recovered from it: "My greatest experience was a recovery. Wagner is merely one of my sicknesses" (*CW*, 155).

In Nietzsche's vocabulary, *decadent* and *modern* are often used synonymously, so it would be incorrect, within a Nietzschean context, to say that Nietzsche recovered from decadence to modernity. But surely Nietzsche embodies the iconoclastic spirit of modernity as few nineteenth-century writers do; for this reason he is a model figure of transition who allows us to see with some clarity modernity emerging *from* decadence as an opposition *to* decadence. Both the negative elements of decadence (Schopenhauerean pessimism, negation of life, sickliness) and the "positive," compensatory elements (redemptive idealism, aesthetic sublimation, refined artificiality) are denied by Nietzsche in favor of his new Dionysianism. But the clearest instance of Nietzsche's modernity (and the word *modernity* need not be qualified here) is his rejection of Christian metaphysics and morality, which, we recall, he equates with the spirit of decadence. On this subject Nietzsche does not hesitate to use the word *no*, but the syllable in the mouth of Dionysian man is different from the decadent's negative:

> I know the pleasure in destroying to a degree that accords with my powers to destroy—in both respects I obey my Dionysian nature which does not know how to separate doing No from saying Yes. I am the first immoralist: that makes me the annihilator *par excellence*. . . .
>
> Fundamentally my term *immoralist* involves two negations. For one, I negate a type of man that has so far been considered supreme: the good, the benevolent, the beneficent. And then I negate a type of morality that has become prevalent and predominant as morality itself—the morality of decadence, or, more concretely, *Christian* morality. It would be permissible to

> consider the second contradiction the more decisive one, since I take the overestimation of goodness and benevolence on a large scale for a consequence of decadence, for a symptom of weakness, irreconcilable with an ascending, Yes-saying life: negating *and destroying* are conditions of saying Yes. (*EH,* 327, 328)

In this context, modern man is an immoralist, not because he is immoral, but because he *overcomes* morality and sees that it is based on false or mendacious suppositions about human existence. Cutting through the lies (as Nietzsche puts it [*EH,* 326]) of Christian metaphysics in order to examine the problematic nature of the human condition more honestly is one of the basic intellectual programs of modernism, one that André Gide, for example, pursued in earnest, and it is strikingly unlike the programs of decadence. The decadent is merely inquisitive, but not questioning; he may be curious, but not searching; and he can only be intrigued by the human condition, never disturbed. Even though the decadent hero of the nineteenth century is the ancestor of the intellectual hero of the twentieth, there is a gap between them that Nietzsche bridges so that others may cross the divide.

When Gide made the passage from decadence to modernity, his transition in many ways paralleled Nietzsche's. Both revolted against the severe moral constraints of Protestant Christianity, both employed the metaphors of sickness and health in detailing that revolt (indeed, both experienced sickness in youth and so learned the value of health), and both described artificiality and contrivance—in art and life—while endorsing a return to naturalness and spontaneity. Wallace Fowlie cautions against citing Nietzsche as *the* dominant influence on the young Gide; Rimbaud and Goethe are similar advocates of instinct and spontaneity whom Gide knew earlier and more deeply than he knew Nietzsche.[15] (Some similarities between the work of the late Nietzsche and the early Gide might be attributable to the common influence of Goethe.) Nevertheless, Jean Delay has convincingly shown that Gide had read Nietzsche earlier than Gide himself admitted.[16] Furthermore, Delay has argued that Gide assimilated enough of Nietzsche by the time he wrote *L'Immoraliste* to make a strong case for the philosopher's influence on that book. Indeed, the very title of the text, as Walter Kaufmann notes (see *CW,* 177 n. 1), is a specifically Nietzschean term. For all this probable influence, however, *L'Immoraliste* is still Gide's novel and not Nietzsche's, and as such the artistic reaction to decadence is different from the philosophical. "Whatever Nietzsche's literary genius, it was no literary aspiration that made him 'set up Dionysus over and against the Crucified.' Nietzsche was primarily a philosopher, Gide an artist."[17] In his response to decadence, Gide may have followed Nietzsche's map, but it led him over a different terrain. It remains to be shown what new aesthetic issues Gide encountered in making his passage to modernity over that terrain.

The example of Gide's *L'Immoraliste* presents us with an outgrowth of decadence different in kind from Joyce's response in the *Portrait.* As we have seen, Joyce's reaction to the aestheticism of Pater and the decadentism of Moore is muted with irony, but the *Portrait* remains, nonetheless, a continuation or development of an earlier aesthetic. In the context of Joyce, modernism takes on a certain thematic coloration traceable to the decadent focus on artistic and erudite subject matter. This in combination with Joyce's stylistic innovations results in a variety of modernism characterized by both a thematics and a poetics of complexity. That is, complexity takes on aesthetic value, and comes to be valued by readers, just as "beauty" or "the sublime" had been valued in the past. If this modernist sense of complexity cannot be seen as *directly* derived from Joyce's decadent/aesthetic precursors, neither can it be regarded as an oppositional or negative reaction to them. In making a new type of fiction, Joyce turned toward Pater and Moore, not away from them. Gide, on the other hand, follows the scenario described by Nietzsche in reacting to decadence and setting off in a new direction. More emphatically than did Joyce, Gide reminds us that modern art is something new, and made in the spirit of newness. Decadence likewise recognizes modernity as newness, but to the decadent mind it is a negative newness that threatens the high culture of the past. Thus the decadent responds to modernity by seeking refuge in earlier forms of artistic expression, and his refuge is made more secure the more erudite and artificial his tastes become. This attitude is completely rejected in *L'Immoraliste,* and not simply at the thematic level. In more than one way Gide's text gives meaning to modernity as a form of antidecadence, a negation of negation, a rejection of an earlier aesthetic stance.

Gide's rejection of decadence is significant because of his earlier affiliation with writers associated with symbolism, notably Mallarmé, who incorporated a deep sense of decadence into his poetry. Indeed, in the early nineties Gide showed signs of continuing in the same general direction as his symbolist forebears. His first book, *Les Cahiers d'André Walter* (1891), is a lyrical and introspective text whose dual themes of mysticism and eroticism are exercised against the biographical background of Gide's love for his cousin Madeleine. Adolescent struggles of spirit and flesh are in general unremarkable in literature, but *André Walter* involved enough use of symbol and myth to arouse Mallarmé's interest, and Gide was admitted to the Tuesday evening sessions at the poet's home. In 1891 Gide also met Oscar Wilde, who is widely regarded as the model for the hedonist Menalque who appears in both *Les Nourritures terrestres* (1897) and *L'Immoraliste.* These two biographical facts are singled out to illustrate Gide's affiliation with two very different literary sensibilities, and the differences become especially evident when we focus on the topic of decadence. The meaning of decadence when applied to Mallarmé is quite different from the decadence of Wilde. As we have seen, *The Picture of Dorian Gray* is only incidentally related to decadence, as the real subject of that work is hedonistic degradation. Mallarmé's decadence is allied more closely to the intellect than to the senses, being a Schopenhauerean rejection of life and despair over the imminence of death.[18] At the outset of his career, Gide is situated nearer the decadence of Mallarmé, but then moves toward the "decadence" of Wilde in the mid- and late nineties, significantly modifying that "decadence" in the process. Gide does not simply shift from the intellectual decadence of Mallarmé to the sensual degradation of Wilde; he transforms the idea of degradation into a type of immorality that is not self-destructive but self-defining.

In making this transition, Gide moves from sickness to health, metaphorically equivalent to a passage from decadence to modernity. Passages from the *Journal* clearly indicate Gide's awareness of decadence as a starting point, as he meditates on the value of sickness. Addressing "l'utilité de la maladie," Gide notes that ill health encourages intellectual unrest, and that the greatest philosophers and artists have achieved their greatness not in spite of illness but because of it.[19] In this, Gide echoes the Goncourt brothers' decadent formula that the sick man is the superior man, and that illness is a source of genius. And like the Goncourts, the Gide of the early *Journal* notes a connection between sickliness and the creation of unusual and particularly exquisite beauty: "By suppressing the puny [des malingres], you suppress the rare variety—a well-known fact in botany or at least in *floriculture:* the most beautiful flowers often being produced by apparently puny plants."[20] The sensibility here is clearly decadent, but there is another aspect of Gide's attitude toward sickliness that is not at all like the typical nineteenth-century notion of the alliance of illness and art. Gide's insistence on *unrest*—"La maladie source d'inquiétude"—introduces a paradoxical element of vigor that is missing from the Goncourt brothers' idea of decadence.[21] "Ill health offers man a new restlessness that he is called on to legitimize,"[22] Gide says, and the statement is the beginning of the rejection of the decadent attitude. In Gide's view, sickness creates an occasion that calls the self into question, something rather more complicated that the simple assurance of superiority that the Goncourts found in their own illnesses. Such sickness as the Goncourts cultivated legitimized nothing more than a withdrawal from life. The attitude toward illness detailed in Gide's early *Journal,* on the other hand, introduces a dynamic element into an idea conventionally associated with decadence; as such it promises an eventual removal from decadence.

The publication of *Les Nourritures terrestres* in 1897 made Gide's break with the decadent sensibility complete, for the work is an exuberant assertion of naturalness and healthful sensuality. Gide's 1927 introduction to the book states as much: "I wrote this book at a time when our literature was terribly imbued with a close and artificial atmosphere, and it seemed to me urgent that it should be brought down to earth once more and step again with bare feet simply on the common ground."[23] *Les Nourritures terrestres,* however, does not illustrate so well as *L'Immoraliste* the *process* of transition from artificiality to spontaneity, from sickness to health, from a kind of decadence to something new and modern. In *Les Nourritures terrestre,* the rejection of decadence and sickly artificiality is an accomplished fact. The narrator of *Les Nourritures* announces at the outset of the book that he has not come by his newfound sense of freedom and instinctual delight in the real world without a struggle, but the details of the process are not elaborated: "While other people were publishing or working, I, on the contrary, devoted three years of travel to forgetting all that I had learned with my head. This unlearning ["désinstruction"] was slow and difficult; it was of more use to me than all the learning imposed by men, and was really the beginning of an education."[24] *L'Immoraliste* may be read as the narrative of the process of *désinstruction* leading to liberation that *Les Nourritures* merely alludes to in passing. Moreover, the fact that *L'Immoraliste* is a narrative makes the later work the logical text to discuss as an illustration of the interaction of decadence and modernity in the context of the novel. *Les Nourritures terrestre* is a generically undefinable Nietzschean dithyramb[25] that bears little, if any, resemblance to the form of the novel. *L'Immoraliste* is at least a *récit* if not a *roman,* and the return to narrative is one of several indications that Gide has put the aesthetic of decadence behind him.

L'Immoraliste, then, is an antidecadent text in both its thematics and its poetics. It must be understood, however, that a complexity of response underlies the term *antidecadent,* as was the case with Nietzsche. Gide does not reject all of decadence outright; instead, he selects from, qualifies, and ultimately transvalues certain elements customarily regarded as decadent. The most obvious evidence of this assertion at the thematic level involves the action of the hero, Michel. At the beginning of the narrative he is a sickly academic who has rejected life for ancient ruins and rare books. He is himself the author of an erudite text entitled *Essai sur les cultes phrygiens,* published under his father's name (26).[26] Michel also subordinates himself to his father even in his marriage: "I had married her [Marceline] without loving her, mostly to please my father who, on his deathbed, was wracked by the thought of leaving me alone" (8). ["Je l'avais épousée sans amour, beaucoup pour complaire à mon père, qui, mourant, s'inquiétait de me laisser seul" (24).] His wife Marceline is at first merely a "camarade" (30), and the marriage remains unconsummated for some time. The honeymoon trip to northern Africa is little more than an archaeological excursion: Michel wishes to visit the site of ancient Carthage and several Roman ruins (31). During the course of the honeymoon trip Michel becomes extremely ill; he coughs blood profusely and resigns himself to death: "I was exhausted. I simply let myself go.—'After all, what did life have in store for me? I worked to the end, did my duty resolutely, devotedly. The rest . . . what does it matter?' I thought . . ." (19). ["J'étais las. Je m'abandonnai, simplement.—'Après tout, que m'offrirait la vie? J'avais bien travaillé jusqu'au bout, fait résolument et passionnément mon devoir. Le reste . . . ah! que m'importe?' pensais-je . . ." (36).] Through all this run several clearly identifiable decadent strains: the fascination with earlier decadent civilizations; the replacement of real life by artifice and erudition; the acceptance of illness; and the suggestion of homosexuality.

This last theme becomes more pronounced as the novel progresses. When Marceline takes Michel to Biskra he is near death; she gradually nurses him back to health, but it is only partially because of Marceline's ministrations that Michel recovers. Michel's return to health is paralleled by his growing interest in the Arab boys whom Marceline invites to their lodgings. The hero's attraction to the Arab boy Bachir is central to the development of health and homosexuality as parallel themes:

> The next day, Bachir returned. He sat down as he had before, took out his knife, and in trying to whittle a hard piece of wood stuck the blade into his thumb. I shuddered, but he only laughed, holding up the shiny cut and happily watching the blood run out of it. When he laughed, he showed his brilliant white teeth, then licked the wound with delight; his tongue was pink as a cat's. How healthy he was! That was what beguiled me about him: health. The health of that little body was beautiful. (24)

> [Le lendemain, Bachir revint. Il s'assit comme l'avant-veille, sortit son couteau, voulut tailler un bois trop dur, et fit si bien qu'il s'enfonça la lame dans le pouce. J'eus un frisson d'horreur. Il en rit, montra la coupure brillante et s'amusa de voir couler son sang. Quand il riait, il découvrait des dents très blanches; il lécha plaisamment sa blessure; sa langue était rose comme celle d'un chat. Ah! qu'il se portrait bien! C'était là ce dont je m'éprenais en lui: la santé. La santé de ce petit corps était belle. (43–43).]

The phallic image of the cut thumb is followed in the next paragraph by a description of a game of marbles that figuratively signifies homosexual interplay:

> The next day, he brought marbles. He wanted me to play with him. Marceline was out; she would have stopped me. I hesitated, looked at Bachir; the child grabbed my arm, thrust the marbles into my hand, forced me. I soon began to wheeze from bending over, but tried to play all the same. Bachir's pleasure enchanted me. At last I could bear no more. I was covered with sweat. (24)

> [Le jour suivant, il apporta des billes. Il voulut me faire jouer. Marceline n'était pas là; elle m'eût retenu. J'hésitai, regardai Bachir; le petit me saisit le bras, me mit les billes dans la main, me força. Je m'essoufflais beaucoup à me baisser, mais j'essayai de jouer quand même. Le plaisir de Bachir me charmait. Enfin je n'en pus plus. J'étais en nage. (43)]

It is on this episode that the text pivots. Michel, exhausted from playing with Bachir, suffers a hemorrhage that seems a final expulsion of sickness from the body: "[I]t was a thick, hideous clot I spat onto the floor with disgust" (25) ["[C]'était un gros affreux caillot que je crachai par terre avec dégoût" (43–44)]. Michel examines the clot of blood and experiences a sudden epiphany: "I stared at it. The blood was ugly, blackish—something slimy hideous. I thought of Bachir's beautiful, quick-flowing blood. And suddenly I was seized by a desire, a craving, something wilder, more imperious than I had ever felt before: to live!" (25). ["Je regardai. C'était un vilain sang presque noir, quelque chose de gluant, d'épouvantable. Je songeai au beau sang rutilant de Bachir. Et soudain me prit un désir, une envie, quelque chose de plus furieux, de plus impérieux que tout ce que j'avais ressenti jusqu'alors: vivre!" (44).] With this exclamation the sense of decadence in the novel begins to recede, and a theme that in earlier fiction had been treated in the dual context of sickness and artificiality is associated with health and naturalness. The theme of homosexuality, while not explicit in *L'Immoraliste,* is implied by both the action and the imagery at work in the novel. The very end of the novel states the theme in language requiring the last effort of interpretation (213–14), and what is significant is that homosexuality is suddenly a subject that is *outside* the realm of decadence.

From that pivotal point in the text—Michel's "vivre!"—several elements signal a thoroughgoing opposition to the decadent frame of mind. For example, Michel's first excursion away from the sickbed is not to view the ruins of some ancient civilization, but to walk in a garden among palm trees along a path of pink clay, "a plastic soil on which bare feet leave their imprint" (39) ["un sol plastique où les pieds nus restent inscrits" (60)]. At first he makes these excursions with Marceline, but soon ventures out alone and acquaints himself with the young Arab goatherds who play flutes and drink wine made from the sap of palm trees (62–63). Nothing could be further from the idea of decadence than this pastoral idyll. Significantly, Michel is unable to resume his intellectual pursuits, with one exception: he rereads Theocritus and discovers that the pastoral pleasures of the mythic past are available to him in the present (72–73). In general, however, Michel finds his education an encumbrance: "My erudition, which awakened at each step, encumbered me, frustrating my joy" (50). ["Mon érudition, qui s'éveillait à chaque pas, m'encombrait, empêchant ma joie" (73)]. What had once been the decadent's obsessive delight—his study of past cultures—becomes an impediment to pleasure: "When . . . I tried to resume my studies, to immerse myself once more in the detailed inspection of the past, I found that something had if not suppressed at least altered my enjoyment of it: the sense of the present" (49). ["Quand . . . je voulus reprendre mes études, me replonger comme jadis dans l'examen minutieux du passé, je découvris que quelque chose en avait, pour moi, sinon supprimé, du moins modifié le goût; c'était le sentiment du présent" (72).] When Michel's health returns completely, however, he returns to academe one last time, but he does so mainly to disseminate his new philosophy of life through a series of lectures. His first lecture is about the decline of Latin civilization, one of the main topics of decadence. But unlike the decadent, Michel has no appreciation of the artistic and sexual refinements a deliquescent culture affords; on the contrary, such decay is not found to be refined or deliquescent at all:

> Discussing the decline of Latin civilization, I described artistic culture as rising like a secretion to the surface of a people, at first a symptom of plethora, the superabundance of health, then immediately hardening, calcifying, opposing any true contact of the mind with nature, concealing beneath the persistent appearance of life the diminution of life, forming a rind in which the hindered spirit languishes, withers and dies. Finally, carrying my notion to its conclusion, I said that Culture, born of life, ultimately kills life. (92–93)

> [A propos de l'extrême civilisation latine, je peignais la culture artistique, montant à fleur de peuple, à la manière d'une sécrétion, qui d'abord indique pléthore, surabondance de santé, puis aussitôt se fige, durcit, s'oppose à tout parfait contact de l'esprit avec la nature, cache sous l'apparence persistante de la vie la diminution de la vie, forme gaine où l'esprit gêné languit et bientôt s'étiole, puis meurt. Enfin, poussant à bout ma pensée, je disais la Culture, née de la vie, tuant la vie. (126–27)]

The metaphor comparing culture to a hard shell or rind ("gaine") that inhibits the spirit's contact with nature echoes an earlier passage in which Michel expresses the desire for *désinstruction.* He imagines a more natural, primal man within himself that his erudite education has crusted over: "And I had already glimpsed him, faint, obscured by their encrustations, but all the more valuable, all the more urgent. I scorned henceforth that secondary, learned being whom education had pasted over him. Such husks must be stripped away" (51). ["Et il m'apparaissait déjà, grâce aux surcharges, plus fruste et difficile à découvrir, mais d'autant plus utile à découvrir et valeureux. Je méprisai dès lors cet être secondaire, appris, que l'instruction avait dessiné par-dessus. Il fallait secouer ces surcharges" (74).] This metaphor is followed by another: "And I would compare myself to a palimpsest; I shared the thrill of the scholar who beneath more recent script discovers, on the same paper, an infinitely more precious ancient text" (51). ["Et je me comparais aux palimpsestes; je goûtais la joie du savant, qui, sous les écritures plus récentes, découvre sur un même papier un texte très ancien infiniment plus précieux (74).] These passages are perhaps the clearest repudiation of the decadent mentality in the text. The last quotation, moreover, suggests a relationship between the text of *L'Immoraliste* and the idea of decadence that goes beyond mere thematic preoccupation. The metaphor comparing the self to a palimpsest under which some earlier, more authentic text lies, obscured by the factitious text of excessive culture, is manifested at the structural level as well, affecting the form of the work as a whole.

As we have seen, the idea of decadence usually implies a heightened sense of textuality at the expense of narrative unity. Bourget's theory of decadence, which Nietzsche echoes, indicates a progressively reductive focus on the literary work as a whole, with greater stylistic concentration coming to rest on individual units of the text—and less concentration on the totality of the text, on the relationship of individual units to one another. We have seen that Flaubert's *Salammbô* is so stylistically concentrated or dense as to be virtually opaque: we are faced with a text first and a story second; a narrative exists, but the language of the text diverts our interest from it. In Huysmans's *A Rebours,* the idea of decadence is so at odds with the operation of the conventional narrative that the text is free to indulge in itself *as text* and not as an effort toward some narrative end. At the philosophical level, the concept of decadence by its very nature is opposed to any narrative projection through time. Except for the isolated instance of *décadisme* (with its avant-garde implications), decadence is without futurity: whatever is beyond decadence is no longer decadence. In formalist terms, a decadent novel sacrifices or severely limits the development of character. Gide's *L'Immoraliste* presents us with a character who *does* develop, who is situated within the context of narrative. Thus, Michel's recovery of health involves more than a repudiation of one of the thematic aspects of decadence: the development of character requires a narrative, and the fact of the narrative removes us from the structural and textual implications of decadence. *L'Immoraliste,* in fact, calls the very idea of a "text" into question. In comparing the self to a palimpsest, Michel rejects the erudite, factitious text of culture for another text, one that is ancient, more precious—nearer to some mythic origin, a natural text like the "inscriptions" (*inscrits*) of bare feet on the earth that Michel discovers when he leaves his sickbed. The whole of *L'Immoraliste,* in fact, questions the idea of textuality by its very form. The work is a *récit* (15), and its status as a *récit* has a dual relationship to the denial of decadence. First, as *récit* the work is by definition a tale or narrative; second, it is a *récit* that is recited, a spoken narrative. Writing is one of the artificial encrustations of culture that Michel breaks out of and denies. Michel's story is spoken, introduced by the words "Michel dit" (17). At this point the text is presented to the reader as if it were an exact *transcription* of Michel's oral—and natural—*récit.*

This presentation, ironically, is nevertheless an artifice: the masquerading of *écriture* as *parole.* But the artifice is not Michel's; instead, it is the artifice of the unnamed friend who, in the company of two of Michel's other friends, Denis and Daniel, listens to Michel's story underneath the clear night sky of "Sidi b. M." This unnamed friend then puts the *récit* on paper as part of an urgent plea to his brother, who has some position of power, to find an occupation for Michel: such strength and intelligence, the writer feels, should be put to use in the service, perhaps, of the state. There are few clues to the identity of this anonymous friend with the remarkable talent for transcription. Together with Denis, Daniel, and Michel, he has entered into a pact: if one friend calls for help, the other three must come to his aid. Allusions to the past suggest that the friendship among the four men developed at school and that they shared similar intellectual interests, with Michel being the most learned and earnest of the four. One passage, however, indicates a striking similarity between the anonymous writer and Michel. Michel, we recall, had to tend to his dying father before he could, in effect, begin his own life. The unnamed transcriber of Michel's narrative reminds his brother that he, too, had to care for his sick father while others were free to pursue their own lives: "I, as you know, was obliged to remain at our father's bedside" (4). ["[M]oi retenu, tu le sais, auprès de notre père malade" (17).] The similarity of the two events stands out all the more since the death of Michel's father is mentioned at the outset of the *récit.* The unnamed writer may therefore be seen as a double of the teller, as writing itself is often imagined as the derivative double of speech. The conception of writing as an artifice inferior to the more natural and original phenomenon of speech has a long history, beginning at least as early as Plato's *Phaedrus* and continuing through the works of Rousseau.[27] *L'Immoraliste* contributes to the tradition that holds the spoken word above the written word, contrasting the natural utterance of language to its "unnatural" inscription. The unnamed writer, it is clear, is disconcerted by Michel the teller, who has deliberately removed himself from writing as part of a program to regain health and authenticity, to find the lost, original man in himself. *L'Immoraliste* questions *écriture* as it questions culture, convention, artifice. In this sense Gide's rejection of decadence is complete, since decadence necessarily embraces *écriture* as a means of exercising artifice. At the end of *L'Immoraliste,* Michel voices his disdain for those who write, and endorses the art of those who speak—and sing—of things that are beautiful because they are *natural:*

> A land liberated from works of art. I despise those who can acknowledge beauty only when it's already transcribed, interpreted. One thing admirable about the Arabs: they live their art, they sing and scatter it from day to day; they don't cling to it, they don't embalm it in *works*. Which is the cause and the effect of the absence of great artists. I have always believed the great artists are the ones who dare *entitle to beauty* things so natural that when they're seen afterward people say: Why did I never realize before that this too was beautiful? . . . (158–59)

> [Terre en vacance d'oeuvres d'art. Je méprise ceux qui ne savent reconnaître la beauté que transcrite déjà et toute interprétée. Le peuple arabe a ceci d'admirable que son art, il le vit, il le chante et le dissipe au jour le jour; il ne le fixe point et ne l'embaume en aucune oeuvre. C'est la cause et l'effet de l'absence de grands artistes. J'ai toujours cru les grands artistes ceux qui osent donner droit de beauté à des choses si naturelles qu'elles font dire après à qui les voit: "Comment n'avais-je pas compris jusqu'alors que cela aussi était beau? . . . (200)]

Despite the celebration of the natural and uncultivated beauty of the primitive that this passage evokes, it would be a mistake to argue that Gide's reaction to decadence is simply a recrustation of romanticism. Even though Gide indulges in a Rousseauistic suspicion of the various manifestations of education and culture, especially writing, such neoromanticism is only one aspect of *L'Immoraliste.* In other ways the work is as removed from romanticism as it is from the artificialities of decadence. Throughout the narrative, a sense of hesitancy and uncertainty arises as Michel discovers his new self and begins his revolt against his earlier way of life. Michel is not at all certain that his program of "immorality"—his spontaneous experimentation with forbidden elements of society—is the best course of action. Is he or is he not responsible for the death of Marceline, who in nursing him back to health contracts his disease and dies? Does he or does he not prefer the Arab boy with whom he lives to the prostitute who is the boy's sister? At the end of *L'Immoraliste,* Michel is still questioning his actions and attitudes, and ruminating upon the moral issues that arise when human beings are confronted with total freedom. The absence of any external or objective criteria for human conduct is clear enough in *L'Immoraliste,* but what is to serve in place of this absence is not so clear. This combination of lucidity and uncertainty has more to do with modernism than romanticism, and thus *L'Immoraliste,* however antidecadent and neoromantic it may appear, is ultimately a modern novel.

By calling *L'Immoraliste* a modern novel, we set up the text against a background of decadence and use that background to delimit the meaning of modernism, to some degree. The same procedure applies to Joyce's *Portrait* as well, where the modernity of the work is likewise gauged against the text's relationship to literary decadence. Yet how is this possible? After all, a different relationship to decadence has been demonstrated in each case, and one may wonder how modernity follows from such dissimilar responses to decadent literature. The authors of both texts, however, are engaged in *distancing* themselves from decadence, and the process makes up the main mechanism of transition. Joyce's *Portrait* is distanced from the brief tradition of decadent aestheticism by means of irony, and we have only to contrast Edward Dayne and Stephen Dedalus to get a measure of that distance. Gide's *L'Immoraliste* is removed from decadence both philosophically and technically, as the development of Michel manifests, a process made abundantly clear when that character is compared to an unmitigated decadent such as Des Esseintes. The argument, then, is that modernity takes shape partly because certain writers of the early twentieth century distanced themselves from decadence in special ways, and that the modern novel assumes significantly different forms in the English and French traditions because of differences in the experience of decadence in each tradition. A quality of high artifice and narrative density appears in the modern novel as it developed in England and America that is often absent from the modern novel in France, with its strong tradition of the lucid, straightforward *récit.* In a sense, some characteristics of the modern novel in English-speaking countries—narrative discontinuity, heightened description, erudite allusiveness—had already had their day in France in the form of *le style de décadence.* This is not to say that the decadent style described by Bourget and the modernist style exercised by Joyce are equivalent, but similarities do exist. The absence of anything like *le style de décadence* in the richly realistic nineteenth-century English novel means at least two things: that the reaction to realism was retarded in a way that it was not in France, and that a negative reaction to decadent *écriture* really did not occur in English and American manifestations of the modern novel. A work like *Nightwood* (1937) by Djuna Barnes, for example, with its congested narrative, its neurasthenic characters, and its displays of bizarre erudition, is an obvious instance of the presence of decadent elements in continental American fiction some fifty years after their appearance in France. On the other hand, Céline's *Voyage au bout de la nuit* (1932) presents us with a more energetic "immoralist" than Gide's Michel, but an immoralist nonetheless, and Céline's novel is cast in the form of a "spoken" narrative that has considerable precedence in Gide's antidecadent *récit* thirty years earlier. Thus, we can see two quite different responses to decadence perpetuated in fiction well into the twentieth century. To say that Joyce and Gide were influential is nothing new, but by contrasting their work in relation to decadence, we can see the influence behind the influence, tradition in transition, and out of this, modernity emerging.

7

The Decline of Decadence

In 1896, Max Beerbohm published *The Happy Hypocrite,* a brief fable set in the time of Regency London but suggestive of Beerbohm's own Edwardian era as well. Lord George Hell is the happy hypocrite of the title, a thirty-five-year-old libertine whose decadence is in the hedonistic mold of "Caligula, with a dash of John Falstaff" (8).[1] He is also a gambler and a dandy, his delight in fine clothing being such "that he used to dress on week-days quite as gorgeously as good people dress on Sundays" (5). One night he attends the theater with his corrupt Italian mistress la Gambogi, but falls in love with the innocent actress Jenny Mere, who makes her debut in an oriental "operette" called *The Fair Captive of Samarcand.* Lord George goes backstage and proposes to the sixteen-year-old Miss Mere on the spot. She rejects him, however, because his face is the visible emblem of his inner corruption, and Jenny Mere can only love the pure of face: "I can never be the wife of any man whose face is not saintly," she says (19). Lord George remedies this problem by having a famous mask-maker fit him with a new face of wax that conveys the appropriate impression of saintliness and beauty. Thus equipped, he leaves the corrupt city for the innocent countryside and just happens to cross paths with Miss Mere, who immediately falls in love with him, or rather, with his saintly appearance (not knowing that he is that same George Hell she only recently rejected). Lord George repeats the proposal, is accepted, and the two are married, Lord George signing the name "George Heaven" (48) on the marriage license. A changed man, the wealthy aristocrat instructs his lawyer to give away his money, mainly to those made needy by Lord George earlier when he cheated them at cards. "George Heaven" is all set to live the simple life with his beloved Jenny when La Gambogi somehow finds him and complains of his neglect. When she discovers that he is married, she accepts the turn of events readily enough, but asks that he remove the mask so she can see the face of her former lover one last time. Lord George refuses. All of this baffles poor innocent Jenny, who is quite astounded to see her husband's former mistress ripping a waxen mask from his face. To La Gambogi's surprise, the face of Lord George is identical to the mask she has just removed: "Line for line, feature for feature, it was the same. 'Twas a saint's face" (62). Lord George does not know that his face has changed until he sees it reflected in the eyes of Jenny, who forgives the deception, still ignorant of the real reason for the mask: "I am not angry. 'Twas well that you veiled from me the full glory of your face, for indeed I was not worthy to behold it too soon" (63). In the end, the happy hypocrite is "happier than he had ever been" (63).

This little fable, subtitled "A Fairy Tale for Tired Men," is less saccharine than it seems when it is read for what it is: a parody of *The Picture of Dorian Gray* that reverses the moralistic plot of Wilde's novel and rewards deception and corruption with an innocent young thing. It is true that Lord George repents of his past life, but so does Dorian Gray at one point, except that the burden of his sins is so great that he is destroyed by them anyway. The moment Lord George is fitted with his new mask, his corrupt past melts away, as though Beerbohm were taking Wilde's artistic doctrine of "The Truth of Masks" as literally as possible: there is no difference whatsoever between reality and appearance, or life and art. Moreover, evil is made good by the skill of a clever artisan—no moral anguish or religious conversion is necessary. The irony at the end of the story is that Jenny, really a perfect model of innocent goodness, thinks of herself as having been unworthy of the corrupt lord until the moment his "true" face appears: "Let the time of my probation be over. Kiss me with your own lips" (63). Having tired of the taste of wax, now the lovers will kiss in earnest, and Beerbohm ends with the reminder that this "ideal" love between a thirty-five-year-old libertine and a sixteen-year-old naïf is hardly distinguishable from pedophilia: "So he took her in his arms, as though she had been a little child, and kissed her with his own lips" (63). Indeed, the romance of George Hell and Jenny Mere is partly Beerbohm's own fantasy-romance with an actress named Cissie Loftus. S. N. Behrman says that "she was a little girl of sixteen" when Beerbohm fell in love with her, and that he called her "Mistress Mere" because she was "a mere child."[2]

Beerbohm's reverse parody of Wilde in *The Happy Hypocrite* suggests a kind of moral weightlessness that turns good and evil into extremely simple conventions. Innocence and corruption are little more than contrary modes of public behavior that one may simply choose at will with a minimum of emotional or moral involvement. It is to the advantage of the happy hypocrite that he put off corruption and put on innocence, so that is what he does: he exchanges one set of moral conventions for the other. In this sense, Beerbohm's fable of *The Happy Hypocrite* can be read as a more general fable of hypocrisy itself, as literary decadence enters a new phase at the end of the century. Even the technique of parody is allied with hypocrisy in one sense, because parody, too, leads a double life, masking one text with another. The face of *Dorian Gray* must show through the mask of *The Happy Hypocrite,* otherwise the parody does not work. The moral dualism that is hypocrisy and the artistic dualism that is parody both rely on the clarity of the conventions that each takes as its object. Part of what I am calling the decline of decadence in fiction takes parody as its structure and hypocrisy as its subject. No doubt this decline is allied in some way with the triumph of the bourgeois world that the aristocratic decadent finds so distasteful. Paradoxically, at the end of the century, the decadent sensibility is displaced from the realm of the aristocrat to that of the common man. Beerbohm's fable is, in part, evidence of this trend. Lord George abandons aristocratic corruption for something like bourgeois respectability, a change not only of morals but of class, and hypocrisy is the means whereby this change comes about. The element of degradation or corruption in Beerbohm's story is treated with irony (the "corrupt" George Hell is a gambler; the "innocent" George Heaven is a pedophile), but decadence here is clearly allied with hypocrisy.

This alliance is evidence of significant changes in the sociology of literary culture in the late nineteenth century. Max Beerbohm wrote his stories and essays for the popular press of the Edwardian era, for a new type of literary magazine that aimed for a style of wit and humor just shy of the more overt satire of the anti-aesthetic *Punch.* Perhaps as a result of this broader audience, the meaning of decadence modulates away from aestheticism proper and toward improper aestheticism. In Beerbohm, "decadence" is mainly misbehavior, transgression of gentlemanly, Edwardian codes that are only made to be violated. This sense of decadence as moral transgression (which may be slight, as in Beerbohm, or excessive, as in Mirbeau) corresponds to an important sociological change in nineteenth-century society, namely, the waning of aristocratic influence. When decadence was the exclusive province of the aristocracy, or when it was represented as such, corruption in whatever form was a private affair. Des Esseintes, for example, is completely isolated from society and his behavior is intended only to gratify his jaded tastes, not to shock the moralistic onlooker. When decadence enters bourgeois society, an inevitable quality of hypocrisy emerges. Des Esseintes had no public life, no contact with the bourgeois world of politics, business, religion. For decadence to survive in the bourgeois world, a radical polarity must develop between the private pursuit of aesthetic and hedonistic refinements and the public maintenance of bourgeois respectability.

The literary effect of this new "bourgeois" decadence is always parodic, whether by accident or design. Pierre Bourdieu argues that an "automatic *effect of parody*" is achieved anytime a work from the past is presented in the context of a new "cultural field." Although Bourdieu speaks here of an actual presentation of an earlier work (e.g., the performance of a forgotten play before a contemporary audience), he does so to make the point that anytime an earlier form of artistic expression is repeated "in a sociologically non-congruent context" it is bound to appear "incongruous or even absurd." This is so because the artistic conventions that once gave the work its life are much more perceptible and their arbitrary nature more obvious.[3] Although most decadent writers of the 1880s and many of those in the 1890s were self-conscious about the conventions they employed, the literary effect falls just short of parody: not even excess is exaggeration. Huysmans knew what he was doing when he had his character Des Esseintes strike the pose of the dandified aesthete. Now we will see what decadence looks like when the pose is held a little too long.

Octave Mirbeau was born the same year as Huysmans (1848), but *Le Jardin des supplices* (translated as *Torture Garden,* 1931) was published in 1899, fifteen years after *A Rebours.* While I have argued that decadence as an aesthetic program extends well into the modernist period, as a Parisian fashion it does not. Considered from this local perspective, the span of fifteen years that separates Huysmans's novel from Mirbeau's is quite a long time. Had *Le Jardin des supplices* appeared in the 1880s, Mirbeau would be much easier to "place" in the brief history of French decadentism. Indeed, most critics have trouble situating the novel squarely in the decadent tradition. John R. Reed, for example, calls *Le Jardin des supplices* "a good example of a bad Decadent novel" that "may be read as a satire" or as "a species of parody."[4] Brian Stableford calls its "a key work of quasi-Decadent fantasy" that is "too full of righteous wrath to be reckoned properly neurasthenic." He also reads the novel as the last word in Baudelairean sinfulness, saying that Mirbeau's unnamed "anti-hero" is "a portrait of the Decadent in search of distraction to end all such portraits," and who "represents the true culmination of this particular aspect of the Decadent adventure. Afterwards, there really was nowhere else to go in search of intensity-through-sin."[5]

Reading *Le Jardin des supplices* as the extremity of excess or as the "Decadence of Decadence" is certainly defensible.[6] However, such a reading fails to take account of how thoroughly the literary landscape had changed in France in the 1890s. Indeed, the decade of the nineties witnessed profound shifts in attitude on the part of a number of writers affiliated with decadence. Jean Pierrot divides the change into two stages: "a wave of anarchist agitation" between 1890 and 1894, and the subsequent wave of official repression that led to the stern nationalism at the end of the century.[7] The anarchist stage follows logically from Baju's *décadisme,* but it differs from the earlier movement in that the writers associated with the anarchy of the 1890s were less interested in aesthetic matters or in the "psychology" of belatedness. Along with former members of the symbolist school (such as Verhaeren and Paul Adam), Mirbeau contributed articles on the political philosophy of anarchy to such journals as *L'En Dehors* and *Entretiens politiques et littéraires.* However, Pierrot cautions against taking this alliance of politics and literature as genuine evidence of active social involvement: "[T]he reasons for this sympathy with anarchism were much more intellectual than political. If some groups of young writers were favorably inclined to the movement, it was above all because they regarded it as providing a political equivalent of the individualism they were advocating in literature. They saw anarchy not as a popular movement but, on the contrary, as an aristocratic one" (252, 253). This observation is useful to an informed reading of Mirbeau. Despite all the criticism of nationalism and colonialism in *Le Jardin des supplices,* the book is not likely to be mistaken either for an endorsement of wholesale anarchistic reform or for the enlightened discourse of modernity. Actual amelioration of social wrongs seems the farthest thing from Mirbeau's mind, even though his satire of society is rhetorically intense. In fact, the satire is so completely an exercise in righteous indignation that it lacks moral force altogether.

The peculiar moral status of *Le Jardin des supplices* can perhaps be understood by thinking of Mirbeau as a representative figure of what might be called "the return to Zola." As we have seen, naturalism and decadence are divergent traditions after the Goncourt brothers. In fact, as a literary phenomenon in its own right, decadence did not really begin until Huysmans abandoned Zola's naturalist school for the decadent aestheticism represented by Des Esseintes. Mirbeau's decadentism was transformed by his anarchistic involvement in the early 1890s, and then further transformed by his return to Zola in the late 1890s, when he enlisted in the cause of Dreyfus. While Mirbeau's interest in the Dreyfus case was evidently earnest, his moral indignation was hardly as well grounded as Zola's. Mirbeau, in fact, had earlier gained a reputation as an anti-Semitic journalist, attacking the Rothschilds by name in the weekly newspaper *Les Grimaces,* where he also made France appear "the victim of speculators in league with the Jews, and accused his country of having made Judaism a state religion." However, in 1896, Mirbeau did a "political about-face" and became a Dreyfusard, attacking anti-semitism as vigorously as earlier he had promoted it.[8] A decadent Dreyfusard is, to say the least, a curiosity because of the contradiction involved in elitist literary leanings and humanitarian interests. By contrast, no contradiction is involved in Zola's opposition to anti-Semitism. His naturalism was always characterized, in part, by a sense of moral seriousness that makes his involvement with the Dreyfus affair perfectly consistent with his earlier literary practice. As a decadent, however, Mirbeau lacked the moral pedigree of a Médan naturalist. A decadent novel simply does not work as a platform for moral or political issues, no matter how well-meaning an author may be. Without question, in *Le Jardin des supplices,* Mirbeau takes appropriate moral positions against chauvinism, anti-Semitism, and colonialism. But in doing so he is merely miming the gestures of morality and ventriloquizing the rhetoric of reform. Mirbeau perhaps illustrates the thesis that a morality of decadence is not possible, but decadent morality is: that is, morality is decadent when it becomes purely a matter of style.

The Dreyfus affair is mentioned only once in *Le Jardin des supplices,* and then only as an example of the innate barbarism of outwardly civilized human beings (23).[9] The observation is made at a curious soirée where "novelists, poets, philosophers, and doctors" (15) are gathered to discuss the topic of murder over after-dinner drinks and cigars. The reference to the Dreyfus affair comes amid this broadly satirical attack on the hypocrisy of those with "cultivated minds and disciplined natures" (22). One of the dinner guests argues that only "peasants . . . are always inclined toward murder," and that this inclination has an outlet at carnival shooting galleries, where, for a sou, one can take aim at cardboard figures of human beings and indulge in the fantasy of actual murder:

> For, the little fellow of cardboard, sawdust, or wood which moves back and forth amid the scenery is no longer a toy to them, or a bit of lifeless material. Watching it pass back and forth, they unconsciously endow it with warm blood, sensitive nerves, thought. . . . They even go so far as to ascribe political and religious convictions to it, contrary to their own; accusing it of being a Jew, an Englishman, or a German, in order to add a particular hate to this general hatred of life, and thus augment the instinctive pleasure of killing by a personal vengeance, intimately relished. (22)

To refute the notion that this fantasy of murder is limited to the lower classes, another guest mentions a number of aristocratic distractions that partake of the same fantasy: "Fencing, dueling, violent sports, the abominable pigeon-shoot, bull fighting, the various manifestations of patriotism, hunting—everything which is in reality only a reversion to the period of old time barbarity" (22–23). This "philosopher" is thankful for these substitutes, and dreads the day when game vanishes "from our fields and our forests": "It is our safeguard and, after a fashion, our ransom. The day it finally disappears, it will not be long before we take its place, for the exquisite enjoyment of the 'cultivated minds.' The Dreyfus affair affords us an excellent example, and never, I believe, was the passion for murder and the joy of the man-hunt so thoroughly and cynically displayed" (23). In the first section of the novel, this theme is sounded again and again, as when a "scientist" argues: "We restrain the innate need of murder and attenuate physical violence by giving it a legalized outlet: industry, colonial trade, war, the hunt or anti-semitism, because it is dangerous to abandon oneself to it immoderately and outside the law" (17). The satire is clear, but at the same time it is complicated by the hypocrisy of the speaker: he criticizes the brutality of the state even as he is thankful for the "legalized outlets" for murder which the state affords.

All of the speakers in the opening section of *Le Jardin des supplices* freely accept that they are all assassins at heart and are grateful for the civilization that keeps their murderous instincts in check. The decadent longing for barbarism that Verlaine expressed in his sonnet "Langueur" is negated by Mirbeau: in his novel, there is no real difference between the refinements of civilization and the cruelties of barbarism. The desire for renewal, the infusion of new life into a decadent civilization, cannot take place if decadence and barbarism are conflated, or rather, if one is merely the public perversion of private desire. In this formulation, hypocrisy is the order of the day: bourgeois obedience to the law of the land is not incompatible with wholesale corruption. In fact, in Mirbeau's novel corruption is a positive asset to bourgeois respectability.

This satirical theme is made clear in the novel proper, presented in two sections titled "The Mission" and "The Garden." These sections compose an unnamed young poet's contribution to the evening's discussion of murder, which he presents in the form of a manuscript account of earlier political experiences. The poet comes to the group with impeccable decadent credentials. His father was a doctor whose combination of aesthetic and scientific sensibilities recalls the misogyny of Flaubert: "Art! art! Beauty! Do you know what it is? Well, my boy, it is a woman's abdomen, open and all bloody, with the hemostats in place!" (28). The poet has learned this lesson well, and professes a truly classical form of sadism when he says that "great assassins have always been formidable lovers. Their genetic powers equal their criminal powers. They love in the same way they kill! Murder is born of love, and love attains its greatest intensity in murder" (32). Schopenhauer's misogyny has also obtained comparable clarity in the poet's mind: "Woman possesses the cosmic force of destruction, like nature's. She is, in herself alone, all nature! Being the matrix of life, she is by that very fact the matrix of death—since it is from death that life is perpetually reborn, and since to annihilate death would be to kill life at its only fertile source" (35). These formulations are made prior to the poet's reading of his manuscript, so we are well aware of his standing as a decadent figure before his retrospective narrative begins. Even though the other speakers prepare us for the alignment of decadence and bourgeois respectability that the poet embodies in "The Mission," it is still surprising to see this character, who combines aestheticism and sadism with such clarity, as yet another hypocritical figure.

The manuscript the young poet reads is a confessional autobiography in two parts. The first part, "The Mission," tells of the young man's experiences in politics twelve years ago; the second part, "The Garden," concerns the exile made necessary by his political and personal failures: he is asked to go to Asia for two years to acquire "a new virginity" (73). In the first half of the novel, Mirbeau's satire of French politics is painted in broad strokes. The poet enters politics as an alternative to suicide, and runs for office on a single-issue agricultural platform: the production of beets (all the candidate knows about beets is that "you get sugar from them—and alcohol" [41]). His opponent, "one of the indisputable glories of politics," frankly admits that he is a thief: "'I've stolen! I've stolen!' he proclaimed in his professions of faith, his bill posters and confidential circulars" (42–43). This frank approach wins over the working classes. However, the beet-candidate is holding his own until he demands "the right to be virtuous, moral and honest," whereupon his supporters at a mass rally turn against him: "They rushed upon me, grasped me by the throat, and my body was lifted and tossed from hand to hand, like a bundle" (43). After this episode, the poet loses his government support, and when he confronts his friend Eugène Moritain, the cabinet minister who has sponsored him, he discovers that the real reason for his beet-campaign was to ensure the election of his opponent, whose advocacy of thievery makes him the kind of candidate the government really wants. The poet is outraged at first over the way he has been used, but then he is paid a handsome sum to keep his mouth shut, and spends "the following three days in the basest debauchery" (47).

The poet's political failure is mirrored by the success of his friend Moritain, who does not make the mistake of advocating virtue: "He aspired to power only for the material pleasures it could procure, and the money which clever men like he knew how to draw from muddy sources" (55). Moritain is "arrogant and servile according to circumstances and individuals"; he is also "grossly corrupt" and "liked by everyone" (58). However, because his career is entangled with that of his friend the poet, who is not so adept as he at turning corruption into a political asset, Moritain devises a scheme to get his potentially damaging friend out of the country for a while. He obtains government funds for a scientific expedition to Ceylon for the study of "embryology," with the hope of discovering "the protoplasmic *initium* of organized life, or something like that" (74). The poet knows no more about embryology than he does about beets, but he agrees to head the expedition, becoming overnight a "courageous pioneer of progress and a soldier of science" (79).

On the steamer to Ceylon the poet, traveling as a scientist, meets an assortment of European sportsmen who discuss, among other things, the practice of "civilizing" Africans by murdering them (95–96). He also meets and falls in love with a woman named Clara, who persuades the poet to abandon his scientific expedition to India in favor of a personal odyssey to China, a country that is said to be the antithesis of the barbarity of Europe: "In China life is free, joyous, complete, unconventional, unprejudiced, lawless . . . at least for us. No other limits to liberty than yourself . . . or to love, than the triumphant variety of your desire. Europe and its hypocritical, barbaric civilization is a lie. What else do you do there except lie. . . . You live attached in a cowardly fashion to moral and social conventions you despise, condemn, and know lack all foundation" (112). Mirbeau in this passage suggests that China offers the same sort of salvation for the decadent European that northern Africa offers for Gide's "immoralist" Michel, who experiences a neoromantic recovery of original, primary passion when he leaves the Continent. Mirbeau satirizes the typical French expectation of recovering from the sickness of civilization in the exotic Orient in two ways. First, he transposes the romantic pilgrimage to find a more original, authentic condition into the progressive, scientific expedition to discover the "primordial cell" of life in the "pelagic ooze" of India (74). Second, he turns the exotic Orient of French romantic tradition into the scene of the most extreme cruelty imaginable. Mirbeau presents the Orient in this way as a satire of that brand of literary colonialism that imposes its romantic vision of "primitivism" on Africa and Asia in the first place. When Clara and the poet arrive in Canton, what they see, and what Clara calls "Chinese," is essentially an exaggerated vision of the European tradition of decadence and sadism. Despite its "oriental" soil, the *Torture Garden* is overgrown with Baudelaire's flowers of evil and sickness.

This second part of the novel reveals that Clara, who seemed an innocent contrast to the boorish colonialists aboard the steamer, is a perverted monster who delights in witnessing the cruelest scenes of torture and execution. We recall the opening section of the novel, when the poet manages to shock the bourgeois "assassins" at the soirée with his extreme sadism, and now we see how he came by that attitude. The action of the second half of the novel is mainly a description of two closely related events. First, the poet accompanies Clara to a prison where well-to-do visitors, mostly women sporting embroidered gowns, fans, and parasols, feed the inmates rotten meat ("carcasses of all sorts: dead rats, drowned dogs, quartered deer and horses" [138]) which they buy from vendors who advertise the rottenness of their goods by exaggerating the implicit oxymoron of decadence itself: "You can find no better any place else. There is none rottener" (138). The second major event is the visit to a fantastic garden where prisoners are tortured to death amid all kinds of exotic flora. According to Clara, the Torture Garden has an "exquisite attraction" because of "the mingling of torture with horticulture, blood with flowers" (138). The aesthetic pleasure produced by the beauty of the flowers is the perfect complement to the torture that goes on there: "Think of what it must mean to a victim who is going to die under torture. Think how much the torture is multiplied in his flesh and his soul by all the splendor which surrounds him" (170–71).

The flowers themselves owe much to Huysmans's description of plants so bizarre they seem unnatural, although Mirbeau places more emphasis on two qualities Huysmans only touches on: sex and death. The sexual flora includes "the phalliform and vulvoid clusters of the most stupefying arumlilies" (166) and the "thalcitrum" plant, with its "ivory like sheath" in "the shape of a yoni." This plant gives off "a powerful phosphatic odor, an odor of semen" (180–81). The flowers of death are not named, but are described in exhaustive detail: "On high stalks, flecked with black and scaly like snake skins, there were enormous spathes, sort of bell-shaped trumpets the deep violet of putrefaction on the inside, and the greenish yellow of decomposition on the outer, which were like the split thoraxes of dead beasts" (207). These plants, to complement the thalcitrum with its odor of semen, give off a "cadaverous odor" that attracts flies. Clara looks at these plants and makes a comment almost identical to Des Esseintes' observation: "[T]hese flowers are not the creation of any sickly soul, nor of a raving genius . . . they are natural. Didn't I tell you nature loved death" (207). When the poet objects that "nature also creates monsters," Clara gives a telling symbolic interpretation of the cadaverous flowers: "What you call monsters are superior forms, or forms simply beyond your understanding." The flowers, in short, suggest the Nietzschean *Übermensch:* "Isn't a man of genius a monster, like a tiger or a spider, like all individuals who live beyond social lies, in the dazzling and divine immorality of things?" (208).

Clara seems to be a kind of *Übermensch* herself, so far beyond the moral and social systems of Western culture that the poet ultimately begins to long for the hypocrisy of Europe that he has left behind. The poet has particular difficulty keeping up with Clara's sadism. When she chides him for being a timid "European lover . . . in whom Catholicism has stupidly inculcated a fear of nature and a hatred of love," he asks: "Dear Clara, is it really natural for you to seek sensuality in decomposition, and urge your desires to greater heights by horrible spectacles of suffering and death?" (143–44). The flowers of sex and death that grow in the garden of punishments represent the perversion of Clara herself, who calls blood "a precious auxiliary of desire. It's the wine of love" (171). The emblematic nature of the garden is made clear when Clara says that "flowers are violent, cruel, terrible and splendid . . . like love!" (196). Also, Clara is advised to "make love . . . like the flowers" by a Chinese master of torture who concludes a long disquisition of the niceties of his trade with this admonition.

Mirbeau's irony is extremely heavy in his presentation of the Chinese torture-master, in part because the "Chinese" tortures that are described are derived from nineteenth-century decadent European literature. For example, Clara and the poet see two men carrying a litter "on which there stirred a bundle of bleeding flesh; a sort of human being, whose skin, cut in strips, trailed on the ground like rags" (182). This work of the torture-master recalls the flayed body of Mâtho at the end of *Salammbô*. Mirbeau also connects the torture-master to the fin de siècle obsession with hermaphroditism when he boasts that he recently "made a woman out of a man. . . . [I]t was such a good job you couldn't tell the difference, and I myself was fooled looking at him" (186). The greatest torture the garden has to offer is called "The Bell," usually reserved for the execution of aristocrats, in which the condemned man is bound and made to lie beneath a huge bell that is rung until he dies, which takes about forty-two hours (224). Most likely, this torture owes something to Baudelaire's "Spleen IV," the poem in which "relief" from the spleen comes when the furious sound of bells suddenly splits the sky ("Des cloches tout à coup sautent avec furie / Et lancent vers le ciel un affreux hurlement").[10] The bell is also described in a way that suggests a relation to Baudelaire's ambiguous *gouffre*, the fearful abyss of meaninglessness: "[T]he bell was sinister to behold. It was somewhat like an abyss in the air, a hanging void which seemed to rise from earth to sky, and whose bottom, filled with silent shadows, could not be seen" (216). The "existential" element in this description brings home the irony that almost all of this "oriental" torture has European roots.

Indeed, the larger irony at work here is that the garden of "Chinese" torture is a vision of what Europe really is without the civilizing veneer of hypocrisy. The torture-master complains that all of the refinements of Chinese torture are in danger of passing away. In short, torture is in a phase of decadence: "Today we no longer know what torture really is, although I try to carry on its real tradition. I am swamped, and I can't stay its decadence all by myself" (187). The problem, of course, is that new, inferior methods of torture are being introduced by "the Europeans, and particularly the English . . . under pretext of civilization" (188). The satire has a double edge: on the one hand, European influence mitigates the native barbarity of the Chinese; on the other, it introduces the new barbarity of colonial exploitation. In the end, the poet thinks of the Torture Garden as "a symbol to me of the entire earth": "Passions, appetites, greed, hatred, and lies; law, social institutions, justice, love, glory, heroism, and religion: these are its monstrous flowers and its hideous instruments of eternal human suffering" (232). The poet momentarily thinks that a return to France can save him—"I call Europe and its hypocritical civilization to my aid" (232)—but then realizes that no escape from the Torture Garden, in this new metaphorical sense, is possible: "[I]t is in all nature in fact which, urged on by the cosmic forces of love, rushes to murder, hoping thus to find beyond life satiation for the furious desires of life which devour it and overflow it in jets of filthy scum!" (233). Twenty years before Freud, Mirbeau articulates something "beyond the pleasure principle" and suggests, without fully affirming the suggestion, that the hypocrisies of civilization are necessary to the survival of society, just as, thirty years later, Freud will argue that the repression that makes us miserable also has the beneficial effect of allowing us to live.[11]

In *Le Jardin des supplices,* the simple dualism of hypocrisy is eventually complicated to the point that whatever satire Mirbeau may have intended is severely compromised. The satiric reversal that turns Europeans into barbarians loses its force when we discover that what the European colonialist corrupts is a native tradition of Chinese torture. Also, what begins as a parody of decadence seems less like satirical exaggeration and more like perverse celebration as the book goes on. The excesses of sadism and artificiality that Mirbeau describes do not end up subverting the attraction of decadence; rather, they are relished for their own sake by the voyeuristic reader, who becomes the double of the scopophilic Clara and comes to share, not condemn, her depraved tastes through the very act of reading. Even the initial satire that figures bourgeois respectability as a mask for murderous instincts, given outlet through such displays of anti-Semitism as the Dreyfus affair, loses its pungency when the desire for destruction is revealed to be universal. By making it appear universal, Mirbeau depoliticizes anti-Semitism altogether and turns hypocrisy into the natural, or at least the necessary, response to the very political outrages he initially addresses in satirical terms.

The necessity of hypocrisy also animates a decadent work by one of Mirbeau's admirers, the American James Huneker: "Hypocrisy rules the world. In fact, life without hypocrisy is unthinkable. They are inseparable" (*PV,* 210). The sentiment is expressed in Huneker's *Painted Veils,* a novel published in 1920 that is almost forgotten today but whose author had, at one time, a considerable reputation for nurturing European "modernity" in the United States.[12] Huneker follows in the tradition of Paul Bourget and Remy de Gourmont as a sympathetic critic of nineteenth-century decadent literature. In fact, both Bourget and de Gourmont lent their names to Huneker's publisher to advertise his books. De Gourmont singled Huneker out, "among foreign critics," as "the one best acquainted with French literature and the one who judges us with the greatest sympathy and with the most freedom." Bourget found in Huneker's book *Egoists: A Book of Supermen* (1909) "a sympathetic style on diverse problems, artistic and literary." In addition, Maurice Maeterlinck called Huneker's *Iconoclasts: A Book of Dramatists* (1905) "the only book of high and universal critical worth that we have had for years—to be precise, since Georg Brandes." And Brandes himself, the estimable Danish critic and novelist, wrote to Huneker: "I find your breadth of view and its expression more European than American; but the essential thing is that you are an artist to your very marrow."[13] With all these endorsements on his résumé, Huneker could justifiably claim to be the bearer of the torch of European modernism to the benighted rabble of America.

Huneker's most famous protege was H. L. Mencken,[14] who called Huneker "a true cosmopolitan" and believed he had "reported more of interest and value than any other American critic, living or dead." In his essay on Huneker, Mencken credits him with introducing American readers to Ibsen and Nietzsche, and with being one of the few critics to successfully resist "Victorian pedantry, formalism, and sentimentality." "It would be difficult, indeed," Mencken writes, "to overestimate the practical value to all the arts in America of his intellectual alertness, his catholic hospitality to ideas, his artistic courage, and above all, his powers of persuasion."[15] These powers had their effect on Edmund Wilson, who, like Huneker, did much to introduce American readers to European modernity. In one of his memoirs, Wilson writes: "In my youth, we used to read James Huneker, who, chaotic and careless though he was, made you ravenous to devour his favorite writers."[16] Similarly, as an undergraduate T. S. Eliot found Huneker's essays "highly stimulating because of the number of foreign authors, artists, and composers whom he was able to mention, and whom I had then never heard of. . . . I think his work may have performed a useful service for others as well as for myself, in bringing to their attention the names of distinguished contemporaries and men of the previous generation, in the various arts."[17] Eliot's assessment is telling, because Huneker's "modernism" does belong to "the previous generation" of Continental decadents, circa 1890, and to the "Nietzschean egoists" of the first decade or so of the twentieth century.

Even though Huneker was instrumental in introducing a generation of Americans to contemporary European culture, he also contributes to what I am calling the decline of decadence in several ways. First, he continues the trend away from aristocratic, "high" decadence toward a social milieu that mixes the bourgeois and the bohemian. Indeed, this element most likely has something to do with Huneker's eclipse from the American literary landscape, because such a mixture could not survive the proletarian 1930s and the drift toward working-class, social realism. Bernard Smith, a socialist critic of the 1930s, "realized that the bourgeois 1920s was traceable back to the example of the substanceless James Huneker."[18] In *Painted Veils*, Huneker's characters work for a living all right, but as music teachers and newspaper critics (Huneker's dual professions in real life), not stevedores; they also read Schopenhauer and Huysmans, listen to Wagner, and appreciate Whistler's painting. These bourgeois characters with aristocratic tastes know they are practitioners of "Bovarysme, or the desire of man to appear other than he is" (*PV*, 210). In fact, the title of the novel comes from the realization that "Hypocrisy . . . is necessary to screen certain unpleasant realities. . . . It is a pia fraus; painted veils! painted lies" (*PV*, 210–11).

A second contribution to the decline of decadence that Huneker makes is in his merging of two traditions that are, for the most part, quite distinct in the European tradition: decadence and diabolism. The diabolic tradition derives, in part, from John Milton's *Paradise Lost*, or rather from the English romantic poets' (mis)interpretation of Satan as the hero of the poem. This reading fueled the defiant aloofness and proud sense of damnation displayed by the romantic heroes created by Shelley and Byron. In turn, Byron's closet dramas, mainly *Cain* and *Manfred*, inspired the wave of Continental Byronism that led to late nineteenth-century Satanism. Only a small portion of Baudelaire's *Les Fleurs du mal* adds to the tradition, mainly that section of the book called "Révolte," which includes "Les Litanies de Satan" and the undoubtedly Byronic "Abel et Caïn." Diabolism comes into its own only with the publication of Lautréamont's *Les Chants de Maldoror*, Barbey d'Aurevilly's *Les Diaboliques*, and Huysmans's *Là-Bas*. Although the decadent treatment of the religion of art and the diabolic celebration of the religion of Satan are divergent traditions, Huneker offers an amalgamation of the two.

A third element of the decline of decadence that Huneker promotes is the popularization of decadent tastes. As a writer for such publications as *Scribner's Magazine, Harper's Bazaar,* and the New York *Sun,* Huneker had a wide, popular audience for a sensibility that, earlier, had been limited to an elite, even effete, group of readers. This topic will be taken up more fully in the next section of this chapter, but for now it is worth noting that Huneker appears to have facilitated what might be called the manifest destiny of decadence. That is, Huneker took an esoteric, essentially Parisian set of literary tastes, circulated them through the popular press, and influenced other newspaper writers, such as H. L. Mencken and Ben Hecht, who, in turn, disseminated "decadence" to the masses. From Paris to New York to Chicago and eventually to Hollywood, the manifest destiny of decadence comes to rest, if that is the word, in such films as *The Devil is a Woman, Diary of a Chambermaid,* and even *Citizen Kane.*

The three elements that I have singled out here—the movement toward a bourgeois-bohemian version of decadence, the blending of decadence and diabolism, and the popularization of decadence as the appropriately "modern" attitude—are all closely connected in Huneker's work. In his critical essays the alliance of decadence and modernity is something Huneker insists on again and again. In an essay on the opera singer Mary Garden, titled "Superwoman," Huneker writes that she "sounds the complex modern note. She does not represent, she evokes." To be modern, then, is to be a *symboliste.* In this same essay, from a collection called *Bedouins* (1920), Huneker comments on Garden's "muted" performance of Wagner, saying that hers is "a magical Isolde, with more than a hint of the perversely exotic we feel in Aubrey Beardsley's drawings of Isolde and Tristan. The modern note again" (*B,* 10, 14). In this essay, modernity is indistinguishable from the decadent-symbolist aesthetic of the 1880s and 1890s. However, in an essay on George Moore from *Overtones* (1904), decadence is conflated with avant-gardism (though Huneker does not use the term): "I remember well when the Confessions of a Young Man appeared. With what eagerness was it not seized upon by a small section of the community, a section that represented the vanguard of a new movement and recognized a fellow decadent" (*O,* 189). In another *Overtones* essay, "Anarchs of Art," Huneker likens decadence to a "phase of development," a progressive moment in history. In the same essay, he calls Flaubert the father of "the new men," who include "Maupassant, Huysmans, Loti, Barrès, Mirbeau." As the title of this essay suggests, Huneker follows Anatole Baju in thinking of the decadent as a new kind of "progressive," anarchistic figure who practices anarchy "in rebellion against conventional art forms—the only kind of anarchy that interests me" (*O,* 218, 223, 219). As we have seen, Paul Bourget and Nietzsche connect artistic decadence with social anarchy, that is, democracy. Huneker, then was in an ideal position to be an "anarch of art," since he was a "European" decadent living in a democratic country.

In Huneker's novel *Painted Veils,* however, America looks a great deal like Europe. Most of the characters reside in a boardinghouse called Maison Felicé (Monsieur Felicé is Provençal, while Madame is Swiss) and pepper their dialogue with French expressions, or with erudite attributions: "He agreed with Huysmans" (*PV,* 72); "as Nietzsche . . . phrased it" (*PV,* 78); "As Paul Bourget would have said" (*PV,* 109); "as Havelock Ellis says" (*PV,* 127); "Ah! what an ideal is Walter Pater" (*PV,* 145); "I adore D'Annunzio" (*PV,* 269); and so on. The principal male character, Ulick Invern, is said to be "Paris born, of New York stock, but a confirmed Parisian" (*PV,* 23). The same "Parisian" quality is attributed to Invern's friend Alfred Stone, "a young-old man, worn, though not precisely dissipated looking" (*PV,* 17). Even the American cityscape appears through a decadent-tinted optic, as in Huneker's precious description of Atlantic City, New Jersey, a "queer Cosmopolis" that boasts "the attractive ugliness of modern life" (*PV,* 192):

> This architecture might be Byzantine. It suggests St. Marco at Venice, St. Sophia at Constantinople, also a Hindoo palace, with its crouching dome, operatic façade, and its dominating monoliths with the blunt tops of concrete; the exterior decoration is a luxurious exfoliation in hues; turquoise and fawn. It is a dream-architecture, this, with its evocations of Asiatic color and music.
>
> But Atlantic City at night. Alfred recalled it as a picture for such different painters as Whistler or Toulouse-Lautrec. . . . Sumptuous evening toilettes assault your nerves. Wealth envelops you. Apparently there is no poverty, no sickness, no unhappiness in existence. The optimistic exuberance of the American is seen here at its most depressing . . . ; yet if you are not seeking the fly in the ointment you may enjoy it as you would enjoy the gorgeous tableaux of Aïda or Salammbô. (*PV,* 193–94)

Here, the author's decadent aestheticizing of the American scene is somewhat disrupted by the presence of actual Americans, and by the depressing spectacle of the *absence* of poverty, sickness, and unhappiness. But then, Huneker is a "new man," a child of Schopenhauer and Flaubert.

The plot of *Painted Veils,* as is the case with most decadent novels, is less important than the occasions for sophisticated conversation and mannered description that the plot affords. The novel opens when Easter Brandès arrives in New York from Virginia to study opera. She is soon befriended by the "bohemian" music critic Alfred Stone, who introduces her to the leading lights of the Metropolitan Opera. Easter, or Esther (as she is also called), manages to parlay these new connections into a trip to Europe where she becomes a great success and the first American to sing in *Parsifal* at Bayreuth. While Easter is away in Europe, most of the novel concerns the adventures of the Paris-born New York dandy named Ulick Invern. He had fallen in love with Easter before she left for Europe, and in her absence he busies himself with two women, the prostitute Dora and Mona Milton, sister of a friend who is studying to be a priest. Ulick goes back and forth from Dora to Mona while still longing for Easter. He and Mona are both advocates of free love, and Ulick eventually gets Mona pregnant. Unfortunately, Mona is struck by a car and her pregnancy turns into peritonitis, but she survives. When Easter, now singing professionally as "Istar," returns to New York and a triumphant debut at the Metropolitan Opera, Ulick leaves Mona. Easter spurns him, so he turns again to Dora. This makes Easter jealous, and she follows Invern to Dora's apartment at the Sappho House. The expected confrontation between Easter and Dora over Ulick does not take place, however. Instead, the two women put on nightgowns, throw Ulick out of Dora's apartment, and spend the night together. Later, Easter seduces Mona's brother, the pious would-be priest Mel Milton, just for the fun of it. These events, and a few others, turn the usually sober Invern to the bottle. Alfred Stone narrates the denouement that has Ulick Invern returning to Paris, where he dies; Mona marrying the wealthy Paul Goddard, who had been Ulick's rival for the affections of both Easter and Dora; the repentant Milton becoming a missionary to China; and Easter Brandès going on to greater and greater success as "Istar, the Great Singing Whore of Modern Babylon" (*PV*, 306).

Though it includes some of the novel's salacious elements, this summary does not do justice to Huneker's mannered and precious treatment of decadent conventions. At times, Huneker's style borders on namedropping, as one decadent figure after another is rather gratuitously inserted into the narrative. Ulick Invern, we are told, sat at the feet of Huysmans himself, who "made a searching examination into the conscience of his youthful admirer":

> He [Huysmans] related, not without a certain muted pride, the advice of Barbey d'Aurevilly, the same advice Barbey had given Charles Baudelaire:

> that either the author of Là-Bas must prostrate himself at the feet of Jesus crucified, or else blow out his brains. . . .
>
> Huysmans prodded his conscience to such good effect that he . . . went with him when he made the rounds of the bookstalls along the left bank of the Seine. It was during one of these fascinating excursions . . . that Ulick was presented to Remy de Gourmont, another of his favourite writers. . . .
>
> . . . Heine, Schopenhauer, and Nietzsche were to come later. His reactions to the system, or lack of a system, in the case of Nietzsche was like a crisis in a dangerous fever. He alternated between languor and exaltation. Schopenhauer cooled off his naturally buoyant temperament, but Nietzsche gave him ecstasy as if poured from an overflowing goblet. (*PV*, 96–97, 99)

Later, Remy de Gourmont advises Ulick on his French prose style: "You write well in our tongue, though not so well as Arthur Symons, anyhow, better than Oscar Wilde—who hasn't mastered our syntax—but, but—it's not vital, individual, your style. I overhear too many echoes of Flaubert, Goncourt, above all, Huysmans" (*PV*, 104). In such passages, Huneker is doing what Huysmans had done before; that is, he is presenting the reader with a catalogue of decadent works and a guide to a more recent version of the decadent style. However, even Huneker, for all his imitativeness and conventionality, seems aware that the literary decadentism of the 1880s is not the latest word. Indeed, *Painted Veils* is sometimes stylistically innovative, but even the innovations seem derivative, mainly of George Moore. On several occasions, Huneker presents his characters' thoughts directly, using the device of the *monologue intérieur:* "Alfred Stone reflected: She is unusual. Never mind the beauty of her voice; it's her personality that will win out. What curious eyes. Hard as steel when she doesn't like the way things are going. Big heart? Yes—for herself" (*PV*, 24–25). This use of interior monologue is hardly the equal of Joyce's, but it is roughly the equal of Moore's, which means that even Huneker's innovations are belated. Still, such flashes of innovative style make for some odd reading alongside Huneker's deadly dialogue:

> "I mean to be a great dramatic soprano," she confidently asserted.
>
> "Aha!" he vouchsafed. "Rather a modest programme."
>
> "I mean to accomplished it," she retorted. He was visibly impressed. (*PV*, 18–19)

Few readers are likely to be impressed, today, with such passages. But the novel does have some whimsical moments, as when Ulick Invern gives Mona "a book of musical sketches by an author unknown to her. It was entitled Melomaniacs" (*PV*, 217). *Melomaniacs* (1902) is one of Huneker's first books, and the idea of a fictional character reading a book by the author of the novel in which she appears might appeal to the postmodernist, self-conscious reader with a taste for metafictional effects. But no doubt in the early twentieth century, many Americans, reading of these decadent, Europeanized Americans, vouchsafed to forgive Huneker the occasional bathetic expression because of his insistence on a liberating modernity.

In general, the meaning of "modernity" in *Painted Veils* involves two things: a receptive attitude toward the decadent tradition (represented by Flaubert, Huysmans, the Goncourts, Remy de Gourmont, and others) and an advocacy of the new, "egoistic" iconoclasm (represented by Ibsen and Nietzsche). The decadent attitude is allied to the modernity of intellectual ideas and aesthetic tastes, while the iconoclastic stance is a matter of the modernity of morals and behavior. This dual modernity is represented by Ulick Invern, who is both decadent and bohemian. His friend Alfred Stone is mainly bohemian (his taste for Wagner excepted), while his other friend, the priest Mel Milton, is largely decadent because of his literary tastes (which include Baudelaire and Huysmans) and his celibacy, the antinatural negation of life. The treatment of decadence as a form of artistic and intellectual modernity is quite extensive. Ulick Invern "knew the men and women of the early nineties who made Paris a city of artistic and intellectual life" (*PV*, 93). He visits the aging Edmond de Goncourt, who is said to have given the "budding littérateurs" of the younger generation "a new opera-glass through which to view contemporary life" (*PV*, 94). As a drama critic, Invern writes about Ibsen because there is "no one else to write about" (*PV*, 77). And like Ibsen, Invern is a feminist, but the feminism he advocates is mainly limited to sexual liberation: "I am a feminist, . . . but I don't give a rap for the suffrage if it doesn't free women from sexual slavery." This last phrase refers to virginity and monogamy: "If a man can run around, having a good time, and not be reproached with his loose-living, why, by the same token, can't a woman?" (*PV*, 280). Here, Invern the aesthete becomes Invern the iconoclast, passing over from decadence to bohemianism.

Although some characters indulge in more diversified varieties of bohemian behavior (Alfred Stone drinks and gambles), most of them take sexual promiscuity as the principle index of their iconoclastic modernity. On this topic, Huneker's treatment of women is interesting because the female characters clearly surpass the male characters in their capacity for "immorality" and "perversity," as in this description of a lesbian soirée:

> Sprawling on luxurious divans were three or four girls, Allie Wentworth [Easter's lesbian lover] among the rest. A monstrously fat woman with a face that recalled the evil eyes and parrot-beak of an octopus, sat enthroned, and in her puffy lips a long black cigar. Introductions. "We call her Anactoria," cried Allie, pointing at the large lady. "Isn't she a queen?" "Allie," said the other in a thick voice, "Allie, you ought to be spanked." "Spanking is too good for her," interrupted Easter. "Spanking is too expensive nowadays," pertly added the girl, who wore her hair like a pianist. "Spanking," remarked the fat creature, "is for virtuosi only." A roar followed this delightful allusion. (*PV*, 297)

Whether spanking is something that can be done only by virtuosi or whether only musical virtuosi should be spanked is the kind of joke that Baudelaire would never make. Not for nothing are his lesbians called *les femmes damnées,* but no such moral judgment attaches to Huneker's representation of these women.

In his essays, Huneker sometimes goes beyond the narrow notion given voice by Ulick Invern that the liberation of women is mainly limited to sexuality. In "The Eternal Feminine," Huneker asks if women can play the piano as well as men do, which may not seem like a burning question today, but in formulating his opinion on the topic Huneker discounts the sexist theories of Lombroso and others, who contended that the "inferiority" of women is "proved," for example, by a lower brain-weight: "But what is all this testing, weighing, and measuring when faced by the spectacle of a glorious winged creature which sails away on victorious pinions with plumage unruffled by Lombroso and his laboratory logic?" (*O,* 279). This is Huneker's way of saying that women can, indeed, play the piano. However, he argues that the music of some composers is better played by men, and when faced with the larger issue of female liberation, he says, simply: "The woman question,—is it not one to be shunned?" (*O,* 300, 302). In another essay, Huneker's attitude toward the "new woman" is not exactly charitable, as the title "Three Disagreeable Girls" suggests. Actually, the disagreeable women he discusses are all fictional characters (Ibsen's Hedda Gabler, George Moore's Mildred Lawson, and Edith Wharton's Undine Spragg) who are not "new women" after all, even though they are "modern." Huneker gives a backhanded compliment to "the 'feminist' movement" by saying that it "is not responsible for them; there were disagreeable females before the flood." Huneker does allow that "new freedom and responsibilities have evolved new social types," but he comes short of advocating even the limited, sexual brand of feminism that his character Ulick Invern supports (*IA,* 314, 327). Clearly, the novelist of 1920 has more to say about sexual freedom than the essayist of 1904 or even of 1915. What Huneker calls the "new freedom" in his essays is really sexual freedom in the novel, as when Alfred Stone complains that "with their 'new freedom,' as they call it, women are becoming more polyandrous. They, too, needs must have a staff of males for their individuality" (*PV,* 281).

All of this might lead one to believe that women in Huneker's novel fall neatly into the polarities of purity and sensuality, as was the case with D'Annunzio's *Il Piacere,* in which the decadent hero Andrea Sperelli goes back and forth from the virginal Maria to the corrupt Elena. This oscillation, which is partly a representation in sexual terms of the Baudelairean vacillation between *idéal* and *spleen,* does not occur in precisely the same polar fashion in *Painted Veils,* although the plot of Huneker's novel does resemble that of D'Annunzio's, as Ulick Invern alternates between Easter and Mona. These two female characters are opposed, but the opposites they represent are not quite so "Baudelairean." Mona is a freethinker; she does not believe the institution of marriage is necessary for men and women to have sexual relations. She is, potentially, a new woman in a limited "bohemian" sense. The would-be priest Mel Milton is concerned about his sister's tendencies when he tells Ulick Invern that she "is read in the 'modernity' you admire, too deeply for her spiritual repose" (*PV,* 214). However, even though Mona reads decadent literature, she is also antidecadent because of her desire to have children and her general affirmation of life. Mona feels uncomfortable around her brothers' friends because they are all theological students sworn to celibacy; this makes them "neuter persons" or "voluntary eunuchs, enemies of the very source of life." Mona would be "embarrassed if a hermaphrodite had been pointed out to her" because "the anti-natural was to be feared and avoided" (*PV,* 115). To fear the antinatural is to be antidecadent, and therefore antimodern; in fact, to Ulick Invern, Mona does not "seem 'modern' or of the overcultured type" (*PV,* 119). Easter Brandès, on the other hand, personifies the "new freedom" of the "new woman" that Alfred Stone fears and Ulick Invern encourages. Thus, the two women, Easter and Mona, represent the opposition of modernity and antimodernity, with Easter's modernity being more of the iconoclastic, "Nietzschean" variety, which includes some powerful antagonism to religion. The puritanism of the priestly Milton is no match for the seductive powers of Istar, who is based in part on the "superwoman" Mary Garden. In the end, the decadent man, whether priest or *artiste*, does not survive, while the modern woman is triumphant. Summing things up, Alfred Stone says of Ulick Invern that "the North American climate withered the Flowers of Evil of his Baudelaire and all the other decadent ideas and poetry he brought over with him. . . . His Fleurs du Mal wilted" (*PV*, 304). In fact, his flower wilts because of the superwoman Istar, whose "evil" exceeds anything Invern can imagine. By the end of the novel, Alfred Stone is calling Easter Brandès "Dame Lucifer"; that is, the new woman is the new Satan. *Painted Veils* ends with a rather Zarathustran "epitaph for Easter" written by Alfred Stone, which must be quoted at length:

> And because Istar had abhorred the Seven Deadly Virtues, and renounced them at the Last Gate in favor of the Seven Deadly Arts, the Warden of Life Eternal bestowed upon her the immeasurable boon of the Seven Capital Sins, which are: Pride, Covetousness, Lust, Anger, Gluttony, Envy, Sloth. . . . Added to these are the Eighth Deadly Sin, which is Perfume; the Sin Against the Holy Ghost; the sweet sin of Sappho; and the Supreme Sin, which is the denial of the Devil. . . . And Istar, Daughter of Sin, was happy and her days were long in the land, and she passed away in the odour of sanctity. . . . Blessed are the pure of heart; for they shall see God . . . ! (*PV*, 309)

Here, diabolism and "feminism" merge in a way that is, among other things, a contradiction of cultural terms. The theme of the "new woman" is contradicted by the presentation of that theme in Satanic form, which turns the modern woman into yet another nineteenth-century "Medusa" figure. Also, the Nietzschean critique of religion that makes up a good part of the book is contradicted by the rhetorical celebration of Satanism, which always ends up affirming Christianity in the process of negating it. As the example of Baudelaire in his "Révolte" mode shows, Satanism may be a black religion, but it is still religion.

The diabolic element in *Painted Veils* is represented by reference to Ulick Invern's brother Oswald, who has remained in Paris, where he has become "a Manichean, a devil worshipper," which can only come about if one "does not repudiate the authority of the Church" (*PV*, 95). Ulick Invern himself practices a kind of cultural Manichaeanism, alternating his reading between Petronius Arbiter and Thomas à Kempis: "Two books had imaged his reverse aspirations: Petronius, his thirst for an absolute in evil; Thomas à Kempis, his God-intoxicated craving for the Infinite" (*PV,* 310). In the novel, the exploration of this dualistic diabolism is limited to debates between Invern and Mel Milton, and to the rhetorical epitaph on Easter Brandès that closes the book. In some of his short stories, however, Huneker gives narrative form to the blend of diabolism and misogyny that rounds off *Painted Veils.* In a story from *Bedouins* titled "The Supreme Sin," Oswald Invern is introduced to an aristocratic aesthete and diabolist named Count Van Zorn who argues that "the Devil is the mainspring of our moral system. Mock him and you mock God—who created him" (*B,* 185). Oswald, who is a composer, is insulted when Van Zorn claims that "the Devil is the greatest of all musicians," and credits him with the invention of the chromatic scale: "[T]hat's why Richard Wagner admired the Devil in music—what is Parsifal but a version of the Black Mass!" (*B,* 185). Oswald accepts the count's apology when he learns that no insult is intended, that the claim is made in earnest. The count invites Oswald to attend a private concert where, perhaps, Van Zorn will be able to summon up Satan by playing the piano, "for I mingle music and magic," he says (*B,* 186). Sure enough, the count's piano playing and his incantations—"O Satan, have mercy on us!"—succeed, but to Oswald's consternation the spirit that appears before him is a beautiful woman. The apparition looks exactly like the count's mistress, who earlier had insisted that "the Devil is a woman" (*B,* 187). Oswald is moved to say: "Thou art a goddess, not the Devil" (*B,* 199). Without knowing it, by saying this Oswald commits the Supreme Sin of denying the Devil. The count intervenes: "Quickly worship, else be banished forever from the only Paradise!" (*B,* 200). Oswald prays to the Son of Mary and "the apparition crumbled" (*B,* 200). In "The Malefic Vision," another story in *Bedouins,* an organist tells how he assisted a priest named Father Moreau in the performance of a black mass that, once again, succeeds in summoning up Satan Herself: "[A]n Antichrist from some fetid hell, sent to seduce us, curse us, destroy us! My eyes almost burst from their sockets, and the humming of hell's loom roared about me as I met the gaze—of the Woman. And now her eyes were the serpent's eyes, and on her head was the crown of hell and its multiple kingdoms. She was naked, and set against her breasts were sharp swords. She was Mater Malorum, and her breath sowed discord, lust, and cruel murder" (*B,* 270). Decadence has been described as "decline at its peak." If that is true, Huneker's diabolism may be the nadir of decadence, the exhaustion of a sensibility that is tired to begin with. Reading Huneker today, it is impossible to be shocked by his diabolism or even offended by his misogyny, because both are often so formulaic as to be laughable. Nonetheless, Huneker is of considerable historical interest because of his widespread influence on younger American writers, including T. S. Eliot, Edmund Wilson, and Kenneth Burke (author of a sympathetic review of *Painted Veils*),[19] who later on either contributed to the canonization of modernist writers or were canonized as modernists themselves. Huneker helps us to understand how these writers spent their youth.

In a letter to James Huneker's biographer, Ben Hecht writes: "In the years that I read him, 1914 to 1921, . . . I regarded [Huneker] as my alma mater."[20] Hecht also writes, in *A Child of the Century*, that in his youth "there was no finer mental sport than could be found in the pages of Huneker, Brandes, Pollard, Hazlitt, Taine, France, Vance Thompson, Mencken, Francis Hackett, Arthur Symons, and their like" *CC*, 340). This list of essayists, headed by Huneker, includes Huneker's colleague and collaborator, Vance Thompson; his famous protégé, Mencken; his admirer, Georg Brandes; and several other essayists associated with the decadent-aesthetic orbit, including Hippolyte Taine and Arthur Symons. In addition to these essayists, Hecht read, as he says, "constantly," the works of such decadent writers as Flaubert (he singles out *Salammbô*), Huysmans, de Gourmont, Mallarmé, D'Annunzio, and Nietzsche (*CC*, 163). When Mencken suggested that Hecht adopt a pen name, he thought of calling himself Joris Karl, after Huysmans.[21] Margaret Anderson, who started the influential *Little Review* in Chicago, "remarked that Hecht reminded her of a Decadent poet."[22] All of this is evidence of what is hardly common knowledge: that the man who authored "half of the most entertaining movies to come out of Hollywood," according to Pauline Kael,[23] started out his cultural life as a latter-day decadent.

This fact is not that interesting in itself, but placed in the context of the modernist movement Hecht's decadentism becomes much more than a curiosity in the career of a great Hollywood screenwriter. Hecht's decadent writings and his brief affiliation with such important promoters of modernism as Margaret Anderson and Ezra Pound (who called Hecht the "only . . . intelligent man in the whole United States")[24] argue the case that decadence not only contributed to the development of canonical modernism, but to the formation of a lesser, noncanonical brand of modernism as well. In addition, the decadent Hecht suggests a point too large to argue here, so I merely suggest it: that the various dilutions of European high decadence introduced by Huneker and taken up by Hecht eventually trickled down into American popular culture through the medium of the movies.

Most literary histories identify the Chicago Renaissance with the realist-naturalist fiction of Sherwood Anderson, on the one hand; and, on the other, with the imagist movement in poetry that had its outlet in Harriet Monroe's *Poetry: A Magazine of Verse.* By and large, this double focus on naturalism and imagism gives a fairly accurate picture of the modernism of the Midwest. But if one looks in the corners of the canvas another variety of modernism comes into view, one that has a distinctly decadent coloration. Strangely enough, the Book Section of the Chicago *Daily News* was devoted mainly to articles on decadent writers. Hecht says that the Book Section "consisted of reading matter as beyond the ken of the *Daily News* readers as if it had been printed in Chinese," and mentions articles on Proust, Huysmans, Gide, and Nietzsche that appeared alongside essays about Anderson, Dreiser, and Carl Sandburg (*CC,* 341). One of the critics who wrote for the *Daily News* was Burton Rascoe, the former literary editor of the rival *Tribune* and "a midwestern member of the Huneker–Mencken school."[25] Rascoe gave Huneker's *Painted Veils* a favorable review in the *News,* which is further evidence that the newspaper was a forum for decadent literature. The book was described in Rascoe's review (8 December 1920) as follows: "When I read the manuscript the tentative title was ISTAR, with PAINTED VEILS as a substitute. It is something of a twentieth century SATYRICON and this arbiter of taste and elegance a Petronius, who has read Huysmans and whose favorite poem is Baudelaire's FEMMES DAMNÉES. The milieu is that of the artistic bohemia of New York and the European continent in the wan flush of the closing decade of the last century."[26] Rascoe also says in his review that Huneker "is our chief spokesman of modernism, our most thorough cosmopolite" (277). Whether Rascoe, "whose taste Huneker had done so much to mold" was really "the spokesman . . . for the younger generation," as one critic claims,[27] is hard to say, but he did have a hand in steering the lesser lights of the Chicago Renaissance in the direction of decadence.[28]

Decadence was in the popular press, and it was also found in the pages of the literary avant-garde. Margaret Anderson's *Little Review* achieved its greatest reputation as a modernist organ only after the journal was moved to New York, where Anderson published Eliot's *The Waste Land* and more than half of Joyce's *Ulysses.* But the early issues of the *Little Review* boast no such triumphs. The journal in its Chicago phase was notable, however, for its mix of decadent-aesthetic sentiment and avant-garde fervor. "It was youth that spoke in *The Little Review*," writes Hecht, "sometimes even *juvenilia*" (*CC*, 234). The second issue, in fact, opens with a defense against the charge that the premier issue was "juvenile." The defense is made (probably by Anderson herself, since the essay is unsigned) by comparing the *Little Review* to the *Germ*, the magazine published late in 1849 by Dante Gabriel Rossetti and the rest of the Pre-Raphaelite Brotherhood: "*The Germ* was published for four months, and then it died. Like all serious things it could find no immediate audience; like all revolutionary things it was called juvenile and regarded with shyness; and like all original and beautiful things it has managed to stay very much alive."[29] Anderson's identification of the avant-garde leanings of her magazine with those of the *Germ* is interesting because the earlier journal was also a source of inspiration for the aesthetic school and especially for the new aestheticism that is synonymous with the Decadence of the 1890s in England. This kind of confluence of decadentism and avant-gardism occurs with some regularity in the early issues of the *Little Review*. Another example is the persistent note of millenialism that was sounded in the pages of the magazine in response to the Great War. The author of an unsigned essay titled "Armageddon" states outright that "[n]ineteenth century civilization has overwhelmingly and dramatically failed. What shall we build now?"[30] Then, a few months later, in an essay on "Remy de Gourmont" Richard Aldington writes an appreciation of the man "who presents in one person the manifold and often conflicting opinions and ideas of modern culture." Called one of the "children of Mallarmé," de Gourmont is held up to the reader as "one of the best examples of Latin or West European culture now living."[31] Although civilization and culture are not necessarily the same thing, the denunciation of nineteenth-century civilization as the impetus to Armageddon is hard to reconcile with Aldington's lavish praise of the highly cultured child of Mallarmé. What is clear, however, is that most of the youthful cries for newness and revolution in the *Little Review* are heard against a background chorus of decadent voices.

The mix of modernity and decadence is evident in the very first issue of the *Little Review*, which introduced its readers to "the heart of modern man" in an essay that advocates in polemical form the same kind of Nietzschean self-overcoming of decadence that Gide narrated in *L'Immoraliste*. The essay, by George Burman Foster, is titled "The Prophet of a New Culture" and begins with a description of the contemporary, collective sensibility:

> . . . life, bruised and bewildered, is worthless—such is the melancholy mood of modernity. Today life is a burden to many to whom it was once a joy. Decadents, they call themselves, who rediscover the elements of their most personal life in everything that is weary and ailing. We are all more or less infected with this weariness and ennui. The blows which the spirit experiences from opposing sides today are so powerful that no one is in a position to endure them with equanimity. The forces resident within the soul no longer suffice to give support and stability to life. Hence our culture has lost faith in itself. Our civilization is played out.[32]

The writer here expresses the same longing for renewal that Verlaine articulates in his sonnet "Langueur." But unlike Verlaine and the Goncourt brothers, who imagine the infusion of new blood by barbarians from without as the only hope of renewal, Foster argues that renewal can come from within if the weary decadent will only look to Nietzsche as "the prophet of a new culture." Law and morality combine to form "an old hereditary woe with which humanity is weighed down." "Morals and Christianity," to Nietzsche, were "the most dangerous maladies with which men were suffering." The appeal Foster makes to "Nietzsche the Immoralist, Nietzsche the Antichrist" can be read in large philosophical terms as an argument for the transvaluation of values that takes place, for example, in Gide's novel. In *L'Immoraliste,* Michel recovers his physical and cultural health through a neoromantic return to his instinctual origins. But the simplistic, iconoclastic Nietzschean stance taken by Foster in his essay can also be read as simple diabolism. Nietzsche the "Antichrist," whose "irresistible, diabolical curiosity impels him to transvalue all values with which men have reckoned," makes it possible to ask whether " 'good' must not be called evil."[33] If a dose of Baudelaire or Huysmans is added to this "diabolic" version of Nietzsche, the result is not so different from the tired, dualistic Satanism of James Huneker.

The cultural forces directing Ben Hecht toward decadence, or some version of "modernity" that included decadence, were manifold: Huneker's essays and *Painted Veils,* the *Little Review,* the Book Section of the Chicago *Daily News,* not to mention Chicago itself. We should not lose sight of the fact that Hecht was a newspaperman in a city that was rapidly assuming the identity of "a prairie Gomorrah."[34] Also, when Hecht worked as a reporter the job was not defined as it is today: "In those years, a reporter wasn't a college journalism graduate who had been hired by a newspaper to turn out a uniform product, but generally a cynical, whoring, hard-drinking adventurer who was writing poetry or a novel between the stories he was banging out on his tall office Underwood."[35] In both prewar Chicago and during the twenties, "journalists engaged in an off-duty literary bohemianism and intellectualism," and this is certainly true of Hecht.[36] He was also a crime reporter, among other things, and this, as well as an interest in sadomasochism derived from interviews with Wilhelm Stekel (author of early studies on the subject), complemented his interest in literary decadence.[37] The parallelism of Hecht's reportorial and literary interests can be seen in one of his *Little Review* pieces, a review of a translation of Dostoevsky's *The House of the Dead.* In this essay, Hecht envies Dostoevsky's acquaintance with truly great criminals in the prisons of Siberia. By contrast, American criminals are second-rate, "a petty lot given to sentimental regrets and griefs and reforms and periodicals." He also bewails the "monotonously bourgeois" nature of American vice. The longing he expresses for a better class of criminals is not, I think, wholly ironic, nor is the sense of delectation he takes in the degradation of humanity he sees in Dostoevsky:

> The swaggering monstrosities that swilled on vodka and wept at the stars. The bestial grotesques who delighted in the murder of infants for the sake of the warm blood that bathed their hands. The filthy saints and nonchalant parricides. The Herculean villains, the irritable gargoyles innocently steeped in insatiable perversion and dripping with infamy. The arrogant, sadistic artists of torture, human as children, with their pitifully crippled souls; praying before the prison ikons, stealing their comrade's clothes and washing his feet; hating and loving with the simplicity of Pagan gods and the ramified cunning of continental diplomats. The nerveless flagellants, the heartbreaking humorists, the fierce, fanciful executioners. There's company for you! A putrefying company in the very dregs of its depravities.[38]

Here, one of the things that appeals to Hecht is quite close to Huneker's diabolism: the dualism of innocence and perversity, spirituality and depravity, religious ritual and criminal behavior. In a way, the passage suggests the double life that Hecht led himself, as both the hard-boiled crime reporter and the refined decadent writer.

Indeed, most of the fiction Hecht wrote in the 1920s bears the stamp of the cosmopolitan Huneker and the preoccupation with decadent literature that Burton Rascoe construed as "modern." But two of his novels have a special relationship to that brand of diabolic, "Nietzschean" decadence that served only as the backdrop for modernity for some but was the very stage on which the modern age was acted out for others. *Fantazius Mal-*

lare: A Mysterious Oath (1922) and its sequel, *The Kingdom of Evil* (1924), are Hecht's main contributions to the bibliography of decadent literature. The first novel was written as a deliberate challenge to such organizations as Boston's Watch and Ward Society (which had banned Hecht's first novel, *Gargoyles*) and New York's Society for the Suppression of Vice, headed by John Sumner, who succeeded in suppressing books by Sherwood Anderson, Aldous Huxley, and John Dos Passos, as well as the work of Hecht's friend, the poet Maxwell Bodenheim.[39] To ensure that *Fantazius Mallare* would bring the wrath of the censors down on his head, and thereby gain publicity for the book, Hecht had his friend Wallace Smith, another *Daily News* reporter and part-time artist, illustrate the text with Beardsley-like drawings. As added insurance of ignominy, Hecht wrote an eight-page "Dedication" to his enemies, with a design by Smith depicting an erect phallus caught in a "vagina" of thorns or barbed wire, flanked by the figures of two nude men, their bodies tortured and twisted in a lattice of thorns. This design tops each page of the "Dedication," perhaps the most famous part of this obscure book because it is said to have influenced Allen Ginsberg's *Howl*.[40] A sample:

> [T]o the moral ones upon whom Beauty exercises a lascivious and corrupting influence; to the moral ones who have chased God out of their bedrooms; . . . to the prim ones who fornicate apologetically (the Devil can-cans in their souls); . . . to the reformers—the Freudian dervishes who masturbate with Purity Leagues, who achieve involved orgasms denouncing the depravities of others; . . . to the smug ones who walk with their noses ecstatically buried in their own rectums (I have nothing against them, I swear); . . . to the noble ones who advertise their secrets, who crucify themselves on billboards in the quest for the Nietzschean solitude. . . . (*FM,* 11–13, 15–16)

If Hecht's purpose was to outrage the censors, he succeeded, only not as he had hoped. Because the book was printed in a limited edition and sold by subscription only (by the small Chicago firm of Covici-McGee), both Hecht and Smith were accused of violating federal law prohibiting the sale of "lewd, obscene and lascivious" material through the United States mail. Hecht and Smith lost their case and were fined $1,000 each. The affair generated a great deal of publicity, but Hecht did not gain any direct profit from it. In fact, the controversy cost him his job at the *Daily News*.[41]

As for the novel itself, Fantazius Mallare is the name of an artist who is so disgusted with reality that he not only turns against nature, as did Huysmans's hero, but against art as well: "It is unfortunate that I am a sculptor, a mere artist. Art has become for me a tedious decoration for my impotence. It is clear I should have been a God" (*FM,* 31). In the company of Goliath, the black, humpbacked dwarf who works as his servant, Mallare destroys his sculpture and begins to realize his aspiration to be a God by going mad and by using his madness to create illusions that have, for him, all the force of reality. In this, the "egoist" Mallare is like God: "There is but one egoist and that is He who, intolerant of all but Himself, sets out to destroy all but Himself. Egoism is the despairing effort of man to return to his original Godhood; to return to the undisputed and triumphant loneliness which was His when as a Creator He moulded the world to His whims" (*FM,* 35). The plot of the novel begins when Mallare sets out to "retrace my way toward a makeshift of Omnipotence. But for this I will have to find a woman" (*FM,* 42). The woman he finds is Rita, an eighteen-year-old Gypsy girl, who is to serve as raw material for the fantasies of Fantazius Mallare. In order for the project to succeed, the girl must listen to Mallare but never speak, and she must never leave the house. She cooperates, and soon Mallare begins to realize the ambition of his madness: "Mallare, seating himself, studied her with calm. She was his creation. He was giving her life. His mind was beginning to conceive her as a part of the phantoms that lived in him and were his world. This illusion diverted him. His objective sense fast vanishing, he was gradually perceiving her as a tangible outline of his own hallucinations" (*FM,* 51). Things get out of hand when the "phantom," that is, Rita in the flesh, becomes sexually attracted to Mallare. He prefers the world of fantasy, and has the true decadent's disdain for those whose "desires for the infinite sate themselves in the feeble trickle of orgasm" and for the second-rate Nietzschean egoist whose "transvaluations—the ineffable and inarticulate mysteries he fancied himself embracing—turn out to be a woman with her legs wrapped around him" (*FM,* 55). At first, Mallare manages to transform Rita's real-life passion into an element of his own narcissism: "I am the mirror and she is the image alive in me. Her desire is a happy shadow I embrace" (*FM,* 60). But the prospect of actual fleshly contact is so abhorrent to Mallare that he leaves his house one night to walk the streets of the city, where he is accosted by a beggar. Mallare looks at him, and his madness produces the odd hallucination that the beggar is Rita: "You have followed me. . . . Very well. It is useless to explain matters to you. You pursue me with your lecherous body. I have warned you. Now I will kill you" (*FM,* 64). Mallare attacks the beggar and kills him under the delusion that the stranger is Rita, then returns to his home where the real

Rita is still very much alive. When he sees her, he is delighted that his fantasy of the woman has survived the murder of the "reality." "I am a man with a woman inside him," he thinks. "I possess the secret of the hermaphroditic Gods. I am complete" (*FM,* 73). And because Mallare thinks that the woman is not a part of the reality outside of himself, he is free to have sex with her, which, to him, is only a matter of "masturbating with an erotic phantom" (*FM,* 86). This would seem to be the ideal situation for the decadent egoist, except that the phantom will not leave him alone. At first, Mallare wonders whether he can murder his own hallucination of the woman as earlier he murdered the woman herself, but he succeeds in freeing himself of his phantom simply by neglecting her. This tact works until the "phantom" rebels and tries to get vengeance against the neglectful decadent by having intercourse with the servant Goliath in full view of Mallare, who is somewhat baffled that anyone other than himself can even see the image projected from his erotic fantasies, let alone copulate with it. " 'Then how does it come,' I continued thinking, 'that he sees that which is visible only to you? His eyes are fastened on her who is to be seen only inside the caverns of Mallare" (*FM,* 151). Mallare watches as the "hallucination he had loved . . . gave itself to the little monster" until he can watch no longer: "Mallare closed his eyes, a God shuddering before his own atheism" (*FM,* 159–60). Although the question is not that important, it is difficult to tell what happens next. Goliath's "masturbation" with the "phantom" causes her to dissolve "in a suicidal orgasm" (*FM,* 162). Evidently, Rita simply puts on her clothes and leaves, whereupon Mallare has only the company of Goliath, who weeps over the vanished "hallucination," and one he calls his "lodge brother," whom Mallare addresses as "an obvious pathologic symptom—an illusory conscience born to adorn the grief of my senses that fancied they had murdered Rita, the phantom" (*FM,* 165). The book ends with an allusion to Barbey d'Aurevilly's famous comment on Huysmans, that after *A Rebours* the novelist's destiny was either the barrel of a pistol or the foot of the cross. The last pages of Hecht's novel feature a drawing by Wallace Smith of a tormented-looking Mallare crucified upon a blank, black background, opposite the words: "Pity me. This is the cross" (*FM,* 174).

The Kingdom of Evil: A Continuation of the Journal of Fantazius Mallare is set exclusively within what the earlier novel terms "the caverns of Mallare" because "his genius was still able to rear the debris of hallucinations" (*KE,* 2). As the title indicates, the novel is almost entirely a description of Mallare's journal, which begins with a parody of Carl Sandburg's once-famous poem about meteorological conditions in Chicago: "The fog drifted into the city like a great blind moth. It fluttered in the air peering in at high windows. Slowly it stretched its vast wings destroying steeples and housetops" (*KE*, 7). Having disposed of everyday reality, the imaginary journal begins the story of a group of artists, poets, architects, engineers, and scientists—"the high priests of progress" (*KE*, 17)—held captive on an island by one Dr. Sebastien, who has "stolen" them "from the world to build the Kingdom of Evil" (*KE*, 43). Using a substance called "Alphaplasm" (*KE*, 56) and assisted by an army of hermaphrodites, Dr. Sebastien builds a strange organic city: "Spermatazoic towers and venereal rainbows spawn like a foul vegetation" (*KE*, 80). Fantazius Mallare becomes the slave of Dr. Sebastien's mistress Kora, "a whip flourishing andromaniac" (*KE*, 79). The relationship of Mallare and Kora partly reverses the story of Mallare and the Gypsy Rita in the earlier novel, as Kora whips her slave because she is jealous of the fantasies she inspires in him: "A strange rage overcomes me when I see your fawning, worshipful eyes raised to me. I grow angered because your eyes see something hidden from mine. I am jealous of the illusions I inspire in your head" (*KE*, 95). Kora is one unhappy andromaniac, in part because no God exists in the Kingdom of Evil, and in keeping with the diabolic tradition the pleasures of sin are lost if there is no God to sin against. As Kora puts it, "Without a God I cannot endure my corruption nor hide from it" (*KE*, 98). Dr. Sebastien and the hermaphrodite slaves therefore set out to mold a God out of Alphaplasm to please Kora. They succeed in growing a plantlike temple for the God, but molding and growing the God Himself is more difficult, as Mallare and one of his companions observe:

> Around us in every direction were dreadful, nauseating figures; two-headed things with faces drooping at the ends of wilted stalks; creatures with boneless limbs and bodies like pouches; creatures with swollen and pendulous heads riveting them to the earth; animate snail-like masses of flesh, hair-matted and mucous-covered; thick, serpent-like bodies that struggled to stand erect; half-formed heads that raised themselves above appalling disfigurements. I could not believe them alive at first and thought they must be matter that had erupted fungus fashion out of the earth. But staring I detected amid these obscene and tumorous shapes, horrifying human fragments—the arm of a man, the perfect breasts of a woman; human eyes staring out of putrescent and formless growths, human lips red and grimacing

> in swollen smiles. Around us they crept, emitting sounds, clawing at the air with fingers and stumps—a convulsive debris of faces, limbs and fetal distortions moving like foul bags of life. (*KE,* 114)

Finally, a God is created; His name is Synthemus. He is a large plant with a human form that grows to huge size and keeps growing (since the God is supposed to be infinite). The God has no brain, but somehow He manages to let out a bellowing sound that lasts all night long. At first Kora is pleased with the God, but she soon grows tired of Him and His incessant bellowing. As for Mallare, he is about to be sacrificed to Synthemus but is saved when a group of rebels opposed to Dr. Sebastien begin their attack and kill the God, whose decaying body in His temple is described in some detail: "In the center, bent in a colossal bow, stands the God rotted away to a blackened, reeking cadaver. The vast bones of his body glisten through the eaten spaces. Armies of white and swollen maggots move like a continuous and fluttering shadow over this orgie of decay. The monster, crusted with blood, its gigantic entrails gleaming like phosphorescent walls, fills the place with vile exhalations as if He still breathed, as if the tattered and moulded flesh over which the verminous feasters swarm with an exultant hum, still throbbed with a dark and nauseous life" (*KE,* 204–5). This and everything else that is described in the journal is really only a description of Mallare's hallucinations. Kora, for instance, is only "the lust that lives in Mallare" (*KE,* 157), whose "madness is so powerful" (*KE,* 161) it can create hallucinations within hallucinations, fantasy creatures who fantasize that Mallare himself is *their* creation.

Both *Fantazius Mallare* and *The Kingdom of Evil* are literary curiosities, and one of the things that makes them curious is the fusion of French decadence and German expressionism. Hecht was exposed to expressionism firsthand in 1918 when he traveled to postwar Berlin as a correspondent for the *Daily News.* There he met Georg Grosz (whose art Hecht later promoted in America) and also attended several dadaist meetings and concerts.[42] The exposure to dada was less important than that of expressionism, at least with regard to Hecht's literary output. What he shares with expressionism in his two books about Fantazius Mallare is the tendency to represent action as it appears to a participant in the action, and not to an outside observer. (Again, this suggests the dualism of Hecht's career as both artist and reporter.) *The Kingdom of Evil,* in particular, resembles Robert Wiene's classic expressionist film, *The Cabinet of Dr. Caligari.* In the film, the manipulation of the somnambulist Cesar by the evil mountebank Caligari is revealed to be nothing more than the paranoic hallucinations of the young man in the care of Dr. Caligari, who in reality is the head of a mental asylum. Interestingly, Carl Sandburg reviewed *Caligari* in 1921 and said that the film "looks like a collaboration of Rube Goldberg, Ben Hecht, Charlie Chaplin and Edgar Allan Poe."[43] Clearly, the Mallare books and *Caligari* have in common the device of treating hallucination as reality. The difference is that Hecht's madman Mallare has an aesthetic attitude toward his own madness; he is conscious of his hallucinations and tries to shape them to his pleasure. In this he does not always succeed.

Despite the expressionistic technique, the Mallare books take their stock of images, and the character Mallare himself, from the French rather than the German tradition. The English decadence is also represented, mainly in *Fantazius Mallare,* by Hecht's tireless ability to turn out epigrams: "Democracy is the honeymoon of stupidity" (*FM,* 22); "The will to live is no more than the hypnotism of banalities" (*FM,* 25); "To go mad is to succumb to the insanity of others" (*FM,* 41); and so on. The name of the character, originally called "Maldor,"[44] is obviously derived from Lautréamont's Maldoror, as is Mallare's intellectual and artistic detachment from all forms of human suffering, including his own. In *The Kingdom of Evil,* the influence of Huysmans and Baudelaire is manifest, mainly in the description of the abortive creatures made of molded Alphaplasm and in the description of the dead God. The deformed organisms that Mallare comes across in the strange grove seem like Des Esseintes's collection of bizarre, fleshly plants come to life as human fragments, while the extended description of the decaying body of God owes much to Baudelaire's "Une Charogne." In fact, not only is Hecht's imagery similar to Baudelaire's, but also the meaning that the imagery suggests: the death of the soul, the death of God. This meaning is also in harmony with the iconoclastic Nietzscheanism represented in the early issues of the *Little Review* that evidently impressed Hecht rather deeply. Actually, the impression might be better described as shallow rather than deep, since the Nietzschean element in Hecht is as conventional as the hypocritical puritanism he sets it against.

By the time of Huneker and Hecht, the complicated, interdependent paradoxes of decadence—Baudelaire's *idéal* and *spleen,* Wilde's art and life, Nietzsche's health and sickness—have become overtly dualistic but oddly coexistent conventions. In Baudelaire, the mutual dependency of *idéal* and *spleen* notwithstanding, the two states cannot be experienced by the poet at the same time, just as, in Flaubert, there can be no continuity of romanticism and realism without an alternation from one to the other. Similarly, Walter Pater asks the aesthete to measure the power of great art against the flux of everyday experience. Even Huysmans's Satanism in *Là-Bas* derives its force as the contrary, not the negation, of Catholic faith. *The Paradox of Redemptive Satanism* is the title of a book on Baudelaire that says a great deal about the moral complexity of nineteenth-century diabolism: the sinner cannot believe in damnation without also believing in redemption.[45] This element of belief is missing from Huneker's diabolism, which seems animated by nothing more than a simplistic variety of Manichaean rhetoric that turns decadence into "evil." Moreover, the diabolism toward which Huneker aspires is mainly a bourgeois pretense, an effort to "behave" within the imagined boundaries of aristocratic style: "It takes brains to be wicked in the grand manner," he says (*IA,* 328). In Hecht's two Mallare books, there is little active interplay between reality and illusion, as in Baudelaire, where disgust with reality sends the poet off in the direction of *l'idéal,* but only until the attractions of the real world assert themselves again, which, in turn, feed the poet's splenetic guilt and sends him back to the ideal. And so on, back and forth, until he is faced with the abysmal absence he called *le gouffre.* In Hecht, the Baudelairean void is precisely what is missing, especially in his naturalistic novels. In *Gargoyles* and *Eric Dorn,* the principal characters are so "Nietzschean" that morality and immorality, virtue and vice, good and evil, are interchangeable, coexistent, parallel. Such coexistence is possible because belief is no longer possible: good and evil are social conventions that any "Michigan Avenue Nietzsche"[46] can "transvalue" at will.

The dualism of private corruption and public virtue is the single-minded theme of Ben Hecht's *Gargoyles,* published in 1922. The novel opens in 1900, with the young lawyer George Basine recovering from a night of debauchery in the brothels of Chicago and rationalizing away any sense of personal wrongdoing in such behavior. Basine excuses his debaucheries in the name of biological determinism: "He was young and given to evil. This was only natural" (*G,* 10). The memories of the night before do "not conflict with his character as a citizen of virtue. For they were memories which he was prepared at any moment to repudiate and denounce" (*G,* 11–12). Basine leads a double life, alternating between morality and immorality, but his duplicity does not trouble him at all: "The crimes Basine committed—usually no greater than normal violations of the ethical code to which he subscribed—were things that had nothing to do with the real Basine. The real Basine was the Basine whom people knew. The real Basine was a characterization he maintained for the benefit of others. The crimes were his own secret. People didn't know them. Therefore they did not exist. They remained locked away. He did not say to himself, 'Hypocrite! Liar!' " (*G,* 36). The public Basine has a habit of "rewriting life so as to fit himself with the heroic part" (*G,* 15), which yields an "ideal Basine—a nobly edited version of his character" (*G,* 37). Here, a fictional character thinks of himself as the author of himself, rewriting and editing his private immoralities into public virtue. This ideal, "edited" Basine is "a mixture of lies, shams, perversions of fact. But that was only when you considered him in relation to his creator—to its original. In his own mind it was absurd to consider this ideal Basine in relation to its creator as it would have been for a critic of aesthetics to consider the merits of Oscar Wilde's poetry in relation to the degeneracy of the man" (*G,* 37).

This reference to Oscar Wilde is the only explicit link to nineteenth-century decadence in *Gargoyles,* but the general motif of the double life recalls several nineteenth-century novels, including *Dorian Gray.* Where Wilde uses the motif as a vehicle both for aesthetic commentary on the relationship of art and life and for a more deeply coded study of homosexuality, Hecht uses the motif mainly for the purpose of broad social satire, much in the manner of the first section of Mirbeau's *Le Jardin des supplices.* In *Gargoyles,* the same George Basine who frequents bordellos in his youth becomes a respected judge who heads a Vice Commission investigating the immorality of Chicago shopgirls who turn to prostitution because they are underpaid by their legitimate employers. During the investigation Basine begins the seduction of his private secretary, and even though the affair is not consummated, it leads to her ruin anyway.

The smaller hypocrisy of George Basine as immoral champion of morality is complicated by a larger hypocrisy; namely, his full knowledge that the vice campaign is undertaken for the purpose of promoting his own political career. And because the campaign is communicated to the people mainly through the newspapers, Basine's hypocrisy has its cognate in the hypocrisy of society at large: "The public is revelling in the salaciousness of nude photographs, raw statements and your anti-vice propaganda. They are utilizing virtue as a cloak for the sensually tantalizing discussion of morality. . . . The whole business is a cunning debauch offered newspaper readers, a debauch which enables them to appear to themselves and to each other not as debauchees but as high crusaders and civic benefactors behind the banner of Basine" (*G,* 288). This criticism of the campaign comes from a cynical newspaperman named Levine, who seems to be a self-portrait of Hecht himself: "He was a Jew and worked on a newspaper. Lean, vicious-tongued and unkempt, the fantastic skepticism of this man attracted her [Basine's sister Doris]. He was a man without principles, ideas, prejudices. His attitude toward life she sensed to be a pose. But he had been completely consumed by this pose and the pose was one of superiority. His brain was like a magician. It waved words over ideas or problems and they turned inside out. Or they vanished and reappeared again as their opposites" (*G,* 163). Here again is the suggestion that hypocrisy is allied with duplicitous linguistic procedures. Levine, the critic of hypocrisy, is himself something of a hypocrite, who poses as something he is not—but here the pose takes over completely. The passage can be read as a commentary on the decline of decadence. Without principles or ideas, the social or moral decadent has nothing to fall back on except rhetoric; the only way to live *à rebours* is by waving words around until ideas vanish or turn into their opposites.

In *Gargoyles* and in his best-known novel, *Eric Dorn,* Hecht presents characters who are completely duplicitous and absolutely unperturbed over their duplicity. The hero as hypocrite may be Hecht's singular contribution to modern fiction. Both Basine and Eric Dorn wear their moral vacuity lightly, and this moral lightness of being, to vary Milan Kundera's phrase, seemed quite bearable to Hecht himself. *Eric Dorn* is a novel of adultery, a highly autobiographical narrative that recasts Hecht's deception of his first wife Marie Armstrong with Rose Caylor, whom he later married. Hecht's hero gets away with adultery, and murder, while remaining morally unruffled. One year before his death, Hecht defended "the double standard" in sexual relationships, bewailing the openness of society in 1963: "The sexes have lost their mystery for each other. The double standard is practically gone. The double standard made you full of gusto—you had to lie all the time, you had to be a lively hypocrite."[47] Hecht was born too late to go against the grain of religion, but if he could not defy the institution of the church, at least he could defy the institution of marriage. Adultery may be the last refuge of the belated decadent.

Hecht's misogynistic endorsement of hypocrisy merely offends, but his "Nietzschean" vacuity is genuinely disturbing. In 1919, Hecht in the *News* and Burton Rascoe in the *Tribune* carried on a number of literary feuds, and Hecht hit upon the idea of conducting debates between the two of them before a paying audience. One of these took place at the Loeb mansion in Chicago, where Hecht met Mrs. Loeb's son Dickie; she told Hecht that her son was "one of your most ardent followers." "I think he has everything you have ever written," she said. Hecht's first wife Marie recalled that Dickie Loeb "shivered with the intensity of his hero worship, his eyes fired by Ben's audacious eloquence." In 1923, after the publication of *Gargoyles, Eric Dorn,* and *Fantazius Mallare,* and after young Loeb had, no doubt, told his friend Nathan Leopold about meeting and admiring Hecht, the two of them committed the notorious murder. In 1926, the critic Stuart Sherman commented further on the link between Leopold and Loeb and Ben Hecht: "Study the traits of these two young supermen who had lost the faculty of appropriate emotional reaction to experience, who looked at the human pageant, including their own trial, as detached intellectual spectators, and who killed a fourteen-year-old boy 'for fun'; and you will find there every prominent feature of the type of mind described by Mr. Hecht in *Eric Dorn.*"[48] While it will always be true that books do not kill people, people do, there is still something chilling about the whole affair. This feeling is intensified by the icy irony of Hecht's being called in as script-doctor for Alfred Hitchcock's *Rope,* a film based on the Leopold–Loeb murder.[49]

While Ben Hecht as a novelist, and even as a person, may give decadence a bad name, Hecht the screenwriter revives the decadent tradition in ways that are positive and productive, though difficult to analyze in detail. Indeed, the set of circumstances that brings decadence to the masses of America is a cultural phenomenon of vast dimensions. Pauline Kael is probably right in saying that "most of the best Hollywood writers of the 30s had a shared background; they had been reporters and critics, and they knew each other from their early days on newspapers and magazines."[50] What she does not say we have already noted: the newspapers and magazines where Hollywood's future screenwriters worked were often saturated with the belated, cosmopolitan decadence that James Huneker introduced to America. The genealogy of decadence we are tracing here runs from literary Europe in the 1890s to journalistic America in the 1920s to the Hollywood of the 1930s. This cultural transaction (Huysmans to Huneker to Hecht to Hollywood) is instanced by *The Scoundrel,* a film staring Noel Coward that Hecht wrote and directed in 1935.

Coward plays an unlikable publisher who dies in a plane crash and returns to earth seeking someone to mourn for him so that he may rest in peace, as Coward's voice-over says: "You died and no one cried for you. Your body is tossing. There is no rest for those who die unloved, unmourned. Go back before your doom is written for all eternity. . . . Let one heart cry for you and you will rest."[51] The character's name is Anthony Mallare, after Fantazius, an unfeeling rake given to Wildean epigrams such as this one: "Ah, if only women were as charming during a love affair as they are after it's over."[52] *Variety* called *The Scoundrel* "good Hotel Algonquin stuff," and the remark suggests another genealogy of decadence, this one tracing the Algonquin crowd's *New Yorker* back to H. L. Mencken's *Smart Set,* which was inspired by James Huneker's and Vance Thompson's *M'lle New York.* The point is that decadence accounts for a wide range of cultural expression in America, much of it with the kinds of direct links to the European tradition that turn up in *The Scoundrel.* A great many Hollywood films are based directly on decadent works, especially when the director is European. Examples include Renoir's *Diary of a Chambermaid,* based on Mirbeau's novel; von Sternberg's *The Devil is a Woman,* based on a book by Pierre Louÿs; and, less directly, Billy Wilder's *Sunset Boulevard,* in which Norma Desmond, the deranged old star of the silent screen, plans to make her return to fame in a film version of *Salome* that sounds suspiciously similar to Wilde's play. But of these three, von Sternberg's film must be singled out as an exemplary decadent work because of its wildly heterogeneous mix of cultures. Based on a fin de siècle novel inspired by the Spanish art of Goya, the film is directed by a German expressionist, and stars Marlene Dietrich as the Andalusian temptress Concha Perez, a role which Dietrich interprets as a French coquette. As if this French–German–Spanish, fin de siècle–expressionist mixture were not sufficient, Louÿs's *La Femme et le pantin* somehow turns into *The Devil is a Woman,* a title that may be derived from the American James Huneker, and features a soundtrack of "Spanish" music composed by the Russian Rimsky-Korsakov.[53]

But a film does not have to be written by someone like Hecht, whose links to decadence are clear, or based on a decadent novel to be grounded in the decadent tradition. Orson Welles's *Citizen Kane,* for example, is mainly a retrospective account of Charles Foster Kane's moral decline and political corruption. Actually, the film has some incidental connections to the kind of decadence typified by Hecht. Herman J. Mankiewicz who most likely authored most of the script, was Hecht's friend, and Welles himself was familiar with at least one of Hecht's novels. As Welles sat for the two-hour makeup sessions needed to transform him into the older, bloated Kane cloistered in his Xanadu palace, the makeup artist Maurice Seiderman asked an associate to read aloud from *The Kingdom of*

Evil. The makeup artist's ideas for the appearance of the older Kane had been inspired by Hecht's description of Dr. Sebastien in that novel, and he thought that Welles "could better relate to the character that Seiderman was creating and see himself, or Kane, as the 'gigantic man with a large head' who had an expressionless face. [Welles] loved and accepted the mimesis."[54] Indeed, like Fantazius Mallare and other Hechtian heroes, Charles Foster Kane becomes an extremely isolated figure, practicing a radical negation of life as he becomes increasingly removed from any activity in society whatsoever. Such decadence takes place amid Kane's vast accumulation of wealth and his wholesale acquisition of cultural artifacts from all over the world. Through a major segment of the film, Kane's obsession with high culture at any cost is symbolized by his obstinate support of his wife's doomed operatic career. She is a terrible singer. But Kane ignores the obvious reality, pretends that his wife is a great diva, and insists that everyone else do the same. The climax of the film comes as the friend of his youth, who was with him at the start of his career when Kane was a crusader for justice, and who later reminds Kane of the "Declaration of Principles" he made as a young man, tells the truth and gives Kane's wife the terrible review she deserves. Kane treats this honest return to principles and truth as a personal betrayal and fires his friend. He then forces his wife to sing in one pitiful operatic performance after another, and only when she attempts suicide does he stop the charade. The opera in question is a fictional one, but it serves to dramatize Kane's descent into a wasteland of empty pretense, excessive artifice, and cultural decadence: the opera is *Salammbô*. Reaching from antiquity to the twentieth century, from Flaubert's Carthage to Hollywood's "Xanadu," at the western edge of America the manifest destiny of decadence is finally fulfilled.

Postface

No cultural critic would ever think to call the 1990s "the tenth decade of the twentieth century." Once again, we live at the end, in the *last* decade, a "new" fin de siècle. And once again, the French phrase is required to describe this particular ending, as though the passing of the current millennium needs the certification of yet another prior decadence, this one only a hundred years old: "From urban homelessness to imperial decline, from sexual revolution to sexual epidemics, the last decades of the twentieth century seem to be repeating the problems, themes, and metaphors of the *fin de siècle*."[1] So says Elaine Showalter, and Emily Apter concurs: "The nineteenth-century legacy of hereditary taints [and] transmissible diseases of the body and the psyche seems eerily still in place within our own 'fin-de-sièclisms.' "[2] Likewise, in a book titled *France: Fin de Siècle,* Eugen Weber ticks off an extensive list of social and cultural ills common to the ends of both this century and the previous one: "Other objects of late-twentieth-century apprehension caused tremors one hundred years ago: pollution, crowding, noise, nerves, and drugs; threats to environment, to peace, to security, to sanity private and public; the noxious effects of press, publicity, and advertising; the decline of public and private standards; the rising tide of transgressions imperiling law and order. The commonweal, then as now on its last legs, looked on itself as into an abyss and shivered."[3] Such "then as now" comparisons of the last fin de siècle and the current one are subverted somewhat by Continental efforts toward a progressive and unified "Europe" of the future. For this reason, any talk of a contemporary "fin de siècle Europe" is bound to sound a little awkward. Less awkward is the use of the term fin de siècle to refer to American culture and society. Indeed, the practice appears to be on the rise, as Showalter's book *Sexual Anarchy* suggests. Subtitled *Gender and Culture in the Fin de Siècle*, the book is replete with analogies linking late nineteenth-century European culture (mainly British) to recent American developments. Without question, the "Fin de Siècle" of Showalter's subtitle refers equally to Europe then and America now (as in the phrase "fin-de-siècle post-feminist America").[4]

Since America has become the lone "superpower" in the world today, it stands to reason that any time concerns over global decline are voiced, an American accent is sounded. The paradox that places America at the core of both power and decline repeats the strange logic of the nineteenth century, which made Paris and London capitals of both progress and decadence. Some of the comparisons noted above seem particularly relevant to American life (the reference to "urban homelessness," for example) even when they are made in a global or general sense. In fact, likening the current American fin de siècle to the previous European one is almost too easy. Late nineteenth-century Europe had its venereal affliction in syphilis, while late twentieth-century America is plagued by AIDS. Alarmist scientists of the last century warned that the universe would die of heat loss, turning all of earth into an icy wasteland; today, the temperature of extinction has changed, and even an American vice president warns against the dread effects of global warming. A hundred years ago, illness was a fetish that made the convalescent, tubercular woman attractive and turned the chronically sick man into a sensitive genius; lately, a good many Americans of both sexes diet and exercise so obsessively that the concern with physical health borders on perversion. In nineteenth century Britain, the homosexual who left the closet wound up in jail; in twentieth-century America, gay men and women live their lives knowing that the sodomy laws are still on the books, and while homosexuals are rarely prosecuted, they are often persecuted. Similarly, the end of the last century saw women campaigning for basic rights, while the end of this one finds women, once again, in the midst of political struggles everywhere from the academy to the abortion clinic.

These comparisons, however, must be made with care, and with due respect for history. The prior fin de siècle may or may not be an appropriate model for the current one, depending on the issue under consideration. Some of the analogies noted above are quite innocuous, such as the contrary obsessions with sickness and health, or the contrast of the earlier heat-death theory with the current theory of global warming. Upon further reflection, however, one may find that the comparison of the latest American "decadence" with the previous European one sometimes cheapens history by falsely idealizing the present, or vice versa. For example, the women's movement may have stalled a bit of late, but even in its stalled form the political force of a century of feminism means that women have more power now than they did a century ago. On the other hand, the comparison of syphilis to AIDS appears misguided for several different reasons. First, before the tertiary stage of the disease was discovered, the well-educated nineteenth-century syphilitic thought he was suffering from something else, usually "neurasthenia," an "artistic" symptom of excessive refinement or heightened sensitivity. Second, once the tertiary stage was understood, the disease was treatable, and syphilis became little more than an inconvenient, though still painful, consequence of what is now called "unprotected" sex. Surely the appearance of the AIDS virus among so many members of the film, theater, and dance communities in America does not make the disease "artistic," any more than syphilis was an "artistic" disease in fact. Such aestheticizing of sickness is one of the grand myths of decadence that the AIDS epidemic abrogates completely. Turning AIDS into a fin de siècle disease for the sake of cultural commentary is, at best, bad taste. Nonetheless, that the commentary is made at all suggests a need to clarify contemporary American culture by linking it to the tradition of transition known as decadence.

By taking the last fin de siècle as a point of reference for this one, the cultural critic encourages the formation of a sensibility at once belated and futurist, decadent and avant-garde. Something of this temporal ambiguity may also be expressed by the word *postmodernism*. Indeed, Andreas Huyssen makes the point that postmodernism is "in search of tradition while pretending to innovation."[5] Huyssen's discussion of postmodernism reads, at times, like Poggioli's analysis of decadence, especially when he balances postmodernist claims about the end of history against "a search for a viable modern tradition apart from . . . the Proust–Joyce–Mann triad and outside the canon of classical modernism" (169). Although Huyssen does not use the term, his theory of postmodernism nicely accommodates the recent American development known as "multiculturalism," which might be defined as a "search for history" that is "also a search for cultural identities" (172). While it is too early to tell if multiculturalism and postmodernism are different cultural developments that happen to be parallel, or if multiculturalism is simply the most recent phase of postmodernism, at least they have a common base in their opposition to the modernist canon. Another common feature seems to be a focus on cultural heterogeneity, either by way of postmodernist pastiche or multiculturalist diversity. They are also similar in their claims to be in the avant-garde of cultural theory while at the same time seeking the revival of—or at least the reference to—earlier but neglected cultural traditions. Postmodernism is concerned with the detachment of cultural forms from their historical roots, which makes possible the free integration of those forms into new contexts. Multiculturalism likewise recognizes the potential of cultural difference and cultural mixture to new forms of aesthetic expression. The postmodern, multiculturalist project may be carried out for different reasons than Flaubert's revival of ancient Carthage, but the critique of received culture and the revival or construction of alternative traditions has much in common with the dynamics of decadence. For this reason, decadence might be a useful frame of reference for the American "fin de siècle" and the cultural mix of postmodernism and multiculturalism that characterizes it.

If for no other reason, the postmodern condition may be treated as a contemporary decadence because of the "sociological" disposition to compare the end of the twentieth century to the end of the nineteenth. As a cultural condition, postmodernity is like decadence insofar as it is felt to be a transitional age, a new period that marks the end of an earlier era. This meaning derives from *A Study of History* by Arnold Toynbee, who located the transition from the modern to the "post-Modern" period around 1875. Although Calinescu cautions against reading Toynbee's "post-Modern" as a synonym for "decadent," he also says that the historian's "prophetic language suggests irrationality, anarchy, and threatening indeterminacy."[6] Toynbee's emphasis on anarchy, in particular, recalls Nietzsche's revulsion over the allegedly fragmented, anarchistic, and decadent democracies of nineteenth-century modernity. In other words, Nietzsche's decadence and Toynbee's post-Modernity begin at about the same time. (In Toynbee's chronology, then, the artistic and literary developments customarily called "modernism" took place early in the "post-Modern" age.) Later usage of the epithet "post-Modern" ignores Toynbee's time frame and makes the term roughly synonymous with "postwar." Evidently, the publication of the later volumes of *A Study of History* in the years following World War II accounts for the shift in meaning. In other words, because the term "post-Modern" gained currency in the postwar years, it somehow came to refer to that period rather than to the period Toynbee intended.[7] In the 1950s, conservative cultural historians thought of postwar America as a period of declining moral standards in the face of the atomic age, and they used the word "postmodern" to describe this mix of anxiety and "decadence." Evidently, the threat of nuclear annihilation was not something that a person of merely modern sensibilities was equipped to handle.[8] This particular postwar meaning of the postmodern treats modernity as something that is neither good nor bad, but simply obsolete. Much more is at stake in the oft-rehearsed debate over postmodernism conducted by Jürgen Habermas and Jean-François Lyotard. In 1980, Habermas presented postmodernism as a neoconservative reaction to the unfinished business of modernity, or "the project of the Enlightenment." In attacking postmodernism in this way, Habermas was also attacking the French poststructuralist school of Jacques Derrida, Lyotard, and others. Lyotard's counterargument defends postmodernism by criticizing the modernity promoted by Habermas as nothing more than a collection of self-legitimating "metanarratives" (*métarécits*) that perpetuate the myth of human progress. In short, Habermas and Lyotard valorize postmodernism in opposite ways, but both conceive of it as a type of transition, although Habermas views the transition as a temporary modulation away from modernity, while Lyotard imagines that the movement away from the "enlightened" metanarratives of modernity will go on indefinitely.[9]

The foregoing discussion shows that decadence and postmodernism coincide in several ways. Both terms give a special cultural shading to the otherwise neutral process of temporal transition, and, more often than not, both postmodernism and decadence are concerned with the problem of decline. Another point of similarity is the contradictory valorization of the term as used by Habermas and Lyotard. Like decadence, postmodernism can just as easily be "positive" or "negative," depending on the context or the tradition with which it is either aligned or opposed. Usually, the positive and negative poles of postmodernism derive their energy, respectively, from literary theory and social theory. Sometimes, "postmodernism" is restricted to literary developments, while "postmodernity" refers mainly to a sociohistorical condition. Thus, postmodernist literature is generally felt to be a good thing, whereas postmodernity may be symptomatic of something objectionable in the social sphere. For example, the earliest use of "postmodernist" as a critical epithet in the American literary tradition is evidently Randall Jarrell's description in 1946 of Robert Lowell's poetry as "post- or anti-modernist."[10] Jarrell approves of Lowell's abandonment of modernist experimentation and his return to traditional verse forms in *Lord Weary's Castle*. Later, in 1959, Irving Howe uses "post-modern" to describe contemporary American fiction in generally favorable terms. As the American novel becomes increasingly self-conscious and experimental throughout the 1970s, it also becomes part of a postmodernist avant-garde movement that is widely regarded as vigorous and inventive. During this period of "metafiction" or "surfiction," American novels and short stories are not only called postmodern, but "postcontemporary" as well.[11] At this time, critics such as Susan Sontag, Leslie Fiedler, and Ihab Hassan have nothing but praise for postmodernist literature. The simple dichotomy I am presenting here, in which a positive (literary) postmodernism is concurrent with a negative (social) postmodernity, seems at first to be undercut by Harry Levin's alignment of literary postmodernism with cultural or intellectual decline. The preface to Levin's 1960 lecture "What Was Modernism?" identifies the modernist movement with "Humanism and the Enlightenment," which is set in opposition to an "anti-intellectual undercurrent" within modernism itself. When this undercurrent of irrationality "comes to the surface" the phenomenon is said to be "post-modern."[12] Levin's essay preserves what is really a dual dichotomy that opposes modernity to postmodernity and modernism to postmodernism. What Levin does, in fact, is value modernism for its modernity (i.e., Enlightenment) while denigrating postmodernism for its postmodernity (i.e., irrationality). In this regard, Levin anticipates by almost twenty years the arguments of Jürgen Habermas. Also, "What Was Modernism?" is one of the earliest instances of a phenomenon that has since become widespread: the confluence of literary and social theory as a means of making ideologically charged comments about the meaning of modernism. Although Levin is a defender of modernism, the retrospective, revisionist formula he employs has since become a postmodernist strategy in itself.

All of these observations oversimplify the complex relationship of modernism to postmodernism, but they also bring into focus some of the similarities of postmodernism and decadence. As with *decadence,* the term *postmodernism* seems to be a universal antonym, drawing its meaning from whatever it sets itself against. If modernist poetry is experimental, then postmodernist poetry is not. If modernist fiction is not a self-conscious exercise in self-referential metalanguage, then postmodernist fiction is. In philosophy and cultural criticism, postmodernity is either reactionary or progressive, depending on whether the line of argument descends from Habermas or Lyotard. The mysterious ways in which the word works are no doubt a function of the *post-* prefix, which allows the critic to invest the chronological designation with whatever meaning is needed, depending on his or her attitude toward modernism. Regardless of the attitude of the individual critic, however, postmodernism as a cultural condition must always define itself in the shadow of modernism. Postmodernism, it seems, is not only after modernism but *after* it as well, that is, engaged in an active pursuit of a prior condition in order to apprehend the present. Just as the decadence of the nineteenth century was simultaneously a reaction against romanticism and an extension of it, postmodernism also seems to negate and extend the meaning of modernism at the same time. If postmodernism does repeat the dynamics of decadence through a double relationship to prior culture, that activity is confirmed by the history of postmodernism that lies outside the American tradition. The first literary use of the term, as far as I know, occurs in 1934, when the Spanish critic Federico de Onís used the word *postmodernismo* to describe the reaction, dating from 1905, to *modernismo,* which in Spanish and South American literary history refers to a movement that is closely affiliated with French symbolist poetry and includes an element of decadence. In terms of American and English literary history, *postmodernismo* is roughly equivalent to modernism.[13] In other words, the reaction to *modernismo* known as *postmodernismo* partially negates a prior decadence but at the same time extends it into a form of modernity. Thus, the relationship of decadence to romanticism, of *postmodernismo* to *modernismo,* and, now, of postmodernism to modernism argues that cultural transition is not necessarily a succession of revolutions and reactions, of clearly zoned alternations from one mode to another, but modulations comprising contradiction and opposition, confirmation and negation, tradition and experimentation, decadentism and avant-gardism.

The current transition more often than not slights aesthetics in favor of poststructuralist theory, perhaps because the whole notion of aesthetics is itself part of the formalist element within modernism that postmodernism questions. Paradoxically, some of the philosophical principles of poststructuralist postmodernism, such as the idea of linguistic uncertainty or the "substitution" of textuality for reality, are thoroughly anticipated by the experimental nature of some modernist literature, as Derrida acknowledges. His comments on James Joyce's *Finnegans Wake* suggest that modernist aesthetics has left its mark on Derrida's deconstructive practice, the debt to Heidegger notwithstanding.[14] The contribution of modernist aesthetics to postmodernist theory implies the possibility of a further transformation of the new theory into a new aesthetic. There is a chance, in other words, that the linguistic turn of poststructuralist theory will come full circle. Some recent British novels suggest that the circle may be starting to close, and that deconstructive practice has paradoxically provided a model for the construction of a new type of novel. This type of literature can be called postmodernist for *aesthetic* reasons because of the way poststructuralism has been appropriated for fictional rather than for theoretical purposes, as Julian Barnes's novel *Flaubert's Parrot* (1984) illustrates.

By most accounts, Barnes's novel qualifies as postmodern because of its fictional application of deconstructive ideas. For example, Barnes's hero is an obsessive amateur scholar who believes he can recover or "recuperate" the meaning of *Une Coeur simple* by locating the original stuffed parrot that Flaubert used as a model for his description of Félicité's beloved Loulou. The scholar discovers not one "origin" but two, and then dozens.[15] The novel is, in effect, a parable of the deconstructive extension of Ferdinand de Saussure's argument that meaning proliferates from language as a result of its own internal system of differences, and not as a representation of a prior, "present" reality outside of language. Barnes's novel is also interesting because of the confluence of deconstructive practice and decadent culture. The hero of *Flaubert's Parrot,* for instance, is not that different from Des Esseintes in his cultural obsessiveness and connoisseurship. Also, the structure of the book sometimes recalls the encyclopedic nature of Huysmans's *A Rebours* or Flaubert's *Bouvard et Pecuchet.* In addition, Barnes's novel suggests Bourget's idea of *le style de décadence* in that its chapters are detachable from the whole, pages from chapters, and lines from pages. The reader does not come away from *Flaubert's Parrot* with any kind of unified understanding of the book (except, perhaps, that literature is not conducive to "unified understanding"), but with a collection of anecdotes. Clearly, Barnes has one foot in decadence and another in deconstruction.

The "deconstructive novel," as this genre may be termed, is mainly the product of English writers who have been receptive to French theory (Peter Ackroyd, David Lodge, and A. S. Byatt join Julian Barnes in this regard). American postmodernism, by contrast, is not really conducive to the cooperation of theory and aesthetics. In general, aesthetic considerations in the context of American postmodernism take the form of polemical or ideological critiques of modernism. Modernism today, as a literary phenomenon, is faulted for its hermeticism, its formalism, and its elitism, as well as the retrograde politics of such key modernists as Ezra Pound, T. S. Eliot, and Wyndham Lewis. It is tempting to think of this criticism as directed at the decadent element within modernism; namely, that element which privileges high culture and encourages art for art's sake. The only problem with this perspective is the number of decadent writers, such as Oscar Wilde and Anatole Baju, who were *also* socially and politically progressive. When such progressiveness sits side by side with elitist hyperculturalism (and even in Huysmans decadent culture and social progress coexist), the decadent writer no longer appears as the prototype of the retrograde modernist author. Despite this genealogical difficulty, the ideological critique of modernism has many benefits, not the least of which is a healthy redefinition of the term *modernism* itself that makes possible the inclusion of certain figures who at first seem to be unlikely candidates for canonization, but whose connection with modernism, however unorthodox, is undeniable. A good example of one of these "new" modernists is the anarchist Emma Goldman, who was directly affiliated with the modernism of the Chicago Renaissance through her association with Margaret Anderson.[16] Until recently, no cultural place existed for *political* writers with connections to literary modernism. But the carving out of cultural space for the inclusion of a new political modernism, and the criticism of the old modernism as apolitical, overconservative, or even fascistic, does not make the current cultural scene analogous to the end of the nineteenth century. If anything, the recent emphasis in American academic circles on the addition of political and moral discourse to the overall meaning of literature—and the use of political and moral criteria as determinants of value—recalls the middle of the nineteenth century, in both France and England. (For that matter, contemporary moral imperatives recall the middle of the twentieth century, namely Sartre's insistence on political *engagement*.) Both l'art pour l'art in France and "art for art's sake" in England evolved as a reaction to the belief that literature should have either a utilitarian or a moral purpose. Postmodernist multiculturalism, in turn, seems to be a reaction to this reaction.

It is not surprising, given the wish to imagine an American fin de siècle, that the modernists should be compared to the decadents and the multiculturalists to the barbarians.[17] Although modernism is more complex than the monocultural straw man it is set up to be in recent debates over multiculturalism, the image of modernism as predominantly male, misogynistic, elitist, and exclusionary has much in common with nineteenth-century decadentism. If modernism really were such a negative cultural construct, then an infusion of diverse cultural blood would be a welcome revival. However, the decadent : barbarian : : modernist : multiculturalist analogy falls apart if one returns to the actual documents of decadence, such as Gautier's essay on Baudelaire's *Les Fleurs du mal.* Although Gautier was concerned mainly with the search for an idiom appropriate to the experience of modernity, his description of decadent style as a heterogeneous construct of diverse vocabularies anticipates the diverse voices of multiculturalism. Gautier hailed Baudelaire as an innovator who extended the range of literary expression by borrowing from various "technical" vocabularies, instead of writing within the received tradition of a poetic idiom inherited from French *classicisme.* While the language of modernism is much more complex than the limited lexicon of Racine (the lexicon that Gautier praised Baudelaire for enriching), that language is clearly not suited to the multiculturalist expression of life in contemporary America. The problem of idiom that Gautier saw resolved in Baudelaire has reemerged in a new form. Baudelaire might have been able to write a poem about his mulatto mistress using the complex, learned style of decadence, but an avatar of Jeanne Duval would have a hard time writing a poem about Baudelaire using the same style today, in part because the complex, learned idiom of decadence involves colonialist comparisons of a woman's body to an exotic, "oriental" country.

In this hypothetical example, the difficulty arises because of differences between the dominant culture of Baudelaire and the dominated culture of Jeanne Duval. The cultural drama of dominant and dominated, of orthodoxy and heresy, has been thoroughly elaborated by Pierre Bourdieu, whose theories of cultural production are useful to the analysis of postmodernist confrontations between modernists and multiculturalists. According to Bourdieu, the existence of any "field of culture" involves a process of "position taking" and "position making," a process that necessarily requires the *creation* of oppositional cultural stances. The advent of multiculturalism supports Bourdieu's theory that cultural production operates according to the underlying laws he describes. At one time modernism was considered to be the highly iconoclastic art of the young, who are never mainstream or orthodox. However, this is precisely what modernism and its defenders have become as a result of its academic "consecration" (as Bourdieu would say) and the entrance of multiculturalism into the cultural field. The dynamics of the field requires that every new entry oppose an earlier orthodoxy, so that the heretical or heterodox group may gain a measure of cultural "capital" from those who control the "economy" of the cultural field.[18] Multiculturalist literature, as yet too unstable to have evolved a canon of its own, is currently being read *against* canonical modernism, in effect overstabilizing that canon and overdefining modernism itself as monocultural, Eurocentric, patriarchal, fascistic, and so on. Whether this negative valorization of modernism is valid or not is unimportant. What is important is the formation of a new position in the cultural field that appears to repeat the positioning of modernism itself. That is, just as modernism appears as a partial negation of decadence, so multiculturalism appears as a negation of modernism.

Multiculturalism therefore has more in common with modernism than is generally acknowledged, even as contemporary appeals to the nineteenth century as a prior decadence are not wholly different from Flaubert's appeal to ancient Carthage. Part of this appeal always involves a longing to replace contemporary culture with another, imaginary culture that is largely utopian. This desire is also expressed in the multiculturalist wish to revive or include alternative or heterodox cultures that presume to be more tolerant of social and gender differences than institutionalized modernism. Multiculturalist discontent with received culture is, however, different from the discontent of the decadents. The decadent malaise always involves an element of self-loathing, for the decadent sees himself as part and parcel of the very culture he despises. The decadent sigh of belatedness comes from within the gates of a worn-out civilization, while the multiculturalist complaint is heard outside them. Whether the multiculturalist project will succeed is at present unclear, especially if "success" is defined as institutional consecration. Such consecration would inevitably drain multiculturalism of much of the adversarial energy that animates it today. According to Bourdieu's logic, in cultural matters success inevitably fails, the winners lose and the losers win.[19] But regardless of who wins or loses, somehow the cultural millennium never arrives, and the age that succeeds a decadent period is always decadent itself in turn. The postmodernist, multiculturalist condition expresses, I believe, the same paradoxical nostalgia for the millennium that Flaubert felt, except that now the old hope for a new cultural world seems perpetually forestalled by the apocalypse of the past.

Flaubert and Baudelaire both thought of decadence as transition; to them, their age was in decay, but at least it was decaying *forward*. The parallelism of decadence and transition has become more problematic since modernism, in part because of the modernists' uncertainty about the usefulness of cultural and philosophical models based on *archē* and *telos,* origins and ends. Time and again, modernist thinking negates teleology in favor of the here and now, a radical sense of the present that is expressed, for example, through Joyce's idea of the epiphany, Saussure's invention of synchronic linguistics, and the surrealists' cultivation of qualitative *kairos* instead of quantitative *chronos.* In this temporal context, which rejects diachronic or progressive paradigms altogether, any retrospective assessment of modernism as modernity, as an Enlightenment project, seems to me curiously out of place, more a revisionist wish than a reality. Although many versions of modernism are—or were—forms of cultural renewal predicated upon a prior decadence, the very *fact* of modernism raises the question of whether cultural renewal is any longer possible at all. This is a paradox of large dimensions, for modernism identifies culture itself with renewal, and transforms transition into a constant state. *Die Brücke,* the bridge to tomorrow celebrated by various avant-gardes, is also a bridge into the unknown, or rather, the never-to-be-known. This is not to say that the avant-garde bridge leads nowhere, only that the bridge itself is the destination; the act of going, a place to go. The steady state of constant transition and cultural ferment may be the greatest heritage of modernism, although "heritage" is not exactly the right word. If perpetual renewal is indeed the "heritage" of modernism—a heritage that is not only contemporary but futurist—then there is no end to it. The only way to get beyond modernism may be to revise the newness out of it, to regard it in retrospect as decadence, as a predication toward some future renewal. To do this, however, is to repeat the reflex of modernism itself, to assume the cultural attitude of the modernist while calling it something else (postmodernism, antimodernism, multiculturalism, etc.). One of the striking things about analyses of postmodernism is, in fact, the frequency with which postmodernism is treated as a reprise of modernism.[20] Postmodernity may also be an oxymoron, since modernity we have always with us, if to be modern is to be contemporary, present, after everything that has gone before. In this relatively simple but ineluctable sense, there is nothing *later than* modernity, nor can there ever be anything later than modernity. At the same time, such radical contemporaneity seems belated: after all, it was the modernists who were new, not us. It was the modernists who made newness a thing of the past. Today, experimentation seems old-fashioned, and the avant-garde is something that is of interest only to the cultural archaeologist. Hence all future efforts toward a futurist condition, the desire to go forward, to get on with it, to "make it new," and so on, must always seem regressive, retrograde, backward. What is progress *now* but a desire to go backward to a time when it was possible to go forward? Progression *à rebours* illustrates that even those with the best of cultural intentions are destined for decadence.

33. Andreas Huyssen, *After the Great Divide: Modernism, Mass Culture, Postmodernism* (Bloomington: Indiana University Press, 1986), 45.

34. Showalter, *Sexual Anarchy,* 7–8. On this topic, Showalter also quotes Toril Moi, *Sexual/Textual Politics* (London: Methuen, 1985), 167.

35. George J. Becker and Edith Philips, ed. and trans., *Paris and the Arts, 1851–1896: From the Goncourt "Journal"* (Ithaca: Cornell University Press, 1971), 309. Entry dated 8 December 1893.

36. Marie Thérèse Jacquet, ed., *Le Dictionnaire des idées reçues* (Paris: Nizet, 1990), 231: "EPOQUE (LA NOTRE). Tonner contre elle. Se plaindre de ce qu'elle n'est pas poétique. L'appeler époque de transition, de décadence."

37. Charles Baudelaire, *Curiosités esthétiques* (Paris: Conard, 1923), 105–6. Quoted by Smith, "The Concept of Decadence," 642.

2. Decadence and Romanticism

1. Harry Levin, *The Gates of Horn: A Study of Five French Realists* (New York: Oxford University Press, 1966), 285.

2. Ibid., 286.

3. See Martine Frier-Wantiez, *Sémiotique du fantastique: Analyse textuelle de "Salammbô"* (Berne: Peter Lang, 1979). According to Todorov, the generic sine qua non of fantastic literature is a sense of hesitation, felt by the reader, between natural and supernatural explanations of events depicted in the text. See *Introduction à la littérature fantastique* (Paris: Editions du Seuil, 1970), 36. Given this definition, much of *Salammbô* seems to be not fantastic but merely marvelous, as when the mysterious sympathy between Salammbô and the moon is described (see chap. 3; once during an eclipse, we are told, Salammbô almost died), or when Salammbô dies at the end of the novel, not from natural causes, but from touching the forbidden veil of Tanit. It should be noted that Todorov does not mention *Salammbô* in his influential study.

4. "L'Antiquité . . . ne comporte pas, de notre part, le roman historique proprement dit, qui suppose l'entière familiarité et l'affinité avec le sujet." *Nouveaux Lundis* (Paris: Lévy, 1881), 4:80.

5. See *Impressionism* (Secaucus, N.J.: Chartwell Books, 1973), 7. Louis Leroy was a reporter for *Le Charivari* when he "invented" the term.

6. Quotations in French from *Salammbô* (Paris: Gallimard, 1970) are bracketed and followed by parenthetical page citations. Quotations in English are followed by parenthetical references to volume and page numbers of an anonymous translation titled *Salammbô: A Romance of Ancient Carthage,* 2 vols. (New York: Walter Dunne, 1904).

7. Anne Green, "*Salammbô* and Nineteenth-Century French Society," in *Critical Essays on Gustave Flaubert,* ed. Laurence M. Porter (Boston: G. K. Hall, 1986),

Notes

Preface

1. Parenthetical quotations refer to Charles Baudelaire, *Oeuvres complètes* ([Paris]: Editions Gallimard, 1975), 1:31–32.

2. See Roger L. Williams, *The Horror of Life* (Chicago: University of Chicago Press, 1980).

3. Roger Shattuck, *The Banquet Years: The Origins of the Avant-Garde in France, 1885 to World War I,* rev. ed. (New York: Vintage, 1968), 4. See also Jerrold Seigel, *Bohemian Paris: Culture, Politics, and the Boundaries of Bourgeois Life, 1830–1930* (New York: Viking Penguin, 1986) for a discussion of the romantic-bohemian preamble to decadence.

4. Ruth Z. Temple, "Truth in Labelling: Pre-Raphaelitism, Aestheticism, Decadence, Fin de Siècle," *English Literature in Transition* 17 (1974): 218.

5. See Eugen Weber, *France: Fin de Siècle* (Cambridge: Harvard University Press, 1986).

6. See Stephen G. Brush, *The Temperature of History: Phases of Science and Culture in the Nineteenth Century* (New York: Franklin, 1977), especially chap. 5, "The Heat Death," 61–76.

7. Jean Pierrot, *The Decadent Imagination, 1880–1900,* trans. Derek Coltman (Chicago: University of Chicago Press, 1981): "[D]ecadence constitutes the common denominator of all the literary trends that emerged during the last two decades of the nineteenth century" (7). See also George Ross Ridge, *The Hero in French Decadent Literature* (Athens: University of Georgia Press, 1961), where decadence is termed the "common metaphysical concern" of symbolism, naturalism, and realism (2).

8. Geoffrey Hartman, "Toward Literary History," in *In Search of Literary Theory,* ed. Morton W. Bloomfield (Ithaca: Cornell University Press, 1972), 197.

1. The Definition of Decadence

1. Ruth Z. Temple, "Truth in Labelling: Pre-Raphaelitism, Aestheticism, Decadence, Fin de Siècle," *English Literature in Transition* 17 (1974): 214.

2. G. L. Van Roosbroeck, *The Legend of the Decadents* (New York: Institut des Etudes Françaises, 1927), 14.

3. Camille Paglia, *Sexual Personae: Art and Decadence from Nefertiti to Emily Dickinson* (New York: Vintage, 1990), 35, 36, 108, 109, 123, 129, 231, 389, 136, 152, 262.

4. Koenraad W. Swart, *The Sense of Decadence in Nineteenth-Century France* (The Hague: Martinus Nijhoff, 1964), 2–3.

5. Mario Praz, *The Romantic Agony*, 2d ed., trans. Angus Davidson (Oxford: Oxford University Press, 1951), 31.

6. A. E. Carter, *The Idea of Decadence in French Literature, 1830–1900* (Toronto: University of Toronto Press, 1958), 4.

7. Phillip Stephan, *Paul Verlaine and the Decadence, 1882–1890* (Totowa, N.J.: Rowman and Littlefield, 1974), 19.

8. Quoted by Renato Poggioli, *The Theory of the Avant-Garde*, trans. Gerald Fitzgerald (Cambridge: Harvard University Press, 1968), 75.

9. Matei Calinescu, *Five Faces of Modernity: Modernism, Avant-Garde, Decadence, Kitsch, Postmodernism* (Durham: Duke University Press, 1987), 170.

10. See Poggioli, *Theory of the Avant-Garde*, 30, and passim.

11. Calinescu, *Five Faces of Modernity*, 178.

12. "Se dissimuler l'état de décadence ou nous sommes arrivés serait le comble de l'insenséisme. Religion, moeurs, justice, tout décade.... La société se désagrège sous l'action corrosive d'une civilisation déliquescente. . . . Nous vouons cette feuille aux innovations tuantes, aux audaces stupéfiantes, aux incohérences à trente-six atmosphères dans la limite la plus reculée de leur compatibilité avec ces conventions archaïques étiquettées du nom de morale publique. Nous serons les vedettes d'une littérature idéale. . . . En un mot, nous serons les mahdis clamant éternellement le dogme élixirisé, le verbe quintessencié du décadisme triomphant." Noël Richard, *Le Movement décadent: Dandys, esthètes et quintessents* (Paris: Nizet, 1968), 24. Quoted and translated by Calinescu, *Five Faces of Modernity*, 175–76, 339.

13. "La décadence esthétique, elle, doit s'entendre par antiphrase; elle est synonyme de jeunesse fringante et de renouvellement." Noël Richard, *Le Movement décadent*, 259.

14. "Cependant, s'il s'agit de Mallarmé et d'un groupe littéraire, l'idée de décadence a été assimilée à son idée contraire, à l'idee même d'innovation." Remy de Gourmont, *La Culture des idées*, 16th ed. (Paris: Mercure de France, 1916), 116, 117.

15. Jean Pierrot, *The Decadent Imagination, 1880–1900*, trans. Derek Coltman (Chicago: University of Chicago Press, 1981), 5.

16. Calinescu, *Five Faces of Modernity*, 212.

17. "[P]ossiamo . . . considerare entrambi [Baudelaire and Dostoevsky] come i precursori e i capisaldi della nuova sensibilità. E il nuovo che essi rappresentano rispetto alla sensibilità romantica può essere sinteticamente indicato nella decisa apertura ai contenuti e alla logica dell'"inconscio." Il Decadentismo nasce quando, in rapporto alla scoperta dell'inconscio, si arriva all'identificazione di Io e Mondo (l'inconscio è la parte dell'io che partecipa della vita della natura), con la messa in crisi del realismo e del sentimentalismo, che costituiscono le fondamenta stesse del Romanticismo." Elio Gioanola, *Il decadentismo*, 2d ed. (Rome: Edizioni Studium, 1977), 29.

18. "It [the adjective *decadent*] emerges as the underside or logical complement of something else, coerced into taking its place in our vocabularies by the pressure of something that needs an opposite, an enemy." Richard Gilman, *Decadence: The Strange Life of an Epithet* (New York: Farrar, Straus, and Giroux, 1979), 159.

19. Roger L. Williams, *The Horror of Life* (Chicago: University of Chicago Press, 1980), x, xi.

20. Swart, *Sense of Decadence*, 67.

21. Calinescu, *Five Faces of Modernity*, 156.

22. Claude-Marie Senninger, ed., *Baudelaire par Théophile Gautier* (Paris: Klincksieck, 1986), 125.

23. Renato Poggioli, "Qualis Artifex Pereo! or Barbarism and Decadence," *Har vard Library Bulletin* 13, no. 1 (Winter 1959): 141–42, 136–37. Quoted by Geor Ross Ridge, *The Hero in French Decadent Literature* (Athens: University of Geo Press, 1961), 47, 23.

24. Praz, *Romantic Agony*, 401.

25. See José Ortega y Gasset, *The Dehumanization of Art and Other Es Art, Culture, and Literature* (Princeton: Princeton University Press, 1968).

26. Ibid., 10–11.

27. Geoffrey Hartman, "Toward Literary History," in *In Search of L ory*, ed. Morton W. Bloomfield (Ithaca: Cornell University Press, 1972)

28. James M. Smith, "The Concept of Decadence in Ninete French Literature," *Studies in Philology* 50 (1953): 651.

29. Elaine Showalter, *Sexual Anarchy: Gender and Culture at* (New York: Viking Penguin, 1990), 3.

30. Rachel Bowlby, *Just Looking* (New York: Methuen, 19 Showalter, *Sexual Anarchy*, 77.

31. Williams in *The Horror of Life* records that Flaubert Hardy, who described the writer as a "hysterical old woma cites this entry from the Goncourt *Journal* dated 20 Decen like two women who live together, whose health is identi at the same time. Even our migraines develop on the sa

32. Showalter, *Sexual Anarchy*, 11.

115. The other analogies between ancient Carthage and Second Empire France discussed in this paragraph are also taken from Green's essay.

8. Robert Rosenblum, *Paintings in the Musée d'Orsay* (New York: Stewart, Tabori and Chang, 1989), 22.

9. Quoted by Eugen Weber, *France: Fin de Siècle* (Cambridge: Harvard University Press, 1986), 16.

10. Cited by Eugenio Donato in *The Script of Decadence: Essays on the Fictions of Flaubert and the Poetics of Romanticism* (New York: Oxford University Press, 1993), 40.

11. Cited by Donato, *The Script of Decadence*, 44.

12. Ibid., 42.

13. "[Flaubert] passe outre à l'archéologie incontinent; il invente, sur la fin de ces funérailles, des supplices, des mutilations de cadavres, des horreurs singulières, raffinées, immondes. Une pointe d'imagination sadique se mêle à ces descriptions . . ." *Nouveaux Lundis*, 4:71.

14. See Mario Praz, *The Romantic Agony*, 2d ed., trans. Angus Davidson (Oxford: Oxford University Press, 1951), chap. 3, "The Shadow of the Divine Marquis," 97–195.

15. Roger L. Williams, *The Horror of Life* (Chicago: University of Chicago Press, 1980), 171.

16. For a complete discussion of this point, see Williams's chapter on Flaubert in *The Horror of Life*, 110–215.

17. "Ces sortes d'expression datent un livre. Les remarques qu'un de mes honorables confrères, M. Cuvillier-Fleury, a faites à ce propos sur les écrivains de la décadence romaine classique, ses rapprochements avec Lucain, avec Claudien, ont de la justesse." *Nouveaux Lundis*, 4:92.

18. "Eh bien! le coté politique, le caractère des personnages, le génie du peuple, les aspects par lesquels l'histoire particulière de ce peuple navigateur, et civilisateur à sa manière, regarde l'histoire générale et intéresse le grand courant de la civilisation, sont sacrifiés ici ou entièrement subordonnés au côté descriptif exorbitant, à un dilettantisme qui, ne trouvant à s'appliquer qu'à de rares débris, est forcé de les exagérer." *Nouveaux Lundis*, 4:86.

19. Roland Barthes uses the phrase "artifice of reading" in *S/Z*, trans. Richard Howard (New York: Hill and Wang, 1974), 19, to describe the proairetic code, the terms of which are "actions" ordered empirically by the reader, and which usually follow a preexisting logic; that is, the "already done" or the "already read," that which is expected by one familiar with a set of conventions. I use the phrase here to suggest that another set of conventions has evolved with the development of literary modernism, and that other expectations have come into being. The reader of a modernist text now *expects* obscurity and discontinuity, for example, and his appreciation of such elements is an acquired taste, a new artifice of reading.

20. *Nouveaux Lundis*, 4:35.

21. "Le drapeau de la Doctrine sera, cette fois, franchement porté, je vous en réponds! Car ça ne prouve rien, ça ne dit rien, ce n'est historique, ni satirique, ni humoristique." Letter to Edmond and Jules de Goncourt, dated 3 July 1860. *Correspondance* (Paris: Conard, 1927) 4:379.

22. See listing of references to "l'art pour l'art" in Charles Carlut, *La Correspondance de Flaubert: Etude et répertoire critique* (Columbus: Ohio State University Press, 1968), 259–61. Carlut includes the reference cited in note 21, above, in his list (260).

23. See letter dated 16 January 1852, *Correspondance* 2:345.

24. Ruth Z. Temple, "Truth in Labelling: Pre-Raphaelitism, Aestheticism, Decadence, Fin de Siècle," *English Literature in Transition* 17 (1974): 208.

25. "Il n'y a de vraiment beau que ce qui ne peut servir à rien . . ." Théophile Gautier, preface to *Mademoiselle de Maupin*, in *Anthology of Critical Prefaces to the Nineteenth-Century French Novel*, ed. Herbert S. Gershman and Kernan B. Whitworth, Jr. (Columbia: University of Missouri Press, 1962), 104.

26. Robert T. Denommé, *Leconte de Lisle* (New York: Twayne, 1973), 33.

27. Ibid., 41.

28. "Les hymnes et les odes inspirées par la vapeur et la télégraphie électrique m'émeuvent médiocrement, et toutes ces périphrases didactiques, n'ayant rien de commun avec l'art." *Poésies complètes* (Geneva: Slatkine Reprints, 1974), 4:217, 216.

29. ". . . l'examen des faits historiques et des institutions, l'analyse sérieuse des moeurs . . ." *Poésies complètes*, 4:218.

30. ". . . exciteront toujours un intérêt plus profond et plus durable que le tableau daguerréotypé des moeurs et des faits contemporains." *Poésies complètes*, 4:222.

31. "Je vais écrire un roman dont l'action se passera trois siècles avant Jésus-Christ, car j'éprouve le besoin de sortir du monde moderne, où ma plume s'est trop trempée et qui d'ailleurs me fatigue autant à reproduire qu'il me dégoûte à voir." Letter to Mademoiselle Leroyer de Chantepie, dated 18 March 1857. *Correspondance*, 4:164.

32. Victor Brombert, *The Novels of Flaubert: A Study of Themes and Techniques* (Princeton: Princeton University Press, 1966), 105.

33. Ibid.

34. Ibid., 102–3.

35. Quotations from Gautier's "L'Art" refer to the text in *The Penguin Book of French Verse*, ed. Anthony Hartley et al. (Baltimore: Penguin, 1975), 397–400.

36. See note 49 below.

37. Brombert, *Novels of Flaubert*, 105–6.

38. Levin, *Gates of Horn*, 277.

39. Stratton Buck, *Gustave Flaubert* (New York: Twayne, 1966), 90.

Notes

Preface

1. Parenthetical quotations refer to Charles Baudelaire, *Oeuvres complètes* ([Paris]: Editions Gallimard, 1975), 1:31–32.

2. See Roger L. Williams, *The Horror of Life* (Chicago: University of Chicago Press, 1980).

3. Roger Shattuck, *The Banquet Years: The Origins of the Avant-Garde in France, 1885 to World War I*, rev. ed. (New York: Vintage, 1968), 4. See also Jerrold Seigel, *Bohemian Paris: Culture, Politics, and the Boundaries of Bourgeois Life, 1830–1930* (New York: Viking Penguin, 1986) for a discussion of the romantic-bohemian preamble to decadence.

4. Ruth Z. Temple, "Truth in Labelling: Pre-Raphaelitism, Aestheticism, Decadence, Fin de Siècle," *English Literature in Transition* 17 (1974): 218.

5. See Eugen Weber, *France: Fin de Siècle* (Cambridge: Harvard University Press, 1986).

6. See Stephen G. Brush, *The Temperature of History: Phases of Science and Culture in the Nineteenth Century* (New York: Franklin, 1977), especially chap. 5, "The Heat Death," 61–76.

7. Jean Pierrot, *The Decadent Imagination, 1880–1900,* trans. Derek Coltman (Chicago: University of Chicago Press, 1981): "[D]ecadence constitutes the common denominator of all the literary trends that emerged during the last two decades of the nineteenth century" (7). See also George Ross Ridge, *The Hero in French Decadent Literature* (Athens: University of Georgia Press, 1961), where decadence is termed the "common metaphysical concern" of symbolism, naturalism, and realism (2).

8. Geoffrey Hartman, "Toward Literary History," in *In Search of Literary Theory,* ed. Morton W. Bloomfield (Ithaca: Cornell University Press, 1972), 197.

1. The Definition of Decadence

1. Ruth Z. Temple, "Truth in Labelling: Pre-Raphaelitism, Aestheticism, Decadence, Fin de Siècle," *English Literature in Transition* 17 (1974): 214.

2. G. L. Van Roosbroeck, *The Legend of the Decadents* (New York: Institut des Etudes Françaises, 1927), 14.

3. Camille Paglia, *Sexual Personae: Art and Decadence from Nefertiti to Emily Dickinson* (New York: Vintage, 1990), 35, 36, 108, 109, 123, 129, 231, 389, 136, 152, 262.

4. Koenraad W. Swart, *The Sense of Decadence in Nineteenth-Century France* (The Hague: Martinus Nijhoff, 1964), 2–3.

5. Mario Praz, *The Romantic Agony*, 2d ed., trans. Angus Davidson (Oxford: Oxford University Press, 1951), 31.

6. A. E. Carter, *The Idea of Decadence in French Literature, 1830–1900* (Toronto: University of Toronto Press, 1958), 4.

7. Phillip Stephan, *Paul Verlaine and the Decadence, 1882–1890* (Totowa, N.J.: Rowman and Littlefield, 1974), 19.

8. Quoted by Renato Poggioli, *The Theory of the Avant-Garde*, trans. Gerald Fitzgerald (Cambridge: Harvard University Press, 1968), 75.

9. Matei Calinescu, *Five Faces of Modernity: Modernism, Avant-Garde, Decadence, Kitsch, Postmodernism* (Durham: Duke University Press, 1987), 170.

10. See Poggioli, *Theory of the Avant-Garde*, 30, and passim.

11. Calinescu, *Five Faces of Modernity*, 178.

12. "Se dissimuler l'état de décadence ou nous sommes arrivés serait le comble de l'insenséisme. Religion, moeurs, justice, tout décade. . . . La société se désagrège sous l'action corrosive d'une civilisation déliquescente. . . . Nous vouons cette feuille aux innovations tuantes, aux audaces stupéfiantes, aux incohérences à trente-six atmosphères dans la limite la plus reculée de leur compatibilité avec ces conventions archaïques étiquettées du nom de morale publique. Nous serons les vedettes d'une littérature idéale. . . . En un mot, nous serons les mahdis clamant éternellement le dogme élixirisé, le verbe quintessencié du décadisme triomphant." Noël Richard, *Le Movement décadent: Dandys, esthètes et quintessents* (Paris: Nizet, 1968), 24. Quoted and translated by Calinescu, *Five Faces of Modernity*, 175–76, 339.

13. "La décadence esthétique, elle, doit s'entendre par antiphrase; elle est synonyme de jeunesse fringante et de renouvellement." Noël Richard, *Le Movement décadent*, 259.

14. "Cependant, s'il s'agit de Mallarmé et d'un groupe littéraire, l'idée de décadence a été assimilée à son idée contraire, à l'idee même d'innovation." Remy de Gourmont, *La Culture des idées*, 16th ed. (Paris: Mercure de France, 1916), 116, 117.

15. Jean Pierrot, *The Decadent Imagination, 1880–1900*, trans. Derek Coltman (Chicago: University of Chicago Press, 1981), 5.

16. Calinescu, *Five Faces of Modernity,* 212.

17. "[P]ossiamo . . . considerare entrambi [Baudelaire and Dostoevsky] come i precursori e i capisaldi della nuova sensibilità. E il nuovo che essi rappresentano rispetto alla sensibilità romantica può essere sinteticamente indicato nella decisa apertura ai contenuti e alla logica dell'"inconscio.' Il Decadentismo nasce quando, in rapporto alla scoperta dell'inconscio, si arriva all'identificazione di Io e Mondo (l'inconscio è la parte dell'io che partecipa della vita della natura), con la messa in crisi del realismo e del sentimentalismo, che costituiscono le fondamenta stesse del Romanticismo." Elio Gioanola, *Il decadentismo,* 2d ed. (Rome: Edizioni Studium, 1977), 29.

18. "It [the adjective *decadent*] emerges as the underside or logical complement of something else, coerced into taking its place in our vocabularies by the pressure of something that needs an opposite, an enemy." Richard Gilman, *Decadence: The Strange Life of an Epithet* (New York: Farrar, Straus, and Giroux, 1979), 159.

19. Roger L. Williams, *The Horror of Life* (Chicago: University of Chicago Press, 1980), x, xi.

20. Swart, *Sense of Decadence,* 67.

21. Calinescu, *Five Faces of Modernity,* 156.

22. Claude-Marie Senninger, ed., *Baudelaire par Théophile Gautier* (Paris: Klincksieck, 1986), 125.

23. Renato Poggioli, "Qualis Artifex Pereo! or Barbarism and Decadence," *Harvard Library Bulletin* 13, no. 1 (Winter 1959): 141–42, 136–37. Quoted by George Ross Ridge, *The Hero in French Decadent Literature* (Athens: University of Georgia Press, 1961), 47, 23.

24. Praz, *Romantic Agony,* 401.

25. See José Ortega y Gasset, *The Dehumanization of Art and Other Essays on Art, Culture, and Literature* (Princeton: Princeton University Press, 1968), 3–54.

26. Ibid., 10–11.

27. Geoffrey Hartman, "Toward Literary History," in *In Search of Literary Theory,* ed. Morton W. Bloomfield (Ithaca: Cornell University Press, 1972), 201.

28. James M. Smith, "The Concept of Decadence in Nineteenth-Century French Literature," *Studies in Philology* 50 (1953): 651.

29. Elaine Showalter, *Sexual Anarchy: Gender and Culture at the Fin de Siècle* (New York: Viking Penguin, 1990), 3.

30. Rachel Bowlby, *Just Looking* (New York: Methuen, 1985), 7. Quoted by Showalter, *Sexual Anarchy,* 77.

31. Williams in *The Horror of Life* records that Flaubert agreed with one Dr. Hardy, who described the writer as a "hysterical old woman" (213). Williams also cites this entry from the Goncourt *Journal* dated 20 December 1866: "We are now like two women who live together, whose health is identical, whose periods come at the same time. Even our migraines develop on the same day" (66).

32. Showalter, *Sexual Anarchy,* 11.

33. Andreas Huyssen, *After the Great Divide: Modernism, Mass Culture, Postmodernism* (Bloomington: Indiana University Press, 1986), 45.

34. Showalter, *Sexual Anarchy,* 7–8. On this topic, Showalter also quotes Toril Moi, *Sexual/Textual Politics* (London: Methuen, 1985), 167.

35. George J. Becker and Edith Philips, ed. and trans., *Paris and the Arts, 1851–1896: From the Goncourt "Journal"* (Ithaca: Cornell University Press, 1971), 309. Entry dated 8 December 1893.

36. Marie Thérèse Jacquet, ed., *Le Dictionnaire des idées reçues* (Paris: Nizet, 1990), 231: "EPOQUE (LA NOTRE). Tonner contre elle. Se plaindre de ce qu'elle n'est pas poétique. L'appeler époque de transition, de décadence."

37. Charles Baudelaire, *Curiosités esthétiques* (Paris: Conard, 1923), 105–6. Quoted by Smith, "The Concept of Decadence," 642.

2. Decadence and Romanticism

1. Harry Levin, *The Gates of Horn: A Study of Five French Realists* (New York: Oxford University Press, 1966), 285.

2. Ibid., 286.

3. See Martine Frier-Wantiez, *Sémiotique du fantastique: Analyse textuelle de "Salammbô"* (Berne: Peter Lang, 1979). According to Todorov, the generic sine qua non of fantastic literature is a sense of hesitation, felt by the reader, between natural and supernatural explanations of events depicted in the text. See *Introduction à la littérature fantastique* (Paris: Editions du Seuil, 1970), 36. Given this definition, much of *Salammbô* seems to be not fantastic but merely marvelous, as when the mysterious sympathy between Salammbô and the moon is described (see chap. 3; once during an eclipse, we are told, Salammbô almost died), or when Salammbô dies at the end of the novel, not from natural causes, but from touching the forbidden veil of Tanit. It should be noted that Todorov does not mention *Salammbô* in his influential study.

4. "L'Antiquité . . . ne comporte pas, de notre part, le roman historique proprement dit, qui suppose l'entière familiarité et l'affinité avec le sujet." *Nouveaux Lundis* (Paris: Lévy, 1881), 4:80.

5. See *Impressionism* (Secaucus, N.J.: Chartwell Books, 1973), 7. Louis Leroy was a reporter for *Le Charivari* when he "invented" the term.

6. Quotations in French from *Salammbô* (Paris: Gallimard, 1970) are bracketed and followed by parenthetical page citations. Quotations in English are followed by parenthetical references to volume and page numbers of an anonymous translation titled *Salammbô: A Romance of Ancient Carthage,* 2 vols. (New York: M. Walter Dunne, 1904).

7. Anne Green, "*Salammbô* and Nineteenth-Century French Society," in *Critical Essays on Gustave Flaubert,* ed. Laurence M. Porter (Boston: G. K. Hall, 1986),

115. The other analogies between ancient Carthage and Second Empire France discussed in this paragraph are also taken from Green's essay.

8. Robert Rosenblum, *Paintings in the Musée d'Orsay* (New York: Stewart, Tabori and Chang, 1989), 22.

9. Quoted by Eugen Weber, *France: Fin de Siècle* (Cambridge: Harvard University Press, 1986), 16.

10. Cited by Eugenio Donato in *The Script of Decadence: Essays on the Fictions of Flaubert and the Poetics of Romanticism* (New York: Oxford University Press, 1993), 40.

11. Cited by Donato, *The Script of Decadence,* 44.

12. Ibid., 42.

13. "[Flaubert] passe outre à l'archéologie incontinent; il invente, sur la fin de ces funérailles, des supplices, des mutilations de cadavres, des horreurs singulières, raffinées, immondes. Une pointe d'imagination sadique se mêle à ces descriptions . . ." *Nouveaux Lundis,* 4:71.

14. See Mario Praz, *The Romantic Agony,* 2d ed., trans. Angus Davidson (Oxford: Oxford University Press, 1951), chap. 3, "The Shadow of the Divine Marquis," 97–195.

15. Roger L. Williams, *The Horror of Life* (Chicago: University of Chicago Press, 1980), 171.

16. For a complete discussion of this point, see Williams's chapter on Flaubert in *The Horror of Life,* 110–215.

17. "Ces sortes d'expression datent un livre. Les remarques qu'un de mes honorables confrères, M. Cuvillier-Fleury, a faites à ce propos sur les écrivains de la décadence romaine classique, ses rapprochements avec Lucain, avec Claudien, ont de la justesse." *Nouveaux Lundis,* 4:92.

18. "Eh bien! le coté politique, le caractère des personnages, le génie du peuple, les aspects par lesquels l'histoire particulière de ce peuple navigateur, et civilisateur à sa manière, regarde l'histoire générale et intéresse le grand courant de la civilisation, sont sacrifiés ici ou entièrement subordonnés au côté descriptif exorbitant, à un dilettantisme qui, ne trouvant à s'appliquer qu'à de rares débris, est forcé de les exagérer." *Nouveaux Lundis,* 4:86.

19. Roland Barthes uses the phrase "artifice of reading" in *S/Z,* trans. Richard Howard (New York: Hill and Wang, 1974), 19, to describe the proairetic code, the terms of which are "actions" ordered empirically by the reader, and which usually follow a preexisting logic; that is, the "already done" or the "already read," that which is expected by one familiar with a set of conventions. I use the phrase here to suggest that another set of conventions has evolved with the development of literary modernism, and that other expectations have come into being. The reader of a modernist text now *expects* obscurity and discontinuity, for example, and his appreciation of such elements is an acquired taste, a new artifice of reading.

20. *Nouveaux Lundis,* 4:35.

21. "Le drapeau de la Doctrine sera, cette fois, franchement porté, je vous en réponds! Car ça ne prouve rien, ça ne dit rien, ce n'est historique, ni satirique, ni humoristique." Letter to Edmond and Jules de Goncourt, dated 3 July 1860. *Correspondance* (Paris: Conard, 1927) 4:379.

22. See listing of references to "l'art pour l'art" in Charles Carlut, *La Correspondance de Flaubert: Etude et répertoire critique* (Columbus: Ohio State University Press, 1968), 259–61. Carlut includes the reference cited in note 21, above, in his list (260).

23. See letter dated 16 January 1852, *Correspondance* 2:345.

24. Ruth Z. Temple, "Truth in Labelling: Pre-Raphaelitism, Aestheticism, Decadence, Fin de Siècle," *English Literature in Transition* 17 (1974): 208.

25. "Il n'y a de vraiment beau que ce qui ne peut servir à rien . . ." Théophile Gautier, preface to *Mademoiselle de Maupin,* in *Anthology of Critical Prefaces to the Nineteenth-Century French Novel,* ed. Herbert S. Gershman and Kernan B. Whitworth, Jr. (Columbia: University of Missouri Press, 1962), 104.

26. Robert T. Denommé, *Leconte de Lisle* (New York: Twayne, 1973), 33.

27. Ibid., 41.

28. "Les hymnes et les odes inspirées par la vapeur et la télégraphie électrique m'émeuvent médiocrement, et toutes ces périphrases didactiques, n'ayant rien de commun avec l'art." *Poésies complètes* (Geneva: Slatkine Reprints, 1974), 4:217, 216.

29. ". . . l'examen des faits historiques et des institutions, l'analyse sérieuse des moeurs . . ." *Poésies complètes,* 4:218.

30. ". . . exciteront toujours un intérêt plus profond et plus durable que le tableau daguerréotypé des moeurs et des faits contemporains." *Poésies complètes,* 4:222.

31. "Je vais écrire un roman dont l'action se passera trois siècles avant Jésus-Christ, car j'éprouve le besoin de sortir du monde moderne, où ma plume s'est trop trempée et qui d'ailleurs me fatigue autant à reproduire qu'il me dégoûte à voir." Letter to Mademoiselle Leroyer de Chantepie, dated 18 March 1857. *Correspondance,* 4:164.

32. Victor Brombert, *The Novels of Flaubert: A Study of Themes and Techniques* (Princeton: Princeton University Press, 1966), 105.

33. Ibid.

34. Ibid., 102–3.

35. Quotations from Gautier's "L'Art" refer to the text in *The Penguin Book of French Verse,* ed. Anthony Hartley et al. (Baltimore: Penguin, 1975), 397–400.

36. See note 49 below.

37. Brombert, *Novels of Flaubert,* 105–6.

38. Levin, *Gates of Horn,* 277.

39. Stratton Buck, *Gustave Flaubert* (New York: Twayne, 1966), 90.

40. The term *figure* here does not mean "trope" but is used in the sense of "figuration" discussed by Tzvetan Todorov in "How to read?" in *The Poetics of Prose,* trans. Richard Howard (Ithaca: Cornell University Press, 1977), 234–46. In Todorov's extended sense *figure* does not refer to standard rhetorical devices but to "linguistic relations we can perceive and designate" (243) and that allow us to organize our reading of a text in a certain way.

41. A "readerly" text would be one that is familiar on a first reading because it conforms to "a plurality of other texts, of codes which are infinite" that the reader brings to the text. The phrase quoted is taken from Barthes's *S/Z,* where the question of "readerly" and "writerly" texts is discussed at length (3–11).

42. Quoted by Maurice Z. Shroder, "On Reading *Salammbô,*" *L'Esprit Créateur* 10 (Spring 1970): 30.

43. Levin, *Gates of Horn,* 278.

44. Georg Lukács, *The Historical Novel,* trans. Hannah Mitchel and Stanley Mitchel (Lincoln: University of Nebraska Press, 1983), 188–89.

45. Georg Lukács, *The Theory of the Novel* (Cambridge: MIT Press, 1971), 88.

46. Erich Auerbach, *Mimesis: The Representation of Reality in Western Literature,* trans. Willard R. Trask (Princeton: Princeton University Press, 1968), 483.

47. Nathalie Sarraute, "Flaubert," trans. Maria Jolas, *Partisan Review* 33 (1966): 203.

48. Ibid., 194–95.

49. "[L]e système de Chateaubriand me semble diamétralement opposé au mein. Il partait d'un point de vue tout idéal; il rêvait des martyrs *typiques.* Moi, j'ai voulu fixer un mirage en appliquant à l'Antiquité les procédés du roman moderne . . ." *Nouveaux Lundis* 4:436. The reference to Flaubert as a "Chateaubrianized Balzac" appears in *Correspondance,* 2:316, letter to Louise Colet. The reference is made in the context of *Madame Bovary,* not *Salammbô,* but the point at issue is the mixture of romanticism and realism that Flaubert identified, respectively, with Chateaubriand and Balzac.

3. Decadence and Naturalism

1. Letter from Joyce to Grant Richards dated 31 May 1906. Richard Ellmann, ed., *Selected Letters of James Joyce* (New York: Viking, 1975), 86.

2. Koenraad W. Swart, *The Sense of Decadence in Nineteenth-Century France* (The Hague: Martinus Nijhoff, 1964), 96.

3. Hippolyte Taine, *Histoire de la littérature anglaise* (Paris: Librairie Hachette, 1873), 1:xv.

4. Elliot M. Grant, *Emile Zola* (New York: Twayne, 1966), 43–44.

5. A. E. Carter, *The Idea of Decadence in French Literature, 1830–1900* (Toronto: University of Toronto Press, 1958), 52.

6. "L'homme aujourd'hui ressemble à ces grandes capitales qui sont les chefs-

d'oeuvre et les nourrices de sa pensée et de son industrie; le pavé y couvre la terre, les maisons offusquent le ciel, les lumières artificielles effacent la nuit, les inventions ingénieuses et laborieuses encombrent les rues, les visages actifs et flétris se pressent le long des vitrines; les souterrains, les égouts, les quais, les palais, les arcs de triomphe, l'entassement des machines étalent et multiplient le magnifique et douloureux spectacle de la nature maîtrisée et défigurée." *La Fontaine et ses fables* (Paris: Librairie Hachette, 1853), 168–69. Quoted by Carter, *Idea of Decadence*, 52.

7. Jean Pierrot, *The Decadent Imagination, 1880–1900,* trans. Derek Coltman (Chicago: University of Chicago Press, 1981), 13.

8. Schopenhauer's *Die Welt als Wille und Vorstellung* (1819) was not fully translated into French until 1886, but the work of the philosopher was known through critical commentaries and scholarly interpretations as early as 1870, when an article by Challemel-Lacour appeared in *Revue des deux Mondes.* Théodule Ribot's *La Philosophie de Schopenhauer* was published in 1874, and articles and books about the German philosopher came forth steadily throughout the period of the naturalist school and the so-called decadent movement. See Pierrot, *Decadent Imagination,* 55–60.

9. "Oui, je nie la vie, je dis que la mort de l'espèce est préférable à l'abomination continue qui la propage." *La Faute de l'Abbé Mouret* (Paris: Marpon et Flammarion, 1890), 188–89.

10. Pierrot, *Decadent Imagination,* 56.

11. Phillip Stephan, *Paul Verlaine and the Decadence, 1882–1890* (Totowa, N.J.: Rowman and Littlefield, 1974), 9–10.

12. "Mon goût si l'on veut est dépravé. J'aime les ragoûts littéraires fortement épicés, les oeuvres de décadence où une sorte de sensibilité maladive remplace la santé plantureuse des époques classiques." Quoted by Mario Praz, *The Romantic Agony,* 2d ed., trans. Angus Davidson (Oxford: Oxford University Press, 1951), 323–24.

13. Stephan, *Paul Verlaine,* 9–10.

14. Roger L. Williams, *The Horror of Life* (Chicago: University of Chicago Press, 1980), 90.

15. "Songez que notre oeuvre, et c'est peut-être son originalité . . . repose sur la maladies nerveuse." Quoted by Paul Bourget, *Essais de psychologie contemporaine* (Paris: Plon, 1926), 2:161–62.

16. Carter, *Idea of Decadence,* 80.

17. Ibid., 65.

18. "Les dispositions d'esprit qui font qu'un homme se distingue des autres hommes par l'originalité de ses pensées et de ses conceptions . . . prennent leur source dans les même conditions organiques que les divers troubles moraux dont la *folie* et l'*idiotie* sont l'expression la plus complète." *La Psychologie morbide dans*

ses rapports avec la philosophie de l'histoire ou de l'influence des névropathies sur le dynamisme intellectuel (Masson, 1859), v. Quoted by Carter, *Idea of Decadence,* 65.

19. Williams, *Horror of Life,* 93.

20. Ibid., 94.

21. Pierrot, *Decadent Imagination,* 52.

22. Stephan, *Paul Verlaine,* 25.

23. "Cette rhétorique, issue de la peinture et la sculpture, est un instrument merveilleux pour exécuter certaines analyses, celles, par exemple, des troubles du système nerveux. Sous l'influence de ces troubles, l'émotion morale est accompagnée d'un cortège de fortes impressions physiques, et, comme cet énervement est la maladie même de l'époque, les frères de Goncourt ont employé leurs procédés de style avec un bonheur rare dans les fortes études de détraquements qui s'appellent *Manette Salomon, Madame Gervaisais, Germinie Lacerteux.* Ces monographies de névroses n'auraient jamais pu être rédigées dans la langue nous a transmise Voltaire." Quoted by Stephan, *Paul Verlaine,* 26.

24. Matei Calinescu, *Five Faces of Modernity: Modernism, Avant-Garde, Decadence, Kitsch, Postmodernism* (Durham: Duke University Press, 1987), 169.

25. "L'anémie nous gagne voilà le fait positif. Il y a dégénérescence du type humain. . . . Peut-être cela a-t-il été la maladie de l'empire romain, dont certains empereurs nous montrent une face dont les traits, même dans le bronze, semblent avoir coulé. . . . Mais alors il y avait de la ressource. Quand une société était perdue, épuisée au point de vue physiologique, il lui arrivait une invasion de barbares qui lui transfusait le jeune sang d'Hercule. Qui sauvera le monde de l'anémie du XIXe siècle? Sera-ce dans quelques centaines d'années une invasion d'ouvriers dans la société . . . ?" *Charles Demailly* (Paris, 1900), 283. Quoted by Swart, *Sense of Decadence,* 112–13.

26. *Journal* entry dated 3 September 1855. Quoted by Williams, *Horror of Life,* 72.

27. Williams, *Horror of Life,* 72.

28. "Depuis que l'humanité va, son progrès, ses acquisitions sont toutes de sensibilité. Elle se nervosifie, s'hystérise, chaque jour. Et quant à cette activité, . . . savez-vous si ce n'est pas d'elle que découle la mélancholie moderne? Savez-vous si la tristesse de ce siècle-ci ne vient pas du surmenage, de son mouvement, de son prodigieux effort, de son travail enragé, de ses forces cérébrales tendues à se rompre, de son excès de production dans tous le sens?" *Journal,* (Paris: Fasquelle and Flammarion, 1956), 6:207. Quoted (337–38 n. 28) and translated (168) by Calinescu, *Five Faces of Modernity.* No date for the journal entry is indicated.

29. Williams, *Horror of Life,* 72, 74.

30. "J'ai donné la formule complète du naturalisme dans *Germinie Lacerteux.*" Entry dated 1 June 1891. *Journal: Mémoires de la vie littéraire,* ed. Robert Ricatte (Paris: Fasquelle and Flammarion, 1956), 3:589.

31. See Ernest Raynaud, "Les Frères de Goncourt," *Le Décadent,* 1 January 1889, 5–9; and 15 January 1889, 22–28.

32. See Richard B. Grant, *The Goncourt Brothers* (New York: Twayne, 1972), 62–63, and Williams, *Horror of Life,* 83, for an account of Rose Malingre's life.

33. "*Germinie Lacerteux* est le livre type qui a servi de modèle à tout ce qui a été fabriqué depuis nous, sous le titre de réalisme, naturalisme, etc." Quoted by J.-H. Bornecque and P. Cogny, *Réalisme et naturalisme: L'Histoire, la doctrine, les oeuvres* (Paris: Librairie Hachette, 1958), 39.

34. Parenthetical page citations refer to *Germinie Lacerteux,* trans. Leonard Tancock (New York: Viking Penguin, 1984) and the French text edited by Gerard Delaisement (Paris: La Boîte à Documents, 1990).

35. Erich Auerbach, *Mimesis: The Representation of Reality in Western Literature,* trans. Willard R. Trask (Princeton: Princeton University Press, 1968), 512.

36. "La passion des choses ne vient pas de la bonté ou de la beauté pure de ces choses. On n'adore que la corruption. On sera passionné d'une femme pour sa putinerie, sa méchanceté, une certaine voyoucratie mauvaise de tête ou de coeur ou de sens. On se passionnera pour un certain faisandé de mots. Au fond, ce qui passionne la corruption, c'est le caprice des êtres ou des choses." Entry dated 30 August 1866. *Journal,* 2:32.

37. "Mais pourquoi, me dira-t-on, choisir ces milieux? Parce que c'est dans le bas qu'au milieu de l'effacement d'une civilisation se conserve le caractère des choses, des personnes, de la langue, de tout. . . . Pourquoi encore? Peut-être parce que je suis un littérateur bien né et que le peuple, la canaille si vous le voulez, a pour moi l'attrait de populations inconnues et non découvertes, quelque chose de l'*exotique,* que les voyageurs vont chercher avec mille souffrances dans les pays lointains." Entry dated 3 December 1871. *Journal,* 2:476. Translated by George G. Becker and Hedley H. Rhys, *Paris and the Arts, 1851–1896: From the Goncourt "Journal"* (Ithaca: Cornell University Press, 1971), 118–19.

38. Auerbach, *Mimesis,* 509.

39. Williams, *Horror of Life,* 65.

40. Quoted by Marcel Sauvage, *Jules et Edmond de Goncourt: Précurseurs* (Paris: Mercure de France, 1970), 160–61. Sauvage does not identify the source of the passage.

41. Sauvage, *Jules et Edmond de Goncourt,* 161.

42. Quoted and translated by Emily Apter, *Feminizing the Fetish: Psychoanalysis and Narrative Obsession in Turn-of-the-Century France* (Ithaca: Cornell University Press, 1991), 163 n. 25.

43. Ibid., 163.

44. Max Nordau, *Degeneration,* 2d ed. (New York: Appleton, 1912), 27–28.

45. "C'est somme toute dans la peinture en prose (j'allais dire dans le *plein-airisme* impressionniste) que les Goncourt atteignent le plus sûrement leur

poésie: de même que leur réalisme trouve la plénitude artistique dans le rendu à la fois 'sténographique' et expressif du langage populaire. Ils accordent subtilement leurs paysages aux états d'âme des personnages: c'est le printemps quand il fait printemps dans l'âme de Germinie,—c'est l'automne boueux quand son âme agoniste et son corps contracte la pthisie dans la poursuite du passé ou dans l'attente d'un mâle,— l'hiver est descendu à l'heure de sa mort, la niege est là pour recouvrir la maigre poignée de terre qu'on a jetée sur son corps." Enzo Caramaschi, *Réalisme et impressionnisme dans l'oeuvre des frères Goncourt* (Pisa: Libreria Goliardica, n.d.), 283.

46. Calinescu, *Five Faces of Modernity*, 175.

4. Decadence and Aestheticism

1. Ian Small, ed., introduction to *The Aesthetes: A Sourcebook* (London: Routledge and Kegan Paul, 1979), v.

2. Graham Hough, *The Last Romantics* (London: Duckworth, 1949), 187.

3. Maurice Beebe, *Ivory Towers and Sacred Founts: The Artist as Hero in Fiction from Goethe to Joyce* (New York: New York University Press, 1964), 147.

4. Jean Pierrot, *The Decadent Imagination, 1880–1900,* trans. Derek Coltman (Chicago: University of Chicago Press, 1981), 17–18. Bracketed French phrases refer to *L'Imaginaire décadent (1800–1900)* (Paris: Presses Universitaires de France, 1977), 28.

5. Ellen Moers, *The Dandy: Brummell to Beerbohm* (London: Secker and Warburg, 1960), 13.

6. Beebe, *Ivory Towers and Sacred Founts,* 151.

7. Pierrot, *Decadent Imagination,* 33–34.

8. See part 2 of Ruth Z. Temple, *The Critic's Alchemy: A Study of the Introduction of French Symbolism into England* (New York: Twayne, 1953), 77–117.

9. Michael Levey, *The Case of Walter Pater* ([London:] Thames and Hudson, 1978), 76.

10. For a thorough examination of this neglected aspect of Pater's work, see John J. Conlon, *Walter Pater and the French Tradition* (London: Associated University Presses, 1982).

11. Hough, *Last Romantics,* 188.

12. Ruth Z. Temple, "Truth in Labelling: Pre-Raphaelitism, Aestheticism, Decadence, Fin de Siècle," *English Literature in Transition* 17 (1974): 218.

13. Small, ed., introduction to *The Aesthetes,* xvii–xviii.

14. George Du Maurier, "Fleur des Alpes; or, Postlethwaite's Last Love," in Small, ed., *The Aesthetes,* 174–75. Originally published in *Punch* 74 (25 December 1880).

15. Temple, "Truth in Labelling," 210.

16. *Oxford English Dictionary,* s.v. "aesthetic."

17. Harold Bloom, "Walter Pater: The Intoxication of Belatedness," *Yale French Studies* 50 (1974): 164.

18. Small, ed., introduction to *The Aesthetes,* xv–xvi.

19. Bloom, "Walter Pater," 172.

20. Hough, *Last Romantics,* 197.

21. "[B]ecause . . . Pater had recommended art for art's sake and then experience for experience's sake, . . . his programme for individual aesthetic discrimination *could* modulate into a programme for decadence: experience for its own sake could very easily become (as in the case of Dorian Gray and his creator) *illicit* experience for its own sake." Small, ed., introduction to *The Aesthetes,* xvii.

22. Mario Praz also suggests that aestheticism has an intermediate place between romanticism and decadence, but that place is described in ethical terms: "[T]he theory of Art for Art's sake steadily gained ground, and, by criticizing all literary inspiration that was dictated by ethical ideals as being due to the intrusions of the practical, destroyed such barriers as damned up the morbid tendencies of Romantic sensibility, thus leading to the progressive cooling of the passionate quality with which the first of the Romantics had invested even morbid themes, and finally to the crystallization of the whole of the movement into set fashion and lifeless decoration" *The Romantic Agony,* 2d ed., trans. Angus Davidson (Oxford: Oxford University Press, 1951), xxii.

23. Bloom, "Walter Pater," 166.

24. Parenthetical page citations to Wilde's work refer to *The Complete Works of Oscar Wilde* (New York: Harper and Row, 1989).

25. Praz, *Romantic Agony,* 359.

26. *Webster's Ninth New Collegiate Dictionary,* s.v. "-ism."

27. Harold Bloom, *The Ringers in the Tower: Studies in Romantic Tradition* (Chicago: University of Chicago Press, 1971), 193.

28. Gerald Monsman, *Walter Pater's Art of Autobiography* (New Haven: Yale University Press, 1980), 51–52.

29. William E. Buckler, "*Déjà vu* Inverted: The Imminent Future in Walter Pater's *Marius the Epicurean,*" *Victorian Newsletter* 55 (Spring 1979): 2.

30. Ibid., 1.

31. Quoted by Levey, *Case of Walter Pater,* 162–63.

32. Bloom, *Ringers in the Tower,* 188.

33. Monsman, *Walter Pater's Art of Autobiography,* 52.

34. Iain Fletcher, *Walter Pater* ([London:] Longmans, Green, 1959), 25.

35. Bracketed page citations refer to Claude-Marie Senninger, ed., *Baudelaire par Théophile Gautier* (Paris: Klincksieck, 1986).

36. Anthony Ward, *Walter Pater: The Idea in Nature* (London: MacGibbon and Key, 1966), 137.

37. Monsman, *Walter Pater* (Boston: Twayne, 1977), 72.

38. Monsman, *Walter Pater's Art of Autobiography,* 56.
39. Bloom, *Ringers in the Tower,* 190.

5. Decadence and *Décadisme*

1. "Mille chemins s'ouvrent, mille possibilitiés offrent à partir de 1884, au moment où Huysmans publie *A Rebours.* Esthètes, mystiques, captifs d'un absolu purement verbal, hommes ravagés par les sens, littérateurs pourront également se réclamer de ce livre. Dans ces broussailles, Huysmans se fraye un chemin qu'il est seul à pouvoir suivre." François Livi, *J.-K. Huysmans: "A Rebours" et l'esprit décadent* ([Brussels]: La Renaissance du Livre, 1976), 48.

2. "[B]y 1881 Huysmans had already begun writing *A Rebours,* and its appearance in 1884 not only began his break with Zola but also constituted the manifesto of a new esthetic." Jean Pierrot, *The Decadent Imagination, 1880–1900,* trans. Derek Coltman (Chicago: University of Chicago Press, 1981), 4.

3. A. E. Carter, *The Idea of Decadence in French Literature, 1830–1900* (Toronto: University of Toronto Press, 1958), 20.

4. See note 2.

5. Parenthetical page citations refer to *A Rebours* (Paris: Garnier-Flammarion, 1978) and *Against Nature,* trans. Robert Baldick (Baltimore: Penguin, 1959).

6. See Carter, *Idea of Decadence,* 17; and Matei Calinescu, *Five Faces of Modernity: Modernism, Avant Garde, Decadence, Kitsch, Postmodernism* (Durham: Duke University Press, 1987), 172–73.

7. George Ross Ridge, *The Hero in French Decadent Literature* (Athens: University of Georgia Press, 1961), 48. Passivity and ennui are the dominant characteristics of the decadent hero as defined by Ridge and other critics. However, such characteristics are not limited to the fictional heroes of late nineteenth-century France. In *The Demon of Noontide: Ennui in Western Literature* (Princeton: Princeton University Press, 1976), Reinhard Kuhn provides an exhaustive history of ennui in Western literature, from medieval acedia to the existential angst of the twentieth century. What is significant about the decadent hero is the centrality of the character type, as Kuhn says: Des Esseintes "is another reincarnation of the sophisticated and blasé man of the world, who since the time of the Roman gentleman of Lucretius, has appeared at intervals throughout the course of the history of literature. In this novel, the incidental figure becomes the central one" (324).

8. Pierrot, *Decadent Imagination,* 60.

9. Ibid., 61–62.

10. "Des Esseintes n'est plus un être organisé à la manière d'Obermann, de René, d'Adolphe, ces héros de romans humains, passionnés et coupables. C'est une méchanique détraquée. Rien de plus. . . . En écrivant l'autobiographie de son héros, il [Huysmans] ne fait pas que la confession particulière d'une personnalité dépravée et solitaire, mais, du même coup, il nous écrit la nosographie d'une

société putrifiée de matérialisme.... Certes! pour qu'un décadent de cette force pût produire et qu'un livre comme celui de M. Huysmans pût germer dans une tête humaine, il fallait vraiment que nous fussions devenus ce que nous sommes,—une race à sa dernière heure." Quoted by Mario Praz, *The Romantic Agony*, 2d ed., trans. Angus Davidson (Oxford: Oxford University Press, 1951), 305.

11. "Appliquer à la joie, au se sentir vivre, l'idée d'hyperacuité des sens, appliquée par Poe à la douleur. Opérer une création par la pure logique de contraire. Le sentier est tout tracé, à rebours." Quoted by Praz, *Romantic Agony*, 323.

12. Carter, *Idea of Decadence*, 86.

13. Victor Brombert, *The Intellectual Hero: Studies in the French Novel, 1880–1955* (Chicago: University of Chicago Press, 1961), 17.

14. Any influence of the Russian novelist on Huysmans's conception of Des Esseintes as a purely cerebral hero is unlikely, as the French vogue for the Russian novel occurred after the publication of *A Rebours*. See Pierrot, *Decadent Imagination*, 92.

15. Calinescu, *Five Faces of Modernity*, 158.

16. Ibid., 170.

17. Parenthetical page citations refer to Claude-Marie Senninger, ed., *Baudelaire par Théophile Gautier* (Paris: Klincksieck, 1986).

18. The article on Baudelaire was reprinted in 1883 in Bourget's *Essais de psychologie contemporaine*. See Calinescu, *Five Faces of Modernity*, 170.

19. Ibid., 173.

20. "Effectivement la phrase de Huysmans, comme sa pensée. est toujours en équilibre instable: la locution adverbiale constitue un moyen excellent pour accentuer cette insécurité. Mais ce ne sont là que des modifications superficielles. Huysmans s'attaque surtout à la structure de la phrase en modifiant aussi souvent que possible l'ordre sujet-verbe-complément." Livi, *J.-K. Huysmans*, 98.

21. John R. Reed, *Decadent Style* (Athens: Ohio University Press, 1985), 19–20.

22. A translation is substituted for the original passage quoted by Carter, *Idea of Decadence*, 135, which is placed in brackets.

23. The vocabulary of Huysmans has been extensively examined by Marcel Cressot in *La Phrase et le vocabulaire de J.-K. Huysmans* (Paris: E. Droz, 1938).

24. Dean de la Motte, "Writing against the Grain: *A rebours*, Revolution, and the Modern Novel," in *Modernity and Revolution in Late Nineteenth-Century France*, ed. Barbara T. Cooper and Mary Donaldson-Evans (Newark: University of Delaware Press, 1992), 19.

25. Laurence M. Porter, "Literary Structure and the Concept of Decadence: Huysmans, D'Annunzio, and Wilde," *Centennial Review* 22 (Spring 1978): 190.

26. Northrop Frye, *Anatomy of Criticism: Four Essays* (Princeton: Princeton University Press, 1957), 311.

27. Joseph Halpern, "Decadent Narrative: *A Rebours*," *Stanford French Review* 2 (Spring 1978): 94.

28. Ibid.

29. See Joseph Frank, "Spatial Form in Modern Literature," in *The Widening Gyre: Crisis and Mastery in Modern Literature* (New Brunswick: Rutgers University Press, 1963), 3–62; and Sharon Spencer, *Space, Time and Structure in the Modern Novel* (Chicago: Swallow Press, 1974).

30. David Mickelsen, "*A Rebours:* Spatial Form," *French Forum* 3 (1978): 48.

31. Ibid., 49.

32. Spencer, *Space, Time and Structure,* 2.

33. Calinescu, *Five Faces of Modernity,* 172.

34. "Se dissimuler l'état de décadence où nous sommes arrivés serait le comble de l'insenséisme. Religion, moeurs, justice, tout décade.... La société se désagrège sous l'action corrosive d'une civilisation déliquescente. L'homme moderne est un blasé. Affinements d'appétits, de sensations, de goût, de luxe, de jouissances; névrose, hystérie, hypnotisme, morphinomanie, charlatanisme scientifique, schopenhauérisme à outrance, tels sont les prodromes de l'évolution sociale." Quoted by Carter, *Idea of Decadence,* 109.

35. Ibid., 110.

36. Calinescu, *Five Faces of Modernity,* 175.

37. *Ouevres complètes de Paul Verlaine* (Paris: Albert Messein, 1938), 1:359.

38. "*Décadisme* est un mot de génie, une trouvaille amusante et qui restera dans l'histoire littéraire; ce barbarisme est une miraculeuse enseigne. Il est court, commode, "à la main," *handy,* éloigne précisement l'idée abaissante de décadence, sonne littéraire sans pédanterie.... Le membre de phrase souligné dans ce passage détermine bien, je crois, ce que nous entendons, vous et moi, en Décadisme, qui est proprement une littérature éclatant par un temps de décadence, non pour marcher dans les pas de son époque, mais bien tout "à rebours," pour s'insurger contre, réagir par le délicat, l'éléve, le raffiné si l'on veut,... contre les platitudes et les turpitudes, littéraires et autres, ambiantes." *Le Décadent,* 1 January 1888, 1–2.

39. "la lumière si longtemps attendue par les jeunes écrivains pour prendre leur direction." *Le Décadent,* 15 January 1888, 1–2.

40. Calinescu, *Five Faces of Modernity,* 176–77.

41. Ibid., 176.

42. Koenraad W. Swart, *The Sense of Decadence in Nineteenth-Century France* (The Hague: Martinus Nijhoff, 1964), 165.

43. "Loin d'être pessimistes, les Décadents bajutiens sont des hommes d'action, animés de la foi au progrès." Noël Richard, *Le Movement décadent: Dandys, esthètes, et quintessents* (Paris: Nizet, 1968), 252.

44. Renato Poggioli, *The Theory of the Avant-Garde,* trans. Gerald Fitzgerald (Cambridge: Harvard University Press, 1968), 75–76.

45. Elaine Showalter, *Sexual Anarchy: Gender and Culture at the Fin de Siècle* (New York: Viking Penguin, 1990), 16.

46. Graham Hough, "George Moore and the Nineties," in *Edwardians and Late*

Victorians, ed. Richard Ellmann (New York: Columbia University Press, 1966), 25–26.

47. See Giovanni Gullace, *Gabriele d'Annunzio in France: A Study in Cultural Relations* (Syracuse: Syracuse University Press, 1966), 12–13.

48. See Ernest Boyd, introduction to *The Child of Pleasure* (New York: Modern Library, 1925), viii; parenthetical page citations of the text in English refer to this translation by Georgina Harding, first published in 1898. Parenthetical page citations to the Italian text refer to *Il Piacere* in *Prose di romanzi,* vol. 1, 8th ed. (Milan: Mondadori, 1968).

49. Praz, *Romantic Agony,* 334ff.

50. Frank Norris, *McTeague: A Story of San Francisco* (New York: Norton, 1977), 44.

51. Parenthetical page citations from *The Picture of Dorian Gray* and other works by Wilde refer to *The Complete Works of Oscar Wilde* (New York: Harper and Row, 1989).

52. Sergio Pacifici, *The Modern Italian Novel: From Capuana to Tozzi* (Carbondale: Southern Illinois University Press, 1973), 44.

53. Richard Aldington, introduction to *The Portable Oscar Wilde* (New York: Penguin, 1977), 29, 30.

54. Edouard Roditti, "Fiction as Allegory: *The Picture of Dorian Gray,*" in *Oscar Wilde: A Collection of Critical Essays,* ed. Richard Ellmann (Englewood Cliffs, N.J.: Prentice-Hall, 1969), 48–49.

55. Ibid., 49.

56. John Eglinton, ed. and trans., *Letters from George Moore to Ed. Dujardin: 1886–1922* (1929; repr., New York: Folcroft, 1970), 20–21.

57. Parenthetical page citations refer to George Moore, *Confessions of a Young Man,* ed. Susan Dick (Montreal: McGill-Queen's University Press, 1972).

58. Dick, ed., introduction, to *Confessions of a Young Man,* 4–5.

59. Leon Edel, introduction to *We'll to the Woods No More,* trans. Stuart Gilbert (New York: New Directions, 1957), xiii.

60. Eglinton, ed., *Letters,* 20.

61. Dick, ed., *Confessions of a Young Man,* 253–54 n. 1.

62. Richard Ellmann, *James Joyce,* rev. ed. (Oxford: Oxford University Press, 1982), 126.

6. Decadence and Modernism

1. Ibsen's "notion of artistic honesty carried to the point where it is almost self-defeating encouraged Joyce in his own rigorous self-examination. For him as for Ibsen, truth was then more an unmasking than a revelation. He approved also of the quality of aloofness in Ibsen that led him to leave his country and call himself

an exile." Richard Ellmann, *James Joyce*, rev. ed. (Oxford: Oxford University Press, 1982), 54.

2. Ellmann says that Joyce was "distrustful of the direction" that Moore's work was taking (circa 1902), but that "in English there was no one writing . . . fiction whom he admired more." Ibid., 98.

3. See Robert M. Scotto, "'Visions' and 'Epiphanies': Fictional Technique in Pater's *Marius* and Joyce's *Portrait*," *James Joyce Quarterly* 11 (Fall 1973): 41–50; Alan D. Perlis, "Beyond Epiphany: Pater's Aesthetic Hero in the Works of Joyce," *James Joyce Quarterly* 17 (Spring 1980): 272–79; and Richard Poirier, "Pater, Joyce, Eliot," *James Joyce Quarterly* 26 (Fall 1988): 21–35.

4. "Aesthetic hero" is the phrase used by Perlis in "Beyond Epiphany," who comments as follows: "At the core of Pater's theory of visions is the Aesthetic Hero, a fictional embodiment of the life of the sensations. The touchstone of the Hero's success in his sensitive reaction to impressions from the external world; his responsiveness, rather than his initiative, indicates the heightened level of his visionary experience" (272). Perlis does not note the points of difference, however, between Pater's Marius and Joyce's Dedalus. Like Robert M. Scotto, whose article Perlis mentions, Perlis resorts to the unfinished *Stephen Hero* to construct the argument that Pater and Joyce shared a similar aesthetic. This leaves untouched the question of Pater's relationship to the *Portrait*, the finished work. See also Scotto, "'Visions' and 'Epiphanies,'" 41–50.

5. S. L. Goldberg, *The Classical Temper: A Study of James Joyce's "Ulysses"* (London: Chatto and Windus, 1963), 52.

6. Hugh Kenner, *Dublin's Joyce* (London: Chatto and Windus, 1955), 145.

7. David Daiches, *Literary Essays* (Edinburgh: Oliver and Boyd, 1956), 173.

8. For example, James T. Farrell in 1945 called Stephen Dedalus the "artistic image of James Joyce himself." "Joyce's *Portrait of an Artist as a Young Man*," in *James Joyce: Two Decades of Criticism*, ed. Seon Givens (New York: Vanguard, 1948), 175.

9. John Gross, *James Joyce* (New York: Viking, 1970), 39.

10. William York Tindall, *A Reader's Guide to James Joyce* (New York: Noonday, 1959), 66–67.

11. Ellmann, *James Joyce*, 142.

12. See Richard Ellmann, ed., *Selected Letters of James Joyce* (New York: Viking, 1975), 23.

13. David S. Thatcher, *Nietzsche in England, 1890–1914: The Growth of a Reputation* (Toronto: University of Toronto Press, 1970), 136.

14. Matei Calinescu, *Five Faces of Modernity: Modernism, Avant-Garde, Decadence, Kitsch, Postmodernism* (Durham: Duke University Press, 1987), 187.

15. Wallace Fowlie, *André Gide: His Life and Art* (New York: Macmillan, 1965), 32, 36.

16. Gide denied having read Nietzsche prior to the composition of *Les Nourritures terrestres* in the preface to the German edition of the work. See Jean Delay, *The Youth of André Gide,* trans. June Guicharnaud (Chicago: University of Chicago Press, 1963), 468.

17. Delay, *Youth of André Gide,* 470.

18. For this interpretation of decadence as despair, see Anna Balakian, *The Symbolist Movement: A Critical Appraisal* (New York: New York University Press, 1977), 115.

19. André Gide, *Journal: 1889–1939* (Editions Gallimard, 1951), 98.

20. "Par la suppression des malingres, on supprime la variété rare—fait bien connu en botanique ou du moins en *floriculture;* les plus belles fleurs étant données souvent par les plantes de chétif aspect." *Journal,* 99. Translation by Justin O'Brien, *The Journals of André Gide* (New York: Knopf, 1947), 1:80.

21. Gide, *Journal,* 98.

22. "La maladie propose à l'homme une inquiétude nouvelle, qu'il s'agit de légitimer." *Journal,* 98. Translation by O'Brien, *Journals,* 1:80.

23. "J'écrivais ce livre à un moment où la littérature sentait furieusement le factice et le renfermé; où il me paraissait urgent de la faire à nouveau toucher terre et poser simplement sur le sol un pied nu." *Les Nourritures terrestres* (Editions Gallimard, 1917–36), 11–12. Translation by Dorothy Bussy, *The Fruits of the Earth* (New York: Knopf, 1949), 3.

24. "Tandis que d'autres publient ou travaillent, j'ai passé trois années de voyage à oublier au contraire tout ce que j'avais appris par la tête. Cette désinstruction fut lente et difficile; elle me fut plus utile que toutes les instructions imposées par les hommes, et vraiment le commencement d'une éducation." *Les Nourritures terrestres,* 19. Translation by Bussy, *Fruits of the Earth,* 11.

25. Fowlie, *André Gide,* 46.

26. Parenthetical page citations reference *L'Immoraliste* ([Paris]: Mercure de France, 1963). Parenthetical references are also made to the translation by Richard Howard, *The Immoralist* (New York: Vintage, 1970).

27. Although Jacques Derrida reverses the traditional relationship of writing to speech, proposing instead an "archē-writing" that had always existed as anterior to the natural or spoken language, he nevertheless provides a fairly complete history of the subordination of writing to speech in *Of Grammatology,* trans. Gayatri Spivak (Baltimore: Johns Hopkins University Press, 1976). See in particular part 1, sec. 2, "Linguistics and Grammatology."

7. The Decline of Decadence

1. Parenthetical page citations refer to *The Happy Hypocrite: A Fairy Tale for Tired Men* (New York: John Lane, 1922).

2. S. N. Behrman, *Portrait of Max: An Intimate Memoir of Sir Max Beerbohm*

(New York: Random House, 1960), 227. Behrman adds that Miss Loftus was billed as "the mimetic marvel" because of her ability to imitate, "with exquisite delicacy, popular singers of indelicate songs." Beerbohm was "riven by the thought of these ribaldries' emerging from the lips of innocence." No doubt this contributed to the theme of hypocrisy in the fictionalization of the attraction.

3. Pierre Bourdieu, *The Field of Cultural Production: Essays on Art and Literature,* ed. Randall Johnson (New York: Columbia University Press, 1993), 31.

4. John R. Reed, *Decadent Style* (Athens: Ohio University Press, 1985), 49, 50.

5. Brian Stableford, *The Dedalus Book of Decadence (Moral Ruins)* (Cambs, England: Dedalus, 1990), 48–49.

6. Stableford, *Dedalus Book of Decadence,* discusses Mirbeau in a chapter titled "Fin de Siècle: The Decadence of Decadence."

7. Jean Pierrot, *The Decadent Imagination, 1880–1900,* trans. Derek Coltman (Chicago: University of Chicago Press, 1981), 253.

8. Emily Apter, *Feminizing the Fetish: Psychoanalysis and Narrative Obsessions in Turn-of-the-Century France* (Ithaca: Cornell University Press, 1991), 153.

9. Parenthetical page citations refer to Octave Mirbeau, *Torture Garden,* trans. Alvah C. Bessie (New York: Citadel, 1948). Because I am concerned here only with the main lines of Mirbeau's narrative, rather than with fine points of style, I have not supplied the French text. But see *Le Jardin des supplices,* 2d ed., ed. Michel Delon (Paris: Gallimard, 1991).

10. Charles Baudelaire, *Oeuvres complètes,* ([Paris]: Editions Gallimard, 1975), 1:75.

11. Sigmund Freud, *Civilization and its Discontents,* trans. James Strachey (New York: Norton, 1961), 33: Freud discusses the "contention [that] holds that what we call our civilization is largely responsible for our misery, and that we should be much happier if we gave it up and returned to primitive conditions. I call this contention astonishing because, in whatever way we may define the concept of civilization, it is a certain fact that all the things with which we seek to protect ourselves against the threats that emanate from the sources of suffering are part of that very civilization."

12. "The New York critic . . . was, in his heyday before World War One, the important bridge between modernist European culture and the United States." Doug Fetherling, *The Five Lives of Ben Hecht* (Toronto: Lester and Orpen, 1977), 40.

13. These blurbs from de Gourmont, Bourget, Maeterlinck, and Brandes appear on an unnumbered page in the back of a posthumous collection of Huneker's essays, titled *Variations* (New York: Scribner, 1922). The book was first published in 1921.

14. "Ever since he had read Huneker in Baltimore at the turn of the century, Mencken had considered him the critic in America from whom he could learn the most. . . . 'If a merciful Providence had not sent James Gibbons Huneker into the world,' he observed in 1909, 'we Americans would still be shipping union suits

to the heathen, reading Emerson, sweating at Chautauquas and applauding the plays of Bronson Howard. In matters exotic and scandalous he is our chief of scouts, our spiritual adviser.' " Arnold T. Schwab, in *James Gibbons Huneker: Critic of the Seven Arts* (Stanford: Stanford University Press, 1963), 234–35.

15. H. L. Mencken, *A Book of Prefaces,* 3d ed. (New York: Knopf, 1920), 161, 163.

16. Edmund Wilson, *The Shores of Light: A Literary Chronicle of the Twenties and Thirties* (New York: Farrar, Straus and Giroux, 1952), 713.

17. Schwab, *James Gibbons Huneker,* 197. Schwab quotes a letter to him from Eliot dated 4 January 1952.

18. Marcus Klein, *Foreigners: The Making of American Literature, 1900–1940* (Chicago: University of Chicago Press, 1981), 137.

19. Schwab, *James Gibbons Huneker,* 271–72.

20. Ibid., 197. Letter dated 7 September 1953. In his autobiography, Hecht also calls H. L. Mencken his "alma mater." See the photo caption facing page 356 of *A Child of the Century* (New York: Simon and Schuster, 1954).

21. William MacAdams, *Ben Hecht: The Man Behind the Legend* (New York: Scribner, 1990), 68.

22. Ibid., 35.

23. Quoted by Fetherling, *Five Lives of Ben Hecht,* 87.

24. MacAdams, *Ben Hecht,* 43.

25. Schwab, *James Gibbons Huneker,* 272.

26. Burton Rascoe, "A Note about Painted Veils," in *Painted Veils* (New York: Avon, 1954), 274. The review is reprinted, along with additional comments by Rascoe, in this paperback edition.

27. Schwab, *James Gibbons Huneker,* 273.

28. Hecht says that he and Burton Rascoe feuded in print over the merits of James Joyce's *Ulysses* when publication of the novel began in the *Little Review.* Hecht, writing in the *Daily News,* defended Joyce, while Rascoe, writing in the *Tribune,* attacked him. See *CC,* 342. Rascoe's position suggests that he remained more decadent than avant-garde.

29. *Little Review* 1, no. 2 (April 1914): 1.

30. *Little Review* 1, no. 6 (September 1914): 4.

31. Richard Aldington, "Remy de Gourmont," *Little Review,* 2, no. 3 (May 1915): 11.

32. George Burman Foster, "The Prophet of a New Culture," *Little Review* 1, no. 1 (March 1914), 14.

33. Foster, "Prophet of a New Culture," 16–17.

34. Fetherling, *Five Lives of Ben Hecht,* 21.

35. MacAdams, *Ben Hecht,* 16.

36. Fetherling, *Five Lives of Ben Hecht,* 21.

37. MacAdams, *Ben Hecht,* 17.

38. Ben Hecht, "The Serman [*sic*] in the Depths (Phosphorescent Gleams of Spiritual Putrefactions)," *Little Review* 2, no. 3 (May 1915): 40.

39. Fetherling, *Five Lives of Ben Hecht,* 52.

40. Ibid., 53.

41. Ibid., 54.

42. MacAdams, *Ben Hecht,* 46, 47.

43. Quoted by Fetherling, *Five Lives of Ben Hecht,* 29.

44. MacAdams, *Ben Hecht,* 68.

45. See Pierre Emmanuel, *Baudelaire: The Paradox of Redemptive Satanism* (Tuscaloosa: University of Alabama Press, 1967).

46. MacAdams, *Ben Hecht,* 59, uses this apt phrase in a description of Eric Dorn.

47. Ibid., 279.

48. Quoted by MacAdams, *Ben Hecht,* 54. The account of the Hecht–Rascoe debate at the Loeb mansion is also taken from MacAdams.

49. Ibid., 55.

50. Pauline Kael, "Raising Kane," in *The Citizen Kane Book* (New York: Limelight, 1984), 9.

51. Quoted by Jeffrey Brown Martin, *Ben Hecht: Hollywood Screenwriter* (Ann Arbor, Mich.: UMI Research Press, 1985), 130.

52. Quoted by Martin, *Ben Hecht,* 126.

53. See Herman G. Weinberg, *Josef von Sternberg: A Critical Study* (New York: Dutton, 1967), 64.

54. Frank Brady, *Citizen Welles: A Biography of Orson Welles* (New York: Doubleday, 1989), 254. The reference to Dr. Sebastien appears on page 13 of Hecht's novel: "He is a gigantic man with a large head. His face is expressionless. When he looks at me he seems made of wax."

Postface

1. Elaine Showalter, *Sexual Anarchy: Gender and Culture at the Fin de Siècle* (New York: Viking Penguin, 1990), 1.

2. Emily Apter, *Feminizing the Fetish: Psychoanalysis and Narrative Obsessions in Turn-of-the-Century France* (Ithaca: Cornell University Press, 1991), xi–xii.

3. Eugen Weber, *France: Fin de Siècle* (Cambridge: Harvard University Press, 1986), 5–6.

4. Showalter, *Sexual Anarchy,* 126.

5. Andreas Huyssen, *After the Great Divide: Modernism, Mass Culture, Postmodernism* (Bloomington: Indiana University Press, 1986), 170.

6. Matei Calinescu, *Five Faces of Modernity: Modernism, Avant-Garde, Decadence, Kitsch, Postmodernism* (Durham: Duke University Press, 1987), 136, 135.

7. Calinescu, *Five Faces of Modernity,* 267, notes that Toynbee's work was summarized in 1946, and that the appeal of a postmodern age "seemed limited to poets, artists, and literary critics, who often interpreted it as applying to the immediate postwar period."

8. See Elwyn Judson Trueblood, *The Dawn of the Post-Modern Era: Dimensions*

of Human Life in the Last Half of the Twentieth Century (New York: Philosophical Library, 1954). Trueblood says the postwar period demands "a different kind of person—whom we may well call post-modern man—who can conserve the values of previous periods while at the same time orienting himself to new perspectives and fresh obligations" (2). Trueblood also bewails "the decadent state of Western civilization" and "our present degraded position" (9).

9. The point of departure for the Habermas–Lyotard debate is Lyotard's *La Condition postmoderne* (Paris: Minuit, 1979) and the Adorno Prize speech delivered by Habermas and printed as "Modernity vs. Postmodernity" in *New German Critique* 22 (Winter 1981): 3–14. For a discussion of the debate, see Huyssen, *After the Great Divide,* 199–206, and Calinescu, *Five Faces of Modernity,* 273–75.

10. Randall Jarrell, *Poetry and the Age* (New York: Knopf, 1953), 216.

11. See Irving Howe's "Mass Society and Postmodern Fiction," *Partisan Review* 26 (1959): 420–36. The term *post-contemporary* is used by Jerome Klinkowitz in *Literary Disruptions: The Making of a Post-Contemporary American Fiction,* 2d ed. (Urbana: University of Illinois Press, 1980).

12. Harry Levin, *Refractions: Essays in Comparative Literature* (Oxford: Oxford University Press, 1966), 271.

13. For further explanations of *modernismo* and *postmodernismo,* see entries under those headings in Federico Carlos Sainz de Robles, *Ensayo de un diccionario de la literatura,* 3d ed. (Madrid: Aguilar, 1965).

14. See Jacques Derrida, "Two Words for Joyce," in *Poststructuralist Joyce: Essays from the French,* ed. Derek Attridge and Daniel Ferrer (Cambridge: Cambridge University Press, 1984), 145–59.

15. See Julian Barnes, *Flaubert's Parrot* (London: Jonathan Cape, 1984).

16. See Suzanne Clark, *Sentimental Modernism* (Bloomington: Indiana University Press, 1991), for a discussion of Emma Goldman and modernism.

17. "The favorite all-purpose Barbarians, at present, are called 'multiculturalists.'" Robert Hughes, *Culture of Complaint: The Fraying of America* (Oxford: Oxford University Press, 1993), 80.

18. See Pierre Bourdieu, *The Field of Cultural Production: Essays on Art and Literature,* ed. Randall Johnson (New York: Columbia University Press, 1993), especially part 1, 29–141, "The Field of Cultural Production."

19. See Randall Johnson, "Editor's Introduction: Pierre Bourdieu on Art, Literature and Culture," in Bourdieu, *Field of Cultural Production,* 7–8, for an explanation of this logic.

20. For example, Charles Taylor, in *Sources of the Self: The Making of the Modern Identity* (Cambridge: Harvard University Press, 1989), offers a conservative critique of postmodernism that treats the work of Lyotard, Derrida, and Foucault as an exercise in subjectivist freedom that has its roots in modernism: "To the extent that this kind of freedom is held up as the essence of 'post-modernity' . . . it shows this to be a prolongation of the least impressive side of modernism" (489).

Index

"Abel et Caïn" (Baudelaire), 165
Ackroyd, Peter, 199
Adam, Paul, 155
Aesthetic interference, 13–15, 17, 24, 37, 41–42, 58, 79
Aestheticism, xviii, 52–54, 60–61, 65–68, 70–71, 104, 109–10, 124–26
Aldington, Richard, 111, 177
Anarchism, 155, 166–67
Anatomy of Melancholy (Burton), 94
Anderson, Margaret, 175, 176–77, 200; *Little Review*, 176–78
Anderson, Sherwood, 176, 180
Apollinaire, Guillaume, xv
Apter, Emily, 192
Apuleius, 71, 76, 91
A Rebours (Huysmans), xvi, xviii, 15, 17, 44, 47, 68, 82–97, 98, 103, 104, 110, 114, 118, 119, 146, 154, 156, 161, 199
Armstrong, Marie (Mrs. Ben Hecht), 188, 189
Arnold, Matthew, 76, 78
"Art, L' " (Gautier), 35
Art pour l'art, l', 33–34, 35, 64
Auerbach, Erich, 39, 52, 57
"Au Lecteur" (Baudelaire), 131
Avant-gardism, 5–6, 100–101, 121, 203

Baju, Anatole, 7, 48, 98–101, 155, 166, 200; *Décadent, Le*, 48, 98–101
Bakhtin, Mikhail, 94
Balzac, Honoré de, 14, 38, 42, 63, 85
Banville, Théodore de, 46
Barbarism, 12–13, 28, 49, 101, 157–58, 178, 200
Barbey d'Aurevilly, Jules Amédée, 62, 84–85, 90, 182
Barnes, Djuna, 149; *Nightwood*, 149
Barnes, Julian, 199; *Flaubert's Parrot*, 199
Barrès, Maurice, 166
Baudelaire, Charles, xi–xiv, xv, 9, 12, 20, 59, 62, 77, 81, 83, 85–87, 88, 97, 98, 114, 115, 131, 160, 162, 165, 171, 172, 173, 176, 178, 185–86, 201; "Abel et Caïn," 165; "Au Lecteur," 131; "Charogne, Une," xi–xiv, 185; "Femmes Damnées," xiv, 176; "Lesbos," xiv; "Litanies du Satan, Les," 165; *Paradis artificiels, Les*, 62; "Spleen IV," 162
Baumgarten, Alexander Gottlieb, 66
Beardsley, Aubrey, 166, 180
Beckett, Samuel, 96
Bedouins (Huneker), 166, 174
Beebe, Maurice, 61, 62
Beerbohm, Max, 151–53; *Happy Hypocrite, The*, 151–53
Behrman, S. N., 152
Belatedness, 5, 28, 78, 203
Belle époque, xv
Birth of Tragedy, The (Nietzsche), 135
Blake, William, 69
Bloom, Harold, 66, 67, 68, 73, 76
Bodenheim, Maxwell, 180
Bohemianism, xv, 165, 170
Borges, Jorge Luis, 96
Bourdieu, Pierre, 154, 201, 202
Bourget, Paul, 5, 31, 45, 48, 63, 82, 88, 89, 97, 98, 100, 136, 146, 149, 164, 167, 199
Bouvard et Pecuchet (Flaubert), 94, 199
Brandes, Georg, 164, 175
Brombert, Victor, 35, 36, 87
Brummel, George Bryan (Beau), 62
Bruno, Giordano, 80
Burke, Kenneth, 175
Burton, Robert, 94; *Anatomy of Melancholy*, 94

Byatt, A. S., 199
Byron, Lord, xvii, 111, 131–32, 165; *Cain,* 131, 165; *Manfred,* 111, 165

Cabinet of Dr. Caligari, The (Wiene), 184–85
Cahiers d'André Walter, Les (Gide), 139–40
Cain (Byron), 131, 165
Calinescu, Matei, 5–6, 11, 89, 99, 136, 195
Camp, Maxime de, 28, 34
Caramaschi, Enzo, 55–56
Carlyle, Thomas, 78
Carter, A. E., 4, 5, 46–47, 91
Case of Wagner, The (Nietzsche), 134, 135–36
Caylor, Rose (Mrs. Ben Hecht), 188
Céline, Louis-Ferdinand, 91, 121, 149–50; *Voyage au bout de la nuit,* 149–50
Chants de Maldoror, Les (Lautréamont), 111, 165
Chaplin, Charlie, 185
Charles Demailly (Goncourt), 48
"Charogne, Une," xi–xiv, 185
Chateaubriand, François René, vicomte de, xii, 4, 42, 64; *Génie du Christianisme,* 64
Child of the Century, A (Hecht), 175
Citizen Kane (Welles), 190–91
Coeur simple, Une (Flaubert), 199
Colet, Louise, 33
Confessions of an English Opium Eater (De Quincey), 62
Confessions of a Young Man (Moore), xviii, 102, 113–18, 121, 129–32, 133, 166
Couture, Thomas, 27; *Romains de la décadence, Les,* 27
Coward, Noel, 189
"Critic as Artist, The" (Wilde), 69

Daiches, David, 128
Dandyism, xviii, 61–62
D'Annunzio, Gabriele, xviii, 13, 102, 103–9, 118, 119, 121, 172, 175; *Piacere, Il,* 102, 103–9, 119, 172
Darwin, Charles, xii–xiii, 44; *Origin of Species,* xii, 44
Darwinism, xii–xiii, 44
Décadent, Le (Baju, ed.), 48, 98–101
Decadentismo, 9
Decadent style. *See Style de décadence, le*
Décadisme, xviii, 6–7, 82–83, 97–101, 133
"Decay of Lying, The" (Wilde), 69
Deconstruction, 198–99
Degeneration, 30–31, 46–50, 55, 140–41
Degradation, 108–9, 111–13, 131, 140, 179
Dehumanization, 15–16
Delacroix, Eugène, 3
Delay, Jean, 138
De Profundis (Wilde), 112
De Quincey, Thomas, 62–63; *Confessions of an English Opium Eater,* 62
Derrida, Jacques, 196, 198
Devil is a Woman, The (von Sternberg), 190
Diabolism, xv–xvi, 111, 165, 173–74, 178, 183, 186
Dick, Susan, 118
Dickens, Charles, 14, 38
Dictionnaire des idées reçues, Le (Flaubert), 20
Dietrich, Marlene, 190
Disraeli, Benjamin, 111; *Vivian Grey,* 111
Donato, Eugenio, 29
Dos Passos, John, 180
Dostoevsky, Fyodor Mikhaylovich, 9, 87, 179; *House of the Dead, The,* 179
Douglas, Lord Alfred, 111
Dowson, Ernest, 60, 65
Dreyfus affair, 156, 157, 163
du Bellay, Joachim, 80
Dujardin, Edouard, 89, 113, 114, 116–17, 118; *Lauriers sont coupés, Les,* 116–17, 118
Du Maurier, George, 65
Duval, Jeanne, 201

Ecce Homo (Nietzsche), 134
Egoists: A Book of Supermen (Huneker), 164
Eliot, T. S., 17, 121, 164, 175, 176, 199; *Waste Land, The,* 176
Ellmann, Richard, 121
Ennui, 99, 178
Eric Dorn (Hecht), 186, 188, 189
Exiles (Joyce), 121
Expressionism, 184–85

Fantazius Mallare: A Mysterious Oath (Hecht), 179–82, 189
Faute de l'Abbé Mouret, La (Zola), 45
Feminism, 18–19, 170, 171–72, 173
"Femmes Damnées" (Baudelaire), xiv, 176
Ferron, Henri de, 44
Fiedler, Leslie, 197
Fin de siècle, xv–xvi, 101–2, 104, 192–94
Finnegans Wake (Joyce), 198
Flaubert, Gustave, xv, xvii–xviii, 14, 15, 18–19, 20, 21, 22–42, 43, 63, 81, 83, 87, 94, 97, 118, 119, 146, 158, 162, 166, 170, 175, 186, 195, 199; *Bouvard et Pecuchet,* 94, 199; *Coeur-simple, Une,* 199; *Dictionnaire des idées re-*

çues, Le, 20; *Madame Bovary*, 22, 39; *Salammbô*, xviii, 14, 15, 21, 22–42, 43, 59, 87, 119, 146, 162, 175, 191
Flaubert's Parrot (J. Barnes), 199
Foster, George Burman, 177–78
Fowlie, Wallace, 138
Fragonard, Jean-Honoré, 58
Franco-Prussian War, 3, 44
Frank, Joseph, 96
Freud, Sigmund, 163
Frye, Northrop, 94

Garden, Mary, 166, 173
Gargoyles (Hecht), 180, 186–88, 189
Gaston de Latour (Pater), 79–81
Gautier, Théophile, 4, 12, 25, 34, 35, 59, 63, 64, 76–77, 88–89, 98, 201; "Art, L'," 35; *Mademoiselle de Maupin*, 34, 98
Génie du Christianisme (Chateaubriand), 64
Germinal (Zola), 53
Germinie Lacerteux (Goncourt), xviii, 14, 15, 43, 47, 50–58, 59, 84, 119
Gide, André, xvii, xviii, 102, 120–21, 133, 138, 139–50, 141, 160, 176, 177; *Cahiers d'André Walter, Les*, 139–40; *Immoraliste, L'*, xviii, 102, 138, 139–50, 160, 177, 178; *Journal*, 140; *Nourritures terrestres, Les*, 140, 141
Ginsberg, Allen, 180
Gionola, Ello, 9
Gobineau, Compte de, 27
Goethe, Johann Wolfgang von, xvii, 138
Goldberg, Rube, 185
Goldberg, S. L., 125
Goldman, Emma, 200
Goncourt, Jules and Edmond de, xv, xviii, 14, 15, 18, 20, 33, 43–58, 59, 84, 119, 140–41, 170, 178; *Charles Demailly*, 48; *Germinie Lacerteux*, xviii, 14, 15, 43, 47, 50–58, 59, 84, 119; *Journal*, 46, 50, 52, 55; *Madame Gervaisais*, 48; *Manette Salomon*, 48
Gourmont, Remy de, 7, 164, 170, 175, 177
Goya, Francisco, 55, 190
Grosz, Georg, 184

Habermas, Jürgen, 196, 197
Halpern, Joseph, 94, 95
Happy Hypocrite, The (Beerbohm), 151–53
Hartman, Eduard von, 45
Hartman, Geoffrey, xvii, 17
Hassan, Ihab, 197
Haussmann, Baron Georges-Eugène, 27
Hecht, Ben, xvi, 166, 175–91; *Child of the Century, A*, 175; *Eric Dorn*, 186, 188, 189; *Fantazius Mallare: A Mysterious Oath*, 179–82, 189; *Gargoyles*, 180, 186–88, 189; *Kingdom of Evil: A Continuation of the Journal of Fantazius Mallare, The*, 180, 182–84
Heraclitus, 69
Heredia, José Maria de, 46
Hermaphroditism, 104–5, 162
Hervieu, Paul, 46
Histoire de la littérature anglaise (Taine), 44
Hitchcock, Alfred, 189
Hoffmann, Ernst Theodor Amadeus, 111
Homosexuality, xiv, 98, 111–12, 142–44, 170
Hough, Graham, 60, 67, 102
House of the Dead, The (Dostoevsky), 179
Houssaye, Arsène, 28
Howe, Irving, 196
Hugo, Victor, 14, 20, 34, 63, 64; *Orientales, Les*, 34
Huneker, James Gibbons, xvi, 163–75, 176, 178, 179, 185, 186, 189, 190; *Bedouins*, 166, 174; *Egoists: A Book of Supermen*, 164; *Iconoclasts: A Book of Dramatists*, 164; *Melomaniacs*, 170; *Overtones*, 166; *Painted Veils*, 163, 165, 167–75, 176
Huxley, Aldous, 180
Huysmans, Joris-Karl, xvi, xviii, 14, 15, 17, 44, 46, 47, 68, 82–97, 98, 100, 101, 103, 104, 110, 114, 118, 119, 121, 146, 154, 156, 161, 165, 166, 168, 170, 175, 176, 178, 180, 185, 186, 199, 200; *A Rebours*, xvi, xviii, 15, 17, 44, 47, 68, 82–97, 98, 103, 104, 110, 114, 118, 119, 146, 154, 156, 161, 199; *Là-Bas*, xvi, 165, 186; *Marthe*, 46; *Soeurs Vatard, Les*, 46
Huyssen, Andreas, 18–19, 194

Ibsen, Henrik, 121, 164, 170, 171
Iconoclasts: A Book of Dramatists (Huneker), 164
Igitur (Mallarmé), 87
Immoraliste, L' (Gide), xviii, 102, 138, 139–50, 160, 177, 178
Impressionism, 23, 54–56
Ivanov, Vyacheslav, 5

Jardin des supplices, Le (Mirbeau), 154–63, 187
Jarrell, Randall, 196
Jarry, Alfred, xv
Jean Paul (Johann Paul Friedrich Richter), 111
Johnson, Lionel, 60

Johnson, Samuel, 68–69
Jourdain, Frantz, 46
Journal (Gide), 140
Journal (Goncourt), 46, 50, 52, 55
Joyce, James, xvii, xviii, 16, 17, 43, 60, 89, 96, 102, 118, 120, 121–23, 139, 149, 176, 198, 202; *Exiles,* 121; *Finnegans Wake,* 198; *Portrait of the Artist as a Young Man, A,* xviii, 102, 120, 121, 122–33, 139, 149; *Stephen Hero,* 124–26; *Ulysses,* 96, 176
Juvenal, 27

Kael, Pauline, 175, 189
Kafka, Franz, 19
Kaufmann, Walter, 138
Keats, John, 78
Kenner, Hugh, 125, 127
Kingdom of Evil: A Continuation of the Journal of Fantazius Mallare, The (Hecht), 180, 182–84
Kock, Charles-Paul de, 87
Kundera, Milan, 188

Là-Bas (Huysmans), xvi, 165, 186
La Fontaine et ses fables (Taine), 44
Laforgue, Jules, 46
Lamartine, Alphonse de, 4
Landor, Walter Savage, 78
"Langeur" (Verlaine), 25, 97, 98–99, 157, 179
Lauriers sont coupés, Les (Dujardin), 116–17, 118
Lautréamont, Compte de (Isidore Ducasse), 111, 165, 185; *Chants de Maldoror, Les,* 111, 165
Leconte de Lisle, Charles-Marie, 34; *Poëmes et poésies,* 34
Leopold and Loeb, 189
Leroy, Louis, 23
"Lesbos" (Baudelaire), xiv
Levin, Harry, 22, 38, 197
Lewis, Wyndham, 199
"Litanies du Satan, Les" (Baudelaire), 165
Little Review (Anderson, ed.), 176–78
Livi, François, 83, 90
Lodge, David, 199
Lombroso, Cesare, 171
Loti, Pierre, 166
Louÿs, Pierre, 190
Lowell, Robert, 196
Lucretius, 67
Lukács, Georg, 22, 38–39, 40
Lyotard, Jean-François, 196

McTeague (Norris), 107
Madame Bovary (Flaubert), 22, 39
Madame Gervaisais (Goncourt), 48
Mademoiselle de Maupin (Gautier), 34, 98
Maeterlinck, Maurice, 164
Mallarmé, Stéphane, xv, 7, 8, 46, 83, 87, 89–90, 114, 116, 133, 139, 140, 175, 177; *Igitur,* 87
Manette Salomon (Goncourt), 48
Manfred (Byron), 111, 165
Mangan, James Clarence, 121
Mankiewicz, Herman J., 190
Mann, Thomas, xvii, 38, 102
Marius the Epicurean: His Sensations and Ideas (Pater), xviii, 14, 15, 21, 59, 68, 71–79, 91, 115, 122–26
Marthe (Huysmans), 46
Maturin, Charles Robert, 111; *Melmoth the Wanderer,* 111
Maupassant, Guy de, 166
Melmoth the Wanderer (Maturin), 111
Melomaniacs (Huneker), 170
Mencken, H. L., 164, 175, 190
Michaud, Guy, 8
Mickelson, David, 96
Milton, John, 165; *Paradise Lost,* 165
Mirbeau, Octave, 4, 154–63, 166, 187, 190; *Jardin des supplices, Le,* 154–63, 187
Misogyny, xiv, 18–20, 57, 158, 174–75, 188
Modernism, xvii, xviii–xix, 6, 9, 16, 41–42, 69–70, 78, 95–97, 101–2, 111, 113, 120–21, 132–33, 137–38, 148–50, 164, 170, 175–78, 198–203
Modernismo, 198
Moers, Ellen, 62
Monet, Claude, 23
Monroe, Harriet, 176
Montaigne, Michel de, 80
Moore, George, xviii, 60, 76, 82, 89, 102, 113–18, 120, 121, 124, 129–32, 133, 166, 171; *Confessions of a Young Man,* xviii, 102, 113–18, 121, 129–32, 133, 166
Moreau, Gustave, 3, 104
Moreau de Tours, Dr. Joseph, 47
Multiculturalism, 194–95, 200–202
Musset, Alfred de, 4

Naturalism, xviii, 43–46, 50–52, 176
Nettement, Alfred, 38
Neurasthenia, 47–49, 53, 194
Nightwood (D. Barnes), 149
Nietzsche, Friedrich Wilhelm, xviii, 1, 15, 89, 133–39, 146, 161, 164, 167, 170, 175, 176, 178,

185, 195; *Birth of Tragedy, The,* 135; *Case of Wagner, The,* 134, 135–36; *Ecce Homo,* 134
Nisard, Désiré, 88, 89, 91
Nordau, Max, 55
Norris, Frank, 107; *McTeague,* 107
Nourritures terrestres, Les (Gide), 140, 141

Onís, Federico de, 198
Orientales, Les (Hugo), 34
Origin of Species (Darwin), xii, 44
Ortega y Gasset, José, 13, 15–16
Overtones (Huneker), 166

Paglia, Camille, 1–2, 19
Painted Veils (Huneker), 163, 165, 167–75, 176
Paradis artificiels, Les (Baudelaire), 62
Paradise Lost (Milton), 165
Parnassianism, 33–36
Parody, 152–54
Pateman, Carole, 19
Pater, Walter, xviii, 14, 15, 21, 59–60, 63–65, 66–81, 82, 91, 93, 101, 115, 118, 120, 121, 122–26, 127, 128, 167, 186; *Gaston de Latour,* 79–81; *Marius the Epicurean: His Sensations and Ideas,* xviii, 14, 15, 21, 59, 68, 71–79, 91, 115, 122–26; *Renaissance, The,* 66, 67, 75, 76, 77; "Romanticism," 63–64; "Style," 63
Péladan, Joséphin, 90, 105; *Vice suprême, Le,* 90
Pessimism, xii–xiii, 2–3, 44–45, 84–85
Petronius, 86, 96, 176
Phaedrus (Plato), 147
Piacere, Il (D'Annunzio), 102, 103–9, 119, 172
Picture of Dorian Gray, The (Wilde), xviii, 67, 68, 69, 102, 109–13, 119, 152, 187
Pierrot, Jean, 7–8, 9, 14, 61, 62, 63, 84, 155
Plato, 147; *Phaedrus,* 147
Poe, Edgar Allan, 87, 111, 185; "William Wilson," 111
Poëmes et poésies (Leconte de Lisle), 34
Poggioli, Renato, 6, 7, 10, 12–13, 14, 28, 100–101, 194
Portrait of the Artist as a Young Man, A (Joyce), xviii, 102, 120, 121, 122–33, 139, 149
Postmodernism, xviii, xix, 194–200
Postmodernismo, 198
Poststructuralism, 198–99
Pound, Ezra, 17, 175, 199
Pradet, Paul, 98
Praz, Mario, xiv, 3, 4, 9, 13, 29, 85, 103, 105
Pre-Raphaelitism, 63, 66, 104, 177
Progress, 11–12, 34
Proust, Marcel, xvii, 102, 176

Quinet, Edgar, 28

Rabelais, François, 94
Racine, Jean, 63, 201
Rascoe, Burton, 176, 179, 188
Raynaud, Ernest, 50, 98
Realism, xii, xiii, 41, 149
Reed, John R., 90, 154
Renaissance, The (Pater), 66, 67, 75, 76, 77
Renoir, Jean, 190
Richard, Noël, 7, 9, 100
Rimbaud, Arthur, 138
Rimsky-Korsakov, Nikolay Andreyevich, 190
Roditi, Edouard, 111
Romains de la décadence, Les (Couture), 27
Romanticism, xi, xii, xvii, xviii, 3–5, 28–29, 34–35, 42, 63–64, 68, 78, 131–32, 147–48
"Romanticism" (Pater), 63–64
Ronsard, Pierre de, 79–80
Rossetti, Dante Gabriel, 66, 177
Rousseau, Jean-Jacques, 4, 45, 63, 147

Sably, Lucien de, 98
Sade, Marquis de, 3, 29
Sadism, xviii, 3, 29–30, 158, 160–62
Sainte-Beuve, Charles-Augustine, 22, 23, 26, 29, 32, 33, 38, 42, 54, 63, 64, 88, 91
Salammbô (Flaubert), xviii, 14, 15, 21, 22–42, 43, 59, 87, 119, 140, 162, 175, 191
Sand, George, 20
Sandburg, Carl, 183, 185
Sarraute, Nathalie, 40
Sartre, Jean-Paul, 200
Satanism. *See* Diabolism
Saussure, Ferdinand de, 199, 202
Sauvage, Marcel, 53, 54
Schopenhauer, Arthur, 10, 18, 45, 95, 96, 103, 114, 134, 158, 165
Scott, Sir Walter, 23, 39
Seiderman, Maurice, 190
Shakespeare, William, 31
Shattuck, Roger, xv
Shelley, Percy Bysshe, 114, 115, 131–32, 165
Sherman, Stuart, 189
Showalter, Elaine, 18, 19, 192, 193
Small, Ian, 60, 67
Smith, Bernard, 164
Smith, Wallace, 180, 182
Soeurs Vatard, Les, 46
Sontag, Susan, 197
Soul of Man Under Socialism, The (Wilde), 69

Southey, Robert, 78
Spencer, Sharon, 96
"Spleen IV" (Baudelaire), 162
Stableford, Brian, 154–55
Stekel, Wilhelm, 179
Stendhal (Marie-Henri Beyle), 14, 63
Stephan, Phillip, 4–5
Stephen Hero (Joyce), 124–26
Sternberg, Josef von, 190; *Devil is a Woman, The,* 190
Stevenson, Robert Louis, 111; *Strange Case of Dr. Jekyll and Mr. Hyde, The,* 111
Strange Case of Dr. Jekyll and Mr. Hyde, The (Stevenson), 111
"Style" (Pater), 63
Style de décadence, le, 5, 25, 31, 36, 76–77, 88–92, 135–37, 146, 149, 201
Sumner, John, 180
Sunset Boulevard (Wilder), 190
Swart, Koenraad W., 2–3, 4, 5
Swinburne, Algernon Charles, 10, 60, 63, 65, 116
Symbolism, 8, 139–40, 166
Symons, Arthur William, 60, 61, 65, 104, 175

Taine, Hippolyte, 28, 44–45, 175; *Histoire de la littérature anglaise,* 44; *La Fontaine et ses fables,* 44
Temple, Ruth Z., 65
Tennyson, Alfred, 65
Thérèse Raquin (Zola), 44
Thompson, Vance, 175, 190
Thoreau, Henry David, 93
Todorov, Tzvetan, 22
Tolstoy, Leo, 14
Toynbee, Arnold, 195
Transition, xvi–xvii, xix, 13, 14–21, 58, 78–81, 83, 137–38, 141, 149–50, 196, 198, 202–3
"Truth of Masks, The" (Wilde), 69

Ulysses (Joyce), 96, 176

Vajarnet, Luc, 98
Van Roosbroeck, G. L., 1
Verhaeren, Emile, 155
Verlaine, Paul, 8, 10, 25, 46, 79, 97, 98–99, 114, 115, 157, 179; "Langeur," 25, 97, 98–99, 157, 179
Vice suprême, Le (Péladan), 90
Vivian Grey (Disraeli), 111
Voyage au bout de la nuit (Céline), 149–50

Wagner, Richard, 114, 117, 134, 136–37, 165, 166, 168, 174
Waste Land, The (Eliot), 176
Watteau, Antoine, 58
Weber, Eugen, xvi, 192
Welles, Orson, 190–91; *Citizen Kane,* 190–91
Wharton, Edith, 171
Whistler, James Abbott McNeill, 60, 165
Wiene, Robert, 184; *Cabinet of Dr. Caligari, The,* 184–85
Wilde, Oscar, xviii, 20, 60, 61, 67, 68–69, 82, 109–13, 116, 118, 119, 121, 124, 133, 140, 152, 153, 185, 187, 200; "Critic as Artist, The," 69; "Decay of Lying, The," 69; *De Profundis,* 112; *Picture of Dorian Gray, The,* xviii, 67, 68, 69, 102, 109–13, 119, 152, 187; "Truth of Masks, The," 69; *Soul of Man Under Socialism, The,* 69
Wilder, Billy, 190; *Sunset Boulevard,* 190
Williams, Roger, xiv, 11, 29, 46, 49
"William Wilson" (Poe), 111
Wilson, Edmund, 164, 175
Wordsworth, William, 67, 78

Zola, Emile, xviii, 43, 44, 45, 46, 47, 52, 53, 81, 83, 156; *Faute de l'Abbé Mouret, La,* 45; *Germinal,* 53; *Thérèse Raquin,* 44